Learning Swift
Building Apps for macOS, iOS, and Beyond

Jon Manning, Paris Buttfield-Addison, and Tim Nugent

Beijing · Boston · Farnham · Sebastopol · Tokyo

Learning Swift

by Jon Manning, Paris Buttfield-Addison, and Tim Nugent

Printed in the United States of America.

Published by O'Reilly Media, Inc., 1005 Gravenstein Highway North, Sebastopol, CA 95472.

O'Reilly books may be purchased for educational, business, or sales promotional use. Online editions are also available for most titles (*http://oreilly.com/safari*). For more information, contact our corporate/institutional sales department: 800-998-9938 or *corporate@oreilly.com*.

Editor: Rachel Roumeliotis	**Indexer:** Ellen Troutman-Zaig
Production Editor: Melanie Yarbrough	**Interior Designer:** David Futato
Copyeditor: James Fraleigh	**Cover Designer:** Karen Montgomery
Proofreader: Amanda Kersey	**Illustrator:** Rebecca Demarest

May 2016: First Edition
March 2017: Second Edition

Revision History for the Second Edition

2017-03-28: First Release

See *http://oreilly.com/catalog/errata.csp?isbn=9781491967065* for release details.

978-1-491-96706-5

[LSI]

Table of Contents

Part III.   An iOS App

Part IV.   Extending Your Apps

Preface

Welcome to *Learning Swift*! This book will help you put the Swift programming language into practice by walking you through the development of a note-taking application for the Apple iOS, macOS, and watchOS platforms.

Swift is a pretty amazing modern language, taking the best from other newer languages without reinventing the wheel. Swift is easy to write, easy to read, and really hard to make mistakes in.

Our philosophy is that the best way to learn Swift is to build apps using it! To build apps, though, you need a great framework, and Apple has several: Cocoa, Cocoa Touch, and WatchKit, to name only a few. This book could quite easily be titled *Learning Cocoa and Cocoa Touch with Swift*, or something similar, because the frameworks are just as important as the language itself. At the time of writing, Swift is currently at version 3, and has a bright future ahead of it.

Resources Used in This Book

We recommend following the book by writing code yourself as you progress through each chapter. If you get stuck, or just want to archive a copy of the code, you can find what you need via our website (*http://www.secretlab.com.au/books/learning-swift-3*).

As this book teaches you how to build a real-world app, we primarily focus on showing you the coding side of things. We're not going to ask you to paint your own icons, so we've provided them for you. You can also download them from our website.

Audience and Approach

This book is solely focused on Swift 3 and does not cover the use of Objective-C. We might mention it occasionally, but we don't expect you to know how to use it. We first cover the basics of the Swift 3 language, and then move on to teach as much of the language as we can, as well as the use of the Cocoa, Cocoa Touch, and watchOS frameworks, through the construction of a complete app for both macOS and iOS. As a reminder, Swift is the programming language, Cocoa is the framework for macOS apps, Cocoa Touch is the framework for iOS apps, and somewhat predictably, watchOS is the framework for the Apple Watch.

This book's approach differs from that of other programming books that you may have encountered. As we've mentioned, we believe that the best way to learn Swift is to build apps using it. We assume that you're a reasonably capable programmer, but we don't assume you've ever developed for iOS or macOS, or used Swift or Objective-C before. We also assume that you're fairly comfortable navigating macOS and iOS as a user.

Organization of This Book

In this book, we'll be talking about Cocoa and Cocoa Touch, the frameworks used on macOS and iOS, respectively. Along the way, we'll also be covering Swift, including its syntax and features.

In Part I, "Swift Basics", we begin with a look at the tools used for programming with Swift, as well as the Apple Developer Program. Then we move on to the basics of the Swift programming language and structuring a program for Apple's platforms, as well as common design patterns.

Chapter 1 covers the basics of Apple's developer program and guides you through a simple Swift app.

Chapter 2 explores all the basics of Swift and prepares you for using it to build more complex applications.

Chapter 3 discusses Swift's object-oriented features, as well as the structure of a good app.

In Part II, "A macOS App", we build a simple note-taking application for Macs, targeting macOS. Along the way, we discuss the design of the app, how it's structured, how it uses documents, and how to build all the features.

Chapter 4 starts off our macOS notes app and sets up the document model and icon.

Chapter 5 goes into detail on working with documents in macOS apps.

Chapter 6 connects the app to iCloud and finishes up the macOS app.

In Part III, "An iOS App", we build a fully featured iOS note-taking application as a companion for the macOS app from Part II.

Chapter 7 starts off our iOS app and sets up the same document model for iOS.

Chapter 8 connects the iOS app to iCloud.

Chapter 9 creates an interface on iOS for displaying our notes.

Chapter 10 sets up the iOS app to handle attachments.

Chapter 11 adds image support to the iOS app.

Chapter 12 adds sharing and searching support to the iOS app.

Chapter 13 adds audio, video, and location attachments to the iOS app.

Chapter 14 finishes the iOS app with a whole lot of polish!

In Part IV, "Extending Your Apps", we add a watchOS app and explore bug hunting and performance tuning.

Chapter 15 adds a watchOS app to the iOS app, allowing for Apple Watch support.

Chapter 16 explores debugging and performance tuning.

Conventions Used in This Book

The following typographical conventions are used in this book:

Italic
> Indicates new terms, URLs, email addresses, filenames, and file extensions.

`Constant width`
> Used for program listings, as well as within paragraphs to refer to program elements such as variable or function names, databases, data types, environment variables, statements, and keywords.

`Constant width bold`
> Shows commands or other text that should be typed literally by the user.

`Constant width italic`
> Shows text that should be replaced with user-supplied values or by values determined by context.

 This element signifies a tip or suggestion.

 This element signifies a general note.

This element indicates a warning or caution.

Using Code Examples

Supplemental material (code examples, exercises, errata, etc.) is available for download at our website (*http://secretlab.com.au/books/learning-swift*).

This book is here to help you get your job done. In general, if example code is offered with this book, you may use it in your programs and documentation. You do not need to contact us for permission unless you're reproducing a significant portion of the code. For example, writing a program that uses several chunks of code from this book does not require permission. Selling or distributing a CD-ROM of examples from O'Reilly books does require permission. Answering a question by citing this book and quoting example code does not require permission. Incorporating a significant amount of example code from this book into your product's documentation does require permission.

We appreciate, but do not require, attribution. An attribution usually includes the title, author, publisher, and ISBN. For example: "*Learning Swift, Second Edition* by Jonathon Manning, Paris Buttfield-Addison, and Tim Nugent (O'Reilly). Copyright 2017 Secret Lab, 978-1-491-96706-5."

If you feel your use of code examples falls outside fair use or the permission given above, feel free to contact us at *permissions@oreilly.com*.

O'Reilly Safari

 *Safari* (formerly Safari Books Online) is a membership-based training and reference platform for enterprise, government, educators, and individuals.

Members have access to thousands of books, training videos, Learning Paths, interactive tutorials, and curated playlists from over 250 publishers, including O'Reilly Media, Harvard Business Review, Prentice Hall Professional, Addison-Wesley Professional, Microsoft Press, Sams, Que, Peachpit Press, Adobe, Focal Press, Cisco Press, John Wiley & Sons, Syngress, Morgan Kaufmann, IBM Redbooks, Packt, Adobe Press, FT Press, Apress, Manning, New Riders, McGraw-Hill, Jones & Bartlett, and Course Technology, among others.

For more information, please visit *http://oreilly.com/safari*.

How to Contact Us

Please address comments and questions concerning this book to the publisher:

O'Reilly Media, Inc.
1005 Gravenstein Highway North
Sebastopol, CA 95472
800-998-9938 (in the United States or Canada)
707-829-0515 (international or local)
707-829-0104 (fax)

We have a web page for this book, where we list errata, examples, and any additional information. You can access this page at *http://bit.ly/learning-swift*.

To comment or ask technical questions about this book, send email to *bookquestions@oreilly.com*.

For more information about our books, courses, conferences, and news, see our website at *http://www.oreilly.com*.

Find us on Facebook: *http://facebook.com/oreilly*

Follow us on Twitter: *http://twitter.com/oreillymedia*

Watch us on YouTube: *http://www.youtube.com/oreillymedia*

Acknowledgments

Jon thanks his mother, father, and the rest of his crazily extended family for their tremendous support.

Paris thanks his mother, without whom he wouldn't be doing anything nearly as interesting, let alone writing books.

Tim thanks his parents and family for putting up with his rather lackluster approach to life.

We'd all like to thank our editors, Rachel Roumeliotis and Brian MacDonald—their skill and advice were invaluable to completing the book. Likewise, all the O'Reilly Media staff we've interacted with over the course of writing the book have been the absolute gurus of their fields.

A huge thank you to Tony Gray and the Apple University Consortium (AUC) (*http://www.auc.edu.au*) for the monumental boost they gave us and others listed on this page. We wouldn't be writing this book if it weren't for them. And now you're writing books, too, Tony—sorry about that!

Thanks also to Neal Goldstein, who deserves full credit and/or blame for getting us into the whole book-writing racket.

We're thankful for the support of the goons at MacLab (who know who they are and continue to stand watch for Admiral Dolphin's inevitable apotheosis), as well as professor Christopher Lueg, Dr. Leonie Ellis, and the rest of the staff at the University of Tasmania for putting up with us. "Apologies" to Mark Pesce. He knows why.

Additional thanks to Rex S., Nic W., Andrew B., Jess L., and Ash J., for a wide variety of reasons. And very special thanks to Steve Jobs, without whom this book (and many others like it) would not have reason to exist.

Thanks also to our tech reviewers, with special thanks to Chris Devers and Tony Gray for their thoroughness and professionalism.

Finally, thank *you* very much for buying our book—we appreciate it! And if you have any feedback, please let us know. You can email us at *lab@secretlab.com.au* and find us on Twitter at @thesecretlab (*http://twitter.com/thesecretlab*).

PART I

Swift Basics

CHAPTER 1

Getting Started

This book teaches the Swift 3 programming language by exploring the development of three applications for Apple platforms: macOS, iOS, and watchOS. This book's approach might differ from what you're used to, because our philosophy is that the best way to learn Swift is to build apps using it! The vast majority of the code in this book will be part of the apps we're building—a full note-taking app for macOS, iOS, and watchOS—rather than individual pieces of sample code. You can see the final product in Figure 1-1.

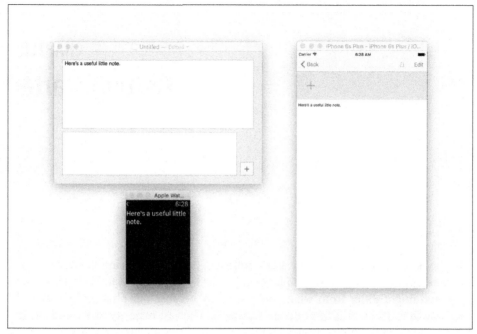

Figure 1-1. Our finished app, for macOS, iOS, and watchOS

Our app is fully functional, but we do make some deliberate design and feature decisions along the way to constrain the scope a little (the book is almost 500 pages!). As we mentioned in the Preface, we assume that you're a reasonably capable programmer, but we don't assume you've ever developed for iOS or macOS, or used Swift or Objective-C before. We also assume that you're fairly comfortable navigating macOS and iOS as a user.

> We recommend that you work through this book front to back, building the macOS app, then the iOS app, then the watchOS app, even if you're only interested in one of the platforms. By approaching the book this way, you'll get the best understanding of what building a real app with Swift requires.

Programming with Swift, and using the Cocoa and Cocoa Touch frameworks to develop macOS and iOS apps, respectively, involves using a set of tools developed by Apple. In this chapter, you'll learn about these tools, where to get them, how to use them, how they work together, and what they can do. At the end of this chapter, you'll make a very simple Swift application for iOS. Then we dive into the details of the Swift language and Apple's frameworks in the following two chapters.

The Apple development tools have a long and storied history. Originally a set of standalone application tools for the NeXTSTEP OS, they were eventually adopted by Apple for use as the official macOS tools. Later, Apple largely consolidated them into one application, known as Xcode, though some of the applications (such as Instruments and the iOS simulator) remain somewhat separate, owing to their relatively peripheral role in the development process. You'll notice the prefix NS on many of the classes you use for Cocoa and Cocoa Touch development with Swift. This prefix comes from the NeXTSTEP heritage of many of Apple's frameworks.

In addition to the development tools, Apple offers developers a paid membership in its Developer Program (*https://developer.apple.com/programs/*), which provides resources and support. The program allows access to online developer forums and specialized technical support for those interested in talking to the framework engineers. If you are just interested in learning Swift and exploring the development tools, you can do so for free. You will need a paid membership, however, if you wish to use developer services like iCloud in your apps or to distribute anything you build through either the iOS or macOS App Store.

Swift is open source, but this doesn't really mean much when it comes to using it to develop apps for macOS, iOS, and watchOS. There's an excellent community of people working on the language that you can find at the Swift website (*http://swift.org*).

With the introduction of Apple's curated App Stores for macOS, iOS, and watchOS, as well as emerging Apple platforms like tvOS, the Developer Program has become the official way for developers to provide their credentials when submitting applications to Apple—in essence, it is your ticket to selling apps through Apple. In this chapter, you'll learn how to sign up for the Apple Developer Program, as well as how to use Xcode, the development tool used to build apps in Swift.

The Apple Developer Program

The paid Apple Developer Program (*https://developer.apple.com/programs/*) provides access to beta development tools, beta operating system releases, and distribution ability through Apple's app store. It also allows you to use some of the cloud-dependent features of the platforms, such as iCloud, CloudKit, In-App Purchase, and App Groups.

We will be using a lot of cloud-dependent features, including iCloud, in the apps we build throughout this book. You will not be able to run these apps if you do not have a paid membership.

It isn't necessary to be a member of the Apple Developer Program if you don't intend to submit apps to the app stores, or don't need the cloud-dependent features. We strongly recommend joining, though, if you intend to build apps for any of Apple's platforms, as the other benefits are substantial:

- Access to the Apple Developer Forums (*https://developer.apple.com/devforums/*), which are frequented by Apple engineers and designed to allow you to ask questions of your fellow developers and the people who wrote the OS.
- Access to beta versions of the OS before they are released to the public, which enables you to test your applications on the next version of the macOS, iOS, watchOS, and tvOS platforms, and make necessary changes ahead of time. You also receive beta versions of the development tools.
- A digital signing certificate (one for each platform) used to identify you to the App Stores. Without this, you cannot submit apps to the App Store, making a membership mandatory for anyone who wants to release software either for free or for sale via an App Store.

That said, registering for the Developer Program isn't necessary to view the documentation or to download the current version of the developer tools, so you can play around with writing apps without opening your wallet.

Registering for the Apple Developer Program

To register for the Developer Program, you'll first need an Apple ID. It's quite likely that you already have one, as the majority of Apple's online services require one to identify you. If you've ever used iCloud, the iTunes store (for music or apps), or Apple's support and repair service, you already have an ID. You might even have more than one (one of this book's authors has four). If you don't yet have an ID, you'll create one as part of the registration process. When you register for the Developer Program, the membership gets added to your Apple ID.

If you don't want to register for the paid developer program, you can skip to "Downloading Xcode" on page 7 for instructions on installing Xcode, the developer tools.

Once again, keep in mind that you won't be able to build the apps that we teach in this book if you don't have a paid membership, as we use cloud-dependent features such as iCloud.

There are alternatives to many of Apple's tools—such as the Google Maps SDK for iOS, or cloud-storage services from Amazon and Microsoft. However, you'll still need a paid membership through Apple to put apps in the iTunes App Store.

Once you're on the Apple Developer Program (*https://developer.apple.com/programs/*) website, simply click Enroll, and follow the steps to enroll.

You can choose to register as an individual or as a company. If you register as an individual, your apps will be sold under your name. If you register as a company, your apps will be sold under your company's legal name. Choose carefully, as it's very difficult to convince Apple to change your program's type.

If you're registering as an individual, you'll just need your credit card. If you're registering as a company, you'll need your credit card as well as documentation that proves you have authority to bind your company to Apple's terms and conditions.

For information on code signing and using Xcode to test and run your apps on your own physical devices, see Apple's App Distribution Guide (*http://bit.ly/app_dist_guide*). We don't cover this in the book, as it's a process that changes often.

Apple usually takes about 24 hours to activate an account for individuals, and longer for companies. Once you've received confirmation from Apple, you'll be emailed a link to activate your account; when that's done, you're a full-fledged developer!

Downloading Xcode

To develop apps for either platform, you'll use Xcode, Apple's integrated development environment. Xcode combines a source code editor, debugger, compiler, profiler, iOS simulator, Apple Watch simulator, and more into one package. It's where you'll spend the majority of your time when developing applications.

At the time of writing, Xcode is only available for Mac, but who knows what the future holds for the iPad Pro?

You can get Xcode from the Mac App Store. Simply open the App Store application and search for "Xcode," and it'll pop up. It's a free download, though it's rather large (several gigabytes at the time of writing).

Once you've downloaded Xcode, it's straightforward enough to install it. The Mac App Store gives you an application that on first launch sets up everything you need to use Xcode. Just launch the downloaded app, and follow the prompts, and you'll be up and running in no time.

 This book covers Swift 3, which is available only if you're using Xcode 8 or later. Make sure you're using the latest version of Xcode from the Mac App Store. It's good practice to use the latest Xcode at all times.

Creating Your First Project with Xcode

Xcode is designed around a single window. Each of your projects will have one window, which adapts to show what you're working on.

To start exploring Xcode, you'll first need to create a project by following these steps:

1. Launch Xcode. You can find it by opening Spotlight (by pressing ⌘-space bar) and typing **Xcode**. You can also find it by opening the Finder, going to your hard drive, and opening the *Applications* directory. If you had any projects open previously, Xcode will open them for you. Otherwise, the "Welcome to Xcode" screen appears (see Figure 1-2).

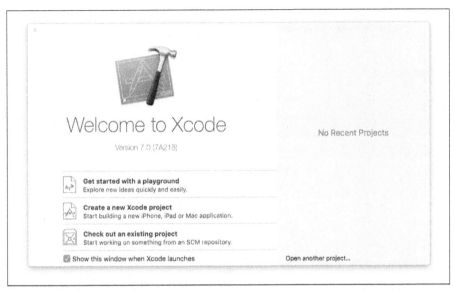

Figure 1-2. The "Welcome to Xcode" screen

2. Create a new project by clicking "Create a new Xcode project" or go to File→New→Project.

You'll be asked what kind of application to create. The template selector is divided into two areas. On the lefthand side, you'll find a collection of application categories. You can choose to create an iOS, watchOS, or macOS application from the project templates, which will set up a project directory to get you started.

Because we're just poking around Xcode at the moment, it doesn't really matter what we select, so choose Application under the iOS header and select Single View Application. This creates an empty iOS application and displays the project settings window shown in Figure 1-3.

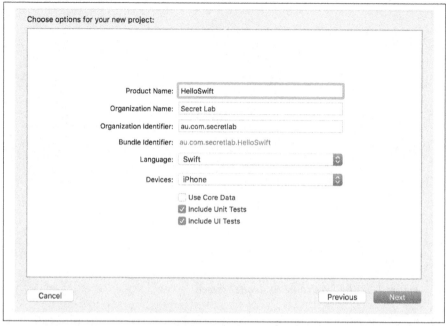

Figure 1-3. The project settings window

3. Name the application. Enter **HelloSwift** in the Product Name section.

4. Enter information about the project. Depending on the kind of project template you select, you'll be asked to provide different information about how the new project should be configured.

   At a minimum, you'll be asked for the following information, no matter which platform and template you choose:

   The product's name
   This is the name of the project and is visible to the user. You can change this later.

   Your organization's name
   This is the name of your company or group. It's not directly used by Xcode, but new source code files that you create will mention it.

   Your organization identifier
   This is used to generate a *bundle ID*, a string that looks like a reverse domain name (e.g., if O'Reilly made an application named MyUsefulApplication, the bundle ID would be *com.oreilly.MyUsefulApplication*).

Bundle IDs are the unique identifier for an application, and are used to identify that app to the system and to the App Store. Because each bundle ID must be unique, the same ID can't be used for more than one application in either of the iOS or Mac App Stores. That's why the format is based on domain names—if you own the site *usefulsoftware.com*, all of your bundle IDs would begin with *com.usefulsoftware*, and you won't accidentally use a bundle ID that someone else is using or wants to use because nobody else owns the same domain name.

If you don't have a domain name, enter anything you like, as long as it looks like a backward domain name (e.g., *com.mycompany* will work).

 If you plan on releasing your app, either to the App Store or elsewhere, it's very important to use a company identifier that matches a domain name you own. The App Store requires it, and the fact that the operating system uses the bundle ID that it generates from the company identifier means that using a domain name that you own eliminates the possibility of accidentally creating a bundle ID that conflicts with someone else's.

If you're writing an application for the Mac App Store, you'll also be prompted for the App Store category (whether it's a game, an educational app, a social networking app, or something else).

Depending on the template, you may also be asked for other information (e.g., the file extension for your documents if you are creating a document-aware application, such as a Mac app). You'll also be asked which language you want to use; because this book is about Swift, you should probably choose Swift! The additional information needed for this project is covered in the following steps.

5. Make the application run on the iPhone by choosing iPhone from the Devices drop-down list.

 iOS applications can run on the iPad, iPhone, or both. Applications that run on both are called "universal" applications and run the same binary but have different user interfaces. For this exercise, just choose iPhone. You should be building universal iOS apps in general, and we'll be doing that when we properly start on iOS in Part III.

6. Leave the rest of the settings as shown in Figure 1-4. Click Next to create the project.

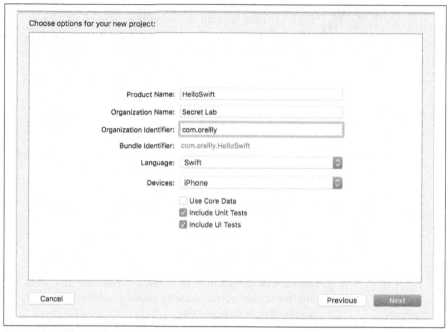

Figure 1-4. The project settings

7. Choose where to save the project. Select a location that suits you. We recommend putting all your work related to this book (and other Swift programming learning you might do) in one folder. You might notice a little checkbox for Source Control; this creates a source code control repository for your code, giving you a place where you can save and manage different versions of your code as you create them. While in general this is a good idea to use, for this example project, make sure this is *unchecked*.

Once you've done this, Xcode will open the project, and you can now start using the entire Xcode interface, as shown in Figure 1-5.

Figure 1-5. The entire Xcode interface

The Xcode Interface

As mentioned, Xcode shows your entire project in a single window, which is divided into a number of sections. You can open and close each section at will, depending on what you want to see.

Let's take a look at each of these sections and examine what they do.

The editor

The Xcode editor (Figure 1-6) is where you'll be spending most of your time. All source code editing, interface design, and project configuration take place in this section of the application, which changes depending on which file you have open.

If you're editing source code, the editor is a text editor, with code completion, syntax highlighting, and all the usual features that developers have come to expect from an integrated development environment. If you're modifying a user interface, the editor becomes a visual editor, allowing you to drag around the components of your interface. Other kinds of files have their own specialized editors as well.

When you first create a project, the editor will start by showing the project settings, as seen in Figure 1-6.

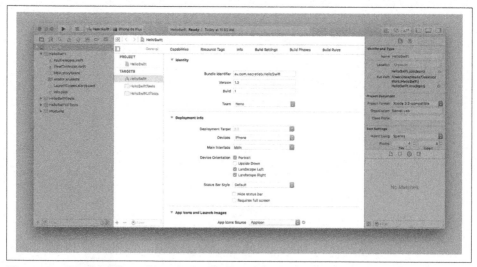

Figure 1-6. Xcode's editor, showing the project settings

The editor can also be split into a *main editor* and an *assistant editor* through the *editor selector*. The assistant shows files that are related to the file open in the main editor. It will continue to show files that have a relationship to whatever is open, even if you open different files.

For example, if you open an interface file and then open the assistant, the assistant will, by default, show related code for the interface you're editing. If you open another interface file, the assistant will show the code for the newly opened files.

At the top of the editor, you'll find the *jump bar*. The jump bar lets you quickly jump from the content that you're editing to another piece of related content, such as a file in the same folder. The jump bar is a fast way to navigate your project.

The toolbar

The Xcode toolbar (Figure 1-7) acts as mission control for the entire interface. It's the only part of Xcode that doesn't significantly change as you develop your applications, and it serves as the place where you can control what your code is doing.

Figure 1-7. Xcode's toolbar

From left to right, after the macOS window controls, the toolbar features the following items:

Run button (Figure 1-8)
    Clicking this button instructs Xcode to compile and run the application.

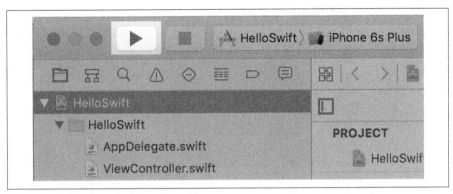

Figure 1-8. The Run button

Depending on the kind of application you're running and your currently selected settings, this button will have different effects:

- If you're creating a Mac application, the new app will appear in the Dock and will run on your machine.
- If you're creating an iOS application, the new app will launch in either the iOS simulator or on a connected iOS device, such as an iPhone or iPad.

  Additionally, if you click and hold this button, you can change it from Run to another action, such as Test, Profile, or Analyze. The Test action runs any unit tests that you have set up; the Profile action runs the application Instruments (we cover this much later, in Chapter 16); and the Analyze action checks your code and points out potential problems and bugs.

Stop button (Figure 1-9)
Clicking this button stops any task that Xcode is currently doing—if it's building your application, it stops; and if your application is running in the debugger, it quits it.

Figure 1-9. The Stop button

Scheme selector (Figure 1-10)

> *Schemes* are what Xcode calls build configurations—that is, what's being built, how, and where it will run (i.e., on your computer or on a connected device).

Figure 1-10. The scheme selector

Projects can have multiple apps inside them. When you use the scheme selector, you choose which app, or *target*, to build.

To select a target, click the lefthand side of the scheme selector.

You can also choose where the application will run. If you are building a Mac application, you will almost always want to run the application on your Mac. If you're building an iOS application, however, you have the option of running the application on an iPhone simulator or an iPad simulator. (These are in fact the same application; it simply changes shape depending on the scheme that you've selected.) You can also choose to run the application on a connected iOS device if it has been set up for development.

Status display (Figure 1-11)

> The status display shows what Xcode is doing—building your application, downloading documentation, installing an application on an iOS device, and so on.

Figure 1-11. The status display

If there is more than one task in progress, a small button will appear on the lefthand side, which cycles through the current tasks when clicked.

Editor selector (Figure 1-12)

> The editor selector determines how the editor is laid out. You can choose to display either a single editor, the editor with the assistant, or the versions editor,

which allows you to compare different versions of a file if you're using a revision control system like Git or Subversion.

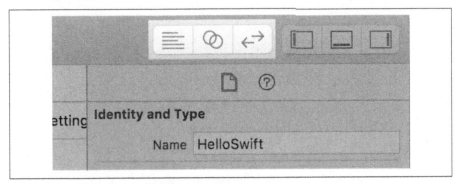

Figure 1-12. The editor selector

 We don't have anywhere near the space needed to talk about using version control in your projects in this book, but it's an important topic. We recommend Jon Loeliger and Matthew McCullough's *Version Control with Git, 2nd Edition* (O'Reilly).

View selector (Figure 1-13)

The view selector controls whether the navigator, debug, and utility panes appear on screen. If you're pressed for screen space or simply want less clutter, you can quickly summon and dismiss these parts of the screen by clicking each of the elements.

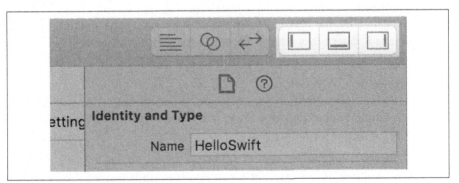

Figure 1-13. The view selector

The navigator

The lefthand side of the Xcode window is the *navigator*, which presents information about your project (Figure 1-14).

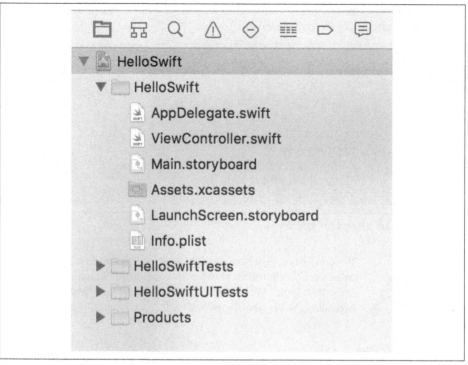

Figure 1-14. The navigator pane has eight tabs at the top

The navigator is divided into eight tabs, from left to right:

Project navigator
> Lists all the files that make up your project. This is the most commonly used navigator, as it determines what is shown in the editor. Whatever is selected in the project navigator is opened in the editor.

Symbol navigator
> Lists all the classes and functions that exist in your project. If you're looking for a quick summary of a class or want to jump directly to a method in that class, the symbol navigator is a handy tool.

Search navigator
> Allows you to perform searches across your project if you're looking for specific text. (The shortcut is ⌘-Shift-F. Press ⌘-F to search the current open document.)

Issue navigator
> Lists all the problems that Xcode has noticed in your code. This includes warnings, compilation errors, and issues that the built-in code analyzer has spotted.

Test navigator

Shows all the unit tests associated with your project. Unit tests used to be an optional component of Xcode but are now built into Xcode directly. Unit tests are discussed much later, in "Unit Testing" on page 469.

Debug navigator

Activated when you're debugging a program, and it allows you to examine the state of the various threads that make up your program.

Breakpoint navigator

Lists all of the breakpoints that you've set for use while debugging.

Report navigator

Lists all the activity that Xcode has done with your project (such as building, debugging, and analyzing). You can go back and view previous build reports from earlier in your Xcode session, too.

Utilities

The utilities pane (Figure 1-15) shows additional information related to what you're doing in the editor. If you're editing a Swift source file, for example, the utilities pane allows you to view and modify settings for that file.

The utilities pane is split into two sections: the *inspector*, which shows extra details and settings for the selected item; and the *library*, which is a collection of items that you can add to your project. The inspector and the library are most heavily used when you're building user interfaces; however, the library also contains a number of useful items, such as file templates and code snippets, which you can drag and drop into place.

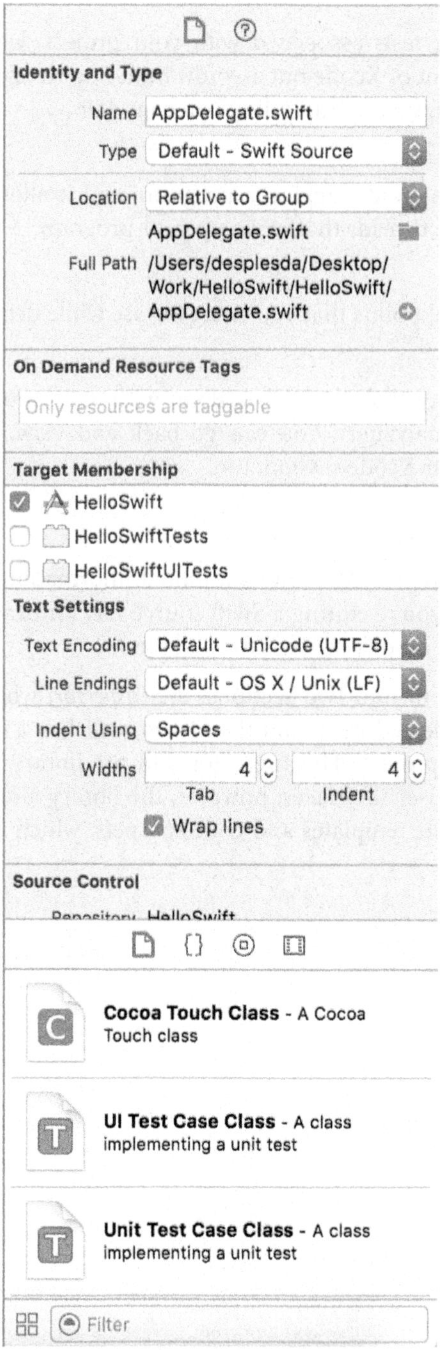

Figure 1-15. The utilities pane, showing information for a source file

The debug area

The debug area (Figure 1-16) shows information reported by the debugger when the program is running. Whenever you want to see what the application is reporting while running, you can view it in the debug area. By default the debug area is not shown unless there is a program running. You can bring up the debug area by using the Xcode Toolbar View selector middle button.

Figure 1-16. The debug area

The area is split into two sections: the lefthand side shows the values of local variables when the application is paused; the righthand side shows the ongoing log from the debugger, which includes any logging that comes from the debugged application.

You can show or hide the debug area by clicking the view selector, at the top right of the window (see Figure 1-17).

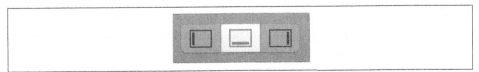

Figure 1-17. The central button in the view selector, which hides and shows the debug area

Developing a Simple Swift Application

Through the bulk of this book, we'll be developing a complex, full-fledged Swift application, spanning three of Apple's platforms: macOS, iOS, and watchOS. But for now, before we even explore how and why Swift itself works, we're going to get a brief taste by building a very, very simple application for iOS.

 If you're more interested in Mac development, don't worry! Exactly the same techniques apply, and we'll be exploring Mac apps in detail later on, in Part II.

This simple application is extremely cutting-edge: it will display a single button that, when tapped, will pop up an alert and change the button's label to "Test!" We're going to build on the project we created earlier in "Creating Your First Project with Xcode" on page 8, so make sure you have that project open.

It's generally good practice to create the interface first and then add code. This means that your code is written with an understanding of how it maps to what the user sees.

To that end, we'll start by designing the interface for the application.

Designing the Interface

When building an application's interface using Cocoa and Cocoa Touch, you have two options. You can either design your application's screens in a *storyboard*, which shows how all the screens link together, or you can design each screen in isolation. As a general rule, storyboards are a better way to create your interfaces even if you only have a single view, as in the case of this first application we are building. The reason is that if you later want to give your application more than one view, it will be easier to do that in a storyboard.

Start by opening the interface file and adding a button. These are the steps you'll need to follow:

1. First, we'll need to open the main storyboard. Because newly created projects use storyboards by default, your app's interface is stored in the *Main.storyboard* file.

    Open it by selecting *Main.storyboard* in the project navigator. The editor will change to show the application's single, blank frame. You may need to pan or zoom the view around to fit it on your monitor.

2. Next, we need to drag in a button. We're going to add a single button to the frame. All user interface controls are kept in the *Object library*, which is at the bottom of the utilities pane on the righthand side of the screen.

    To find the button, you can either scroll through the list until you find Button, or type **button** in the search field at the bottom of the library.

    Once you've located it, drag it into the frame.

3. At this point, we need to configure the button. Every item that you add to an interface can be configured. For now, we'll change only the text on the button.

    Select the new button by clicking it, and select the Attributes Inspector, which is the fourth tab from the right at the top of the utilities pane. You can also reach it by pressing ⌘-Option-4.

    There are many attributes on the button; look for the one labeled Title. The Title attribute has two different components inside it: a drop-down box and a text field containing "Button." In the text field, change the button's Title to "Hello!"

You can also change the button's title by double-clicking it in the interface.

Our simple interface is now complete (Figure 1-18). The only thing left to do is to connect it to code.

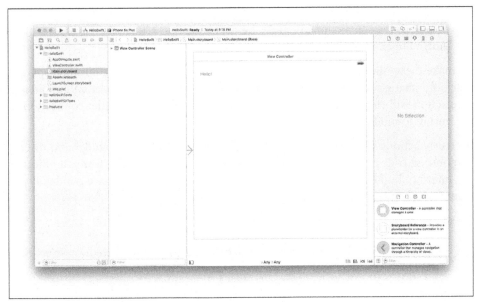

Figure 1-18. Our completed simple interface

Connecting the Code

Applications aren't just interfaces—as a developer, you also need to write code. To work with the interface you've designed, you need to create connections between your code and your interface.

There are two kinds of connections that you can make:

Outlets
> Variables that refer to objects in the interface. Using outlets, you can instruct a button to change color or size, or to hide itself. There are also *outlet collections*, which allow you to create an array of outlets and choose which objects it contains in the interface builder.

Actions
> Methods in your code that are run in response to the user interacting with an object. These interactions include the user touching a finger to an object, dragging a finger, and so on.

To make the application behave as we've just described—tapping the button displays a label and changes the button's text—we'll need to use both an outlet and an action. The action will run when the button is tapped and will use the outlet connection to the button to modify its label.

To create actions and outlets, you need to have both the interface builder and its corresponding code open. Then hold down the Control key and drag from an object in the interface builder to your code (or to another object in the interface builder, if you want to make a connection between two objects in your interface).

We'll now create the necessary connections:

1. First, open the assistant by selecting the second button in the editor selector in the toolbar. The symbol is two interlocking circles.

   The assistant should open and show the corresponding code for the interface *ViewController.swift*. If it doesn't, click the intertwining circles icon (which represents the assistant) inside the jump bar and navigate to Automatic→*ViewController.swift*. Make sure you don't select the assistant symbol in the toolbar, as that will close the assistant editor.

2. Create the button's outlet. Hold down the Control key and drag from the button into the space below the first { in the code.

   A pop-up window will appear. Leave everything as the default, but change the Name to **helloButton**. Click Connect.

   A new line of code will appear: Xcode has created the connection for you, which appears in your code as a property in your class:

   ```
   @IBOutlet weak var helloButton : UIButton!
   ```

3. Create the button's action. Hold down the Control key, and again drag from the button into the space below the line of code we just created. A pop-up window will again appear.

This time, change the Connection from Outlet to Action, set the Name to showAlert, and click Connect.

More code will appear. Xcode has created the connection, which is a method inside the ViewController class:

```
@IBAction func showAlert(sender: Any) {
}
```

4. In the showAlert method you just created, add in the new code:

```
let alert = UIAlertController(title: "Hello!", message: "Hello, world!",
        preferredStyle: UIAlertControllerStyle.alert) ❶
alert.addAction(UIAlertAction(title: "Close",
        style: UIAlertActionStyle.default, handler: nil)) ❷
self.present(alert, animated: true, completion: nil) ❸
self.helloButton.setTitle("Test!", forState: UIControlState.normal) ❹
```

This code does the following things:

❶   It creates a UIAlertController, which displays a message to the user in a pop-up window. It prepares it by setting its title to "Hello!" and the text inside the window to "Hello, world!"

❷   Finally, an action that dismisses the alert is added, with the text "Close".

❸   The alert is then shown to the user.

❹   Finally, it sets the title of the button to "Test!"

The application is now ready to run. Click the Run button in the upper-left corner. The application will launch in the iPhone simulator. Don't worry if the app takes a while to launch the first time; the simulator can take a fair amount of time on first launch.

If you happen to have an iPhone or iPad connected to your computer, Xcode will try to launch the application on the device rather than in the simulator. To make Xcode use the simulator, go to the Scheme menu in the upper-left corner of the window and change the selected scheme to the simulator.

When the app finishes launching in the simulator, tap the button. An alert will appear; when you close it, you'll notice that the button's text has changed.

Using the iOS Simulator

The iOS simulator (Figure 1-19) allows you to test out iOS applications without having to use actual devices. It's a useful tool, but keep in mind that the simulator behaves very differently compared to a real device.

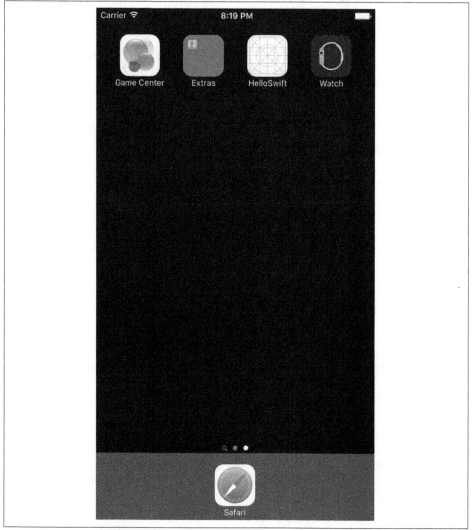

Figure 1-19. The iOS simulator

For one thing, the simulator is a lot faster than a real device and has a lot more memory. That's because the simulator makes use of your computer's resources—if your Mac has 8 GB of RAM, so will the simulator, and if you're building a processor-intensive application, it will run much more smoothly on the simulator than on a real device.

The iOS simulator can simulate many different kinds of devices: everything from the iPad 2 to the latest iPad Pro, and from the Retina display 3.5- and 4-inch iPhone-sized devices to the latest 4.7-inch and 5.5-inch iPhones. It can also test on variable-size devices.

To change the device, open the Hardware menu, choose Device, and select the device you want to simulate. You can also change which simulator to use via the scheme selector in Xcode. Each simulator device is unique, and they do not share information. So if you want to test your application on different simulators, you will need to build it again through Xcode.

 If you change hardware in the simulator while running an app, it will crash and Xcode will alert you. Be wary of changing the hardware in the simulator while testing applications unless you really like crashes.

You can also simulate hardware events, such as the Home button being pressed or the iPhone being locked. To simulate pressing the Home button, you can either choose Hardware→Home, or press ⌘-Shift-H. To lock the device, press ⌘-L or choose Hardware→Lock.

There are a number of additional features in the simulator, which we'll examine more closely as they become relevant to the various parts of iOS we'll be discussing.

Conclusion

In this chapter, we've looked at the basics of the Apple Developer Program, as well as the tools used for building apps. We've also made a really quick and simple iOS app, just to give you a taste of the process. In the next two chapters, we'll look at the Swift programming language, using a feature of Xcode and Swift called Playgrounds to work with Swift code outside the application context.

CHAPTER 2

The Basics of Swift

The Swift programming language was first introduced in June 2014 at Apple's Worldwide Developers Conference (WWDC). Swift was a surprise to everyone: Apple had managed to develop an entire language (as well as all the supporting libraries, developer tools, and documentation) *and* make it work seamlessly with the existing Objective-C language. And on top of that, it was a really good "1.0" language.

In June 2015, Apple announced Swift 2.0, improving the performance of the language, adding a collection of new features, and making the Cocoa and Cocoa Touch platform APIs more Swift-like in style. Swift was open sourced on December 3, 2015, and is now as much a community-run project as an Apple-run one. We can expect Swift to evolve over time, in line with the developments in the Swift Open Source project (*http://www.swift.org*).

 Xcode supports having multiple versions of the Swift language installed. You might have a different version of the language if, for example, you've downloaded a copy of Swift from the open source project. For information on how to get a copy and use it in Xcode, go to the Swift project's Download page (*https://swift.org/download/*).

This book covers Swift 3, which was released in September 13, 2016. The 3.0 release was a very big deal in the Swift community and included numerous changes to the language as well as to the standard library. With the release of Swift 3, future changes to the language aim to be smaller in scope and more backward compatible.

If you have older Swift code that you need to update to the latest stable Swift syntax, Xcode provides a converter. Open the Edit menu and choose Convert→To Latest Swift Syntax to get started.

Swift draws upon an extensive history of language design and has a number of very cool design features that make developing software easier, simpler, and safer. We'll begin this chapter with a high-level overview of what Swift aims to do, and how it sets about doing it, before we dive into the details of the language.

 As Swift develops, it's likely that some of the syntax that we use in this book will become out of date or change (as is true for any programming book). We'll keep the book's page on our site (*http://www.secretlab.com.au/books/learning-swift*) up to date with a changelog for the latest Swift for as long as we're able.

In this chapter, you'll learn the basics of coding in Swift 3.0.

The Swift Programming Language

The Swift programming language has the following goals:

Safety
Swift is designed to be a safe language. Many of the pitfalls of C, such as accidentally working with null pointers, are much harder to encounter. Swift is very strongly typed, and objects aren't allowed to be null except under very specific circumstances.

Modernity
Swift contains a large number of modern language features designed to make it easy to express the logic of your code. These include pattern-matching `switch` statements (see "Switches" on page 39), closures ("Closures" on page 58), and the concept of all values being objects to which you can attach properties and functions ("Extensions" on page 71).

Power
Swift has access to the entire Objective-C runtime and is seamlessly bridged to Objective-C's classes as well as its own standard library. This means that you can use Swift right away to write full iOS and macOS apps—you don't need to wait for anyone to port any features from Objective-C to Swift. And if you've never used Objective-C, then you don't need to worry about Objective-C! You can do everything you need to develop for Apple platforms using Swift.

So, what does Swift look like? Here's an example:

```
func sumNumbers(numbers: Int...) -> Int {   ❶
    var total = 0   ❷
    for number in numbers {   ❸
        total += number   ❹
    }
    return total   ❺
}
let sum = sumNumbers(2,3,4,5)   ❻
print(sum)   ❼
```

This code snippet does the following things:

❶ First, a function called sumNumbers is defined. This function takes one or more Int values, which are integers (whole numbers), and returns a single Int. The Int... denotes that the function takes a variable number of Int values; you can access these values through the numbers variable, which is an array.

❷ Inside the function, the variable total is declared. Note that the type isn't given—the compiler knows that it stores an Int, because it's being set to the integer value of 0.

❸ Next, a for-in loop starts up, which loops over every number that was sent to the method. Notice again that the type of the number variable isn't defined—the compiler infers that, given that numbers is an array of Int values, number should itself be an Int.

❹ The value of number is added to total.

❺ When the loop is complete, total is returned.

❻ The function sumNumbers is called with a collection of integers, and the result is stored in the new variable sum. This variable is *constant*: by defining it with the let keyword, we tell the compiler that its value never changes. Attempting to change the value of a constant is an error.

❼ Finally, we display the value using the print function, which prints values out to the console.

There are a few interesting things to note here:

- You usually don't need to define the type of variables. The compiler will do that for you, based on what values you're using.

- Even though the sumNumbers function takes a variable number of parameters, there's no weird syntax to deal with it (if you're a C or C++ programmer, you might remember struggling with va_start and friends).

- Variables that are declared with the let keyword are constants. The language is designed so that any variables that can be a constant should be one to prevent accidental changes later. Importantly, constants in Swift don't have to be known at compile time. Instead, you can think of them as variables that are set only once.

Swift 2 Versus Swift 3

If you already know Swift 2 and want to quickly get up to speed with what's new in the Swift 3 universe, here's a quick rundown of the main changes:

- The great renaming. Almost every function and property was renamed in some way. All function parameters now have labels unless you say otherwise; redundant words have been omitted; and the NS prefix was mostly dropped, so farewell NSURL and UIColor.redColor(), hello URL and UIColor.red. Additionally, Swift now has rules around how you should be naming your properties and functions, which we'll cover in "Making Your Code Swifty" on page 60.

- C-style for loop and the ++ and -- operators are now gone. After a long debate, both the C-style for loop and the increment and decrement operators were seen as holdovers from old languages. They made Swift trickier to learn for newcomers and just didn't feel right in Swift. You can use for-in, while loops or stride to replace their functionality.

- The private access modifier has been changed. Declaring parts of your code as private means they can only be used when in the same scope as they were declared. A new access modifier called fileprivate was introduced to perform the same functionality private had in Swift 2.

- Swift Package Manager was released. Swift now comes with a nifty package manager to handle downloading and managing distribution of Swift code. If in the past you were using Carthage or Cocoapods, the Swift Package Manager works in a similar fashion. We'll talk more about using the package manager in "Swift Package Manager" on page 80.

If you have a Swift 2 codebase and are not quite ready to move to Swift 3, you can use the version 2.3 released along with Swift 3.0—although you really ought to be moving to Swift 3 as soon as possible.

Playgrounds

The easiest way to learn Swift is to use a *playground*. Playgrounds are environments that let you write Swift code and see its results instantly. You don't need to build and run your code to see the results, and the code doesn't need to be a part of a larger app.

This means that if you want to play around with the language, a function, or even with a piece of a larger app, you don't need to make it part of an entire app.

The remainder of this chapter (but not the remainder of the book!) is written assuming that the code is being run in a playground. You should get used to working in one if you want to follow along! Playgrounds are really useful, and we strongly recommend you use them when experimenting with and learning Swift.

It's really useful to have quick access to a playground when you're learning and ultimately working with Swift. We recommend dragging a playground file (from wherever you saved it in the Finder) to your macOS Dock. That way, you can use it to test Swift code quickly and easily.

To start using a playground, you can create one from the "Welcome to Xcode" screen that appears when Xcode starts up (see Figure 2-1).

You can also choose File→New→New Playground and create a new playground from there. We'll be working with iOS playgrounds in this part.

The difference between iOS and macOS playgrounds is simply the libraries they have access to. For the purposes of these next few chapters, there's not a huge distinction between the two, but if you were making a playground that specifically tested some iOS code, you'd need to create an iOS playground.

When you create a playground, you'll see something that looks like Figure 2-2. On the lefthand side of the window, you can type Swift code. On the righthand side of the window, you'll see the result of each line of code that you write.

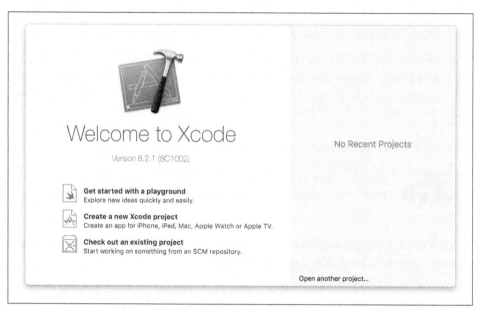

Figure 2-1. The "Welcome to Xcode" screen (click "Get started with a playground" to create a new playground)

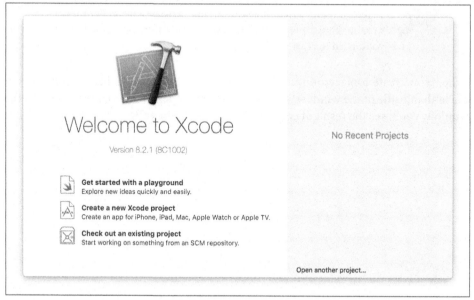

Figure 2-2. An empty playground

Comments

Comments in Swift are nonexecutable text. You can use comments as a note or reminder to yourself. We use comments often in sample code in this book; they are ignored by the compiler.

You can begin a single-line comment with two forward slashes (//) or open a multiline comment using a forward slash and an asterisk (/*) and close it using an asterisk followed by a forward slash (*/). Multiline comments can be nested:

```
// This is a single-line comment.

/* This is a multiple-line
    comment. */

/*
 This is a comment.

 /* This is also a comment, inside the first! */

 Still a comment!
 */
```

 Playgrounds (and only playgrounds) support a rich-text markup within comments that allows you to define headings, lists, and quotes, as well as include images and links. You can learn more about this in Apple's Markup Formatting Reference (*http://apple.co/ 1q1OyWo*).

Variables and Constants

You define a variable in Swift using either the `let` or `var` keywords:

```
var myVariable = 123
let myConstantVariable = 123
```

When you define a variable using `var`, you're allowed to change its value. If you define one using `let`, it's never allowed to change. Swift encourages you to use constants as much as possible, because they're safer—if you know that a value can never change, it won't cause a bug by changing without you knowing about it:

```
myVariable += 5

myConstantVariable += 2
// (ERROR: can't change a constant variable)
```

In addition to letting the compiler infer the type of your variables, you can also explicitly tell the compiler what value the variable should have:

```
// Explicit type of integer
let anExplicitInteger : Int = 2
```

Variables and constants are allowed to initially have no value, but you need to assign a value to them before you try to access them. In other words, if you create a variable and don't give it a value, the only thing you can do with it is to give it a value. After that, you can use it as normal:

```
var someVariable : Int
someVariable += 2
// ERROR: someVariable doesn't have a value, so can't add 2 to it
someVariable = 2
someVariable += 2
// WORKS, because someVariable has a value to add to
```

Unlike many popular languages, Swift doesn't require that you end your lines of code with a semicolon. However, if you want to, that's totally OK.

You can also break your lines of code over multiple lines without problems, like this:

```
var someVariable =
"Yes"
```

The single exception to the rule of not needing to use semicolons is when you want to put multiple statements on a single line. In those cases, you separate the statements with a semicolon:

```
someVariable = "No"; print(someVariable)
```

Operators

To work with the contents of variables, you use *operators*. There's a wide variety of operators built into Swift, the most common of which are the arithmetic operators (+, -, /, *, etc.):

```
1 + 7 // 8
6 - 5 // 1
4 / 2 // 2
4 * 0 // 0
```

In almost all cases, operators can only be used with two values of the same type (see "Types" on page 41). If you try to divide a number by a string, you'll get a compile error.

In addition to these basic operators, you'll also frequently work with *equality* and *inequality* operators. These check to see whether two values are the same:

```
2 == 2 // true
2 != 2 // false
"yes" == "no" // false
"yes" != "no" // true
```

Finally, the third most frequent operator you'll encounter is the . operator, which lets you access methods and properties:

```
true.description // "true"
```

```
4.advanced(by: 3) // 7
```

 We'll be covering methods and properties in more detail in "Classes and Objects" on page 63.

Control Flow

In every program you write, you'll want control over what code gets executed and when. For this, we'll make use of if statements, loops, and so on. The syntax for control flow in Swift is very straightforward and includes some handy additional features as well.

if statements in Swift are pretty much the same as in any other language, though in Swift there's no need to wrap the expression you're checking in parentheses:

```
if 1+1 == 2 {
    print("The math checks out")
}
// Prints "The math checks out", which is a relief
```

In Swift, the body of all if statements—as well as all loops—must be put between two braces ({ and }). In C, C++, Java, and Objective-C, you can omit these braces if you just want to have a single statement in your loop or if statement, like this:

```
if (something)
    do_something(); // NOT allowed in Swift!
```

However, this has led to all kinds of bugs and security problems caused by programmers forgetting to include braces. So, in Swift, they're mandatory.

Loops

When you have a collection of items, such as an array, you can use a for-in loop to iterate over every item:

```
let loopingArray = [1,2,3,4,5]
var loopSum = 0
```

```
for number in loopingArray {
    loopSum += number
}
loopSum // = 15
```

The `number` variable used in the `for-in` loop is implicitly created. You don't need to define a variable called `number` to make it work.

You can also use a `for-in` loop to iterate over a range of values. For example:

```
var firstCounter = 0
for index in 1 ..< 10 {
    firstCounter += 1
}
// Loops 9 times
```

Note the `..<` operator on the second line. This is a *range* operator, which Swift uses to describe a range of numbers from one value to another. There are actually two range operators: two dots and a left angle bracket (`..<`) and *three* dots and no angle bracket (`...`). Called the *half-range operator*, `..<` means a range that starts at the first value and goes up to but does not include the last value. For example, the range `5..<9` contains the numbers 5, 6, 7, and 8. If you want to create a range that *does* include the last number, you instead use the *closed-range operator* (`...`). The range `5...9` contains the numbers 5, 6, 7, 8, and 9. You can use an inclusive range operator in `for-in` loops like so:

```
var secondCounter = 0
for index in 1 ... 10 { // note the three dots, not two
    secondCounter += 1
}
// Loops 10 times
```

You can do a lot with the `for` loop and ranges but sometimes you need a bit more control over how the loop iterates; this is where `stride` comes into play. The `stride` function allows you to precisely control how you iterate over a sequence. So, for example, say you wanted to iterate between 0 and 1, going up by 0.1 each time:

```
for i in stride(from: 0, to: 1, by: 0.1) {
    print(i)
}
```

This is the `stride(from: to: by:)` form, which is exclusive of the final number; there is also an inclusive form `stride(from: through: by:)`.

A `while` loop lets you repeatedly run code while a certain condition remains true. For example:

```
var countDown = 5
while countDown > 0 {
    countDown -= 1
```

```
}
countDown // = 0
```

`while` loops check to see if the condition at the start of the loop evaluates to `true`, and if it does, they run the code (and then return to the start). In addition to `while` loops, the `repeat-while` loop runs the code at least once and *then* checks the condition:

```
var countUp = 0
repeat {
    countUp += 1
} while countUp < 5
countUp // = 5
```

 You can include the values of variables in strings by using the following syntax:

```
let myNumber = 3
let myString = "My number is \(myNumber)"
// = "My number is 3"
```

You can also include the results of expressions:

```
let OtherString = "My number plus 1 is \(myNumber + 1)"
// = "My number plus one is 4"
```

Switches

A *switch* is a powerful way to run code that depends on the value of a variable. Switches exist in other languages, but Swift kicks them into high gear.

To run different code based on the value of an integer, you can use a `switch` statement like this:

```
let integerSwitch = 3

switch integerSwitch {
case 0:
    print("It's 0")
case 1:
    print("It's 1")
case 2:
    print("It's 2")
default: // note: default is mandatory if not all
    // cases are covered (or can be covered)
    print("It's something else")
}
// Prints "It's something else"
```

In Swift, you can use the `switch` statement to handle more than just integers. You can switch on many things, including string values:

```
let stringSwitch = "Hello"
```

```
switch stringSwitch {
case "Hello":
    print("A greeting")
case "Goodbye":
    print("A farewell")
default:
    print("Something else")
}
// Prints "A greeting"
```

You can also switch on *tuples*, variables that are bundles of similar data; they're covered more in "Tuples" on page 47. This functionality is especially powerful, as you can write cases that run when only one of the components matches your condition:

```
let tupleSwitch = ("Yes", 123)

switch tupleSwitch {
case ("Yes", 123):
    print("Tuple contains 'Yes' and '123'")
case ("Yes", _):
    print("Tuple contains 'Yes' and something else")
case (let string, _):
    print("Tuple contains the string '\(string)' and something else")
default:
    break
}
// Prints "Tuple contains 'Yes' and '123'"
```

Finally, you can also use ranges in switches to create code that runs when the value you're testing falls between certain ranges:

```
var someNumber = 15

switch someNumber {
case 0...10:
    print("Number is between 0 and 10")
case 11...20:
    print("Number is between 11 and 20")
case 21:
    print("Number is 21!")
default:
    print("Number is something else")
}
// Prints "Number is between 11 and 20"
```

Switches in Swift work a little differently than switches in C and Objective-C. In Swift, the execution of a section in a `switch` statement doesn't automatically "fall through" into the next section, which means you don't need to include a `break` keyword at the end of your section.

If you *do* want execution to fall through from one case into the next, you use the `fallthrough` keyword, like so:

```
let fallthroughSwitch = 10

switch fallthroughSwitch {
case 0..<20:
    print("Number is between 0 and 20")
    fallthrough
case 0..<30:
    print("Number is between 0 and 30")
default:
    print("Number is something else")
}
// Prints "Number is between 0 and 20"
(and then)
// "Number is between 0 and 30"
```

Additionally, `switch` statements are required to be *exhaustive*. This means that the `switch` statement must cover all possible values. If you're switching using a `Bool` type, which can either be `true` or `false`, you *must* provide handlers for both values. If you don't, it's a compiler error.

However, it's sometimes not possible to cover all cases. With integers, for example, it's impossible to write a case for all possible numbers. In these cases, you provide a `default` case, which is shorthand for "every other possible value." So, to recap: in Swift, you either provide a case for all possible values, or you provide a default case.

If multiple cases in a `switch` statement overlap—for example, `case 0...10` and `case 5...15`—then the first matching case will be used.

Types

Swift out of the box includes a variety of types to cover many basic situations:

`Int`
> Represents whole numbers (e.g., `1`)

`Double`
> Represents decimal numbers (e.g., `1.2`)

`String`
> Represents a list of characters (e.g., `"hello world"`)

Bool

Represents Boolean state (i.e., `true` or `false`)

These aren't the only basic types that come with Swift, but they're the ones you'll run into the most.

You don't need to define what type the variable is. Swift will infer its type from its initial value. This means that when you define a variable and set it to the value 2, that variable will be an `Int`:

```
// Implicit type of integer
var anInteger = 2
```

Most types can't be combined, because the compiler doesn't know what the result would be. For example, you can't add a `String` to an `Int` value, because the result is meaningless:

```
// ERROR: Can't add a string to an integer
anInteger += "Yes"
```

Working with Strings

In Swift, strings are sequences of Unicode characters. This means that they're able to store pretty much any character that has ever been a part of a human language, which is great news for making your app translatable to other languages.

Creating a string in Swift is easy. You can create an empty string by creating a string literal with nothing in it:

```
let emptyString = ""
```

You can also create an empty string by using the `String` type's initializer:

```
let anotherEmptyString = String()
```

To check to see if a string is empty, you use the `isEmpty` property:

```
emptyString.isEmpty // = true
```

You can also combine strings by using the + and += operators:

```
var composingAString = "Hello"
composingAString += ", World!" // = "Hello, World!"
```

Internally a string is a sequence of `Character` objects, each representing a Unicode character. To loop over every character in a string, you can use a `for-in` loop:

```
var reversedString = ""
for character in "Hello".characters {
    reversedString = String(character) + reversedString
}
reversedString // = "olleH"
```

To work out how many characters are in a string, you use the count function:

```
"Hello".characters.count // = 5
```

The count function actually works on any collection, including arrays and dictionaries.

Note that the number of characters in a string is *not* the same as the number of bytes. Unicode characters can range in size from 1 byte to 4 bytes, depending on their type (emoji, for example, are 4 bytes).

To change the case of a string, you use the uppercased and lowercased functions, which return modified versions of the original string:

```
string1.uppercased() // = "HELLO"
string2.lowercased() // = "hello"
```

Comparing Strings

To compare two different strings, you just use the == operator. This operator checks the contents of two strings to see if they contain the same characters:

```
let string1 : String = "Hello"
let string2 : String = "Hel" + "lo"

if string1 == string2 {
    print("The strings are equal")
}
```

In other languages like C and Objective-C, the == operator checks to see if two values are equal, or if two variables refer to the same location in memory. If you really do want to see if two string variables refer to the same object, you use the === operator (note that it's three equals signs, instead of two):

```
if string1 as AnyObject === string2 as AnyObject {
    print("The strings are the same object")
}
```

AnyObject in Swift means "any object, of any type."

Searching Strings

You can check to see if a string has a given suffix or prefix by using the hasPrefix and hasSuffix methods:

```
if string1.hasPrefix("H") {
    print("String begins with an H")
}
```

```
if string1.hasSuffix("llo") {
    print("String ends in 'llo'")
}
```

Optional Types

It's often very useful to have variables that can sometimes have no value. For example, you might have a variable that stores a number to display to the user, but you don't know what that number is yet. As we've seen already, Swift variables need to have a value. One solution might be to use the number zero to represent "no value"; indeed, many languages, including C, C++, Java, and Objective-C, do just this. However, this creates a problem: there is no way to distinguish between the value zero and no value at all. What if the value you want to show is actually zero?

To deal with this issue, Swift makes a very clear distinction between "no value" and all other values. "No value" is referred to as `nil` and is a different type from all others.

 If you're coming from Objective-C, you might remember that `nil` is actually defined as a `void` pointer to zero. This makes it technically a number, which means, in Objective-C, you can do things like this:

```
int i = (int)(nil)+2;
// Equals 2 (because 0 + 2 = 2)
```

This isn't allowed in Swift, because `nil` and `Int` are different types.

However, recall that all variables in Swift are required to have values. If you want a variable to be allowed to *sometimes* be `nil`, you make it an *optional* variable. This is useful in situations where you don't know if something will occur; for example, when downloading an image from the internet, you do not know if you will get back a valid image file or gibberish. You define optional variables by using a question mark (?) as part of their type:

```
// Optional integer, allowed to be nil
var anOptionalInteger : Int? = nil
anOptionalInteger = 42
```

Only optional variables are allowed to be set to `nil`. If a variable isn't defined as optional, it's not allowed to be set to the `nil` value:

```
// Nonoptional (regular), NOT allowed to be nil
var aNonOptionalInteger = 42

aNonOptionalInteger = nil
// ERROR: only optional values can be nil
```

If you create an optional variable and don't assign it a value, it will default to `nil`.

You can check to see if an optional variable has a value by using an `if` statement:

```
if anOptionalInteger != nil {
    print("It has a value!")
} else {
    print("It has no value!")
}
```

When you have an optional variable, you can *unwrap* it to get at its value. You do this using the ! character.

Note that if you unwrap an optional variable, and it has no value, your program will throw a runtime error, and the program will crash:

```
// Optional types must be unwrapped using !
anOptionalInteger = 2
1 + anOptionalInteger! // = 3

anOptionalInteger = nil
1 + anOptionalInteger!
// CRASH: anOptionalInteger = nil, can't use nil data
```

If you don't want to unwrap your optional variables every time you want to use them, you can declare a variable as an *implicitly unwrapped optional*, like this:

```
var implicitlyUnwrappedOptionalInteger : Int!
implicitlyUnwrappedOptionalInteger = 1
1 + implicitlyUnwrappedOptionalInteger // = 2
```

Implicitly unwrapped optionals are regular optionals: they can either contain `nil`, or not. However, whenever you access their value, the compiler unwraps it.

This lets you use their values directly but can be unsafe, because when an optional is unwrapped and has no value, your program crashes.

Implicitly unwrapped optionals let you get away with not explicitly unwrapping them when you use them, which can make you forget that they can sometimes be `nil`. Use this with caution.

You can use an `if-let` statement to check to see if an optional variable has a value; and if it does, assign that value to a constant (*non*optional) variable, and then run some code. This can save you quite a few lines of code while preserving the safety of first checking to see if an optional variable actually has a value to work with.

An `if-let` statement looks like this:

```swift
var conditionalString : String? = "a string"

if let theString = conditionalString {
    print("The string is '\(theString)'")
} else {
    print("The string is nil")
}
// Prints "The string is 'a string'"
```

Type Casting

Swift is strongly typed. This means that it relies upon objects being of the type it expects when passing arguments to functions. Sometimes you need to check the type of an instance, or treat it as a different type, and that's where *type casting* comes in.

Using the `is`, `as!`, and `as?` operators, you can test for types, as well as downcast—that is, treat an instance as one of its subclassses. (We'll discuss subclasses in "Inheritance" on page 66.)

You can also use these operators to check whether a type conforms to a protocol. We'll touch more on protocols later, in "Protocols" on page 70.

You can use the `is` operator to check if an instance is a certain subclass, for example:

```swift
if thing is String {
  print("Thing is a string!")
}
```

The `as?` operator checks the type of a variable and returns an optional value of the specified type:

```swift
var maybeString = thing as? String

// maybeString is a String?—an optional string.
// If the check didn't work, maybeString will be nil.
```

Using the `as!` operator works in the same way as the `as?` operator, except that it returns a *non*optional value of the specified type. If the value can't be converted to the desired type, your program crashes:

```swift
var definitelyString = thing as! String

// definitelyString is a String and is guaranteed to have a value
```

 The `as!` operator is for when you're absolutely sure that the value you're converting is the right type, and you don't want to work with optionals.

You can convert between certain types in Swift. For example, to convert an Int to a String, you do this:

```
let aString = String(2)
// = "2"
```

Note that not all types can be converted to other types. It depends on the specific types you're trying to convert between, and the precise value of the thing you're trying to convert. For example, the String "2" can be converted to an Int, but the String "Hello" can't.

You also can't convert types by directly assigning variables—you must explicitly cast. Attempting to assign a value of one type to a variable with another produces an error:

```
// ERROR: Can't directly convert between types
let aString = anInteger
```

Tuples

A *tuple* is a simple collection of data. Tuples let you bundle any number of values of any type together into a single value:

```
let aTuple = (1, "Yes")
```

Once you have a tuple, you can get values out of it by index:

```
let theNumber = aTuple.0 // = 1
```

In addition to using indices to get the values out of a tuple, you can also apply labels to values inside tuples:

```
let anotherTuple = (aNumber: 1, aString: "Yes")

let theOtherNumber = anotherTuple.aNumber // = 1
```

Arrays

Arrays are ordered lists of values and are very easy to create in Swift. To create an array, you use square brackets ([ ]):

```
// Array of integers
let arrayOfIntegers : [Int] = [1,2,3]
```

Swift can also infer the type of the array:

```
// Type of array is implied
let implicitArrayOfIntegers = [1,2,3]
```

Arrays can contain a mix of different types of values. However, if you do this, Swift will be forced to assume that it's an array of objects of an unknown type, instead of an array of a single type.

You can create an empty array as well, though you need to manually specify its type if you do this:

```swift
// You can also create an empty array, but you must provide the type
let anotherArray = [Int]()
```

While most of the time your arrays will all be single-value types, you can mix and match types in a single array.

Once you have an array, you can work with its contents. For example, you can append objects to the end of the array using the append function:

```swift
var myArray = [1,2,3]
myArray.append(4)
// = [1,2,3,4]
```

In addition to appending to the end of the array, you can also insert objects at any point in the array. Swift arrays start at index 0, making this code the opposite of append:

```swift
myArray.insert(5, at: 0)
// = [5,1,2,3,4]
```

You can't insert items into an array beyond its bounds. For example, if you tried to insert an item at element 99, it wouldn't work and would throw a runtime error (i.e., your program would crash). Typically, the two most common cases in which you add things to an array are when you add them to the end (using append) and at the start (using insert at index 0).

You can also remove items from an array. Doing so automatically reindexes the array so you don't end up with empty elements inside your arrays. To remove an item, you indicate its index in the array. So to remove the fifth element from the array, you'd do this:

```swift
myArray.remove(at: 4)
// = [5,1,2,3]
```

You can also quickly reverse the contents of an array using the reverse function:

```
myArray.reverse()
// = [3,2,1,5]
```

It is worth noting that in this example, the `reverse` function doesn't reverse `myArray` but instead returns a new array that is the reverse of `myArray`.

Finally, it's often useful to know how many items are in an array. You can work this out using the array's `count` property:

```
myArray.count
// = 4
```

Arrays are frequently in `for-in` loops; see "Control Flow" on page 37.

If you define an array with the `let` keyword, its contents become *immutable* (i.e., it's not allowed to change its contents):

```
let immutableArray = [42,24]
```

When you create an array by using the shorthand of a list of comma-separated values surrounded by square brackets, you are initializing it as an *array literal*. This is just shorthand for the full initializer; `[42, 24]` actually gets compiled to `Array(arrayLit eral: 42, 24)`.

Dictionaries

A *dictionary* is a type that maps *keys* to *values*. Dictionaries are useful for when you want to represent a collection of related information.

In a dictionary, you associate a key with a related value. For example, to store information about the crew of a space station, you could use a dictionary like this:

```
var crew = [
    "Captain": "Benjamin Sisko",
    "First Officer": "Kira Nerys",
    "Constable": "Odo"
];
```

When you have a dictionary, you can access its contents through *subscripting*—that is, using square brackets ([and]) after a variable's name to describe what you want to get from that variable. For example, to get the "Captain" value from the `crew` variable, you do this:

```
crew["Captain"]
// = "Benjamin Sisko"
```

You can also set values in a dictionary using subscripting. For example, to register the fact that Julian Bashir is the station's doctor:

```
crew["Doctor"] = "Julian Bashir"
```

In the previous example, we're talking about a dictionary that uses `String` values for both its keys and its values. However, it doesn't have to be set up this way—dictionaries can actually contain almost any value. For example, you can make a dictionary use `Int` values for both keys and values:

```
// This dictionary uses integers for both keys and values
var aNumberDictionary = [1: 2]
aNumberDictionary[21] = 23
```

You can mix and match different types in your arrays and dictionaries; for example, you can make a dictionary that contains both strings and integers as values:

```
var aMixedDictionary = ["one": 1, "two": "twoooo"] as [String: Any]
// (If you declare a dictionary with different types,
// you need to add the type annotation to reassure the
// compiler that that's actually what you wanted to do)
```

Enumerations

Creating an enumeration is an easy way to group a collection of related or like values and work with them in a safe, clean way. An enumeration is a first-class type that is restricted to a defined list of possible values.

Defining an enumeration is easy. Use the `enum` keyword, name the type, and place each possible case between the braces, using the keyword `case` to differentiate each one:

```
// Enumeration of top-secret future iPads that definitely
// will never exist
enum FutureiPad {
    case iPadSuperPro

    case iPadTotallyPro

    case iPadLudicrous
}
```

Once you've got your enumeration, you can use it like any other variable in Swift:

```
var nextiPad = FutureiPad.iPadTotallyPro
```

You can also change it to a different value of the type:

```
nextiPad = .iPadSuperPro
```

Or use a `switch` statement to match enumeration values:

```
switch nextiPad {
case .iPadSuperPro:
    print("Too big!")

case .iPadTotallyPro:
    print("Too small!")

case .iPadLudicrous:
    print("Just right!")
}
```

You might be familiar with enums, or enumerations, in other programming languages. They're much the same in Swift, with the exception that they don't automatically have a corresponding integer value. The members of an enumeration are values themselves and are of the type of that enumeration. They can, of course, have a corresponding integer number. Because Swift does it this way, enumerations are safe and explicit.

Associated Values

Enumerations in Swift allow you to store associated values. The associated values can be any type, and each member of the enumeration can have a different set of values.

For example, if you wanted to represent two types of weapons that a spaceship in a video game could have, you might do this:

```
enum Weapon {
    case laser
    case missiles
}
```

Using associated values, you could also allow a laser power level, or the range of missiles, to be specified:

```
enum Weapon {
    case laser(powerLevel: Int)
    case missiles(range: Int)
}
```

To work with these associated values, you provide them when assigning to the variable:

```
let spaceLaser = Weapon.laser(powerLevel: 5)
```

Enumerations with associated values aren't so much *containers* for those values as they are a *specialization* of the enumeration's value. Don't think of Laser(powerLevel: 5) as "laser, with the number 5 inside it"; instead, think of it as "a laser of value 5."

You can use the `switch` statement with associated values, which allows you to pattern-match on more specific values in your enumeration:

```swift
switch spaceLaser {
case .laser(powerLevel: 0...10 ):
    print("It's a laser with power from 0 to 10!")
case .laser:
    print("It's a laser!")
case .missiles(let range):
    print("It's a missile with range \(range)!")
}
// Prints "It's a laser with power from 0 to 10!"
```

Sets

A *set* lets you store a collection of unique values of the same type. Sets are unordered and can store anything from integers and strings to classes or structs.

You can create an empty set by using the `Set` type's initializer. When you do, you specify the type of values that will be stored in the set:

```swift
var setOfStrings = Set<String>()
```

Alternatively, you can create a set with an array literal. If you do this, Swift will figure out what type to use, based on the type of values in the array:

```swift
var fruitSet: Set = ["apple", "orange", "orange", "banana"]
```

To be stored in a set, a type must be *hashable*. All the provided types are hashable, but you can also make your own types hashable by making them conform to the Hashable protocol. We talk more about protocols in "Protocols" on page 70.

Objects in a set are unique. If you add the same object twice to a set, it's only included in the set once. For example, in the preceding code, we included the string "orange" twice in the array, bringing it to a total of four items; however, if we ask the set how many objects it contains, it will report only three:

```swift
fruitSet.count
// = 3
```

You can access or modify a set in all the usual ways, including checking its count property, checking if it's empty, and adding and removing items:

```
if fruitSet.isEmpty {
    print("My set is empty!")
}

// Add a new item to the set
fruitSet.insert("pear")

// Remove an item from the set
fruitSet.remove("apple")
// mySet now contains {"banana", "pear", "orange"}
```

You can, of course, also iterate over a set, just like you would with an array or dictionary:

```
for fruit in fruitSet {
    let fruitPlural = fruit + "s"
    print("You know what's tasty? \(fruitPlural.uppercased()).")
}
```

 You can also perform unions, intersections, exclusions, and subtractions, as well as check if sets are supersets or subsets of each other. For more information, check out Apple's Collection Types documentation (*http://apple.co/21TwOIb*).

Functions and Closures

In Swift, you define *functions* to perform tasks with data. Functions let you organize your code into small, repeatable chunks, like so:

```
func sayHello() {
    print("Hello")
}

sayHello()
```

Functions can return a value to the code that calls them. When you define a function that returns a type, you must indicate the type of the data that it returns by using the arrow (->) symbol:

```
func usefulNumber() -> Int {
    return 123
}

usefulNumber()
```

When the usefulNumber function is called, the code between the two braces ({ and }) is run.

Inside a function's parentheses, you can pass it parameters, which it's able to use to do work. When you define parameters for a function, you must also define the type of those parameters:

```
func addNumbers(firstValue: Int, secondValue: Int) -> Int {
    return firstValue + secondValue
}

addNumbers(firstValue: 1, secondValue: 2)
```

A function can return a single value, as we've already seen, but it can also return *multiple* values, in the form of a tuple. In addition, you can attach names to the values in the tuple, making it easier to work with the returned value:

```
func processNumbers(firstValue: Int, secondValue: Int)
    -> (doubled: Int, quadrupled: Int) {
        return (firstValue * 2, secondValue * 4)
}
processNumbers(firstValue: 2, secondValue: 4)
```

When you call a function that returns a tuple, you can access its value by index or by name (if it has them):

```
// Accessing by number:
processNumbers(firstValue: 2, secondValue: 4).1 // = 16
// Same thing but with names:
processNumbers(firstValue: 2, secondValue: 4).quadrupled // = 16
```

By default, all parameters after the first one must have a *label* associated with them, and the label is necessary in calling the function. You can see this in action in the preceding code sample: the second parameter has secondValue: before it. Swift includes this to make it easier to read the code; when parameters have labels, it's a lot easier to remember what each parameter is for.

However, sometimes you don't need a label before parameter names, especially when it's very obvious what the parameters are for. In these cases, you can tell Swift to not require a label before the parameters by placing an underscore before the name:

```
func subtractNumbers(_ num1 : Int, _ num2 : Int) -> Int {
    return num1 - num2
}

subtractNumbers(5, 3) // = 2
```

 The underscore is used throughout Swift to represent the concept "I don't care what this is." It's an idea that appears in several other languages, such as Prolog.

By default, the label for the parameter is the same as the parameter's name. However, if you prefer to, you can provide a custom label for a parameter. To override the default label for a parameter, you put the label before the parameter's name, like so:

```
func addNumber(firstNumber num1 : Int, toSecondNumber num2: Int) -> Int {
    return num1 + num2
}

addNumber(firstNumber: 2, toSecondNumber: 3) // = 5
```

You can also create functions whose parameters have *default* values. This means that you can call these functions and omit certain parameters; if you do, those parameters will use the value used in the function's definition:

```
func multiplyNumbers2 (firstNumber: Int, multiplier: Int = 2) -> Int {
    return firstNumber * multiplier;
}
// Parameters with default values can be omitted
multiplyNumbers2(firstNumber: 2) // = 4
```

Sometimes, you'll want to use functions with a *variable* number of parameters. A parameter with a variable number of values is called a *variadic* parameter. In these cases, you want a function to handle any number of parameters, ranging from 0 to an unlimited number. To do this, use three dots (...) to indicate that a parameter has a variable number of values. Inside the body of the function, the variadic parameter becomes an array, which you can use like any other:

```
func sumNumbers(numbers: Int...) -> Int {
    // In this function, 'numbers' is an array of Ints
    var total = 0
    for number in numbers {
        total += number
    }
    return total
}
sumNumbers(numbers: 2,3,4,5) // = 14
```

When using variable parameters, you can have as many nonvariadic parameters as you like. However, note that you can only have a single variadic parameter, and any parameter listed after a variadic parameter must have an external parameter name.

Normally, function parameters and return values are passed by value; you are given a copy of the parameters and return values. However, if you define a parameter with the inout keyword, you can pass the parameter by reference and directly change the value that's stored in the variable. You can use this to swap two variables using a function, like so:

```
func swapValues(firstValue: inout Int, secondValue: inout Int) {
    (firstValue, secondValue) = (secondValue, firstValue)
}

var swap1 = 2
var swap2 = 3
swapValues(firstValue: &swap1, secondValue: &swap2)
swap1 // = 3
swap2 // = 2
```

When you pass in a variable as an `inout` parameter, you preface it with an ampersand
(&). This reminds you that its value is going to change when you call the function.

Using Functions as Variables

You can store functions in variables. To do this, you first declare a variable as capable
of storing a function that takes certain parameters and returns a value. Once that's
done, you can store *any* function that takes those types of parameters and returns the
same type of value in the variable:

```
var numbersFunc: (Int, Int) -> Int;
// numbersFunc can now store any function
// that takes two ints and returns an int

// Using the 'addNumbers' function from before, which takes two numbers
// and adds them
numbersFunc = addNumbers
numbersFunc(2, 3) // = 5
```

Functions can also receive and use other functions as parameters. This means that
you can combine functions:

```
func timesThree(number: Int) -> Int {
    return number * 3
}

func doSomethingToNumber(aNumber: Int, thingToDo: (Int)->Int) -> Int {
    // We've received some function as a parameter, which we refer to as
    // 'thingToDo' inside this function

    // Call the function 'thingToDo' using 'aNumber', and return the result
    return thingToDo(aNumber);
}

// Give the 'timesThree' function to use as 'thingToDo'
doSomethingToNumber(aNumber: 4, thingToDo: timesThree) // = 12
```

Functions can also return *other functions*. This means that you can use a function that
creates a new function, which you can use in your code:

```
// This function takes an Int as a parameter. It returns a new function that
// takes an Int parameter and return an Int.
```

```
func createAdder(numberToAdd: Int) -> (Int) -> Int {
    func adder(number: Int) -> Int {
        return number + numberToAdd
    }
    return adder
}
var addTwo = createAdder(numberToAdd: 2)

// addTwo is now a function that can be called
addTwo(2) // = 4
```

A function can also "capture" a value and use it multiple times. This is a tricky concept, so we'll go into it in a bit of detail. Consider the following example code:

```
func createIncrementor(incrementAmount: Int) -> () -> Int { ❶
    var amount = 0 ❷
    func incrementor() -> Int { ❸
        amount += incrementAmount ❹
        return amount
    }
    return incrementor ❺
}

var incrementByTen = createIncrementor(incrementAmount: 10) ❻
incrementByTen() // = 10 ❼
incrementByTen() // = 20

var incrementByFifteen = createIncrementor(incrementAmount: 15) ❽
incrementByFifteen() // = 15 ❾
```

This example does the following things:

❶ The createIncrementor function takes an Int parameter and returns a function that takes no parameters and returns an Int.

❷ Inside the function, a variable called amount is created and set to 0.

❸ A new function is created inside the createIncrementor function, which takes no parameters and returns an Int.

❹ Inside this new function, the amount variable has the incrementAmount parameter added to it, and then returned. Notice that the amount variable is outside of this function.

❺ The incrementor function is then returned.

❻ The createIncrementor function can then be used to create a new incrementor function. In the first example, one is created with the incremementAmount parameter set to 10.

❼ Each time this function is called, it will return a value that's 10 higher than the last time it was called. The reason it's doing this is because the function that `crea teIncrementor` returned *captured* the variable `amount`; every time it's called, that variable goes up by `incrementAmount`.

❽ The `amount` variable is not shared between individual functions, however. When a new incrementor is created, it has its own separate `amount` variable.

❾ The second function goes up by 15.

This feature of Swift allows you to create functions that act as *generators*, functions that return different values each time they're called.

Closures

Another feature of Swift is that of *closures*, which are small, anonymous chunks of code that you can use like functions. Closures are great for passing to other functions to tell them how they should carry out a certain task.

To give you an example of how closures work, consider the built-in `sort` function. This function takes an array and a closure, and uses that closure to determine how two individual elements of that array should be ordered (i.e., which one should go first in the array):

```
var sortingInline = [2, 5, 98, 2, 13]
sortingInline.sort() // = [2, 2, 5, 13, 98]
```

To sort an array so that small numbers go before large numbers, you can provide a closure that describes *how* to do the sort, like this:

```
var numbers = [2, 1, 56, 32, 120, 13]

// Sort so that small numbers go before large numbers
var numbersSorted = numbers.sorted(by: {
    (n1: Int, n2: Int) -> Bool in return n2 > n1
})
// = [1, 2, 13, 32, 56, 120]
```

Closures have a special keyword, `in`. The `in` keyword lets Swift know where to break up the closure from its definition and its implementation. So in our previous example, the definition was `(n1: Int, n2: Int)->Bool`, and the implementation of that closure came after the `in` keyword: `return n2 > n1`.

 If you come from Objective-C land, the `in` keyword works similar to the ^ syntax in blocks.

A closure, like a function, takes parameters. In the preceding example, the closure specifies the name and type of the parameters that it works with. However, you don't need to be quite so verbose—the compiler can infer the type of the parameters for you, much like it can with variables. Notice the lack of types in the parameters for the following closure:

```
var numbersSortedReverse = numbers.sorted(by: {n1, n2 in return n1 > n2})
// = [120, 56, 32, 13, 2, 1]
```

You can make it even more terse if you don't especially care what names the parameters should have. If you omit the parameter names, you can just refer to each parameter by number (the first parameter is called $0, the second is called $1, etc.).

Additionally, if your closure only contains a single line of code, you can omit the return keyword:

```
var numbersSortedAgain = numbers.sorted(by: {
    $1 > $0
}) // = [1, 2, 13, 32, 56, 120]
```

Finally, if a closure is the last parameter in a function call, you can put it outside the parentheses. This is purely something that improves readability and doesn't change how the closure works:

```
var numbersSortedReversedAgain = numbers.sorted {
    $0 > $1
} // = [120, 56, 32, 13, 2, 1]
```

The line breaks in this code are optional, too. You could also do this:

```
var numbersSortedReversedOneMoreTime = numbers.sorted { $0 > $1 }
// = [120, 56, 32, 13, 2, 1]
```

Just like functions, closures can be stored in variables. In that case, you can call them just like a function:

```
var comparator = {(a: Int, b:Int) in a < b}
comparator(1,2) // = true
```

The defer Keyword

Sometimes, you'll want to run some code, but at a later date. For example, if you're writing code that opens a file and makes some changes, you'll also need to ensure that the file is closed when you're done. This is important, and it's easy to forget when you start writing your method.

The defer keyword lets you write code that will run at a later time. Specifically, code you put in a defer block will run when the current flow of execution leaves the current scope—that is, the current function, loop body, and so on:

```
func doSomeWork() {
    print("Getting started!")
    defer {
        print("All done!")
    }
    print("Getting to work!")
}

doSomeWork()
// Prints "Getting started!", "Getting to work!" and "All done!", in that order
```

 defer is a resource management technique, not a means of implementing asynchronous code!

The guard Keyword

There are often cases where your code needs to check to see if a certain condition holds. For example, if you're writing a method to withdraw money from a bank account, you can't go ahead with the operation if the bank account's balance is too low.

The guard keyword lets you define a test that needs to pass; alternatively, if it doesn't pass, a block of code is run. This might sound very similar to the if statement, but it has a twist: the block of code that runs if the test doesn't pass is *required* to exit the current flow of execution. That is, if it's inside a function, it has to return from that function; it's a compiler error if it doesn't. This guarantees that if the condition doesn't hold, the code following the guard statement will not be executed:

```
guard 2+2 == 4 else {
    print("The universe makes no sense")
    return // this is mandatory!
}
print("We can continue with our daily lives")
```

Making Your Code Swifty

With the release of version 3.0 the Swift community has made some guidelines to follow when designing, creating, and naming your code and APIs. The full guidelines can be seen on the API Design Guidelines website (*https://swift.org/documentation/api-design-guidelines/*) and are well worth checking out, but the cornerstone of it all is clarity. Some general rules to remember:

- When writing functions, remember that you will only write it once but will use it many times, so keep the names as simple and unambiguous as possible. For example, the `remove(at:)` function on arrays removes an element at the index passed in. Using it like `anArray.remove(at: 2)` is clear and unambiguous, whereas if it were just `anArray.remove(2)` we wouldn't know if it were removing the element at index 2 or removing the object 2 from the array.

- Where possible, make your functions read like an English sentence; `anArray.insert(x at: y)` reads better than `anArray.insert(x index: y)`. Additionally, when making mutating and nonmutating functions, make the mutating functions sound like verbs and name the nonmutating form with the "-ed" or "-ing" suffix, so `anArray.sort()` would modify the `anArray` variable whereas `anArray.sorted()` would return a sorted copy.

- Finally, avoid abbreviations, acronyms, and obscure terms. Unless they are domain specific to what you are writing, they are just going to make it harder to understand later on.

Conclusion

In this chapter, we've looked at the basics of programming with Swift. In the next chapter, we'll dive into some of the language's more advanced components, such as objects, memory management, working with data, and error handling. After that, we'll continue our exploration of Swift through the construction of three apps.

CHAPTER 3

Swift for Object-Oriented App Development

The previous chapter looked at the basic building blocks of programming in Swift. In this chapter, we're going to look at some of the more advanced features of Swift, such as memory management, working with files and external data, and error handling. We'll also touch on interoperating with Apple's older programming language, Objective-C.

Swift's features allow it to be used as an *object-oriented* programming language. This means that you do the majority of your work by creating and manipulating *objects*— chunks of data and code that represent a thing that can perform some useful work or store some useful data.

Classes and Objects

In Swift, as with Objective-C, Java, and C++ (and many other languages), you define templates for your objects using *classes*. Classes in Swift look like this:

```
class Vehicle {

}
```

Classes contain both *properties* and *methods*. Properties are variables that are part of a class, and methods are functions that are part of a class.

The Vehicle class in the following example contains two properties: an optional String called color, and an Int called maxSpeed. Property declarations look the same as variable declarations do in other code:

```
class Vehicle {

    var color: String?
    var maxSpeed = 80

}
```

Methods in a class look the same as functions anywhere else. Code that's in a method can access the properties of a class by using the `self` keyword, which refers to the object that's currently running the code:

```
class Vehicle {

    var color: String?
    var maxSpeed = 80

    func description() -> String {
        return "A \(self.color) vehicle"
    }

    func travel() {
        print("Traveling at \(maxSpeed) kph")
    }
}
```

 If you are wondering what the \() inside the string is, this is *string interpolation*, which lets you make strings from myriad types. We talk more about strings in "Working with Strings" on page 42.

You can omit the `self` keyword if it's obvious that the property is part of the current object. In the previous example, `description` uses the `self` keyword, while `travel` doesn't.

When you've defined a class, you can create instances of the class (called an object) to work with. Instances have their own copies of the class's properties and functions.

For example, to define an instance of the `Vehicle` class, you define a variable and call the class's initializer. Once that's done, you can work with the class's functions and properties:

```
var redVehicle = Vehicle()
redVehicle.color = "Red"
redVehicle.maxSpeed = 90
redVehicle.travel() // prints "Traveling at 90 kph"
redVehicle.description() // = "A Red vehicle"
```

Initialization and Deinitialization

When you create an object in Swift, a special method known as its *initializer* is called. The initializer is the method that you use to set up the initial state of an object and is always named `init`.

Swift has two types of initializers, *convenience initializers* and *designated initializers*. A designated initializer sets up everything you need to use that object, often using default settings where necessary. A convenience initializer, as its name implies, makes setting up the instance more convenient by allowing for more information to be included in the initialization. A convenience initializer must call the designated initializer as part of its setup.

In addition to initializers, you can run code when removing an object, in a method called a *deinitializer*, named `deinit`. This runs when the retain count of an object drops to zero (see "Memory Management" on page 87) and is called right before the object is removed from memory. This is your object's final opportunity to do any necessary cleanup before it goes away forever:

```swift
class InitAndDeinitExample {
    // Designated (i.e., main) initializer
    init () {
        print("I've been created!")
    }
    // Convenience initializer, required to call the
    // designated initializer (above)
    convenience init (text: String) {
        self.init() // this is mandatory
        print("I was called with the convenience initializer!")
    }
    // Deinitializer
    deinit {
        print("I'm going away!")
    }
}

var example : InitAndDeinitExample?

// using the designated initializer
example = InitAndDeinitExample() // prints "I've been created!"
example = nil // prints "I'm going away"

// using the convenience initializer
example = InitAndDeinitExample(text: "Hello")
// prints "I've been created!" and then
//   "I was called with the convenience initializer"
```

An initializer can also return `nil`. This can be useful when your initializer isn't able to usefully construct an object. For example, the `URL` class has an initializer that takes a string and converts it into a URL; if the string isn't a valid URL, the initializer returns nil.

To create an initializer that can return nil—also known as a *failable initializer*—put a question mark after the init keyword, and return nil if the initializer decides that it can't successfully construct the object:

```
// This is a convenience initializer that can sometimes fail, returning nil
// Note the ? after the word 'init'
convenience init? (value: Int) {
    self.init()

    if value > 5 {
        // We can't initialize this object; return nil to indicate failure
        return nil
    }

}
```

When you use a failable initializer, it will always return an optional:

```
var failableExample = InitAndDeinitExample.init(value: 6)
// = nil
```

Properties

Classes store their data in *properties*. Properties, as previously mentioned, are variables or constants that are attached to instances of classes. Properties that you've added to a class are usually accessed like this:

```
class Counter {
    var number: Int = 0
}
let myCounter = Counter()
myCounter.number = 2
```

However, as objects get more complex, it can cause a problem for you as a programmer. If you wanted to represent vehicles with engines, you'd need to add a property to the Vehicle class; however, this would mean that *all* Vehicle instances would have this property, even if they didn't need one. To keep things better organized, it's better to move properties that are specific to a subset of your objects to a new class that *inherits* properties from another.

Inheritance

When you define a class, you can create one that *inherits* from another. When a class inherits from another (called the *parent* class), it incorporates all its parent's functions and properties. In Swift, classes are allowed to have only a single parent class. This is the same as Objective-C, but differs from C++, which allows classes to have multiple parents (known as *multiple inheritance*).

To create a class that inherits from another, you put the name of the class you're inheriting from after the name of the class you're creating, like so:

```
class Car: Vehicle {

    var engineType : String = "V8"

}
```

Classes that inherit from other classes can *override* functions in their parent class. This means that you can create subclasses that inherit most of their functionality, but can specialize in certain areas. For example, the Car class contains an engineType property; only Car instances will have this property.

To override a function, you redeclare it in your subclass and add the override keyword to let the compiler know that you aren't accidentally creating a method with the same name as one in the parent class.

In an overridden function, it's often very useful to call back to the parent class's version of that function. You can do this through the super keyword, which lets you get access to the superclass's functions:

```
class Car: Vehicle {

    var engineType : String = "V8"

    // Inherited classes can override functions
    override func description() -> String  {
        let description = super.description()
        return description + ", which is a car"
    }

}
```

Computed properties

In the previous example, the property is a simple value stored in the object. This is known in Swift as a *stored property*. However, you can do more with properties, including creating properties that use code to figure out their value. These are known as *computed properties*, and you can use them to provide a simpler interface to information stored in your classes.

For example, consider a class that represents a rectangle, which has both a width and a height property. It'd be useful to have an additional property that contains the area, but you don't want that to be a third stored property. Instead, you can use a computed property, which looks like a regular property from the outside, but on the inside is really a function that figures out the value when needed.

To define a computed property, you declare a variable in the same way as you do for a stored property, but add braces ({ and }) after it. Inside these braces, you provide a get section, and optionally a set section:

```
class Rectangle {
    var width: Double = 0.0
    var height: Double = 0.0
    var area : Double {
        // computed getter
        get {
            return width * height
        }

        // computed setter
        set {
            // Assume equal dimensions (i.e., a square)
            width = sqrt(newValue)
            height = sqrt(newValue)
        }
    }
}
```

When creating setters for your computed properties, you are given the new value passed into the setter passed in as a constant called newValue.

In the previous example, we computed the area by multiplying the width and height. The property is also settable—if you set the area of the rectangle, the code assumes that you want to create a square and updates the width and height to the square root of the area.

Working with computed properties looks identical to working with stored properties:

```
var rect = Rectangle()
rect.width = 3.0
rect.height = 4.5
rect.area // = 13.5
rect.area = 9 // width & height now both 3.0
```

Observers

When working with properties, you often may want to run some code whenever a property changes. To support this, Swift lets you add *observers* to your properties. These are small chunks of code that can run just before or after a property's value changes. To create a property observer, add braces after your property (much like you do with computed properties), and include willSet and didSet blocks. These blocks each get passed a parameter—willSet, which is called before the property's value changes, is given the value that is about to be set, and didSet is given the old value:

```
class PropertyObserverExample {
    var number : Int = 0 {
        willSet(newNumber) {
            print("About to change to \(newNumber)")
        }
        didSet(oldNumber) {
            print("Just changed from \(oldNumber) to \(self.number)!")
        }
    }
}
```

Property observers don't change anything about how you actually work with the property—they just add further behavior before and after the property changes:

```
var observer = PropertyObserverExample()
observer.number = 4
// prints "About to change to 4", then "Just changed from 0 to 4!"
```

Lazy properties

You can also make a property *lazy*. A lazy property is one that doesn't get set up until the first time it's accessed. This lets you defer some of the more time-consuming work of setting up a class to later on, when it's actually needed. To define a property as lazy, you put the `lazy` keyword in front of it. *Lazy loading* is very useful to save on memory for properties that may not be used—there is no point in initializing something that won't be used!

You can see lazy properties in action in the following example. In this code, there are two properties, both of the same type, but one of them is lazy:

```
class SomeExpensiveClass {
    init(id : Int) {
        print("Expensive class \(id) created!")
    }
}

class LazyPropertyExample {
    var expensiveClass1 = SomeExpensiveClass(id: 1)
    // Note that we're actually constructing a class,
    // but it's labeled as lazy
    lazy var expensiveClass2 = SomeExpensiveClass(id: 2)

    init() {
        print("First class created!")
    }
}

var lazyExample = LazyPropertyExample()
// prints "Expensive class 1 created", then "First class created!"

lazyExample.expensiveClass1 // prints nothing, it's already created
lazyExample.expensiveClass2 // prints "Expensive class 2 created!"
```

In this example, when the `lazyExample` variable is created, it immediately creates the first instance of `SomeExpensiveClass`. However, the second instance isn't created until it's actually used by the code.

Protocols

A *protocol* can be thought of as a list of requirements for a class. When you define a protocol, you're creating a list of properties and methods that classes can declare that they have.

A protocol looks very much like a class, with the exception that you don't provide any actual code—you just define what kinds of properties and functions exist and how they can be accessed.

For example, if you wanted to create a protocol that describes any object that can blink on and off, you could use this:

```
protocol Blinking {

    // This property must be (at least) gettable
    var isBlinking : Bool { get }

    // This property must be gettable and settable
    var blinkSpeed: Double { get set }

    // This function must exist, but what it does is up to the implementor
    func startBlinking(blinkSpeed: Double) -> Void
}
```

Once you have a protocol, you can create classes that *conform* to a protocol. When a class conforms to a protocol, it's effectively promising to the compiler that it implements all of the properties and methods listed in that protocol. It's allowed to have more stuff besides that, and it's also allowed to conform to multiple protocols.

To continue this example, you could create a specific class called `Light` that implements the `Blinking` protocol. Remember, all a protocol does is specify *what* a class can do—the class itself is responsible for determining *how* it does it:

```
class TrafficLight : Blinking {
    var isBlinking: Bool = false

    var blinkSpeed : Double = 0.0

    func startBlinking(blinkSpeed : Double) {
        print("I am a traffic light, and I am now blinking")
        isBlinking = true

        // We say "self.blinkSpeed" here, as opposed to "blinkSpeed",
        // to help the compiler tell the difference between the
        // parameter 'blinkSpeed' and the property
```

```
            self.blinkSpeed = blinkSpeed
        }
    }

    class Lighthouse : Blinking {
        var isBlinking: Bool = false

        var blinkSpeed : Double = 0.0

        func startBlinking(blinkSpeed : Double) {
            print("I am a lighthouse, and I am now blinking")
            isBlinking = true

            self.blinkSpeed = blinkSpeed
        }
    }
```

The advantage of using protocols is that you can use Swift's type system to refer to any object that conforms to a given protocol. This is useful because you get to specify that you only care about whether an object conforms to the protocol—the specific type of the class doesn't matter since we are using the protocol as a type:

```
    var aBlinkingThing : Blinking
    // can be ANY object that has the Blinking protocol

    aBlinkingThing = TrafficLight()

    aBlinkingThing.startBlinking(blinkSpeed: 4.0) // prints "I am now blinking"
    aBlinkingThing.blinkSpeed // = 4.0

    aBlinkingThing = Lighthouse()
```

Extensions

In Swift, you can *extend* existing types and add further methods and computed properties. This is very useful in two situations:

- You're working with a type that someone else wrote, and you want to add functionality to it but either don't have access to its source code or don't want to mess around with it.

- You're working with a type that you wrote, and you want to divide its functionality into different sections for readability.

Extensions let you do both with ease. In Swift, you can extend *any* type—that is, you can extend both classes that you write, as well as built-in types like Int and String.

To create an extension, you use the extension keyword, followed by the name of the type you want to extend. For example, to add methods and properties to the built-in Int type, you can do this:

```
extension Int {
    var double : Int {
        return self * 2
    }
    func multiplyWith(anotherNumber: Int) -> Int {
        return self * anotherNumber
    }
}
```

Once you extend a type, the methods and properties you defined in the extension are available to *every* instance of that type:

```
2.double // = 4
4.multiplyWith(anotherNumber: 32) // = 128
```

You can only add computed properties in an extension. You can't add your own stored properties.

You can also use extensions to make a type conform to a protocol. For example, you can make the Int type conform to the Blinking protocol described earlier:

```
extension Int : Blinking {
    var isBlinking : Bool {
        return false;
    }

    var blinkSpeed : Double {
        get {
            return 0.0;
        }
        set {
            // Do nothing
        }
    }

    func startBlinking(blinkSpeed : Double) {
        print("I am the integer \(self). I do not blink.")
    }
}
2.isBlinking // = false
2.startBlinking(blinkSpeed: 2.0)
// prints "I am the integer 2. I do not blink."
```

Access Control

Swift defines four levels of access control, which determines what information is accessible to which parts of the application:

Public

Public classes, methods, and properties are accessible by any part of the app. For example, all of the classes in UIKit that you use to build iOS apps are public.

Internal

Internal entities (data and methods) are only accessible to the *module* in which they're defined. A module is an application, library, or framework. This is why you can't access the inner workings of UIKit—it's defined as internal to the UIKit framework. Internal is the default level of access control: if you don't specify the access control level, it's assumed to be internal.

Fileprivate

Fileprivate entities are only accessible to the file in which it's declared. This means that you can create classes that hide their inner workings from other classes in the same module, which helps to keep the amount of surface area that those classes expose to each other to a minimum.

Private

Private entities are only accessible to the current declaration scope, and this is the most restrictive access modifier. This means you can create functions and objects that can hide their internals from everything else in the module and file. By marking something private, you create functionality you never want others to touch, even inside extensions. This means you can declare a method as private inside a class, and an extension of that class cannot access that method.

The kind of access control that a method or property can have depends on the access level of the class that it's contained in. You can't make a method more accessible than the class in which it's contained. For example, you can't define a private class that has a public method.

To specify the access level for a class, you add the appropriate keyword before the `class` keyword. To define a `public` class called `AccessControl`, for instance, you'd write the following:

```
public class AccessControl {

}
```

By default, all properties and methods are `internal`. You can explicitly define a member as `internal` if you want, but it isn't necessary:

```
// Accessible to this module only
// 'internal' here is the default and can be omitted
internal var internalProperty = 123
```

The exception is for classes defined as `private` or `fileprivate`—if you don't declare an access control level for a member, it's set as `private` or `fileprivate`, not `inter` nal. It is *impossible* to specify an access level for a member of an entity that is more open than the entity itself.

When you declare a method or property as public, it becomes visible to everyone in your app:

```
// Accessible to everyone
public var publicProperty = 123
```

If you declare a method or property as private, it's only accessible from within the scope in which it's declared:

```
// Only accessible in this class
private var privateProperty = 123
```

The difference between private and fileprivate may not be obvious at first glance, but private is far more restrictive than fileprivate. Using private means only within the scope it's declared can it be used, so even code inside extensions will be restricted:

```
class AccessObject {
    func doAThing()
    {
        print("doing a thing")
    }
}
extension AccessObject {
    private func doAPrivateThing() {
        print("doing a private thing")
    }
    fileprivate func doAFilePrivateThing() {
        print("doing a fileprivate thing")
        // can call private functions here
        // as we are in the same scope
        doAPrivateThing()
    }
}

let accessDemo = AccessObject()
accessDemo.doAThing()
accessDemo.doAFilePrivateThing()
// the following won't work
// accessDemo.doAPrivateThing()
```

Finally, you can render a property as read-only by declaring that its setter is filepri vate. This means that you can freely read and write the property's value within the source file that it's declared in, but other files can only read its value:

```
// The setter is fileprivate, so other files can't modify it
fileprivate(set) var privateSetterProperty = 123
```

Operator Overloading

An operator is actually a function that takes one or two values and returns a value. Operators, just like other functions, can be overloaded. For example, you could represent the + function like this:

```
func + (left: Int, right: Int) -> Int {
    return left + right
}
```

 The preceding example actually calls itself in an infinitely recursive way, which hangs your app. Don't actually write this code.

Swift lets you define new operators and overload existing ones for your new types, which means that if you have a new type of data, you can operate on that data using both existing operators, as well as new ones you invent yourself.

For example, imagine you have an object called Vector2D, which stores two floating-point numbers:

```
class Vector2D {
    var x : Float = 0.0
    var y : Float = 0.0

    init (x : Float, y: Float) {
        self.x = x
        self.y = y
    }
}
```

If you want to allow adding instances of this type of object together using the + operator, all you need to do is provide an implementation of the + function:

```
func +(left : Vector2D, right: Vector2D) -> Vector2D {
    let result = Vector2D(x: left.x + right.x, y: left.y + right.y)

    return result
}
```

You can then use it as you'd expect:

```
let first = Vector2D(x: 2, y: 2)
let second = Vector2D(x: 4, y: 1)

let result = first + second
// = (x:6, y:3)
```

For information on how to create your own custom operators, see the "Advanced Operators" (*http://apple.co/1r1RiTJ*) section of *The Swift Programming Language*.

Generics

Swift is a statically typed language. This means that the Swift compiler needs to definitively know what type of information your code is dealing with. This means that you can't pass a string to code that expects to deal with a date (which is something that can happen in Objective-C!).

However, this rigidity means that you lose some flexibility. It's annoying to have to write a chunk of code that does some work with strings, and another that works with dates.

This is where *generics* come in. Generics allow you to write code that doesn't need to know precisely *what* information it's dealing with. An example of this kind of use is in arrays: they don't actually do any work with the data they store, but instead just store it in an ordered collection. Arrays are, in fact, generics.

To create a generic type, you name your object as usual, and then specify any generic types between angle brackets. T is traditionally the term used, but you can put anything you like. For example, to create a generic Tree object, which contains a value and any number of child Tree objects, you'd do the following:

```
class Tree <T> {

    // 'T' can now be used as a type inside this class

    // 'value' is of type T
    var value : T

    // 'children' is an array of Tree objects that have
    // the same type as this one
    private (set) var children : [Tree <T>] = []

    // We can initialize this object with a value of type T
    init(value : T) {
        self.value = value
    }

    // And we can add a child node to our list of children
    func addChild(value : T) -> Tree <T> {
        let newChild = Tree<T>(value: value)
        children.append(newChild)
        return newChild
    }
}
```

Once a generic type is defined, you can create a specific, nongeneric type from it. For example, the `Tree` generic type just defined can be used to create a version that works with `Ints` and one that works with `Strings`:

```
// Tree of integers
let integerTree = Tree<Int>(value: 5)

// Can add children that contain Ints
integerTree.addChild(value: 10)
integerTree.addChild(value: 5)

// Tree of strings
let stringTree = Tree<String>(value: "Hello")

stringTree.addChild(value: "Yes")
stringTree.addChild(value: "Internets")
```

Subscripts

When you work with arrays and dictionaries, you use square brackets, [and], to indicate to Swift what part of the array or dictionary you want to work with. The term for this is *subscripting*, and it's something that your own classes and types can adopt.

You do this using the `subscript` keyword, and define what it means to get and set values via a subscript. For example, let's say you want to access the individual bits inside an 8-bit integer. You can do this with subscripting, like so:

```
// Extend the unsigned 8-bit integer type
extension UInt8 {

    // Allow subscripting this type using UInt8s;
    subscript(bit: UInt8) -> UInt8 {

        // This is run when you do things like "value[x]"
        get {
            return (self >> bit & 0x07) & 1
        }

        // This is run when you do things like "value[x] = y"
        set {
            let cleanBit = bit & 0x07
            let mask = 0xFF ^ (1 << cleanBit)
            let shiftedBit = (newValue & 1) << cleanBit
            self = self & mask | shiftedBit
        }
    }
}
```

With this in place, you can access the individual bits inside the number by reading and writing them:

```
var byte : UInt8 = 212

byte[0] // 0
byte[2] // 1
byte[5] // 0
byte[6] // 1

// Change the last bit
byte[7] = 0

// The number is now changed!
byte // = 84
```

Structures

For the most part, structures are very similar to classes: you can put properties and methods in them, they have initializers, and they generally behave in an object-like way, just like a class does. However, there are two main things that differentiate them from classes:

- Structures do not have inheritance—that is, you cannot make a structure inherit its methods and properties from another.

- When you pass a structure around in your code, the structure is always *copied*.

Structures are declared as follows:

```
struct Point {
    var x: Int
    var y: Int
}
```

 In Swift, structures are *value types*, which are always copied when passed around. Some value types in Swift include `Int`, `String`, `Array`, and `Dictionary`, all of which are implemented as structures.

Additionally, structures in Swift get a compiler-provided initializer, called the *memberwise initializer*, if you don't provide one yourself:

```
let p = Point(x: 2, y: 3)
```

Modules

In Swift, code is grouped into *modules*. When you define a framework or application, all of the code that's added to it is placed within that target's module. To get access to the code, you use the `import` keyword:

```
import AVFoundation
```

Depending on your programming background, you are probably used to including code to make sure you don't accidentally include something multiple times. In Swift you don't have to worry about this. Modules are clever enough to handle potential import conflicts, letting you focus on making great apps!

The Swift Standard Library, Foundation, Cocoa, and Cocoa Touch

The different features you work with in Swift come from different places, or *libraries*, depending on how platform-specific they are. These are the four main libraries you'll access:

The Swift Standard Library
> Contains all of the lowest-level types and functions that you'll be working with, including `Int`, `String`, math functions, arrays, and dictionaries.
>
> You don't need to do anything special to access the standard library; all Swift programs have access to it.

Foundation
> A slightly higher-level library that provides more tools and types, such as `NSNotificationCenter`, which is used to broadcast application-wide notifications, and `JSONSerialization`, which allows you to read and write JSON data.
>
> You import the Foundation library with the `import Foundation` statement, at the top of your file.

Cocoa
> Specific to macOS and includes features like buttons, windows, image views, and menus.
>
> You import Cocoa with the `import Cocoa` statement.

Cocoa Touch
> On iOS, provides equivalent tools and functionality from Cocoa: views, touch input, sensor capabilities, and so on.
>
> You import Cocoa Touch with the `import UIKit` statement.

If you import Cocoa or Cocoa Touch, you'll also import Foundation. You don't need to import both.

There are also equivalent libraries for tvOS and watchOS. There are also some third-party tools and libraries for Swift, but these are well beyond the scope of this book.

Swift Package Manager

When you do need to get access to other people's code and libraries, you could manually download the Swift files and add them to your codebase. This is error prone, however, and requires you to handle downloading not only the code you want, but all the code it also needs to run. A better way would be to use a tool to handle all this. For iOS development there are two popular tools to do this: Carthage and Cocoapods. Apple wanted something that everything can use. This is why it made the Swift Package Manager.

The Swift Package Manager is simple enough to use: you create a package file that describes what you want to include, you tell the package manager to resolve the dependencies and download the code, and the package manager then downloads and builds the code into a library you can use in your project. Let's take a look at using the Swift Package Manager to download some code we can then use. For this, we will use the example package manager project Apple created and made available for people to experiment with on GitHub (*https://github.com/apple/example-package-dealer*).

We will be recreating the project from scratch instead of using their completed one, but the goal will be to create a Swift program that can create a standard deck of playing cards, shuffle the deck, and then deal out some cards, displaying what is on each card. Most of the work is done for us; we just need to write some code to hook all the bits together. The library we will be downloading is called `DeckOfPlayingCards`; this is our only dependency. `DeckOfPlayingCards`, however, has two dependencies, `PlayingCard` and `FisherYates`. `PlayingCard` represents a single card and `FisherYates` is a little function to shuffle an array into a random order.

First thing we need to do is make a package file; this tells the package manager what we need downloaded and built. Open Xcode, go to File→New File, and select Swift File. When the save dialog box appears, name it *Package.swift* and save it in a sensible spot.

You have to name your package file *Package.swift*. If you don't, the Swift Package Manager won't be able to find it!

Open *Package.swift* and replace it with the following:

```
import PackageDescription

let package = Package(
    name: "Dealer",
    dependencies:
[
    .Package(
        url:"https://github.com/apple/example-package-deckofplayingcards.git",
        majorVersion: 3)
]
    )
```

Let's take a look at what this is doing. First, it is importing the `PackageDescription` module; this module allows us to define a `Package` object that will tell the Package Manager what to download. Then we are creating a new `Package` object, which has two parameters: a name of the package (`Dealer`), and then what dependencies our package will need. In this case we only need the `DeckOfPlayingCards` dependency, so we set the URL of where we can get the `DeckOfPlayingCards` and then a version number. All Swift packages use the semver (*http://semver.org*) semantic versioning system, so we can specify major, minor, and patch versions; but in this case we will just use the major version of 3. It is worth noting that the dependencies are an array; we can have as many packages as we want, and we can also have greater control over the modules being downloaded, including excluding certain modules, setting ranges for the versions, or even making multiple build targets that chain into one another. For this example, though, we want to keep it simple.

Now we need to write a small program to make use of all modules we're about to download. Inside Xcode, create a new Swift file by going to File→New File and select Swift File. This time we will name it *main.swift* and save it with the package file. Open *main.swift* and replace it with the following:

```
import DeckOfPlayingCards

var deck = Deck.standard52CardDeck()
deck.shuffle()

for _ in 0...5
{
 guard let card = deck.deal() else
 {
     print("No More Cards!")
     break
 }
 print(card)
}
```

This program is pretty straightforward: first we import the `DeckOfPlayingCards` module, then we create a new deck of cards and shuffle them. Then we enter a for loop that runs five times, printing out cards after doing a quick check that the deck hasn't run out of cards.

So with our package ready, and our program to use it complete, it is time to build this. We are going to be building and running the project through the command line; as it stands the Swift Package Manager works better through the command line. Future and better integration with Xcode is coming sometime down the track:

1. Open `Terminal.app`.

2. Navigate to where you saved the two Swift files by typing `cd <path/to/where/you/saved/your/files>` and then pressing Return.

3. Build the program by typing `swift build`.

   This will tell the Swift Package Manager to read our *Package.swift* file, download all the required dependencies, and then build them. Once it has done that it will also build our *main.swift* program into a little executable program we can run in the terminal.

    This is because we specified the single Swift file *main.swift*, which tells the Swift tools we want an executable built. You can also have the Swift tools generate an Xcode project; to do this, change the command to `swift package generate-xcodeproj` and it will download the packages and make a new Xcode project with them included.

4. Run our little program by typing `.build/debug/Dealer`; this will run the program called Dealer (the name we set back in the *Package.swift* file) inside the *.build/debug/* folder. The output will look something like:

   ♠8
   ♣7
   ♠9
   ♠J
   ♣2
   ◇5

We just used the Swift Package Manager and a teensy bit of our own code to write a small program. This is only scraping the surface of what the Swift Package Manager can do; it is a very powerful tool with hundreds of options, and it is well worth taking a full look at it at the official site on GitHub (*https://github.com/apple/swift-package-manager*).

Data

In Cocoa, you'll frequently find yourself working with chunks of arbitrary data that you need to save to or load from disk, or that you've downloaded from the network. Cocoa represents these as `Data` objects.

You can get a `Data` object in a variety of ways. For example, if you have a string that you want to convert to a `Data` object, you can use the string's `dataUsingEncoding` method, like so:

```
let stringToConvert = "Hello, Swift"
let data = stringToConvert.data(using: String.Encoding.utf8)
```

Loading Data from Files and URLs

You can also load data from a URL or file location on disk. If the file is one of the resources built into your project, you first need to work out where on disk it's being stored; once you have that, you can load its contents into memory.

To get the location of a built-in file, you first use the `Bundle` class to determine where a given file is being stored on disk using the `path forResource` method. Once you've done that, you construct a `Data` object by providing it either a URL or a filepath:

```
// Loading from URL
if let URL = URL(string: "https://oreilly.com") {
    let loadedDataFromURL = try? Data(contentsOf: URL)
}

// Loading from a file
if let filePath = Bundle.main
    .path(forResource: "SomeFile", ofType: "txt") {
        let loadedDataFromPath = NSData(contentsOfFile:filePath)
}
```

Using `Data(contents0)` this way to get data over the network will cause pauses and slowdowns because the code will wait for the data to be loaded. If you're making an app that loads data over the network, consider using a dedicated library that specializes in doing it, like AlamoFire (*https://github.com/Alamofire/Alamofire*).

A *bundle*, represented by the `Bundle` class, is an object that bundles up all the resources that your apps can use. You can use `Bundle` to load and unload code, images, audio, or almost anything imaginable without having to deal directly with the filesystem.

Serialization and Deserialization

You can also convert an object to data to make it easier to save, load, or send the object. To do this, you first make an object conform to the NSObject and NSCoding protocols, and then add two methods—encodeWithCoder and an initializer that takes an NSCoder:

```
class SerializableObject : NSObject, NSCoding {

    var name : String?

    func encode(with aCoder: NSCoder) {
        aCoder.encode(name!, forKey:"name")
    }

    override init() {
        self.name = "My Object"
    }

    required init(coder aDecoder: NSCoder) {
        self.name = aDecoder.decodeObject(forKey: "name") as? String
    }
}
```

An object that conforms to NSCoding can be converted to an NSData object, and also be loaded from one, via the NSKeyedArchiver and NSKeyedUnarchiver classes. The trick is in the encode method and in the special initializer: in the encode method, you take the NSCoder that's passed in as a parameter and store any values that you want to keep in it. Later, in the initializer, you pull those values out.

Converting these objects to and from data is very straightforward and looks like this:

```
let anObject = SerializableObject()

anObject.name = "My Thing That I'm Saving"

// Converting it to data
let objectConvertedToData =
NSKeyedArchiver.archivedData(withRootObject: anObject)

// Converting it back
// Note that the conversion might fail, so 'unarchiveObjectWithData' returns
// an optional value. So, use 'as?' to check to see if it worked.
let loadedObject =
NSKeyedUnarchiver.unarchiveObject(with: objectConvertedToData)
    as? SerializableObject

loadedObject?.name
// = "My Thing That I'm Saving"
```

Error Handling

It's normal for computer programs to generate errors. When that happens, you need to be ready to handle them, and Swift makes this particularly easy and robust.

If you programmed using Objective-C or Swift 1.0, you might be familiar with a different error-handling system. Previously, an NSError object would be passed as a pointer; when something could fail, you'd pass in an NSError object as a parameter, and if there was an error you could fill the object with information.

This was powerful, as it allowed the return value of a method to be separated from any potential error information. But it was easy to forget to look inside the NSError object. Swift 2.0 replaces this system, and while it expects a little more from programmers now, it is much clearer to read, gives you greater safety by making sure all errors are caught, and requires less messing around with pointers.

In Swift, errors can be any type that conforms to the Error protocol. The Error protocol doesn't have any required functions or properties, which means that any class, enum, or structure can be an error. When your code encounters an error, you *throw* an error.

 For compatibility in Swift, the Objective-C error type NSError is an Error, which means it can be thrown like every other Error.

For example, let's define an enumeration for problems that can relate to a bank account. By making the enumeration an Error, we can throw it as an error:

```
enum BankError : Error {
    // Not enough money in the account
    case notEnoughFunds

    // Can't create an account with negative money
    case cannotBeginWithNegativeFunds

    // Can't make a negative deposit or withdrawal
    case cannotMakeNegativeTransaction(amount:Float)
}
```

Functions that can throw errors must be marked with the throws keyword, which goes after the function's return type:

```
// A simple bank account class
class BankAccount {

    // The amount of money in the account
    private (set) var balance : Float = 0.0
```

```
// Initializes the account with an amount of money.
// Throws an error if you try to create the account
// with negative funds.
init(amount:Float) throws {

    // Ensure that we have a non-negative amount of money
    guard amount > 0 else {
        throw BankError.cannotBeginWithNegativeFunds
    }
    balance = amount
}

// Adds some money to the account
func deposit(amount: Float) throws {

    // Ensure that we're trying to deposit a non-negative amount
    guard amount > 0 else {
        throw BankError.cannotMakeNegativeTransaction(amount: amount)
    }
    balance += amount
}

// Withdraws money from the bank account
func withdraw(amount : Float) throws {

    // Ensure that we're trying to deposit a non-negative amount
    guard amount > 0 else {
        throw BankError.cannotMakeNegativeTransaction(amount: amount)
    }

    // Ensure that we have enough to withdraw this amount
    guard balance >= amount else {
        throw BankError.notEnoughFunds
    }

    balance -= amount
}
}
```

When you call any function, method, or initializer that throws, you are required to
wrap it in a do-catch block. In the do block, you call the methods that may potentially
throw errors; each time you do, you preface the potentially throwing call with try. If
the method call throws an error, the do block stops executing and the catch clause
runs:

```
do {
    let vacationFund = try BankAccount(amount: 5)

    try vacationFund.deposit(amount: 5)

    try vacationFund.withdraw(amount: 11)
```

```
} catch let error as BankError {

    // Catch any BankError that was thrown
    switch (error) {
    case .notEnoughFunds:
        print("Not enough funds in account!")
    case .cannotBeginWithNegativeFunds:
        print("Tried to start an account with negative money!")
    case .cannotMakeNegativeTransaction(let amount):
        print("Tried to do a transaction with a negative amount of \(amount)!")
    }

} catch let error {
    // (Optional:) catch other types of errors
}
```

However, it can sometimes be cumbersome to wrap calls to methods that can throw errors in a do-catch block. Sometimes you may not care about the specifics of the error; you just care if there was an error or not. This is where the try? statement comes in. If you preface a call to something that can throw an error with try?, and it *does* throw an error, the result will be nil:

 This means that the return type of any call that you try? will be an optional.

```
let secretBankAccountOrNot = try? BankAccount(amount: -50) // = nil
```

Finally, there are sometimes cases where your program *needs* the method call to succeed and guarantee a returned value. If you call a method with try!, and it throws an error, your program will simply crash. (This has the same effect as using try? to receive an optional and then using the force-unwrap operator (!) on that optional.)

```
let secretBankAccountOrNot = try! BankAccount(amount: -50) // crash!
```

The try? and try! statements do *not* need to be in a do-catch block. If you do put them in one, any errors won't be caught by the catch block; they'll still just either evaluate to nil or crash.

Memory Management

Objects in Swift are *memory managed*. When an object is being used, Swift keeps it in memory; when it's no longer being used, it's removed from memory.

The technique that Swift uses to keep track of which objects are being used and which are not is called *reference counting*. When an object is assigned to a variable, a counter called the *retain count* goes up by 1. When the object is no longer assigned to that variable, the retain count goes down. If the retain count ever reaches 0, that means that no variables are referring to that object, and the object is then removed from memory.

The nice thing about Swift is that this all happens at the compiler level. As the compiler reads your code, it keeps track of when objects get assigned to variables and adds code that increments and decrements the retain count.

However, this automatic memory management has one potential snag that you need to keep an eye out for: *retain cycles*.

A retain cycle is where you have two objects that refer to each other, but are otherwise not referred to by any other part of the application. Because those objects refer to each other, their retain count is not zero, which means they stay in memory; however, because no variable in the rest of the application refers to them, they're inaccessible (and consequently useless).

Swift solves this using the concept of *weak* references. A weak reference is a variable that refers to an object, but doesn't change the retain count of that object. You use weak references when you don't particularly care whether an object stays in memory or not (i.e., your code isn't the *owner* of that object).

To declare a weak reference in Swift, you use the `weak` keyword, like so:

```
class Class1 {
    init() {
        print("Class 1 being created!")
    }

    deinit {
        print("Class 1 going away!")
    }
}

class Class2 {
    // Weak vars are implicitly optional
    weak var weakRef : Class1?
}
```

The topic of memory management can get complex if you're doing more advanced things. If you'd like to learn more about it, see the section "Automatic Reference Counting" in *The Swift Programming Language* (*http://apple.co/21TDi9O*).

Design Patterns in Cocoa and Cocoa Touch

Cocoa is built around a number of design patterns whose purpose is to make your life as a developer more consistent and (one hopes) more productive. Three key patterns are the *model-view-controller* (MVC) pattern, upon which most of Cocoa and Cocoa Touch is built; the *delegation* pattern, which allows both your code and Cocoa to be highly flexible in determining what code gets run by whom; and *notifications*, which allow your code to watch for important events that happen within your app. We'll be working with notifications in a very hands-on sense later in the book (in Chapters 13 and 14); at the moment, let's dive in to model-view-controller and delegation!

Model-View-Controller

The model-view-controller design pattern is one of the fundamental design patterns in Cocoa. Let's take a look at what each of these parts means:

Models
> Objects that contain data or otherwise coordinate the storing, management, and delivery of data to other objects. Models can be as simple as a string or as complicated as an entire database—their purpose is to store data and provide it to other objects. They don't care what happens to the data once they give it to someone else; their only concern is managing how the data is stored.

Views
> Objects that work directly with the user, providing information to them and receiving input back. Views do not manage the data that they display—they only show it to the user. Views are also responsible for informing other objects when the user interacts with them. Like data and models, views do not care what happens next—their responsibility ends with informing the rest of the application.

Controllers
> Objects that mediate between models and views and contain the bulk of what some call the "business logic" of an application—the actual logic that defines what the application is and how it responds to user input. At a minimum, the controller is responsible for retrieving information from the model and providing it to the view; it is also responsible for providing information to the model when it is informed by the view that the user has interacted with it.

For an illustration of the model-view-controller design pattern in action, imagine a simple text editor. In this example, the application loads a text file from disk and presents its contents to the user in a text field. The user makes changes in the text field and saves those changes back to disk.

We can break this application down into model, view, and controller objects:

- The model is an object that is responsible for loading the text file from disk and writing it back out to disk. It is also responsible for providing the text as a string to any object that asks for it.

- The view is the text field, which asks another object for a string to display and then displays the text. It also accepts keyboard input from the user; whenever the user types, it informs another object that the text has changed. It is also able to tell another object when the user has told it to save changes.

- The controller is the object responsible for instructing the model object to load a file from disk, and it passes the text to the view. It receives updates from the view object when the text has changed and passes those changes to the model. Finally, it can be told by the view that the user has asked to save the changes; when that happens, it instructs the model to do the work of actually writing the file out to disk.

Breaking the application into these areas of responsibility enables us to more easily make changes to it.

For example, if the developer decides that the next version of the application should add the ability to upload the text file to the internet whenever the file is saved, the only thing that must be changed is the model class—the controller can stay the same, and the view never changes.

Likewise, clearly defining which objects are responsible for which features makes it easier to make changes to an application while maintaining a clear structure in the project. If the developer decides to add a spell-checking feature to the application, that code should clearly be added to the controller, as it has nothing to do with how the text is presented to the user or stored on disk. (You could, of course, add some features to the view that would allow it to indicate which words are misspelled, but the bulk of the code would need to be added in the controller.)

The majority of the classes described in this chapter, such as NSData, arrays, and dictionaries, are model classes; all they do is store and present information to other classes. NSKeyedArchiver is a controller class; it takes information and performs logical operations on it. NSButton and UITextField are examples of view objects; they present information to the user and do not care about how the data is managed.

The model-view-controller paradigm becomes very important when you start looking at the more advanced Cocoa features, like the document architecture and bindings, both of which are covered throughout this book.

Delegation

Delegation is Cocoa's term for passing off some responsibilities of an object to another. An example of this is the UIApplication object, which represents an application on iOS. This object needs to know what should happen when the application moves to the background. Many other languages handle this problem by subclassing —for example, in C++, the UIApplication class would define an empty placeholder method for applicationDidEnterBackground, and then you as a developer would subclass UIApplication and override the applicationDidEnterBackground method.

However, this is a particularly heavy-handed solution and causes additional problems—it increases the complexity of your code, and also means that if you want to override the behavior of two classes, you need separate subclasses for each one.[1] Swift's answer to this problem is built around the fact that an object can determine, at runtime, whether another object is capable of responding to a method.

Let's say Object A wants to let Object B know that something is going to happen or has happened and stores a reference to Object B as an instance variable. This reference to Object B is known as the delegate. When the event happens, Object A checks to see if the delegate object (Object B) implements a method that suits the event—for delegates of the UIApplication class, for example, the application delegate is asked if it implements the applicationDidEnterBackground method. If it does, that method is called.

Because of this loose coupling, it's possible for an object to be the delegate for multiple objects. For example, an object could become the delegate of both an audio playback object and an image picker, and be notified both when audio playback completes and when an image has been captured by the camera.

Because the model-view-controller pattern is built around a very loose coupling of objects, it helps to have a more rigidly defined interface between objects so that your application can know with more certainty how one object expects others to behave.

The specific messages used by delegates are often listed in protocols. For example, if your object wants to be the delegate of an AVAudioPlayer object, it should conform to the AVAudioPlayerDelegate protocol.

Working with delegates in Swift is easy. Imagine you have two classes, and you want one of them to act as the delegate for another:

```swift
// Define a protocol that has a function called handleIntruder
protocol HouseSecurityDelegate {

    // We don't define the function here, but rather
    // indicate that any class that is a HouseSecurityDelegate
    // is required to have a handleIntruder() function
    func handleIntruder()
}
```

---

1 C++'s answer to this problem is multiple inheritance, which has its own problems.

```
class House {
    // The delegate can be any object that conforms
    // to the HouseSecurityDelegate protocol
    var delegate : HouseSecurityDelegate?

    func burglarDetected() {
        // Check to see if the delegate is there, then call it
        delegate?.handleIntruder()
    }
}

class GuardDog : HouseSecurityDelegate {
    func handleIntruder() {
        print("Releasing the hounds!")
    }
}

let myHouse = House()
myHouse.burglarDetected() // does nothing

let theHounds = GuardDog()
myHouse.delegate = theHounds
myHouse.burglarDetected() // prints "Releasing the hounds!"
```

The burglarDetected method needs to check that a security delegate exists for the house before calling its handleIntruder method. It does this using a Swift feature called *optional chaining*, which lets you access something that depends on an optional having a value, without specifically testing the optional first. If the optional has a value, in this case a houseSecurityDelegate, its handleIntruder method is called. If the optional is nil, nothing happens. You can use optional chaining to access the properties, method, or subscripts of your classes, structures, and enumerations in this way.

Structuring an App

Before we wrap up this part and begin our long, deep dive into building real-world apps, it's worth looking at the big picture of how apps are built, both on macOS and iOS.

iOS and macOS are built on the idea of *event-driven programming*. Anything that your app does is in response to an event of some kind. On macOS, events include the mouse moving or clicking, keyboard input, and the window resizing; on iOS, they include touch input and sensor input. On both iOS and macOS, events can also include timers firing or the screen refreshing.

At their core, apps are about the *run loop*, an infinite loop that waits for an *event* to fire, and then takes appropriate actions. Most of those actions are handled by the built-in parts of your app; for example, swiping your finger on a list will cause the list to adjust its position. However, there are several events that your code handles. For example, when a button is clicked, as part of handling this event, the code calls a method that you write.

The Application Delegate

The delegation pattern is used a lot for event handling. Every time the operating system needs to let your app know that an interesting event has happened, the application delegate object—which you write—has a method called on it. The application delegate object—usually shortened to *app delegate*—is just an instance of a class that conforms to the NSApplicationDelegate (on macOS) or UIApplicationDelegate (on iOS) protocol. When you create a project, Xcode adds a file that contains a class that implements the correct protocol for your platform.

The app delegate contains methods like application(_, didFinishLaunchingWithOptions:); these methods are called when events happen (like when the application finishes launching). You provide code in these methods to run when the events occur.

Window Controllers and View Controllers

Window controllers are objects that manage a window's contents on macOS, and *view controllers* manage a view's contents on both iOS and macOS. On iOS a view controller is usually fullscreen, but on macOS that may not be the case (although the view that controller manages is usually the full size of the window containing it).

 When working with documents, you'll be provided with a window controller that allows you to keep your logic in the document class. We'll look at this in more detail in Chapter 4.

View controllers can manage other view controllers; for example, navigation controllers are a view controller that manages multiple *child* view controllers. View controllers exist on iOS and macOS, while window controllers exist only on macOS (because the concept of windows really only exists on macOS).

Windows in Swift are the individual windows of the application (i.e., the entire box that the application shows on the screen). A view, on the other hand, is contained inside a window and represents and is responsible for the elements within. In iOS you will have a single window per application, and multiple views will be shown inside that window. In macOS your application might have multiple windows, each with its own views.

Nibs and Storyboards

When an application starts, it loads its interface. The interface is stored inside a file, and there are two types of files: *nib files* and *storyboard files*. Both are used in the interface builder to design and lay out an interface.

Nib files contain a collection of objects, and are generally used to represent a single window or view; they also contain nonvisible objects, such as controller objects, when needed.

Storyboards take this idea and extend it by storing multiple interfaces—that is, views and windows—and letting you describe how you get from one interface to another, using connections called *segues*.

Conclusion

In this chapter, you've learned about how to work with object-oriented programming in Swift and how to get some more real-world tasks done using the functionality provided by Cocoa and Cocoa Touch. In the next part of this book, we'll use these skills to start building actual apps.

PART II

A macOS App

CHAPTER 4

Setting Up the macOS Notes App

In Part I, we looked at the Apple Developer Program, the tools you use for developing on Apple platforms, and the fundamentals of the Swift language. Now we're actually going to build some apps!

In this chapter, we'll start building *Notes*. Notes is a Mac app that lets you write notes, which contain text plus a number of other attachments: images, locations, videos, sounds, contacts, and more. We'll be creating an iOS counterpart for Notes later on, in Part III.

We're not going to be doing any coding in this chapter, but it's still important! We'll be doing all the setup to make a real, working macOS app, using Xcode, by the end of the chapter (it won't do much, though!).

The kind of setup that we'll be doing in this chapter is fundamental to the creation of most Swift-based applications for macOS and iOS. One of the most striking things about developing for Apple's platforms using Xcode and Swift is just how much work is done for you. Just one or two years ago, the setup we'll accomplish in this chapter would have taken lines upon lines of code.

Even if you're only interested in learning to use Swift to create iOS applications, we suggest that you work through the chapters (there are only three!) that cover the creation of the macOS application anyway. You'll gain a better understanding of using Swift with Xcode to build applications, and you'll be better equipped to work on the iOS application once we start on that, in Part III.

Designing the macOS Notes App

When we first sat down to build this app, the only thing we had figured out so far was that we wanted to "make a notes app that lets you add attachments." To determine how this would work overall, we started drawing *wireframes*.

 A wireframe is a very rough drawing of the app that you're about to make. It's much faster to get your ideas down on paper (digital or physical) than it is to actually implement the app itself, and the act of drawing your ideas helps you organize your thoughts.

The application that we used to make these wireframes was *OmniGraffle*, a fantastic vector drawing tool that's very well suited for wireframes. You don't need any software at all to get started figuring out an app idea, however—pencil and paper will work just as well.

 The wireframes were drawn several weeks before we started writing this book, not once we had a finished app ready. This means, just like wireframes for real-world products, they differ slightly from the finished product. This is OK when your development team is small, such as when it's just you and maybe one other, because in this case, the goal of wireframing isn't to create a perfect blueprint for others to implement, but rather to get a solid understanding of how your app needs to work.

This book isn't here to teach you how to design wireframes or conceptualize the applications that you'll build, but we have to start somewhere. Programming without considering what you're building, in our experience, leads to poor-quality software. That's why we're starting with wireframes and showing them to you.

The process for figuring out how the wireframes needed to come together came from the OmniGraffle equivalent of doodling: we drew rectangles on the page, pretended they were windows, and asked ourselves how we'd use the app. When we (inevitably) ran up against a limitation in the design, we went back to the design and added, removed, or changed the content of the screen. We continued to go back and forth on this design until we were sure that the app's design was usable.

You can see the wireframe for the app in Figure 4-1.

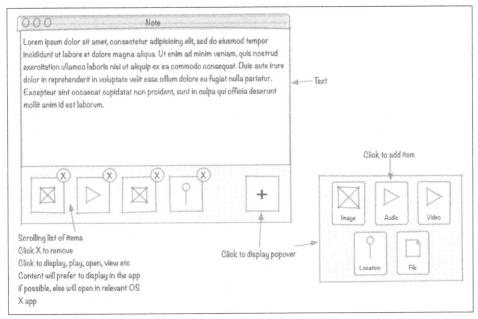

Figure 4-1. The macOS app's wireframes

On macOS, each document is given its own window. The app itself has no "main window"; instead, the only visible component will be the document windows.

The focus of the app is the text editor, which takes up the majority of the space. Underneath it, a horizontally scrolling list of all of the attachments is shown. For each attachment in the document, we'll show a preview image. Next to the list of attachments, we'll show a button that allows the user to attach new items to the document; when it's clicked, a popover will appear that presents the various options available. Above this button, we'll add a button that opens the location attachment, if one is present.

By the end of these chapters, the app outlined in the wireframes will be a real, working app, as shown in Figure 4-2.

Figure 4-2. The macOS app

The Mac app has several key features:

- It uses the macOS document model, which means that it gets a number of useful behaviors for free, including versioning and autosave, plus the ability to associate its document types with the app (meaning that when you double-click a file, it will open in the app).

- Documents contain text that can be formatted—that is, you can italicize and bold text, change the color of letters, and so on.

- Documents can also store attachments. When you add an attachment, it's displayed in a list underneath the text area.

- You can add attachments by either clicking an Add button, which presents a window that lets you select the file you want to add, or by dragging and dropping the file into the list of attachments.

- Double-clicking an attachment presents a Quick Look window that allows you to view the contents of the file.

- You can open the location that's attached to the document (which we'll examine in quite a bit more detail when we build the iOS app in Part III) in the Maps application.

Let's get started!

Creating the macOS Project

The first thing we need to do is create an Xcode project for our macOS app. We'll be working in this project for most of the rest of the book, including the iOS app, which will be added as a target in the same project. If you need a refresher on Xcode and the development tools, see Chapter 1.

1. Launch Xcode, as shown in Figure 4-3.

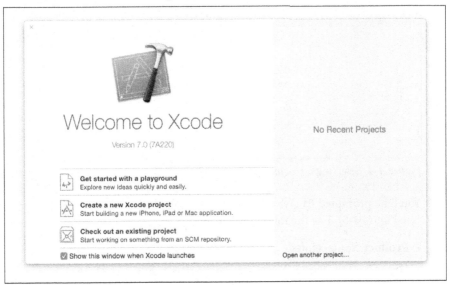

Figure 4-3. The "Welcome to Xcode" screen

2. Click the "Create a new Xcode project" button.

The list of project templates will appear. Click Application under the macOS heading, in the left column (which includes categories for Apple's other platforms, such as iOS, tvOS, and watchOS), and then select Cocoa Application (Figure 4-4). Click Next.

The other templates provide a default setup for different types of application. You can do everything provided by each template manually, if you want. They're just a collection of provided files and code. The templates shown in Figure 4-4 are those provided by Apple, and they ship with Xcode.

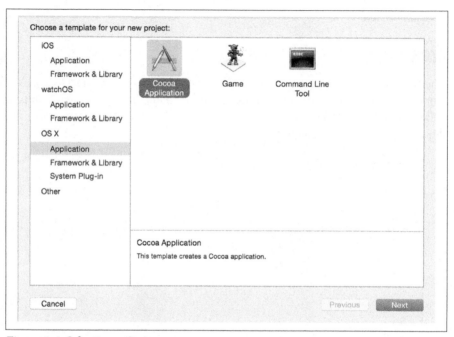

Figure 4-4. Selecting a Cocoa app

3. You'll be prompted to give the project a name, plus some additional information (see Figure 4-5). Use the following settings:

- **Product Name**: Notes

- **Organization Name**: Your company's name. Enter your own name if you're not making this app for a company.

- **Organization Identifier**: Your domain name, reversed; for example, if you own mycompany.com, enter `com.mycompany`. (Customize this based on your domain name; if you don't have one, enter `com.example`.)

Choose options for your new project:

Product Name:	Notes
Organization Name:	Secret Lab
Organization Identifier:	au.com.secretlab
Bundle Identifier:	au.com.secretlab.Notes
Language:	Swift

☐ Use Storyboards
☑ Create Document-Based Application

Document Extension:	note

☐ Use Core Data
☑ Include Unit Tests
☑ Include UI Tests

Cancel   Previous   Next

Figure 4-5. Configuring the Cocoa app

The organization name and the product name are used to create the app's *bundle identifier*. A bundle identifier is a period-separated string that uniquely identifies a bundle of code and resources. For example, if you use `com.example` as your organization identifier, the bundle ID will be `com.exam ple.Notes`.

Bundle identifiers are used everywhere in the macOS and iOS ecosystem. A bundle identifier forms the basis of your *app ID*, which is the unique string that identifies your app on the App Store. Bundle IDs are used to distinguish between apps. Your app's bundle ID is also used as the basis of other IDs, such as the uniform type identifier (UTI) for your documents, which we'll cover in "Defining a Document Type" on page 106.

- **Language:** Swift

We're setting the language to Swift, because—well—this is a Swift book! You can set this to Objective-C if you want, though! But the rest of the book will make absolutely no sense if you do.

- **Use Storyboards:** Off

We're not turning storyboards on here because we're going to use the other means of creating a UI, nibs, for the macOS app. We'll use storyboards when we build the iOS app, in Part III. We're deliberately using both UI techniques so you'll get experience with both. We'll explain more about nibs versus storyboards in "A Basic UI" on page 125.

- **Create Document-Based Application:** On

  This setting asks Xcode to provide the basics of a document-based application to us, in the template that it generates for the project. This will give us a `Docu` `ment` class that we can build from. A document-based application is one that handles multiple documents, each with its own window. Much of this infrastructure is provided for free by Apple's document architecture. You can learn more about this in the documentation (*http://bit.ly/abt_cocoa_doc_architec ture*).

- **Document Extension:** *note*

  Since our Notes app will work with documents that represent notes, we set the file extension for the basic document-based application that Xcode is going to generate to something that makes sense. In this case, we'll be making a Notes app that works with *.note* files. We'll talk about this more throughout the remainder of this chapter.

- **Use Core Data:** Off

  Core Data is a framework provided by Apple that lets you store data in a manner similar to a database, but local to your app. We're not using Core Data in this book, as it's a topic that warrants a book all on its own. Additionally, the limits of Core Data are quite easy to hit, and it's often more useful, as well as more of a learning experience, to build storage infrastructure for your app from scratch. If we'd turned this on, stubs for Core Data, as well as a data model, would be added to the project that Xcode will generate for us. If you really must, you can learn more about Core Data in the documentation (*http:// apple.co/21THwOU*). Don't say we didn't warn you!

- **Include Unit Tests:** On

- **Include UI Tests:** On

  Leaving these two on creates stubs for unit tests and UI tests, respectively. We'll touch on these subjects much later, in Chapter 16.

If you're using macOS Yosemite, note that UI tests will run only on macOS 10.11 El Capitan or later. You can *create* a project that includes UI tests on Yosemite, but you won't be able to run them.

4. Click the "Next" button, and Xcode will ask you where you'd like to save the project (which will be a folder with the same name as you put in the Product field), and then it will create a project for you to work with.

Now that the project has been set up, we need to provide more information about the documents that this app will be working with.

We recommend that you store this project (and, indeed, anything else that you might work on) in Git, or a similar version control system. It's out of the scope of this book to explore Git, but we strongly recommend you take some time to explore it if you're not already using it. Xcode has some basic support for Git built in, which you can read about in Apple's documentation (*http://apple.co/21TI7zS*).

5. Select the Notes project at the top of the Project Navigator (Figure 4-6). If you need a refresher on the Xcode interface, flip back to "The Xcode Interface" on page 13.

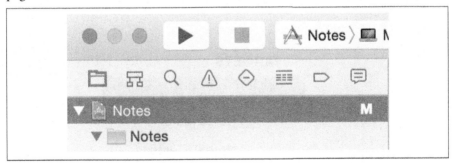

Figure 4-6. Selecting the project

The main editor will show information about the overall project.

There's a lot that you get for free just by creating the project. In addition to the app itself, you get an application that is capable of working with document-like objects. If you run the application right now, you'll already be able to create new "documents" by pressing ⌘-N, though you won't yet be able to save them to disk.

Defining a Document Type

We'll now provide some more information about the document type. Notes will be a document-based application, which means it will behave like other document-based applications on macOS, such as Pages or TextEdit.

1. Select the Notes application from the list of targets. As a reminder, a project can contain multiple targets, each of which collects the code, user interface, and other resources required to generate a product. We first mentioned targets back in "The Xcode Interface" on page 13.

   If you don't see the list of targets, make sure the Notes project (it has a blueprint icon) is selected in the Project Navigator, and then click the icon that looks like a square with a vertical line inside it, at the top left of the editor (Figure 4-7). This will toggle the projects and targets list (Figure 4-8).

Figure 4-7. Opening the targets list

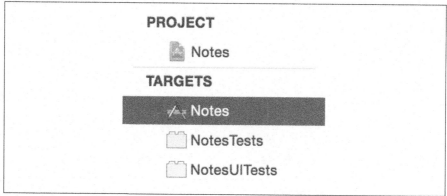

Figure 4-8. Selecting the Notes target

2. Select the Info tab from the top of the editor, shown in Figure 4-9.

Figure 4-9. The Info tab

3. Scroll down to the Document Types section, and open it by clicking the triangle. There's already the beginnings of a document type laid out, because we asked Xcode to create a document-based application, and it knows that such an application will need a document type.

   We need to add a little more description, including a proper name for the document, as well as an identifier similar to our organization identifier, so our document type won't collide with any other possible files with a *.note* extension:

   a. Set Name to **Note**.

   b. Set Identifier to your organization identifier, plus *.Note*. For example, if your organization identifier is `com.example`, the document's identifier is `com.example.Note`.

   This defines this document as conforming to this uniform type identifier, which is the method by which the system works out the types of files.

A uniform type identifier looks very similar to a bundle identifier: it's a period-separated string. For example, the UTI for PDF files is *com.adobe.pdf*.

UTIs were invented to deal with the thorny problem of identifying the types of files. If you're given a blob of information, what you can do with it depends on the kind of data that it contains. For example, Adobe Photoshop can open images but not Word documents, and if the user wants to open a Word document, the operating system shouldn't even consider opening it in Photoshop. However, it's not reasonable for the OS to inspect the contents of the file to tell the difference, so we need some kind of *metadata* that describes those contents.

Originally, file types were simply identified by the file extension. For example, the JSON data interchange format uses the file extension *.json*. This worked fairly well, until we hit the problem of *type granularity*.

You see, a JSON file isn't just describable solely as JSON data—it's also a text file, a chunk of binary data, and a file (as opposed to a directory). There are thousands of plain-text formats out there, and a text editor shouldn't have to manually specify each one that it's capable of opening.

This is where UTIs come in. UTIs are a *hierarchy* of types: when a UTI is declared, it also declares all of the other types that it *conforms* to. For example, the UTI for JSON is `public.json`; this UTI also conforms to `public.text`, which represents *plain text* and itself conforms to both `public.data` and `public.content`. This means that, even if you don't know anything about the specifics of the JSON file format, you know that JSON is text.

When you create a new type of document, you add information to the app that *exports* the new UTI. This means that when the app is installed on the system, the operating system will detect the fact that you're declaring a new type of document. In addition, because your app registers itself as one that can also *open* that type of document, the system will record that if the user double-clicks files of that type, your app should be the one that's launched.

When you export a UTI, you provide as much information as possible about it: any icon to use, a textual description of what the type is, all existing UTIs that the new type conforms to, and any other information that the system can use to identify the file. This additional information includes things that other operating systems use, such as file extensions, MIME types, and OSTypes (which were used by Mac OS Classic, the precursor to macOS).

Different kinds of apps work with different kinds of data, and it helps to be familiar with the different types of UTIs that are out there. You can find a list of UTIs that the system defines in Apple's documentation (*http://apple.co/1UCACPq*).

The document type in this app will be one that conforms to the `com.apple.package` type, which means that it's a folder that contains other files, but should be presented to the user as a single file. macOS and iOS make extensive use of packages, since they're a very convenient way to present a file that contains other information. This is perfect for our file format, since it contains attachments.

We'll be talking more about this approach in "Package File Formats" on page 116.

1. Select the box for "Document is distributed as a bundle" (Figure 4-10).

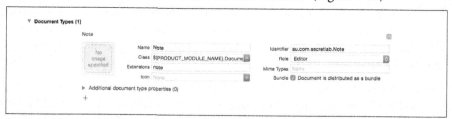

Figure 4-10. Defining a document type

The Note document type that we've just described is a new type that the rest of the system doesn't know about yet. Because we've just invented this new UTI, we need to export it to the system, as shown in Figure 4-11. Let's do that now.

2. Open the Exported UTIs section.

3. Click the + button in this section to add a new entry.

4. Provide the following information, as shown in Figure 4-11:

   a. Set Description to **Note**.

   b. Set Extensions to **note**.

   c. Set Identifier to the same as the identifier you provided earlier (e.g., `com.exam ple.Note`).

   d. Set Conforms To to `com.apple.package`. This tells the system that files of this type are actually folders ("packages") of files.

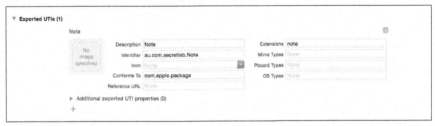

Figure 4-11. Defining a new uniform type identifier

5. Run the app by clicking the play button in the upper-left corner of the window, or by pressing ⌘-R on your keyboard. After compiling, the app will launch.

   It doesn't do much, but you can already create new *documents* by pressing ⌘-N, as shown in Figure 4-12. Pretty neat!

It might not seem like you've done a lot, because we haven't done any programming (we did warn you!). But really, you've accomplished a whole lot in this chapter, helped along by parts of the process that Xcode automates. In brief, you've:

- created a brand-new macOS app, complete with support for multiple documents, open in multiple windows.

- defined a brand-new file extension, *.note*, and told the system about it by exporting it as a UTI.

- been given a `Document` class, written in Swift, for you to extend to do what you need. (Did you notice the *Document.swift* file in the Project Navigator? We'll be working with that in the next chapter!)

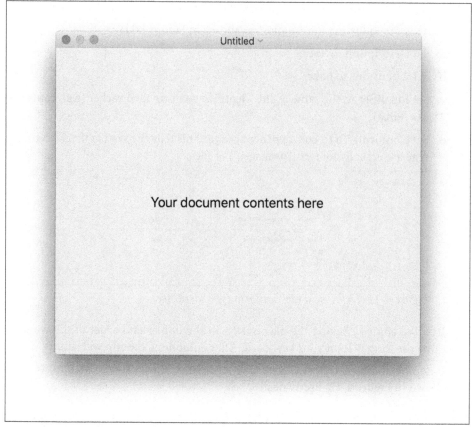

Figure 4-12. The current state of the app

In the next chapter, we'll make the app even better, but there's one last cosmetic thing we need to do first!

Adding the Icon

Finally, we'll add the icon to the application's *asset catalog*. We probably wouldn't really add the application icon at this point in the process, but since we're providing an icon for you to use, and since apps look better with an actual icon instead of the Apple default icon, we thought we'd do it here. It's also a good opportunity to talk about asset catalogs.

In Xcode, an asset catalog is a file that contains the assets that your app uses. It is most commonly used to store images, but can be used to store all sorts of assets: data files, app icons, placeholder images for certain OS features, and various other things.

The predominant use for asset catalogs is storing images. Asset catalogs simplify management of images that your app uses as part of its user interface. Importantly, each image itself is composed of *each of the different versions* that the system could use. A good example of this in practice is the icon that we're about to add.

A macOS app's icon can be presented at a variety of sizes: if it's in the Dock, it will probably be about 64 pixels high; but if it's being shown in List mode in the Finder, it may be only 16 pixels high. This gets even more complicated when you add Retina displays into the mix, where there may be more physical pixels per screen point than a non-Retina screen (that is, an image might report itself as 16 × 16 screen points, but will physically be a 32 × 32 pixel image). For optimal image quality, it's best to provide a separate image file for different sizes—as shown in the following exercise; downscaling a large image or upscaling a small one generally results in a pretty significant drop in image quality:

1. Locate the *macOS Icon.png* and *macOS Icon@2x.png* files in the downloaded resources. As a reminder, these are available via this book's website (*http://www.secretlab.com.au/books/learning-swift/*).

2. Open the *Assets.xcassets* file, and select the AppIcon item in the list of assets.

3. Drag the *macOS Icon.png* file onto the slot labeled 1x Mac 512pt. Next, drag the *macOS Icon@2x.png* file onto the slot labeled 2x Mac 512pt.

The app now has an icon (see Figure 4-13)! You might be wondering what the "1x" and "2x" mean: the 1x icon is the version of the icon for non-Retina displays, and the 2x icon is the version of the icon for Retina displays. The 2x image is double the resolution of the 1x image. You can learn more about Retina displays and macOS apps in Apple's documentation (*http://apple.co/1UCCS9k*).

Rather than requiring you to individually address each possible version of the image, the asset catalog saves you time by creating *image sets* for each image. The application image is an image set, which lets you provide multiple files for a single image. At runtime, the system will select the most appropriate image to use. You still provide the images, but you only have to refer to what the image is representing by name, rather than the specific resolution version. In this case, the system looks for the AppIcon item, in the asset catalog, and knows to use the 1x version for non-Retina displays, and the 2x version for Retina displays.

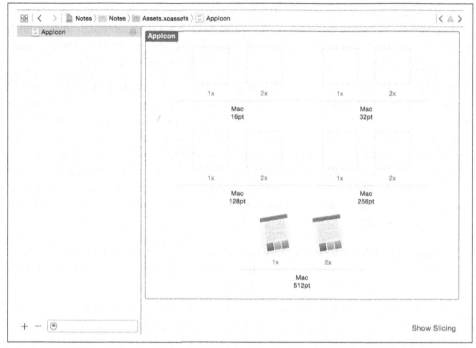

Figure 4-13. The app icon

Conclusion

Now that you've made it to the end of this first chapter on creating macOS apps, let's look back at what you've learned. In addition to developing an idea of how document-based applications work and how this particular app will work, we've done some fairly low-level plumbing of the type system and introduced an entirely new document type. In the next chapter, we'll start adding features to the app and start building an actual, working, feature-full app.

CHAPTER 5

Working with Documents on macOS

Now that we've done the groundwork for the macOS application, we can start adding the features that power it. Here's where we'll actually be doing some programming with Swift.

Because most of the functionality of the app, along with the user interface, comes from the Document class that was automatically provided when we first created the project in Xcode, we'll be spending most of our time working with Document and enhancing its features to meet our needs. We'll be adding support for storing text inside our note document format, creating a user interface to show that text and making sure the app can save and open note files.

Along the way, we'll talk about how documents work on macOS, how to build applications that work with the document system to help users get their work done, and how Swift fits into all of this.

The NSDocument Class

In macOS, documents are represented by the NSDocument class. When you create a new type of document, you subclass this class, inheriting from it, and add the properties and methods that are specific to your situation. For example, later in this chapter, we'll be adding properties that store the text of the note. If you need a refresher about subclassing and inheritance, refer back to "Inheritance" on page 66.

iOS has a similar class, called UIDocument. We'll be looking at UIDo cument in lots of detail in Chapter 9.

The NSDocument class and its many related classes form a framework that allows you to focus on the specifics of how your application needs to work. You don't, for example, need to reimplement common features like a filepicker to let the user choose what file to open. By using NSDocument, you also automatically gain access to advanced features like autosaving and versions.

An instance of NSDocument, or one of its subclasses, represents a single document and its contents. When the application wants to create a new document, it creates a new instance of the class; when that document needs to be saved, the system calls a method that returns an encoded version of the document's contents, which the system then writes to disk. When an existing document needs to be loaded, an instance is created and then given an encoded representation to use.

This means that your NSDocument subclasses never directly work with the filesystem, which allows macOS to do several behind-the-scenes tricks, like automatically saving backup copies or saving snapshots over time.

 NSDocument is not part of the Swift programming language, but is instead part of the AppKit framework. AppKit is the framework Apple provides to build graphical applications for macOS, and it contains windows, buttons, menus, text fields, and so on. You can learn more about AppKit in Apple's documentation (*http:// apple.co/21TU0G6*).

We're going to work with NSDocument, using Swift, through the rest of this chapter, and we'll explain how it fits together as we go.

Storing Data in the Document

In Chapter 4 we created a new project and asked it to set up a "document-based application" for us. Because of this, our project already has a Document class file in place, with some method stubs, as shown here (with comments removed). You'll find this in the *Document.swift* file, which you can open by clicking it in the Project Navigator, located on the left side of the screen. As ever, if you need a refresher on the structure of Xcode's user interface, check back to "The Xcode Interface" on page 13.

When you open *Document.swift* in the editor, you'll see a number of stub functions that the template gave us. Here are the two we are interested in:

```
override func dataOfType(typeName: String) throws -> NSData {
    throw NSError(domain: NSOSStatusErrorDomain, code: unimpErr, userInfo: nil)
}

override func readFromData(data: NSData, ofType typeName: String) throws {
    throw NSError(domain: NSOSStatusErrorDomain, code: unimpErr, userInfo: nil)
}
```

The method stubs provided to us don't really do much at the moment. All we have right now are some methods that get called when a document of whatever type (in our case, a note) gets written to, read from, or displayed. We're going to need to make sure this Document class is actually useful to us.

The throw keyword, in this case, causes an NSError object to be relayed back to the document system, indicating that there was a problem in saving or opening the document. In this case, the problem is that the methods are unimplemented.

The first thing we need to do is customize our Document class to support storing the data that our documents contain. There are two main items that the documents keep: the text and the attachments. The first item is very straightforward; the second is quite a bit trickier.

Storing Text

The Notes application is primarily about storing written text. In just about every programming language under the sun, text is stored in strings, which means that we'll need to add a string property in which to store the document's text.

Strings in Swift are *really* powerful. In Swift, a string is stored as a series of Unicode characters. If you're an old Objective-C programmer, you might (or might not, if you disliked NSString!) be pleased to know that Swift String class is bridged to Foundation's NSString class, which means you can do anything to a Swift String that you could do to an NSString. If you don't know what this means, then you don't need to worry about it!

However, the Notes application should be slightly fancier than a plain-text editor. We want the user to be able to **bold** and *italicize* the text, or maybe ***both***, and regular strings can't store this information. To do so, we'll need to use a different type than String: we'll need to use NSAttributedString.

NSAttributedString is from Foundation, the base layer of classes that were created to support Objective-C, Apple's other programming language. Because of this, NSAttributedString has a few differences around its use compared to the native Swift String class; but in practice, this often doesn't matter.

An *attributed* string is a type of string that contains *attributes* that apply to ranges of characters. These attributes include things like bold, color, and font.

Attributed text is also referred to as *rich text*.

1. Open the *Document.swift* class file containing stubs created by Xcode.

2. Add the following property to the Document class above the init method:

```
// Main text content
var text : NSAttributedString = NSAttributedString()
```

Although in theory you can put your property declarations pretty much anywhere you want, it is standard practice to add them to the top of the class declaration. We talked more about properties in Swift back in Chapter 2.

This NSAttributedString property has a default value of the empty attributed string and will be used to store the text for a note file. NSAttributedString is all you need in order to store and work with formatted text (that is, text with attributes, such as a font and a size) almost anywhere within your apps. User interface elements provided by Apple support NSAttributedString and know how to display it. It's that easy!

Package File Formats

In addition to storing plain text, the Document class also needs to store attachments. These attachments can be *any* file that the user chooses, which means that we need to think carefully about how we approach this.

On most operating systems, documents are represented as single file. This makes a lot of intuitive sense in most situations, since a "document" can be thought of as a single "thing" on the disk. However, if you have a complex document format that contains lots of different information, it can cause a lot of work: the document system needs to read through the file, determine what information is where, and parse it into a usable in-memory representation. If the file is large, this can mean that the system needs to make sure that it doesn't run out of memory while reading the file.

macOS deals with this kind of problem in a simpler, more elegant way. Instead of requiring all documents to be individual files, documents can also be *packages*: folders that contain multiple files. The NSDocument class is capable of working with both flat files and packages in the same way.

A file package allows you to use the filesystem to work with different parts of your document. For example, Apple's presentation tool Keynote uses a package file format to store the content of the slides separately from the images that appear on those slides. Additionally, all applications on macOS and iOS are themselves packages: when you build an application using Xcode, what's produced is a folder that contains, among much else, the compiled binary, all images and resources, and files containing information that describes the capabilities of the application to the operating system.

 Package file formats have a lot of advantages, but they have a single, large disadvantage: you can't directly email a folder to someone. Instead, you have to store the folder in an archive, such as a ZIP file. Additionally, users of other operating systems won't see a package as a single document, but rather as a folder.

To work with package file formats, you use the `FileWrapper` class. A `FileWrapper` is an object that represents either a single file, or a directory of multiple files (each of which can itself be a file wrapper representing a directory).

The `Document` class will contain at least two file wrappers:

- One for the *.rtf* file containing the text, called *Text.rtf*
- One for a folder called *Attachments*, which will store the attachments.

We need two file wrappers in order to store both parts of a note. As we described in Chapter 4, a note is composed of formatted text, plus any number of attachments, which can be arbitrary files. To store the text to disk—which is represented and manipulated within our Swift code as an `NSAttributedString`—we use one file wrapper to store it, saving it using the preexisting *rich-text format* (RTF). To store the attachments, we'll use a folder, called *Attachments*, which will live inside the package that represents an individual *.note* file.

We need to implement methods that load from and save to a file wrapper, as well as the necessary machinery for accessing the contents of the files. We'll implement the first file wrapper, for the text of a note, in this chapter, and the second file wrapper, for attachments, in the next chapter.

However, before we start implementing the `Document` class, we need to do a little bit of preparation. First, we'll define the names of the important files and folders that are kept inside the documents; next, we'll lay out the types of errors that can be generated while working with the documents.

These will be kept inside an `enum`, which we talked about in "Enumerations" on page 50; by using this approach, we'll avoid annoying bugs caused by typos. This enumeration is one that we'll be adding to as we extend the functionality of the `Document` class. Add the following enumeration to the top of *Document.swift* (that is, before the `Docu ment` class):

```
// Names of files/directories in the package
enum NoteDocumentFileNames : String {
    case TextFile = "Text.rtf"

    case AttachmentsDirectory = "Attachments"

}
```

Opening and saving a document can fail. To diagnose *why* it failed, it's useful to build a list of error codes, which will help us figure out the precise causes of failures. The list of errors we've chosen here is derived from Apple's list of possible NSError types (*http://apple.co/21TV6BM*).

In the NSError system (which we discussed back in "Error Handling" on page 85), each possible error is represented by an error *code*: a number that represents the error in question. Rather than having to manually specify the error codes for each thing that could go wrong, we'll use an enumeration; this allows us to focus on the errors themselves instead of having to be reminded that we're really working with numbers.

 Note that the type associated with this enumeration is String. This allows us to associate each value of the enumeration with a corresponding string.

1. Add the following list of possible errors, which is also an enumeration. This enumerator is an Int type, since that's what NSError requires for its error codes. As with the NoteDocumentFileNames enumeration, we want to add this one above the class definition, at the top of the *Document.swift* file:

```
enum ErrorCode : Int {

    /// We couldn't find the document at all.
    case cannotAccessDocument

    /// We couldn't access any file wrappers inside this document.
    case cannotLoadFileWrappers

    /// We couldn't load the Text.rtf file.
    case cannotLoadText

    /// We couldn't access the Attachments folder.
    case cannotAccessAttachments

    /// We couldn't save the Text.rtf file.
    case cannotSaveText

    /// We couldn't save an attachment.
```

```
        case cannotSaveAttachment
    }
```

We're using a triple-slash (///) for our comments in the preceding code for a reason. The triple-slash tells Xcode to treat that comment as documentation. Put triple-slash comments above method names and entries in enums to define what they mean, and Option-click those names to see this documentation.

To save typing, we'll also create a method that prepares an NSError object for us based on the types of errors that can occur while a user is opening or saving a document.

2. Above the Document class definition, implement the err function:

```
let ErrorDomain = "NotesErrorDomain"

func err(_ code: ErrorCode,
         _ userInfo:[AnyHashable: Any]? = nil) -> NSError {
    // Generate an NSError object, using ErrorDomain, and using whatever
    // value we were passed.
    return NSError(domain: ErrorDomain,
                   code: code.rawValue,
                   userInfo: userInfo)
}
```

 The userInfo parameter is a little complex, so let's break it down a bit. The underscore before the parameter's name (user Info) indicates to Swift that calls to this function don't need to label the parameter—they can just call it as err(A, B) instead of err(A, userInfo: B). The type of the parameter is an optional dictionary that maps NSObjects to any object. If this parameter is omitted, this parameter's value defaults to nil.

This function takes our enumeration from before, as well as the object that caused the error, and returns an NSError object.

The NSError class represents something—*anything*—that can go wrong. In order to properly deal with the specific things that can go wrong while someone is working with the document, it's useful to have an NSError that describes what happened. However, the NSError class's initializer is complicated and verbose.

It's easier to instead create a simple little function that you can just pass a value from the ErrorCode enumeration in, as in this example (which is part of the code we'll be writing later), instead of having to pass in the ErrorDomain variable and an Int version of the error code. It saves typing and reduces the chance of accidentally introducing a bug.

You'll be using the err method later in this chapter, when we start making the loading and saving system. Here's what it looks like:

```
// Load the text data as RTF
guard let documentText = NSAttributedString(rtf: documentTextData,
    documentAttributes: nil) else {
    throw err(.cannotLoadText)
}
```

The guard Keyword, and Why It's Great

You'll notice we're using the guard keyword in the previous example. The guard keyword was introduced in Swift 2 and helps you to avoid writing two kinds of painful code: if-pyramids (sometimes called "pyramids of doom"), and early returns.

An if-pyramid looks something like this:

```
if let someObjectA = optionalA {
    if let someObjectB = optionalB {
        if let someObjectC = optionalC {
            // Do something that relies on all three of these optionals
            // having a value
        }
    }
}
```

And an early return looks something like this:

```
if conditionA == "thing" { return }
if conditionB == "thing" { return }
if conditionC == "thing" { return }

// Do something that relies on conditionA, conditionB, and
// conditionC all NOT being equal to "thing"

// Don't forget to include the 'return' statements, or you're in trouble!
```

We suspect that at least one of these looks familiar! The guard keyword lets you avoid this pain. It embodies Swift's philosophy of encouraging, or even forcing, you to write safe code. You tell guard what you want to be the case, rather than what you don't want to be the case; this makes it easier to read the code and understand what's going on.

When you use guard, you provide a condition to test and a chunk of code. If the condition evaluates to false, then the chunk of code is executed. So far, this might seem similar to the if statement, but it has an interesting extra requirement: at the end of the code, you're *required* to exit from the current scope. This means, for example, you'll have to return from the function you're in. For example:

```
guard someText.characters.count > 0 else {
    throw err(.TextIsEmpty)
}
```

Here, we guard on the premise that a variable called someText has more than zero characters. If it doesn't, we throw an error. Again, while guard might not look that different from a bunch of if statements right now, it's a lot easier to read and understand what the code is going to do.

Getting back to the app, there is one more task we need to do before we can start saving and loading files. We'll add a property to the Document class: a FileWrapper that represents the file on disk. We'll be using this later to access the attachments that are stored in the document.

Add the following property to the Document class (this goes inside the class definition):

```
var documentFileWrapper = FileWrapper(directoryWithFileWrappers: [:])
```

The documentFileWrapper will represent the contents of the document folder, and we'll use it to add files to the package. Defining the variable with the default value FileWrapper(directoryWithFileWrappers: [:]) ensures that the variable will always contain a valid file wrapper to work with.

Saving Files

With the groundwork in place, we can now implement the guts of loading and saving. We'll start by implementing the method that saves the content, and then we'll implement the loading method.

The saving method, fileWrapper ofType, an NSDocument method we are going to override, is required to return an FileWrapper that represents a file or directory to be saved to disk. It's important to note that you don't actually write a file yourself; instead, the FileWrapper object merely *represents* a file and its contents, and it's up to macOS to actually commit that object to disk. The advantage of doing it like this is that you can construct whatever organization you need for your package file format without actually having to have files written to disk. You simply create "imaginary" files and folders out of FileWrapper objects and return them from this method, and the system takes care of actually writing them to disk.

Inside the Document class, implement the fileWrapper ofType method, which prepares and returns a file wrapper to the system, which then saves it to disk:

```
override func fileWrapper(ofType typeName: String) throws -> FileWrapper {

    let textRTFData = try self.text.data(
        from: NSRange(0..<self.text.length),
        documentAttributes: [
```

```
                NSDocumentTypeDocumentAttribute: NSRTFTextDocumentType
        ]
    )

    // If the current document file wrapper already contains a
    // text file, remove it - we'll replace it with a new one
    if let oldTextFileWrapper = self.documentFileWrapper
        .fileWrappers?[NoteDocumentFileNames.TextFile.rawValue] {
        self.documentFileWrapper.removeFileWrapper(oldTextFileWrapper)
    }

    // Save the text data into the file
    self.documentFileWrapper.addRegularFile(
        withContents: textRTFData,
        preferredFilename: NoteDocumentFileNames.TextFile.rawValue
    )

    // Return the main document's file wrapper - this is what will
    // be saved on disk
    return self.documentFileWrapper
}
```

This function takes a single parameter: a string, which contains a UTI that describes the kind of file that the system would like returned to it.

In this application, which only works with *one* type of file, we can safely ignore this parameter. In an app that can open and save multiple types of documents, you'd need to check the contents of this parameter and tailor your behavior accordingly. For example, in an image-editing application that can work with both PNG and JPEG images, if the user wants to save her image as a PNG, the typeName parameter would be public.png, and you'd need to ensure that you produce a PNG image.

The method creates a new variable, called textRTFData, which contains the text of the document encoded as an RTF document. The line in which this happens is complex, so let's take a closer look at it:

```
let textRTFData = try self.text.data(
    from: NSRange(0..<self.text.length),
    documentAttributes: [
        NSDocumentTypeDocumentAttribute: NSRTFTextDocumentType
    ]
)
```

This line of code does a lot of work, all at once. It first accesses the self.text property, and accesses the NSAttributedString that contains the document's text. It then calls the data fromRange method to convert this attributed string into a collection of bytes that can be written to disk. This method first requires an NSRange, which represents a chunk of the text; in this case, we want the entire text, so we ask for the range starting at zero (the start of the text) and ending at the last character in the text.

The `data fromRange` method also needs to know *how* the data should be formatted, because there are multiple ways to represent formatted text; we indicate that we want RTF text by passing in a dictionary that contains the `NSDocumentTypeDocumentAttri bute` key, which is associated with the value `NSRTFTextDocumentType`.

This whole line is prefixed with the `try` keyword, which is required because `data fromRange` is capable of failing. However, we don't need to actually deal with this error, because the `fileWrapperOfType` method *itself* is marked as capable of failing (this is the `throws` keyword at the top of the function). In other words, if there is a problem in getting the formatted data, the entire function will immediately return, and the calling function will need to deal with the error object that is generated. (The calling function, in this case, is part of the macOS document system; we don't need to worry about the specifics. But if you're curious, it displays an alert box to users to tell them that there was a problem saving their file.)

At this point, the method is taking advantage of an especially useful combination of Swift's features. Remember that, in Swift, nonoptional variables are required to be non-nil—that is, they have a value. The only way for the `dataFromRange` method to fail to provide a value is to completely fail in its task. This is indicated from the way that `dataFromRange`'s method is declared:

```
func data(from range: NSRange,
          documentAttributes dict: [String : Any] = [:]) throws -> Data
```

Notice how the return type of this method is `Data`, not `Data?` (with a question mark at the end). This indicates that the method will either succeed and give you a value, or completely fail. If it fails, the fact that this method `throws` and that any errors from `data fromRange` are not specifically caught means that the method will immediately return. This means that you don't have to do any `nil` checking or optional unwrapping on the value you get back from `data fromRange`.

Once the `textRTFData` variable has been created, the method then needs to determine whether or not it needs to replace any existing text file. The reason for this is that a `FileWrapper` can have multiple file wrappers inside it *with the same name*. We can't simply say "add a new file wrapper called *Text.rtf*," because if one already existed, it would be added as "*Text 2.rtf*," or something similar. As a result, the document asks itself if it already has a file wrapper for the text file; if one exists, it is removed.

After that, a new file wrapper is created that contains the `textRTFData` that we prepared earlier. This is added to the document's `documentFileWrapper`.

Remember, documentFileWrapper is guaranteed to always exist and be ready to use, because it was defined with a default value.

Finally, the documentFileWrapper is returned to the system. At this point, it's now in the hands of the operating system; it will be saved, as needed, by macOS.

Loading Files

Next, we'll implement the function that loads the data from the various files into memory. This is basically the reverse of the fileWrapperOfType method: it receives a FileWrapper and uses its contents to get the useful information out.

Implement the read from fileWrapper method, which loads the document from the file wrapper:

```
override func read(from fileWrapper: FileWrapper,
    ofType typeName: String) throws {

    // Ensure that we have additional file wrappers in this file wrapper
    guard let fileWrappers = fileWrapper.fileWrappers else {
        throw err(.cannotLoadFileWrappers)
    }

    // Ensure that we can access the document text
    guard let documentTextData =
        fileWrappers[NoteDocumentFileNames.TextFile.rawValue]?
            .regularFileContents else {
        throw err(.cannotLoadText)
    }

    // Load the text data as RTF
    guard let documentText = NSAttributedString(rtf: documentTextData,
        documentAttributes: nil) else {
        throw err(.cannotLoadText)
    }

    // Keep the text in memory
    self.documentFileWrapper = fileWrapper

    self.text = documentText

}
```

This function takes a FileWrapper and uses guard to make sure that we actually have access to our collection of file wrappers; otherwise, it throws one of our errors, from the enumeration we made earlier. It then checks that there is text inside that we can access (again, otherwise throwing an error) and then loads the text into an

NSAttributedString (which stores formatted text, as we discussed earlier). If that fails, then we throw yet another possible error.

If we have successfully made it past the three guard statements, then we have successfully loaded the text. We can now store the loaded text in the text property; we'll also keep the FileWrapper that we just loaded from in the documentFileWrapper property. This is is used later, when the document is saved.

In this book, because the Note file format uses a package file format, we'll be using the methods that are specific to package file format. However, this is only one of the two approaches.

If you're making a document-based application that stores its data in flatfiles, you implement the read from data: and data ofType: methods instead of the read from fileWrapper: and fileWrapper ofType: methods. In the read from data: method, your class is handed an NSData object that contains the raw data loaded from the file that the user wants to open, and it's up to you to interpret the contents of that data:

```
override func read(from data: Data, ofType typeName: String) throws {
    // Load data from "data".
}
```

Conversely, the data ofType method is expected to create and return a Data object that contains the information that should be written out to disk:

```
override func data(ofType typeName: String) throws -> Data {
    // Return an NSData object. Here's an example:
    return "Hello".data(using: String.Encoding.utf8)!
}
```

 Don't implement both the FileWrapper methods and the Data methods in the same class. If you do, you're likely to confuse the system in regards to how your documents are stored.

A Basic UI

Now that the document class has been prepared, we can create a user interface that will let users actually edit their documents. We're going to create a UI at this point, because if we don't, it will be hard to make sure that the app is behaving as expected. macOS apps are very visual (and iOS apps even more so) and are more often than not —as is the case here—intrinsically linked between code and interface.

It's very easy to think of Xcode's interface builder as being a tool that lets you design a layout and then serialize it into some form of markup that describes the position, type, size, and so on of each object.This is not what's happening. The interface you build is actually the real, bona fide interface that your app uses, not a visual representation of it. This has some consequences that we'll touch on as they come up. We also mentioned this back in "Designing the Interface" on page 22.

In macOS and iOS, you design an interface using Xcode's built-in interface builder. The interface builder is a drag-and-drop environment in which you both lay out your interface and also connect it to your code. The interface files are stored either as *nib files* or as *storyboard files*; nib files are simpler to work with than storyboards, but storyboards have more features. We briefly touched on the interface builder earlier, in "Developing a Simple Swift Application" on page 21.

 We'll be using nib files in the macOS app, and storyboard files in the iOS app. The user interface needs of the macOS app are much simpler than those of the iOS app we'll be building later, and this way you get to see the use of nibs and storyboards in one book!

When the application creates or opens a document, it needs to present some kind of interface to the user. It does this by first asking the `Document` instance that it just created for the name of the nib file that will contain the document's UI, by accessing its `windowNibName` property:

```
override var windowNibName: String? {
    // Document supports multiple NSWindowControllers; you should remove
    // this property and override -makeWindowControllers instead.
    return "Document"
}
```

Let's now implement the user interface:

1. Open *Document.xib*, as shown in Figure 5-1.

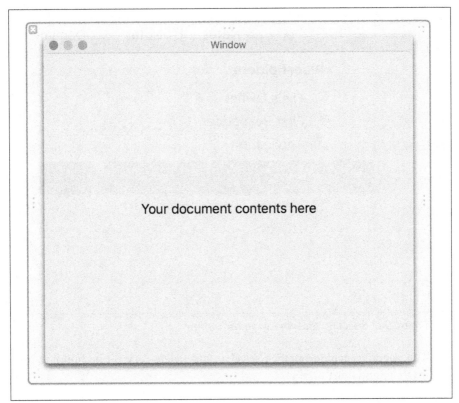

Figure 5-1. The empty Document.xib, opened for the first time

 Nib used to stand for "NeXT Interface Builder," which was the original program that developers used to create their interfaces. The file format was later changed from a custom binary format to XML, which is why the files have the filename extension *.xib*. It's still referred to as "nib." The N in the various NS-prefixed classes has the same origin.

2. Set the window's Full Screen mode to Primary Window (see Figure 5-2). Full-screen support is free, especially when you use constraints, but you need to turn it on. Do this by clicking the icon representing the window in the sidebar of the nib editor (it's below the "A" icon made out of a paintbrush, pencil, and ruler). Then use the Attributes Inspector (one of the tabs on the right side of the screen) to select Primary Window from the drop-down menu next to Full Screen.

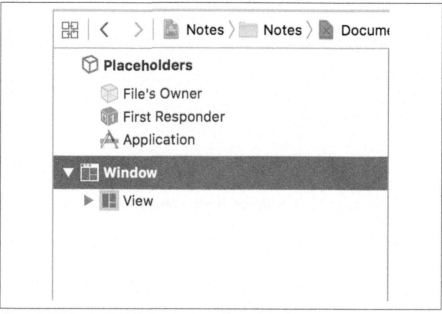

Figure 5-2. Selecting the window in the outline

3. The window includes a label; select it and delete it. We'll be building our own interface and don't need it.

If you need a reminder of where to find the Attributes Inspector, the Object library, or any other part of the Xcode user interface, revisit "The Xcode Interface" on page 13.

4. Search for NSTextView in the Object library (see Figure 5-3).

An NSTextView is used for drawing text (and selecting and modifying text). It's a simple interface to Cocoa's very, very powerful text system. You can read more about it in Apple's documentation (*http://apple.co/1UCYl1H*).

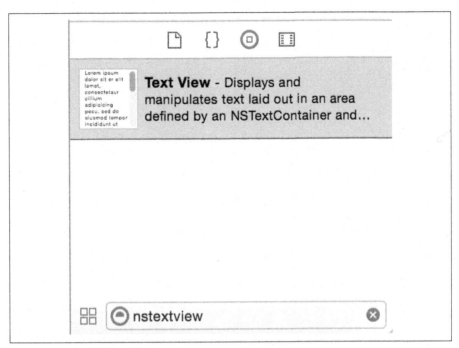

Figure 5-3. An NSTextView

5. Drag it into the interface and resize it to fill the window, leaving a little bit of margin on all sides (Figure 5-4).

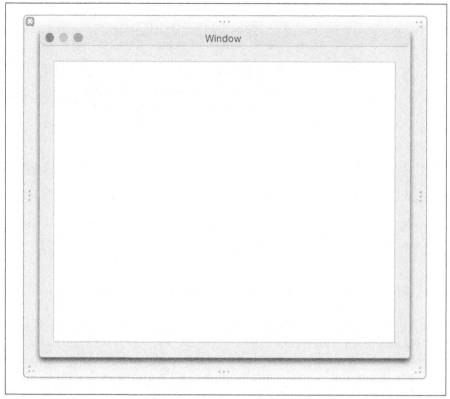

Figure 5-4. Adding the text view

6. Select the text view and open the Editor menu. Choose Resolve Auto Layout Issues→Reset to Suggested Constraints. This will add constraints that define the view's position and size in the window.

> Constraints are rules that define the position and size of the different parts of the user interface. We'll be looking at them in a lot of detail as we build the macOS and iOS apps.

7. If it isn't already open, open the outline by clicking the icon at the lower left of the view (Figure 5-5).

Figure 5-5. The outline button

8. Expand the Bordered Scroll View, and then expand the Clip View that's inside it. Select the Text View (Figure 5-6).

You might also be wondering what's up with the fact that a text view is really a Bordered Scroll View, which contains a Clip View, which contains the Text View itself. The issue is complicated and mostly boils down to "for historical reasons," but the essentials are as follows: the text view simply displays text and allows the user to type, a clip view provides some underlying support for the scroll view, and the scroll view allows users to scroll to access the content of the text view if they type more than can fit in the view.

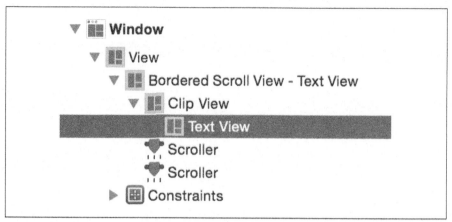

Figure 5-6. Selecting the Text View, inside its parent views

9. Open the Attributes Inspector (if it isn't already visible) and scroll down to the bottom of the list. Turn on Smart Links. This will make any URLs that the user enters appear as clickable links.

Finally, we need to connect the user interface to the underlying Document class. To do this, we'll use *bindings*, which link the value of a user interface element, such as a text field or a label, to a property in another object. When you make changes to the UI element, the property is updated; when the property is updated, the UI element is updated as well.

 Bindings are available only on macOS. On iOS, we'd need to manually register to be notified of changes that the user makes.

10. Open the Bindings Inspector by either clicking the second-to-last button at the top of the utilities pane, or by pressing ⌥-⌘-7 (see Figure 5-7).

Figure 5-7. The Bindings Inspector

11. Open the Attributed String section.

12. Select the Bind To box.

13. Change Bind To to File's Owner.

14. Change Model Key Path to **self.text**.

15. Run the app; you can now enter and save text (Figure 5-8). Close the document and reopen it, and notice that the contents of the document are saved. You also get free undo and revision control—lots of stuff is taken care of for you!

 Bindings are an incredibly powerful technology that's available on macOS. They save you a lot of work in ensuring that your controls and the data that they represent are in sync, and they can be applied to almost every control. In addition to binding individual controls, like the text field in this app, you can bind the content of collection views and table views. We won't be doing that in this app, but you can learn more about it in Cocoa Bindings Programming Topics (*http://apple.co/1UCZypP*).

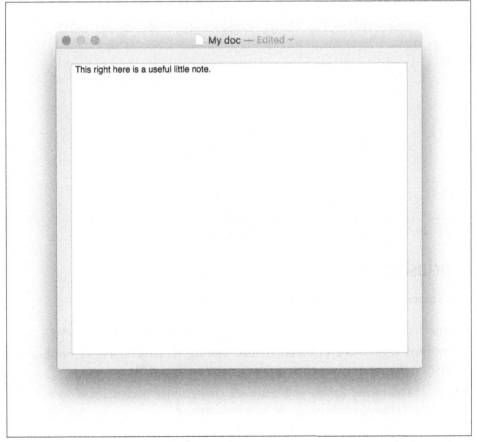

Figure 5-8. The app in its current form

After you've saved a document, locate it in the Finder and right-click it. Choose Show Package Contents, and you'll find the *Text.rtf* file, as shown in Figure 5-9. This is the text file wrapper that we wrote to earlier, when we added code to `fileWrapperOfType` inside the `Document` class.

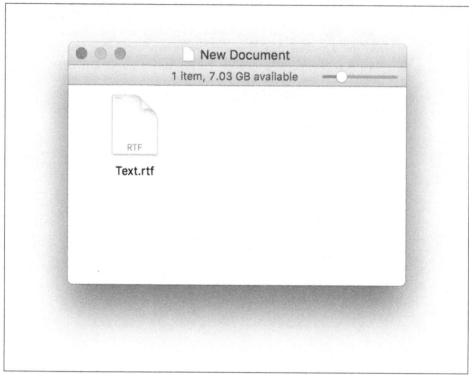

Figure 5-9. The text file inside the document

Conclusion

We've accomplished a lot in this chapter! At a high level, we've:

- manipulated the document model of macOS, which is built on `NSDocument`.
- worked with styled (attributed) text, storing it in memory, in Swift, using `NSAttributedString`, and on disk as a rich-text format file.
- used `FileWrapper` to save and load data, connecting it back to the `Document` class that was created for us by Xcode back in Chapter 4.

In the next chapter, we'll add attachment support to the macOS app.

CHAPTER 6

User Interfaces and iCloud

In its current state, our note-taking app for macOS allows you to view and edit the text in documents. In this chapter, we'll add the ability to work with attachments, and then we'll add support for iCloud.

First, we'll add support for the general concept of attachments—that is, attaching arbitrary files to a notes document, including the user interface; and then we'll expand it, adding support for double-clicking attachments to open them, including attachments that represent a real-world location, and dragging and dropping files on notes to attach them. We'll also add support for Quick Look on our notes file format, allowing users to view the contents of a note from within the macOS Finder.

As you learned in "Package File Formats" on page 116, when we set up the file wrappers for this app, attachments are stored in the document's *Attachments* directory. This means that the Document class needs tools for working with the contents of this directory. It also needs an interface for presenting the attachments and a method of adding new attachments.

In this chapter, we'll use NSCollectionView, some more advanced features of File Wrapper, and NSOpenPanel to select files to add as attachments. The NSCollection View and NSOpenPanel classes are advanced user interface elements of macOS that will allow you to present a grid or list of data, and allow users to pick files from the filesystem for use in your app, respectively.

Updating the UI

The first thing we need to do is update our user interface, adding a collection view to show a list of attachments. In the previous chapter, we wrote code and then created a UI. This time we're going to make a UI, then write code. This is because the UI we're making here is a little more complex than the UI from the last chapter, and we'll need certain parts of it in place before we can connect the code we'll be writing to it:

1. Open *Document.xib*.

2. Resize the text view (using the handles, just like any GUI resize) we added in the last chapter so that there's more margin at the bottom of the window (see Figure 6-1). This margin is where the collection view will go.

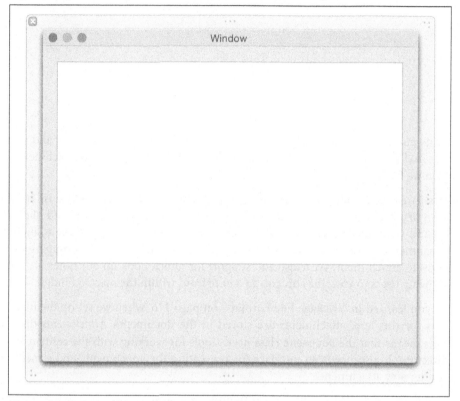

Figure 6-1. Resizing the text view to make room

3. Search for NSCollectionView in the Object library (see Figure 6-2). Drag in a collection view. We're going to use this to display any attachments for the open note document.

   NSCollectionView is provided by AppKit to display a grid of other views. Each view it displays is managed by an NSCollectionViewItem.

   To create the collection view, we also need to create the view for each cell. We only need to create one of these views—the collection view will create and manage multiple copies of them, one for each attachment in the documents.

The closest equivalent for iOS is a UICollectionView, which we'll use later on, in "Collection Views" on page 212.

□ {} ◎ ▦

Collection View - Displays an array of content as a grid of views.

Collection View Item - Manages the relationship between a collection view and the model object.

🔘 NSCollectionView ⊗

Figure 6-2. Finding the NSCollectionView

4. Resize the collection view to fill the margin beneath the text view, but leave some space on the righthand side (see Figure 6-3).

Figure 6-3. Adding the collection view

5. Select the collection view and open the Attributes Inspector. In the Layout options, change it to Flow, which will create a nice, simple, linear layout for our attachments.

6. Select both the text view and the collection view. Open the Editor menu, choose Resolve Auto Layout Issues, and choose Reset to Suggested Constraints.

7. Open *Document.swift* in the Assistant.

8. Hold down the Control key, and drag from the collection view into the `Document` class. Create a new outlet connection called `attachmentsList`. You can now close the Assistant if you need the screen space.

9. Hold down the Control key again, and drag from the collection view to the File's Owner in the outline. Choose "delegate" from the list that appears.

10. Hold down the Control key a third time, and drag from the collection view to the File's Owner. Choose "dataSource" from the list that appears.

Because of the hierarchy of views in our interface, selecting from the interface will often grab a parent object instead of the view we want. It is generally easier to select the correct object from the outline than from the views.

For just a few clicks and some dragging, we have done rather a lot. We added a collection view to our interface and then we used the built-in tool to fix the constraints on our interface. Next, we created an outlet for the collection so we can refer to it in our code. Finally, we hooked up the `delegate` and `dataSource` properties of the collection view to our `Document.swift` class. We've done all of this so we can refer to and configure the collection view in our code.

Document-Filetype-Extension UI

Next, we need to design the view that will be used for each attachment in the collection view. At the same time, we'll create a new class that will act as the manager for the cell's view. We won't be adding any code to this class right away, but it saves a little time to do it now rather than to create the file later:

1. Create a new Cocoa class named `AttachmentCell` by going to File→New→File in the menu or by pressing ⌘-N. Make it a subclass of `NSCollectionViewItem`, and turn on "Also create XIB file for user interface," as shown in Figure 6-4.

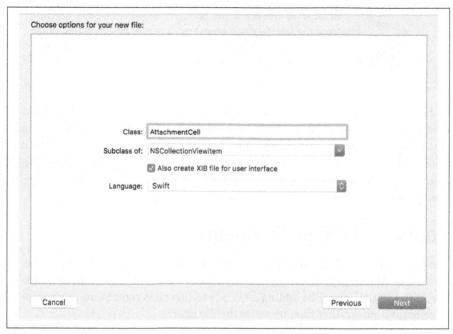

Figure 6-4. Adding the AttachmentCell

2. Open the newly created *AttachmentCell.xib*.

3. Go to the Object library, and search for Collection View Item (Figure 6-5). Drag one into the outline view, at the left.

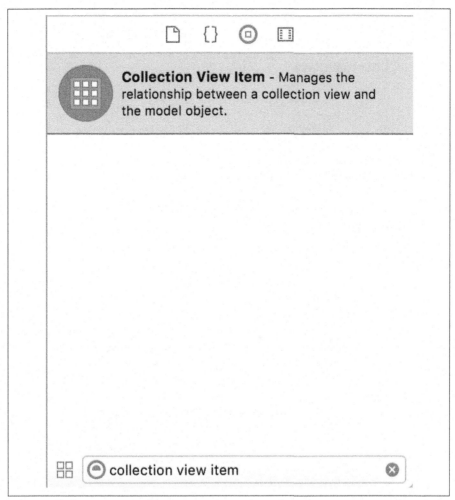

Figure 6-5. Searching for a collection view item

4. We need to make the collection view use the AttachmentCell class, so select it and go to the Identity Inspector. Change its class from NSCollectionViewItem to AttachmentCell (Figure 6-6).

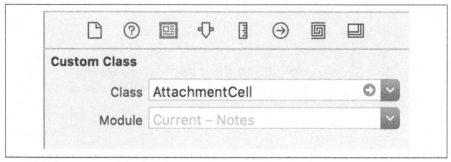

Figure 6-6. Changing the class for the collection view

We'll now add an image view to represent the attachments, and a label to show their file extension.

5. Search for NSImageView in the Objects library (Figure 6-7).

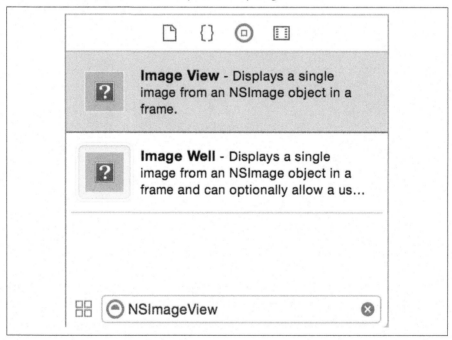

Figure 6-7. The NSImageView in the library

6. Drag in an image view, and place it in the center of the canvas. Resize it to give it a bit of space around the edges (Figure 6-8).

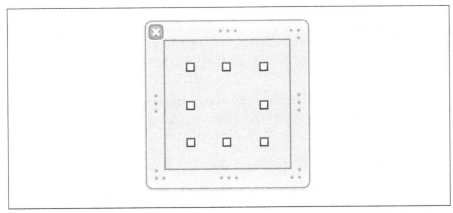

Figure 6-8. Adding the image view

7. Next, we'll add a label to show the file type. Drag in a label from the Object library, and place it beneath the image view.

8. Select the new image view and label, and open the Editor menu. Choose Resolve Auto Layout Issues→Reset to Suggested Constraints.

   Next, we need to tell the collection view item about the image view and text field that we just added. Hold down the Control key, and drag from the attachment cell in the outline to the image view. Select imageView in the menu that appears.

9. Repeat this process, but this time drag from the attachment cell to the label, and select textField in the menu.

10. Repeat this process a third time, and Control-drag from the attachment cell onto the view that contains the image view (not the image view itself). Select view in the menu that appears.

Collection view items already have an outlet set up for an image view and a text field, so you don't need to create them yourself.

The interface for the collection view cells are now ready. It's time to set up the Document class to be able to provide data to the collection view.

Getting an Icon for the Collection View Cells

As part of displaying attachments, we need some kind of picture to show them. We'll also display the file extension of each attachment in the label that you just created.

We're talking about two types of "extension" here: one is the file's extension (e.g., the "rtf" component of a filename *Text.rtf*), and the other is in terms of a Swift extension, which we covered in "Extensions" on page 71. Don't get confused! We often do.

Because attachments are represented by `FileWrapper` objects, we need a way to get a representative image from them. This means extending the `FileWrapper` class to add a method that returns an image. We'll also need a way to get the file's extension so that it can be displayed:

1. Open *Document.swift*.

2. Add the following extension to the top of the file, outside the `Document` class:

```swift
extension FileWrapper {

    dynamic var fileExtension : String? {
        return self.preferredFilename?.components(separatedBy: ".").last
    }

    dynamic var thumbnailImage : NSImage {

        if let fileExtension = self.fileExtension {
            return NSWorkspace.shared().icon(forFileType: fileExtension)
        } else {
            return NSWorkspace.shared().icon(forFileType: "")
        }
    }

    func conformsToType(_ type: CFString) -> Bool {

        // Get the extension of this file
        guard let fileExtension = self.fileExtension else {
            // If we can't get a file extension,
            // assume that it doesn't conform
            return false
        }

        // Get the file type of the attachment based on its extension
        guard let fileType = UTTypeCreatePreferredIdentifierForTag(
            kUTTagClassFilenameExtension, fileExtension as CFString, nil)?
            .takeRetainedValue() else {
            // If we can't figure out the file type
            // from the extension, it also doesn't conform
            return false
        }

        // Ask the system if this file type conforms to the provided type
        return UTTypeConformsTo(fileType, type)
```

```
            }
        }
```

This extends `FileWrapper` to provide a means for getting a thumbnail—in this case, the icon for a specific file extension—for each attachment. The extension is in the *Document.swift* file because of the close relationship the file wrappers have with the document—it makes sense to keep the related functionality together.

The `fileExtension` property takes the name of the `FileWrapper` and splits it up at every . character. It then returns the last item in this list.

The `thumbnailImage` property takes the `fileExtension` and asks the `NSWorkspace`, which represents the environment in which the app is running, to provide the image used for files with this extension. If the extension is `nil`, a generic icon is used.

Finally, `conformsToType` takes the `fileExtension` and asks the operating system's type system to convert the file extension into an object representing that file type. If this succeeds, that type object is used to check whether it conforms to the provided type identifier.

 If you are wondering what the `takeRetainedValue()` function is doing, or why we have these weird-looking values like `kUTTagClass FilenameExtension`, it's because this code is using some libraries that are written in the C programming language, not in Swift. Unfortunately for us, C is not as nice as Swift, so we need to jump through a few hoops and use some weird syntax to get the two languages to play nicely with each other.

Adding Attachments

Finally, we need to add the button, which we'll use to allow users to add new attachments. We'll be adding code to this button shortly to actually make it work. First, do the following:

1. Open *Document.xib*.

2. Search for `NSButton` in the Object library (see Figure 6-9).

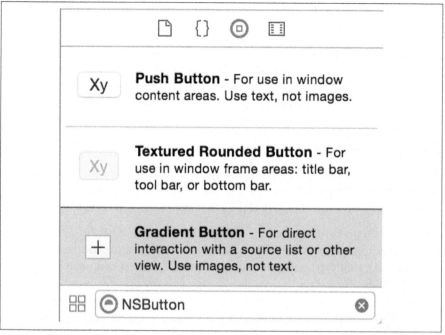

Figure 6-9. The NSButton in the library

3. Drag in a gradient button, and place it in the lower-right corner of the window (Figure 6-10).

4. Resize it to 32 × 32.

5. Select the collection view, the text view, and the button. Open the Editor menu, and choose Resolve Auto Layout Issues→Reset to Suggested Constraints.

Figure 6-10. Adding the button

Next, we'll set up the user interface that appears when this button is clicked. We'll need to create a new class that controls it. We're making a new class, which will come with a XIB file of its own, because this piece of UI will be displayed in a popover. We'll explain popovers in a moment.

6. Open the File menu, and choose New→File.

7. Select the Source item under macOS, and then select Cocoa Class (Figure 6-11). Click Next.

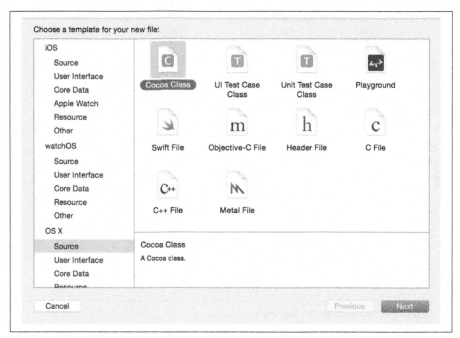

Figure 6-11. Selecting the Cocoa Class file type

8. Name the new class `AddAttachmentViewController`, and make it a subclass of `NSViewController`. Select "Also create XIB file for user interface," and ensure that the language is set to Swift (Figure 6-12).

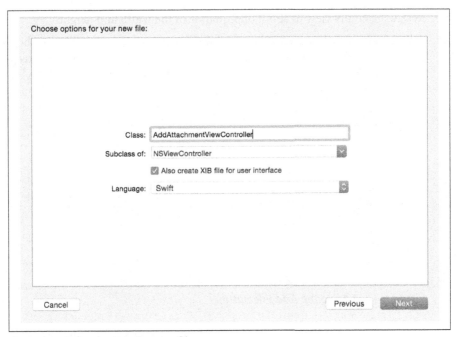

Figure 6-12. Setting up the new file

9. Open *AddAttachmentViewController.xib*. You'll see a brand-new, empty view (Figure 6-13).

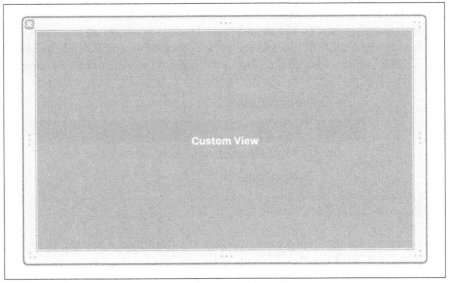

Figure 6-13. The empty AddAttachmentViewController.xib

10. Resize the empty view to about one-quarter of the width and height.

11. Add a new push button to the view and set its text to Add File, as shown in Figure 6-14. Place it in the center of the view, and add constraints that keep it in the center by opening the Editor menu and choosing Resolve Auto Layout Issues→Reset to Suggested Constraints.

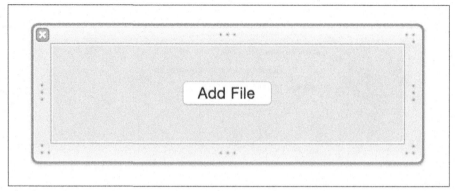

Figure 6-14. Adding the Add File button

12. Now we'll confirm that the File's Owner is correct. Select the File's Owner at the top of the outline (Figure 6-15). File's Owner exists within every nib file. It's a placeholder object that represents the controller object that works with the contents of the nib. Connecting File's Owner to the class `AddAttachmentViewController` (which is inside the *AddAttachmentViewController.swift* file) means the instance of `AddAttachmentViewController` can work with objects (like the user interface elements) inside the nib file. (There is generally an automatic connection between the Swift file and the nib file, because we asked Xcode to "also create XIB file" when we added this class, but it is always worth double checking.)

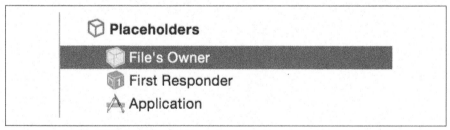

Figure 6-15. The File's Owner

13. Go to the Identity Inspector by clicking the third icon at the top of the utilities pane, or by pressing ⌥-⌘-3 (Figure 6-16).

Figure 6-16. The Identity Inspector

14. Change the class to `AddAttachmentViewController` (Figure 6-17).

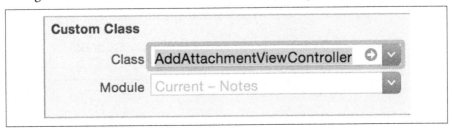

Figure 6-17. Updating the object's class

15. Open the Assistant by clicking the Assistant Editor button, or by pressing ⌥-⌘-↵ (Figure 6-18).

Figure 6-18. The Assistant Editor button

16. Ensure that the Assistant is showing the *AddAttachmentViewController.swift* file by clicking the leftmost segment of the jump bar and choosing Automatic→AddAttachmentViewController.swift (Figure 6-19).

Figure 6-19. Finding AddAttachmentViewController.swift in the jump bar

17. Hold down the Control key, and drag from the Add File button into the `AddAttachmentViewController` class. Release the mouse button, and in the window that appears, create a new `Action` connection named `addFile` (see Figure 6-20). As a reminder, we talked about `Action` connections back in "Connecting the Code" on page 23.

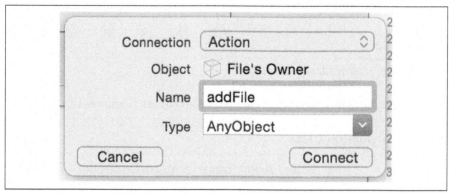

Figure 6-20. Defining a new action method

18. Close the Assistant by pressing either the Standard Editor button (Figure 6-21) or ⌘-↩.

Figure 6-21. The Standard Editor button

19. Open *AddAttachmentViewController.swift*.

20. Add the `AddAttachmentDelegate` protocol to the top of the file:

```
protocol AddAttachmentDelegate {

    func addFile()

}
```

We introduced protocols back in "Protocols" on page 70. Using a protocol for this feature allows us to take advantage of a powerful programming concept that Swift encourages: the idea that objects should know as little about each other as possible. The less an object knows about another, the fewer assumptions it can make about how it's going to behave and what methods and properties it has. This approach means that it becomes a lot less tempting to make an object depend upon the internals of how another object works.

The `AddAttachmentDelegate` protocol defines a single method, `addFile`, because there's only one thing that the `AddAttachmentViewController` needs to know about the `delegate` object: what method to call when the user adds a file. It doesn't need to know that the `delegate` object will be the `Document` object, and it doesn't need to know about any of that object's methods and properties beyond `addFile`.

21. Add a new property to the `AddAttachmentViewController` class:

```
var delegate : AddAttachmentDelegate?
```

22. Update the `addFile` method by adding the following code:

```
@IBAction func addFile(_ sender: AnyObject) {
    self.delegate?.addFile()
}
```

This code provides an action that can be called from a user interface element created in the interface builder, which calls the `addFile` method on the `delegate` object.

Finally, we'll add the ability to display the new attachment screen.

23. Open *Document.xib*, and open *Document.swift* in the Assistant Editor.

24. Hold down the Control key, and drag from the + button into the `Document` class. Create a new action called `addAttachment`.

Storing and Managing Attachments

We now need to implement support for actually storing and managing attachments in these documents:

1. Add the `attachmentsDirectoryWrapper` computed property to the `Document` class, which returns a `FileWrapper` that represents the document's *Attachments* folder. A computed property is essentially a property that behaves like a function: the code inside it runs every time it's accessed. We discussed computed properties, in "Properties" on page 66:

```
fileprivate var attachmentsDirectoryWrapper : FileWrapper? {

    guard let fileWrappers = self.documentFileWrapper.fileWrappers else {
        NSLog("Attempting to access document's contents, but none found!")
        return nil
    }

    var attachmentsDirectoryWrapper =
        fileWrappers[NoteDocumentFileNames.AttachmentsDirectory.rawValue]

    if attachmentsDirectoryWrapper == nil {

        attachmentsDirectoryWrapper =
            FileWrapper(directoryWithFileWrappers: [:])

        attachmentsDirectoryWrapper?.preferredFilename =
            NoteDocumentFileNames.AttachmentsDirectory.rawValue
```

```
self.documentFileWrapper
            .addFileWrapper(attachmentsDirectoryWrapper!)
    }

    return attachmentsDirectoryWrapper
}
```

The `attachmentsDirectoryWrapper` property represents the *Attachments* folder inside the document's package. When you access it, first it does a safety check to get access to the list of file wrappers inside the document. It then checks to see if that list already contains an *Attachments* directory; if it doesn't, a new one is created and added to the document. Last, the file wrapper is returned.

2. Next, add the `addAttachmentAtURL` method, which adds a new attachment to the document:

```
func addAttachmentAtURL(_ url:URL) throws {

    guard attachmentsDirectoryWrapper != nil else {
        throw err(.cannotAccessAttachments)
    }

    self.willChangeValue(forKey: "attachedFiles")

    let newAttachment = try FileWrapper(url: url,
        options: FileWrapper.ReadingOptions.immediate)

    attachmentsDirectoryWrapper?.addFileWrapper(newAttachment)

    self.updateChangeCount(.changeDone)
    self.didChangeValue(forKey: "attachedFiles")
}
```

This method adds an attachment to the document's *Attachments* directory. It works by first getting access to the `attachmentsDirectoryWrapper` (by calling the property that you just added); it then indicates to the system that the `attachedFiles` property will change. A new `FileWrapper` containing the provided file is created and added to the `attachmentsDirectoryWrapper`. Last, the fact that the document's contents were changed is registered.

3. Finally, add the `attachedFiles` property, which returns the list of `FileWrappers` currently inside the document:

```
dynamic var attachedFiles : [FileWrapper]? {
    if let attachmentsFileWrappers =
        self.attachmentsDirectoryWrapper?.fileWrappers {

        let attachments = Array(attachmentsFileWrappers.values)

        return attachments
```

```
        } else {
            return nil
        }
    }
```

The `attachedFiles` property simply gets the dictionary that maps filenames to file wrappers inside the *Attachments* directory and returns the list of file wrappers. The `dynamic` keyword here indicates to any other object that's watching the variable for changes that it can be changed by other parts of the object.

We want to display the Add File button in a popover, so we'll need a property in which to store that popover.

A popover is provided by `NSPopover` and is a piece of user interface that sits on top of existing content. Popovers are available on both macOS and iOS. We'll use an iOS popover later on, in "Adding Attachments" on page 291.

4. Add the following property to the `Document` class:

```
var popover : NSPopover?
```

5. Next, update the `addAttachment` method to include the following code:

```
@IBAction func addAttachment(_ sender: NSButton) {

    if let viewController = AddAttachmentViewController(
        nibName:"AddAttachmentViewController", bundle:Bundle.main
        ) {

        self.popover = NSPopover()

        self.popover?.behavior = .transient

        self.popover?.contentViewController = viewController

        self.popover?.show(relativeTo: sender.bounds,
            of: sender, preferredEdge: NSRectEdge.maxY)
    }

}
```

Note that you need to make the `sender` parameter's type `NSBut ton`. That's important because `showRelativeToRect` expects the `ofView` parameter to be an `NSView` or one of its subclasses.

This method creates an `AddAttachmentViewController` using the *AddAttachmentViewController.xib* file that you designed earlier. Once the file has been created, the popover is set up to display the view controller and is then displayed while attached to the button.

To be notified when the user selects a type of attachment, we need to conform to the `AddAttachmentDelegate` protocol. We'll do this in an extension to help keep the code we're about to add separate from the core functionality of the `Document` class.

6. Add the following extension to `Document.swift` outside of the `Document` class:

```
extension Document : AddAttachmentDelegate {

}
```

7. Add the required `addFile` method to this extension:

```
func addFile() {

    let panel = NSOpenPanel()

    panel.allowsMultipleSelection = false
    panel.canChooseDirectories = false
    panel.canChooseFiles = true

    panel.begin { (result) -> Void in
        if result == NSModalResponseOK,
            let resultURL = panel.urls.first {

            do {
                // We were given a URL - copy it in!
                try self.addAttachmentAtURL(resultURL)

                // Refresh the attachments list
                self.attachmentsList?.reloadData()

            } catch let error as NSError {

                // There was an error adding the attachment.
                // Show the user!

                // Try to get a window to present a sheet in
                if let window = self.windowForSheet {

                    // Present the error in a sheet
                    NSApp.presentError(error,
                        modalFor: window,
                        delegate: nil,
                        didPresent: nil,
                        contextInfo: nil)
```

```
            } else {
                // No window, so present it in a dialog box
                NSApp.presentError(error)
            }
        }
    }
}
```

`addFile` creates an instance of `NSOpenPanel`, a class provided by Apple that lets users browse the filesystem and pick a file. It sets some options on the `NSOpenPanel`, disallowing users to pick more than one file at a time, preventing them from choosing directories and allowing them to pick only individual files.

`addFile` then presents the panel to the user and gets the selected URL. It then calls `addAttachmentAtURL` with the URL of the file the user selected; if this results in an error, it's presented to the user.

8. Update the `addAttachment` method to make the `AddAttachmentViewController` use the document as its delegate:

```
@IBAction func addAttachment(_ sender: NSButton) {

    if let viewController = AddAttachmentViewController(
        nibName:"AddAttachmentViewController", bundle:Bundle.main
    ) {

>       viewController.delegate = self

        self.popover = NSPopover()

        self.popover?.behavior = .transient

        self.popover?.contentViewController = viewController

        self.popover?.show(relativeTo: sender.bounds,
            of: sender, preferredEdge: NSRectEdge.maxY)
    }

}
```

Displaying Data in the Collection View

We now have everything that we need to display content in the collection view, except for the methods that actually deliver data to the collection view itself. Let's add that now!

To provide cells to a collection view, we need to connect its `dataSource` outlet (which we set up earlier) to an object that conforms to the `NSCollectionViewDataSource` protocol. This means that we need to make the `Document` class conform to this protocol. We'll do this using an extension.

1. Add the following code to the *Document.swift* file:

```
extension Document : NSCollectionViewDataSource {

}
```

There are two methods that you need to implement in order to conform to `NSCollectionViewDataSource`. The first tells the system how many items exist, and the second provides an `NSCollectionViewItem` for the collection view to display.

2. Add the following method to the extension you just added:

```
func collectionView(_ collectionView: NSCollectionView,
    numberOfItemsInSection section: Int) -> Int {

    // The number of items is equal to the number of
    // attachments we have. If for some reason we can't
    // access attachedFiles, we have zero items.
    return self.attachedFiles?.count ?? 0
}
```

The `??` operator is called the *nil coalescing* operator. If the value on the lefthand side of the `??` is `nil`, the value on the righthand side is used instead. It's a faster way of saying:

```
if let count = self.attachedFiles?.count {
        return count
} else {
        return 0
}
```

This method is called for each *section* (that is, each group of cells) that exists in the collection view. By default, a collection view only contains a single section, so we ignore the `section` parameter and simply return the number of items in the `attachedFiles` list, or 0 if that list can't be accessed.

Next, we need to add a method that returns an `NSCollectionViewItem` for each attachment.

3. Add the following method to the extension:

```
func collectionView(_ collectionView: NSCollectionView,
    itemForRepresentedObjectAt indexPath: IndexPath)
    -> NSCollectionViewItem {
```

```
// Get the attachment that this cell should represent
let attachment = self.attachedFiles![indexPath.item]

// Get the cell itself
let item = collectionView
    .makeItem(withIdentifier: "AttachmentCell", for: indexPath)
    as! AttachmentCell

// Display the image and file extension in the ecell
item.imageView?.image = attachment.thumbnailImage
item.textField?.stringValue = attachment.fileExtension ?? ""

return item
}
```

This method first uses the `indexPath` parameter, which describes the location in the collection view that we're trying to display, to locate the appropriate attachment. It then calls the `makeItem withIdentifier` method to get a `NSCollection ViewItem` object, which it then casts to an `AttachmentCell`.

The reason this cast works (and why we can use the `as!` operator) is that `makeI temWithIdentifier`'s first parameter is used by macOS to search for a *.xib* file with the same name. If this *.xib* file contains a Collection View Item (which we added earlier), it's returned.

We then use the `imageView` and `textField` properties of the `AttachmentCell` to set up the image view with the icon with the thumbnail image and the label with the file extension.

Now we are ready to test our fancy new attachment system! Run the app and add an attachment. It will appear in the list of attachments (Figure 6-22). If you save the document and then view its contents, it's there!

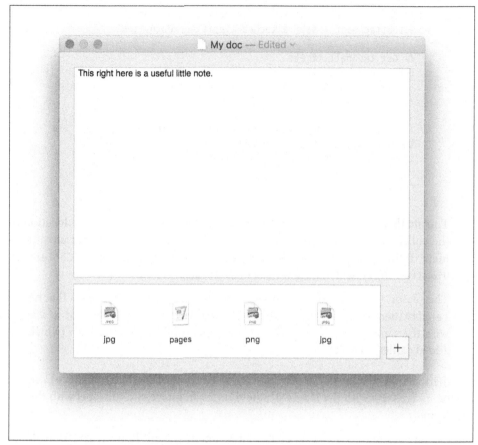

Figure 6-22. Basic attachments are working

Enhancing Attachments

We've got the basics of attachments down, so now we need to add support for some more advanced features in our attachment system, such as the ability to actually open attachments, include Quick Look attachments, view location attachments in the system Maps application, and drag files into the app to attach them.

Opening Attachments

First, we want to be able to double-click an attachment and have that file open up in whatever application is most appropriate for it.

To do this, we need to first recognize a double-click on a collection view item. Next, we need a method of telling the system to open the attachment that the collection view item represents.

To recognize double-clicks, we need to implement the `mouseDown` method in the `AttachmentCell` class. `mouseDown`, which is provided by default with a view, doesn't come with support for double-clicks—the mouse action, not the band (*https://en.wiki pedia.org/wiki/The_Doubleclicks*)—so we'll be adding it. We also need a way for the `AttachmentCells` to tell the `Document` about when this happens.

First, we'll define a protocol for the document to implement.

1. Open *Document.swift*, and add the following protocol to the file:

```
@objc protocol AttachmentCellDelegate : NSObjectProtocol {
  func openSelectedAttachment(_ collectionViewItem : NSCollectionViewItem)
}
```

 Again, we're using a protocol here to limit the amount of information that the `Document` needs to know about whatever object ends up viewing the attachment. It only needs to know how to ask the object to open the attachment.

Next, we'll add an extension to the `Document` class that makes it open whatever attachment is currently selected. This works through a little Apple magic: we use `NSWorkspace`, which is provided to work with other parts of the system your app is running on, such as launching other apps or files and working with connected devices, and ask it to open the URL of the attached file (you can learn more about `NSWorkSpace` in Apple's documentation (*http://apple.co/21UtHj1*)):

```
extension Document : AttachmentCellDelegate {
    func openSelectedAttachment(_ collectionItem: NSCollectionViewItem) {

        // Get the index of this item, or bail out
        guard let selectedIndex = (self.attachmentsList
            .indexPath(for: collectionItem) as NSIndexPath?)?.item else {
            return
        }

        // Get the attachment in question, or bail out
        guard let attachment = self.attachedFiles?[selectedIndex] else {
            return
        }

        // First, ensure that the document is saved
        self.autosave(withImplicitCancellability: false,
                    completionHandler: { (error) -> Void in
            var url = self.fileURL
            url = url?.appendingPathComponent(
                NoteDocumentFileNames.AttachmentsDirectory.rawValue,
                isDirectory: true)
```

```
                url = url?
                    .appendingPathComponent(attachment.preferredFilename!)

                if let path = url?.path {
                    NSWorkspace.shared().openFile(
                        path, withApplication: nil, andDeactivate: true)
                }
            })

        }
    }
```

We'll now make the `AttachmentCell` have a property that lets it keep a reference to an object that conforms to `AttachmentCellDelegate`.

2. Open *AttachmentCell.swift*.

3. Add the following property to the `AttachmentCell` class:

```
    class AttachmentCell: NSCollectionViewItem {

>       weak var delegate : AttachmentCellDelegate?

    }
```

Next, we'll implement `mouseDown`. This method is called whenever the user clicks on the cell's view; in this method, we'll check to see if we've clicked *twice*, and if we have, we'll call the `delegate`'s `openSelectedAttachment` method.

4. Add the following method to `AttachmentCell`:

```
    override func mouseDown(with theEvent: NSEvent) {
        if (theEvent.clickCount == 2) {
            delegate?.openSelectedAttachment(self)
        }
    }
```

Finally, we need to make all `AttachmentCells` use the `Document` as their delegate.

5. Open *Document.swift*.

6. Add the following line of code to the `collectionView(_, itemForRepresentedObjectAt indexPath:)` method:

```
    func collectionView(_ collectionView: NSCollectionView,
        itemForRepresentedObjectAt indexPath: IndexPath)
        -> NSCollectionViewItem {

        // Get the attachment that this cell should represent
        let attachment = self.attachedFiles![indexPath.item]
```

```
// Get the cell itself
let item = collectionView
    .makeItem(withIdentifier: "AttachmentCell", for: indexPath)
    as! AttachmentCell

// Display the image and file extension in the ecell
item.imageView?.image = attachment.thumbnailImage
item.textField?.stringValue = attachment.fileExtension ?? ""
```

>   `// Make this cell use us as its delegate`
>   `item.delegate = self`

```
    return item
}
```

7. You're done! Run the app, and double-click an attachment. It will open!

Adding Attachments via Drag-and-Drop

Next we're going to add support for dragging and dropping files on our app to attach them to notes.

To add support for drag-and-drop in a view, you implement certain methods that define what kinds of content can be dropped onto a view, such as URLs, colors, and text. The collection view has special support for delegating this to another object, so we'll use that.

We need to make the attachments list register for dragging. The best place to do that is in the method windowControllerDidLoadNib, which is called after the interface has loaded, but before it appears on screen. In windowControllerDidLoadNib, all of the views that the user can see are prepared and ready to be displayed, which means it's the earliest chance we have to set up the behavior of our user interface. After window ControllerDidLoadNib has finished, the bindings system kicks in, pulling information from the Document object and displaying the data in the views in the window.

1. Update the windowControllerDidLoadNib method to the Document class:

```
override func windowControllerDidLoadNib(_ windowController:
    NSWindowController) {

    self.attachmentsList.register(forDraggedTypes: [NSURLPboardType])

    self.checkForLocation()

}
```

By calling `register forDraggedTypes` and passing in an array containing the NSURLPboardType value, we're telling the collection view that we will accept NSURLs—that is, links to files on disk—that get dropped on it.

Finally, we need to add methods that the collection view will call when files are dragged. We'll do this by adding an extension to the Document class that makes it conform to the NSCollectionViewDelegate protocol.

 We *could* put these methods directly into the Document class. However, using an extension makes it a *lot* easier to keep the methods that are specific to NSCollectionViewDelegate in a single place.

2. Add the following extension to *Document.swift*:

```swift
extension Document : NSCollectionViewDelegate {

    func collectionView(_ collectionView: NSCollectionView,
        validateDrop draggingInfo: NSDraggingInfo,
        proposedIndexPath proposedDropIndexPath:
            AutoreleasingUnsafeMutablePointer<NSIndexPath>,
        dropOperation proposedDropOperation:
            UnsafeMutablePointer<NSCollectionViewDropOperation>)
        -> NSDragOperation {

        // Indicate to the user that if they release the mouse button,
        // it will "copy" whatever they're dragging.
        return NSDragOperation.copy
    }

    func collectionView(_ collectionView: NSCollectionView,
        acceptDrop draggingInfo: NSDraggingInfo,
        indexPath: IndexPath,
        dropOperation: NSCollectionViewDropOperation) -> Bool {

        // Get the pasteboard that contains the info the user dropped
        let pasteboard = draggingInfo.draggingPasteboard()

        // We need to check to see if the pasteboard contains a URL.
        // If it does, we also need to create the URL from the
        // pasteboard contents. The initializer for this is in the
        // NSURL type (not URL!), so we use that, and then convert
        // it to URL.

        // If the pasteboard contains a URL, and we can get that URL...
        if pasteboard.types?.contains(NSURLPboardType) == true,

            let url = NSURL(from: pasteboard) as? URL
```

```
        {
            // Then attempt to add that as an attachment!
            do {
                // Add it to the document
                try self.addAttachmentAtURL(url)

                // Reload the attachments list to display it
                attachmentsList.reloadData()

                // It succeeded!
                return true
            } catch let error as NSError {

                // Uh-oh. Present the error in a dialog box.
                self.presentError(error)

                // It failed, so tell the system to animate the
                // dropped item back to where it came from
                return false
            }

        }

        return false
    }

}
```

We're implementing two important methods here: the validateDrop method, and the acceptDrop method.

The validateDrop method is called when the user drags something *over* the collection view. We've already told the collection view that it will accept URLs in general; the validateDrop method allows us to be more selective about the URLs that we accept. In this app, we'll accept any old URL, so we'll instantly return NSDragOperation.copy to indicate that we should tell the user that dropping the object will result in it being copied.

The acceptDrop method is called when the user *drops* the file (that is, releases the mouse button while the cursor is over the collection view). At this point, we use the draggingInfo parameter to get information about what was dropped.

In macOS's drag-and-drop system, you don't drop entire files, but rather just NSURL objects that link to files. This means that we first have to access the URL by using the NSURL method's fromPasteboard: initializer. If that works, we use the addAttachmentAtURL method, which we wrote before; if it doesn't work, we use the NSDocument class's built-in presentError method to tell the user about the problem.

Finally, the method returns either `true` or `false` to indicate that the drop was accepted or not. If the drop was not accepted, macOS will animate the dragged object "flying back" to where it was dragged from, which tells the user that the drag failed.

You can now drag and drop files onto the list of attachments (see Figure 6-23)!

Figure 6-23. Drag-and-drop being demonstrated

Adding QuickLook

If a document uses a package file format, you can very easily take advantage of the Quick Look feature of macOS by including a folder called *QuickLook*. If this folder contains a file called *Preview.png* (or *.txt*, *.pdf*, and so on), it will be displayed when the user selects the file in Finder and presses the space bar. We're only going to implement Quick Look for the text component of a note, since displaying all the attachments goes beyond its capabilities.

Additionally, if the *QuickLook* folder contains a file called *Thumbnail.png* (or similar), this will be used as the document's icon.

First, we'll add items to the `NoteDocumentFileNames` enumeration, and then we'll add code to `fileWrapperOfType` that makes it save a copy of the *Text.rtf* file in the *Quick-Look* folder.

1. Add the following items to the `NoteDocumentFileNames` enumeration:

    ```
    // Names of files/directories in the package
    enum NoteDocumentFileNames : String {
        case TextFile = "Text.rtf"

        case AttachmentsDirectory = "Attachments"

    >   case QuickLookDirectory = "QuickLook"
    >
    >   case QuickLookTextFile = "Preview.rtf"
    >
    >   case QuickLookThumbnail = "Thumbnail.png"

    }
    ```

2. Next, add the following method to the `Document` class:

    ```
    func iconImageDataWithSize(_ size: CGSize) -> Data? {

        let image = NSImage(size: size)

        image.lockFocus()

        let entireImageRect = CGRect(origin: CGPoint.zero, size: size)

        // Fill the background with white
        let backgroundRect = NSBezierPath(rect: entireImageRect)
        NSColor.white.setFill()
        backgroundRect.fill()

        if self.attachedFiles?.count >= 1 {
            // Render our text, and the first attachment
            let attachmentImage = self.attachedFiles?[0].thumbnailImage

            let result = entireImageRect.divided(atDistance:
                entireImageRect.size.height / 2.0, from: CGRectEdge.minYEdge)

            self.text.draw(in: result.slice)

            attachmentImage?.draw(in: result.remainder)
        } else {
            // Just render our text
            self.text.draw(in: entireImageRect)
    ```

```
    }

    let bitmapRepresentation =
        NSBitmapImageRep(focusedViewRect: entireImageRect)

    image.unlockFocus()

    // Convert it to a PNG
    return bitmapRepresentation?
        .representation(using: .PNG, properties: [:])

}
```

This method is responsible for preparing an image and then returning it as an NSData object containing a PNG. We first start building the image by creating a new NSImage object, passing in the size of the image we want to create. We then call the lockFocus method, which tells the drawing system that we wish to start drawing into this new image.

Next, we start the drawing itself. We first fill the entire image with a white background and then check to see if we have attachments. If we have any attachments, we draw the first attachment's thumbnail image into the top half of the canvas, and the text of the note into the bottom half; if we have no attachments, we draw just the text.

Once the drawing is done, we create an NSBitmapImageRep object, which allows us to convert the image into a bitmap format, such as PNG. This is necessary, because NSImage can also just as easily be converted to a vector format, like PDF; we need to be specific about what we want to do with the image.

Once the bitmap representation has been created, we call unlockFocus to tell the drawing system that we're done working with the image.

 If you call lockFocus, you must call unlockFocus. If you don't, you'll cause all kinds of problems, because the drawing system won't know that you're done drawing content into your image.

Finally, we can return a Data object by asking the bitmap representation to provide a PNG version of itself, which we then return.

Now that documents are capable of producing a thumbnail image that represents themselves, we can use these thumbnails in the document's Quick Look preview.

3. Add the following code to fileWrapperOfType:

```
override func fileWrapper(ofType typeName: String) throws -> FileWrapper {
```

```
          let textRTFData = try self.text.data(
              from: NSRange(0..<self.text.length),
              documentAttributes: [
                  NSDocumentTypeDocumentAttribute: NSRTFTextDocumentType
              ]
          )

          // If the current document file wrapper already contains a
          // text file, remove it - we'll replace it with a new one
          if let oldTextFileWrapper = self.documentFileWrapper
              .fileWrappers?[NoteDocumentFileNames.TextFile.rawValue] {
              self.documentFileWrapper.removeFileWrapper(oldTextFileWrapper)
          }

>         // Create the QuickLook folder
>
>         let thumbnailImageData =
>             self.iconImageDataWithSize(CGSize(width: 512, height: 512))!
>         let thumbnailWrapper =
>             FileWrapper(regularFileWithContents: thumbnailImageData)
>
>         let quicklookPreview =
>             FileWrapper(regularFileWithContents: textRTFData)
>
>         let quickLookFolderFileWrapper =
>             FileWrapper(directoryWithFileWrappers: [
>             NoteDocumentFileNames.QuickLookTextFile.rawValue: quicklookPreview,
>             NoteDocumentFileNames.QuickLookThumbnail.rawValue: thumbnailWrapper
>             ])
>
>         quickLookFolderFileWrapper.preferredFilename
>             = NoteDocumentFileNames.QuickLookDirectory.rawValue
>
>         // Remove the old QuickLook folder if it existed
>         if let oldQuickLookFolder = self.documentFileWrapper
>             .fileWrappers?[NoteDocumentFileNames.QuickLookDirectory.rawValue] {
>             self.documentFileWrapper.removeFileWrapper(oldQuickLookFolder)
>         }
>
>         // Add the new QuickLook folder
>         self.documentFileWrapper.addFileWrapper(quickLookFolderFileWrapper)

          // Return the main document's file wrapper - this is what will
          // be saved on disk
          return self.documentFileWrapper
      }
```

This method gets the PNG data that contains the document's thumbnail image
and creates a `FileWrapper` to represent a file that stores that data. Next, it takes
the note's text, which has previously already been stored in the `textRTFData` vari-

able, and stores it in a second `FileWrapper`, to represent the document's preview file. Finally, a third `FileWrapper` is created, which represents the folder that contains the thumbnail and preview files.

Next the method checks to see if the document's file wrapper already contains a *QuickLook* folder. If it does, it's removed. Finally, the newly created *QuickLook* folder is added to the document's file wrapper. As a result, when the document is saved, the *QuickLook* folder and its required files are written to disk.

4. Run the app and save the document. Select the document in the Finder, and hit the space bar. You'll see the document's text, as shown in Figure 6-24.

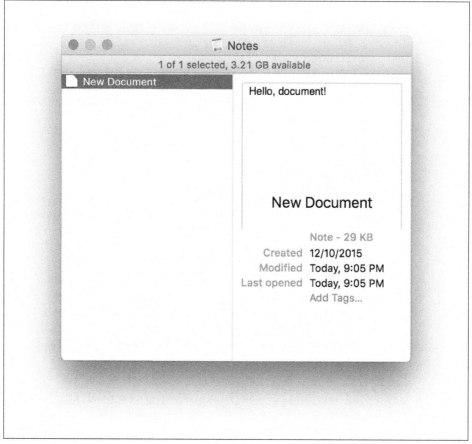

Figure 6-24. Quick Look working on a Notes file

Location

Now we'll add special support to the Document class to make it open locations in the Maps app. It doesn't really make a lot of sense to have a location just be an attachment; after all, what would it represent? Instead, we will make it so that we determine our location once, when we create a new note, and we'll save it separately from the rest of the attachments.

The location will be stored in a file next to the main text document. This file will store the location as a latitude and longitude coordinate pair, in the JSON file format. When a document is created, the application will attempt to get the computer's current location; if it succeeds, it will store the location, and if it fails, it will give up. While the location is being determined, the window will show a spinning activity indicator.

If a document has a location attached to it—either because the location has just been determined, or because a document was opened that already had an attachment—then we'll show a button that, when clicked, opens the location in the Maps application:

1. Open the *Assets.xcassets* file.

2. Drag the *Location.pdf* image into the list of images—we'll use this as our location button.

3. Open *Document.xib*; this will be where we make all our changes to the UI.

4. Drag in a new Gradient button, and place it above the Add Attachment button, in line with the attachments list.

5. Set its height to be 34 points and its width to be 32 points.

6. Set its image to be the *Location* image we just added into the Assets.

7. Add constraints to the button's width, height, distance to upper view, and distance to trailing edge of upper view. This will pin the button to its current position and dimensions.

   With this done our UI should look like Figure 6-25.

8. Next drag in an Indeterminate Circular Progress Indicator (which is a fancy way of saying a spinner) and place it centered over the Location button. We will use this to indicate when location is being determined.

9. Add constraints to the spinner to center it vertically and horizontally with the Location button.

   The last part is to hook the new button and spinner up to some outlets and actions.

10. Inside *Document.swift* connect the spinner to an outlet called locationSpinner.

11. Connect the button to an outlet called `locationButton`.

12. Connect the button's action to an action called `showLocation`.

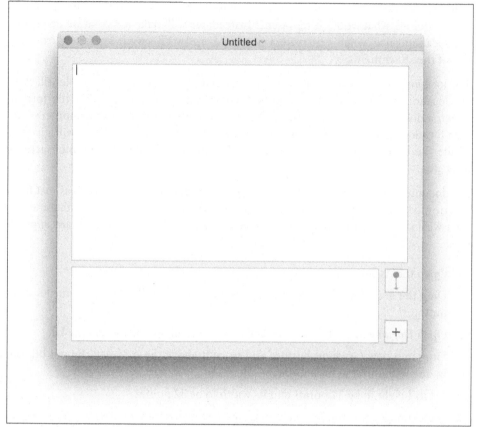

Figure 6-25. The Location button, bottom right, above the Add Attachment button

With that done, we are finished with the changes to our UI and we can start implementing the code:

1. Open *Document.swift* and import the `CoreLocation` and `MapKit` libraries. These give us all the required functionality to determine and show location:

    ```
    import MapKit
    import CoreLocation
    ```

2. Add a new property to the `Document` class:

    ```
    var location : CLLocationCoordinate2D?
    ```

    A `CLLocationCoordinate2D` is a simple struct that represents a spot on the earth as a latitude and longitude. This will represent the location once we determine it.

3. Add a `CLLocationManager` property to the `Document` class. This will be the object that determines the note's location:

```
var locationManager = CLLocationManager()
```

Location managers work by delegate methods: you configure the location manager to determine location, ask it to do so, and then let it go. As determining location can take an indeterminate amount of time, the location manager will inform its delegate when it has a location.

4. Now we'll implement the required delegate methods for our location manager. We are going to be doing this as an extension to the `Document` class to keep it all neat and tidy:

```
extension Document : CLLocationManagerDelegate {
    func locationManager(_ manager: CLLocationManager,
                    didUpdateLocations locations: [CLLocation]) {

        guard let location = locations.first else {
            NSLog("Received didUpdateLocations, but received no locations")
            return
        }

        self.location = location.coordinate

        self.locationSpinner.isHidden = true
        self.locationButton.isHidden = false

        manager.stopUpdatingLocation()
    }

    func locationManager(_ manager: CLLocationManager,
                    didFailWithError error: Error) {
        let alert = NSAlert(error: error)

        alert.runModal()

        self.locationSpinner.isHidden = true
        self.locationButton.isHidden = true
    }
}
```

The first method `locationManager didUpdateLocations` is called when the location manager has determined a location. In this case we are doing a quick check to make sure there is actually a location; if there is, we store it in our location property and then update the UI to stop the spinner spinning and to show the location button. The second method, `locationManager didFailWithError`, is called if the location manager encounters an error. In this case all we do is show it and then update the UI to hide the button and the spinner.

5. Add a new method to check for a location:

```swift
func checkForLocation() {
    // Check to see if we need to add a location
    let raw = NoteDocumentFileNames.locationAttachment.rawValue
    if let locationRawData =
        self.documentFileWrapper.fileWrappers?[raw]?.regularFileContents,
        let locationData = try? JSONSerialization.jsonObject(
            with: locationRawData,
            options: []) as? [String:Double],
        let latitude = locationData?["lat"],
        let longitude = locationData?["long"]
    {
        self.location =
            CLLocationCoordinate2D(latitude: latitude, longitude: longitude)

        locationButton.isHidden = false
        locationSpinner.isHidden = true

        return
    }

    switch CLLocationManager.authorizationStatus() {

    // If we're authorized
    // or we haven't yet gotten permission, start checking
    case .notDetermined:
        fallthrough
    case .authorized:
        locationButton.isHidden = true
        locationSpinner.isHidden = false
        locationSpinner.startAnimation(nil)

        locationManager.delegate = self

        locationManager.startUpdatingLocation()

    // If it's any other state (i.e. denied or restricted), hide all UI
    default:
        locationButton.isHidden = true
        locationSpinner.isHidden = true
    }
}
```

First, this method checks the filewrappers to see if there is already a location. If there isn't, we switch over the authorization status of the location manager. There are a few options here, but basically if the user has denied permission, all we do is hide the button and spinner. If the user has given permission, we tell the location manager that we will be its delegate and to start looking for locations. Finally we hide the button and start our spinner spinning. Now you might notice there is some reference to a NoteDocumentFileNames.locationAttachment type that we haven't yet set up—don't worry about that as we will implement that soon.

6. Add this code to the windowControllerDidLoadNib method:

```
override func windowControllerDidLoadNib(_ windowController:
    NSWindowController) {

    self.attachmentsList.register(forDraggedTypes: [NSURLPboardType])

>   self.checkForLocation()

}
```

7. Now implement the showLocation action we set up earlier:

```
@IBAction func showLocation(_ sender : NSButton) {

    guard let location = self.location else {
        NSLog("Attempted to show the location, but there isn't one")
        return
    }

    // Build a placemark with that coordinate
    let placemark =
        MKPlacemark(coordinate: location,
                    addressDictionary: nil)
    // Build a map item from that placemark...
    let mapItem = MKMapItem(placemark: placemark)
    // And open the map item in the Maps app!
    mapItem.openInMaps(launchOptions: nil)
}
```

This method creates a new MKPlacemark, which is one of those little pins you see on the Maps app, and then opens the placemark inside Maps.

There are just two more changes to make. First, we don't actually support location attachments in the document model, so let's change that now:

1. Add a new value to the NoteDocumentFileNames enumeration:

```
case locationAttachment = "location.json"
```

This is what we used earlier when we checked if we already have a location.

2. Add the following to the fileWrapper ofType method:

```
override func fileWrapper(ofType typeName: String) throws -> FileWrapper {

    let textRTFData = try self.text.data(
        from: NSRange(0..<self.text.length),
        documentAttributes: [
            NSDocumentTypeDocumentAttribute: NSRTFTextDocumentType
```

```
            ]
        )

        // If the current document file wrapper already contains a
        // text file, remove it - we'll replace it with a new one
        if let oldTextFileWrapper = self.documentFileWrapper
            .fileWrappers?[NoteDocumentFileNames.TextFile.rawValue] {
            self.documentFileWrapper.removeFileWrapper(oldTextFileWrapper)
        }

        // Create the QuickLook folder

        let thumbnailImageData =
            self.iconImageDataWithSize(CGSize(width: 512, height: 512))!
        let thumbnailWrapper =
            FileWrapper(regularFileWithContents: thumbnailImageData)

        let quicklookPreview =
            FileWrapper(regularFileWithContents: textRTFData)

        let quickLookFolderFileWrapper =
            FileWrapper(directoryWithFileWrappers: [
            NoteDocumentFileNames.QuickLookTextFile.rawValue: quicklookPreview,
            NoteDocumentFileNames.QuickLookThumbnail.rawValue: thumbnailWrapper
            ])

        quickLookFolderFileWrapper.preferredFilename
            = NoteDocumentFileNames.QuickLookDirectory.rawValue

        // Remove the old QuickLook folder if it existed
        if let oldQuickLookFolder = self.documentFileWrapper
            .fileWrappers?[NoteDocumentFileNames.QuickLookDirectory.rawValue] {
            self.documentFileWrapper.removeFileWrapper(oldQuickLookFolder)
        }

        // Add the new QuickLook folder
        self.documentFileWrapper.addFileWrapper(quickLookFolderFileWrapper)

>       if let oldLocationFileWrapper = self.documentFileWrapper
>           .fileWrappers?[NoteDocumentFileNames.locationAttachment.rawValue] {
>           self.documentFileWrapper.removeFileWrapper(oldLocationFileWrapper)
>       }
>
>       if let location = self.location {
>
>           let locationDictionary = ["lat":location.latitude,
>                               "long": location.longitude]
>       if let locationData = try? JSONSerialization.data(withJSONObject:
>                               locationDictionary, options: [])
>       {
```

```
>          // Save the location data into the file
>          self.documentFileWrapper.addRegularFile(
>              withContents: locationData,
>              preferredFilename:
>                  NoteDocumentFileNames.locationAttachment.rawValue)
>      }

        // Save the text data into the file
        self.documentFileWrapper.addRegularFile(
            withContents: textRTFData,
            preferredFilename: NoteDocumentFileNames.TextFile.rawValue
        )

        // Return the main document's file wrapper - this is what will
        // be saved on disk
        return self.documentFileWrapper
    }
```

This is where we actually load and save our location attachment. In our case what we have is a simple JSON file that stores a latitude and longitude, and we use the built in `JSONSerialization` class to do so.

It's worth noting that there are already established file formats for storing location data, such as GeoJSON or KML, but these are quite large systems designed to handle far more than what we need. This is why we made our own instead of using one of the standards.

With that done, we can now add and show locations in the app!

iCloud

The Mac app is now almost entirely done and dusted, and the last thing to add is integration with iCloud, which will make all documents that you create in the app available on the user's other devices.

To be able to effectively test and develop applications (for both macOS and iOS) that use iCloud, you will need to make sure your devices are set up with your own iCloud account. If iCloud is not enabled, you can't test apps you develop that use iCloud.

iCloud is an online storage and syncing service provided by Apple. It is promoted as a service that makes "all of your data available on all of your devices": the user's mail, settings, documents, and data are all synced via the iCloud server across all devices that are signed in to the same account.

On macOS, an application doesn't need to do a great deal of work to gain access to iCloud's file-syncing services. All you need to do is turn the feature on in Xcode, and macOS will take care of the rest. This is a very short section!

The minimal amount of work required to make a macOS app work with iCloud is almost the opposite of the amount of work required to make an iOS app work with iCloud. macOS and iCloud, for document-based apps, is easy. iOS and iCloud is… not! Sorry!

The Basics of iCloud

iCloud actually exists as three related services:

- iCloud key/value storage allows applications to store simple information, like strings and numbers, in a dictionary-like structure that's synced across all of a user's devices.

- iCloud document storage provides a folder to each application whose contents are synced across devices.

- CloudKit is a cloud-hosted database that allows both applications running on the user's devices as well as external services, like a server that you host, to access the data.

iCloud is designed to provide maximum privacy and safety for the user: your apps are able to access only data made by an app that you own, and iCloud is available only to apps that have been signed by a registered Apple developer.

To add support for storing data in iCloud, you must provision the application for used with iCloud. This isn't as ominous as it sounds (at least for the macOS app):

1. Click the project at the top of the Project Navigator.

2. Select the Notes target, and go to the General tab. Ensure that the team is not set to None; if it is, select your development team. If you don't have a development team, refer to "The Apple Developer Program" on page 5 to learn how to set up your account.

3. Go to the Capabilities tab.

4. Turn iCloud on.

   Xcode will spin for a few moments while it sets up your application for use with iCloud.

5. In the Services section, select iCloud Documents, and deselect everything else (Figure 6-26).

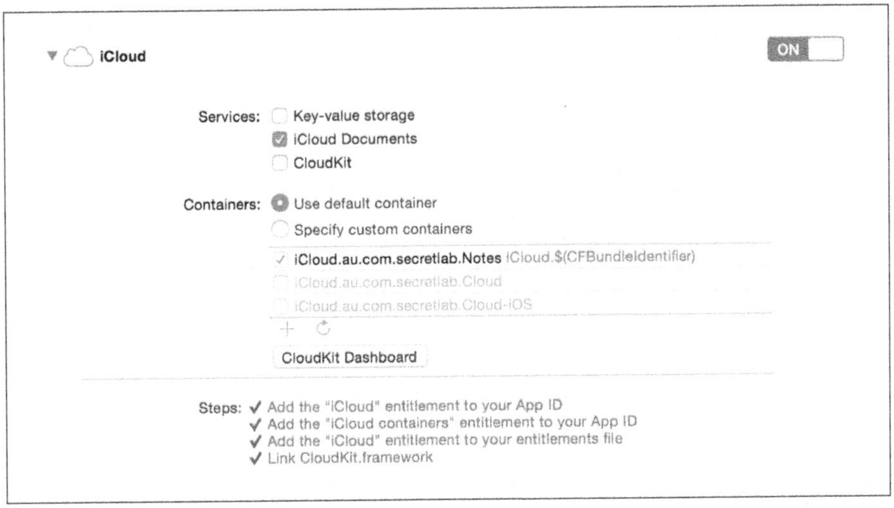

Figure 6-26. Setting up iCloud

Note the name of the iCloud container: in Figure 6-26, it's "iCloud.au.com.secret-lab.Notes," but yours will be different. You'll need this in a moment.

The name of the iCloud container will be used in a moment to ensure that the iCloud Drive folder for this app is visible.

Next, we need to indicate to the system that this application should have a folder in iCloud Drive. iCloud Drive is the users' view of all of the various files they've stored in iCloud, and each application that has access to iCloud can potentially have a folder appear in iCloud Drive.

Having the ability to store documents in iCloud is not the same thing as having a visible folder in the iCloud Drive interface. If you have iCloud Documents turned on, your app can store files in iCloud, but your app won't appear in iCloud Drive. You need to turn it on manually.

6. Go to the Info tab. Add a new entry to the Custom macOS Target Properties list by moving the mouse over anywhere in the list and clicking the + button. Name the new entry NSUbiquitousContainers, and change its type to Dictionary by clicking anywhere inside its second column (Figure 6-27).

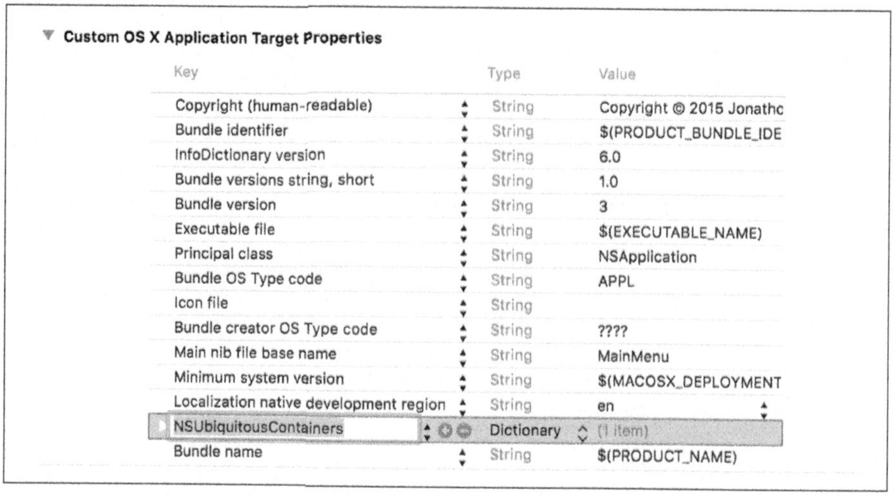

Figure 6-27. Adding a new entry to the custom target properties list

7. Expand the new `NSUbiquitousContainers` entry, and add a new entry inside it by moving the mouse over the row and clicking the + button. This entry should have the same name as your iCloud container from earlier, and its type should be `Dictionary`.

8. Add the following three entries to this dictionary (by moving the mouse over this *additional* row that you just added, and clicking +), as shown in Figure 6-28:

- **NSUbiquitousContainerIsDocumentScopePublic (Boolean):** YES
- **NSUbiquitousContainerSupportedFolderLevels (String):** Any
- **NSUbiquitousContainerName (String):** Notes

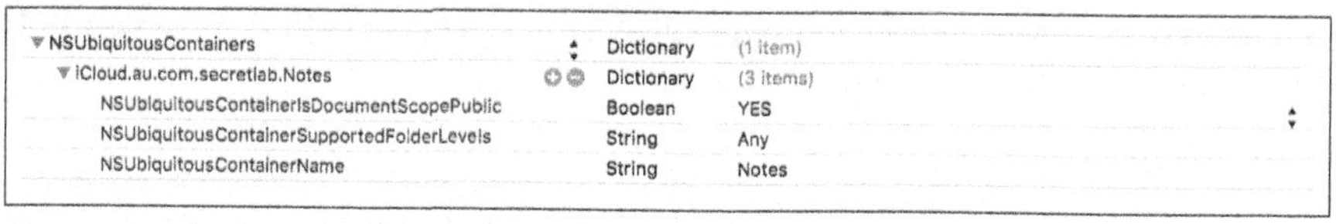

Figure 6-28. The newly added entries

The app is now set up for iCloud. You can save documents in iCloud Drive, and they'll be synced across all devices that have the Notes app installed. When we implement the iOS app in Part III, it will receive the documents as well.

iCloud, being a networked service, can occasionally behave in ways you don't expect. If you're having trouble figuring out why iCloud is doing things you don't want it to, like failing to sync changes to files, there's a debugging tool that you can use to observe what iCloud's doing behind the scenes.

Open the Terminal app, which you'll find in the *Applications→Utilities* folder. Next, type the following and press Return:

```
brctl log --wait --shorten
```

This will start logging all iCloud activity across all applications until you press Control-C.

Conclusion

We've done a huge amount in this chapter! In brief, we've:

- Explored more complex pieces of macOS user interface that are available, such as NSCollectionView (which provides the ability to display a grid of views, and used it to display a list of attachments for our notes) and NSPopover.
- Used outlets and actions, allowing us to easily connect code to the user interface of our apps.
- Created new classes, and subclassed existing classes, to add functionality.
- Implemented Quick Look on our custom file format, allowing users of our app to preview the contents of files using the macOS Finder.
- Added iCloud support.

That's basically everything we're going to do for the macOS app in this book. We're keeping it short and simple. If you're interested in taking it further, we'll provide some suggestions on our website (*http://www.secretlab.com.au/books/learning-swift*).

In the next part of the book, we'll start working with iOS!

PART III

An iOS App

CHAPTER 7

Setting Up the iOS Notes App

People carry their phones everywhere, and they expect to have access to everything, any time. This means that, for a note-taking app like the one we made in Part II, our users are going to want access to the notes that they've been writing while on their phones.

Over the next several chapters, we'll implement an iOS application that allows users to both write new notes while on the go and also access the notes that they've made on their Mac, using the macOS app we built in Part II. Because the Mac app was already set up using iCloud, their documents already exist in the cloud; this means that our iOS application will be able to access them.

By storing documents that were created on the phone in iCloud, users can seamlessly move from their desktop computer to their phone and back again, while having access to all of their documents at the same time. Additionally, if they own more than one iOS device—for example, both an iPhone and an iPad—their documents will exist on all of their devices at the same time.

 You can download the resources for this app, including wireframes, mockups, and icons from this book's website (*http://www.secret lab.com.au/books/learning-swift*).

We'll be doing a lot more coding in this part than we did back in Part II, when we built the macOS app. We'll begin the iOS app by first discussing its design—both its visual design and the design of the software. Next, we'll dive in and begin creating the app, assembling a new Xcode project for it, adding the icon, and adding support for iCloud. We're setting up iCloud up front for the iOS app, instead of at the end, as we did for the macOS app (in "iCloud" on page 177) because iCloud is so tightly integrated with everything in iOS and can't just be turned on as with on macOS. After setting up iCloud, we'll set up the iOS app to work with the same Note document type we created for the macOS app in "Defining a Document Type" on page 106.

Designing the iOS Notes App

The most obvious difference between an iOS device and a Mac is the difference between the two display sizes. An iPhone is *much* smaller than a Mac, and while the iPad is bigger, it's still quite small. Only iPad Pro approaches, and in some cases exceeds, a regular laptop's size.

On top of this difference in size, iOS devices have a second, more important distinction: the user interacts with the interface using a touchscreen. Touchscreens change the way that you interact with any user interface, for a number of reasons. First, because the user's hand is not transparent, anything the user is touching is covered up by the finger that's touching it. On top of that, the rest of the hand that's attached to that finger—the palm, wrist, and so on—also covers up even more of the screen. Additionally, fingertips are significantly less precise than a mouse cursor, which means that everything needs to be bigger if you want the user to actually be able to touch it.

 You might think that it's incredibly obvious that a mobile device is likely to be much smaller than a traditional computer, and you'd be right; but it's amazing how many mobile developers forget this and try to cram everything into a single screen of a mobile app interface.

On top of the constraints imposed by the touchscreen, you have a number of other hardware issues to deal with: the phone relies on a battery, which means that you have to be very economical with the amount of power that the app consumes. Additionally, because users will be switching from WiFi to cell coverage as they move around, your app can't rely on access to the internet.

Finally, there are constraints imposed by iOS itself. Unlike in macOS, there is no Finder application that acts as the *host* for all other apps; instead of working primarily with their documents in the Finder, users work with apps in the home screen. This means that every iOS app that works with files is responsible for presenting the list of the user's files. This includes searching the iCloud container for files that the app should present, as well as identifying when that list of files changes due to other devices making changes to the container.

Starting with iOS 9, users can browse the contents of their iCloud Drive using a built-in app. However, the user may not be using it— the app can be disabled, the user may not have access to iCloud, or the user may simply not know where to find it. The iCloud Drive app is meant to be a secondary method for users to access their files, because the iOS philosophy is that apps "contain" their documents. This means that your app needs to present and manage its own list of documents.

Additionally, not every file that's in the user's iCloud container will be downloaded to the device. This differs from how it works on macOS, which automatically downloads every file. Your app needs to specifically request to download each file that the user wants to access.

With this in mind, we started designing wireframes for the iOS app: the basic layout of each screen for the app, and how they relate (see Figures 7-1 and 7-2).

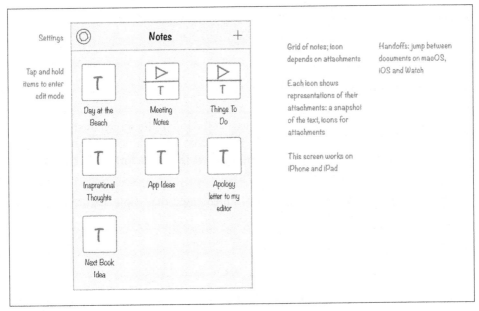

Figure 7-1. The document list

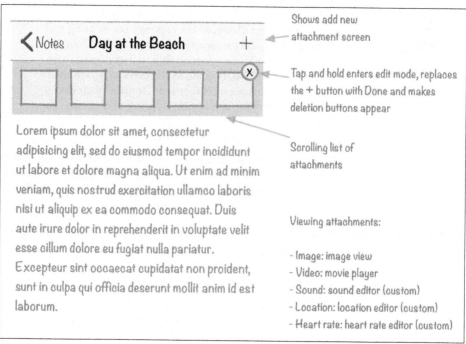

Figure 7-2. A single document

You'll notice that the attachments list appears at the top of the screen, instead of at the bottom. The reason for this is the on-screen keyboard, which occludes everything in the bottom half of the screen; if users want to access their attachments, it's not reasonable to ask them to dismiss the keyboard first.

At the end of these chapters, you'll have implemented the whole application, which will look like Figures 7-3 through 7-5.

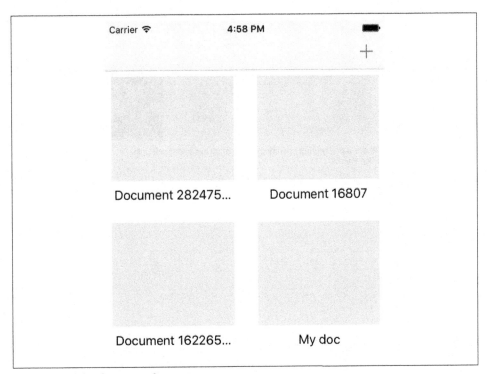

Figure 7-3. The document list

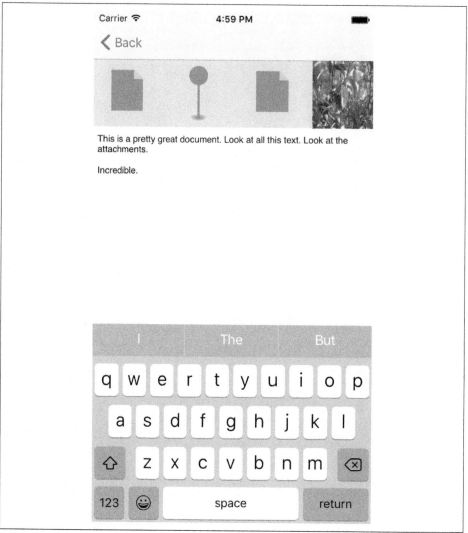

Figure 7-4. A single document

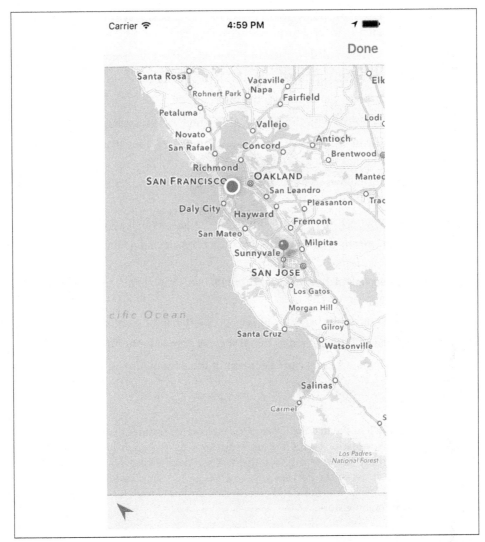

Figure 7-5. Locations

The iOS app will have many features, and we'll be adding all of them over the coming chapters:

- Compatibility with the macOS app's documents: users can start writing a note on macOS and make changes to it on any of their iOS devices.

- Files are stored in either iCloud or locally on the user's device, as per the user's preference.

- Conflict resolution for notes, so users can pick the most recent version if there's a conflict when notes are synchronized between devices.

- Attachments can be added to notes and viewed. These attachments include:

  — images and videos, captured using the device's camera.

  — audio recordings, captured with the microphone.

  — locations, captured with the device's GPS when you create a note.

- Image attachments can be shared via any of the user's apps that support sharing (Twitter, Facebook, Pinterest, and so on).

- Handoff support allows users to instantly move from one device to the next while editing a document.

- Search indexing means that notes appear in Spotlight search results.

- Undo support means that users can instantly revert a change that they've made to the note text.

- Links are detected in note text, and when users tap them, an embedded web browser will appear.

- Users can customize the behavior of the app via the Settings app.

- Images can have filters applied to them, such as grayscale and film effects.

- Text to speech means users can select text in the document and have their device speak it.

 You'll notice that the iOS app has many more features than the Mac app. Most of this is because Mac apps have quite a bit of stuff already taken care of for them: if we double-click an image, it launches in the Preview app, whereas an iOS app has to create its own view controller and present it in an image view. iOS apps just take more work.

Creating the iOS Project

Because it's part of the same collection of products, the iOS app will be added as a target attached to the original project. This allows it to share code with the Mac target, and it keeps everything in one place (if you need a reminder on targets, flip back to "The Xcode Interface" on page 13):

1. Open the File menu, and choose New→Target.

2. In the window that appears, select Application under the iOS heading. Select Single-View Application, and then click Next (see Figure 7-6).

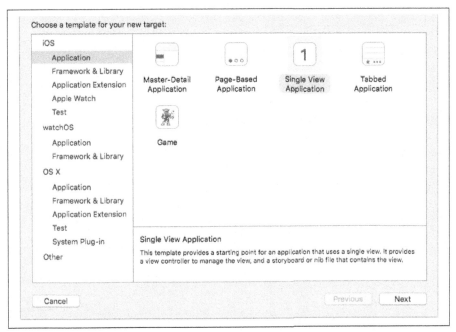

Figure 7-6. Creating the target

Xcode provides a number of different templates for iOS applications, but they're all fundamentally the same. The only difference between most of them is which view controllers are set up ahead of time. We're using a Single-View Application because we'll be building things out piece by piece, and we don't want a lot of boilerplate that we either have to contrive a use for or delete.

The other templates are as they sound: Master-Detail provides the basics of an app with a list down the left side and a detail view on the right side (like Mail); Page-Based provides the basics of an app with multiple views scrolling across the screen (like Weather); Tabbed provides the basics of a tab bar setup (like Music); and Game provides an empty game view, using Apple's SceneKit framework. As you become familiar with the basics of iOS development, you'll typically start most of your apps from the Single-View template, as we do here, because you'll want to define what's going on yourself, rather than rely on a template skeleton.

3. Name the application **Notes-iOS**. Set Devices to Universal, and ensure that Use Core Data is turned off (see Figure 7-7). Click Finish.

Choose options for your new target:

Product Name:	Notes-iOS
Organization Name:	Secret Lab
Organization Identifier:	au.com.secretlab
Bundle Identifier:	au.com.secretlab.Notes-iOS
Language:	Swift
Devices:	Universal
	☐ Use Core Data
	☑ Include Unit Tests
	☑ Include UI Tests
Project:	📄 Notes

Cancel   Previous   **Finish**

Figure 7-7. Finishing up the target

Core Data

Core Data is a database framework that comes bundled with iOS and macOS. Core Data is a huge, powerful, complex system that's designed for working with objects in a database. It's so huge, in fact, that describing it usually fills entire books.

Core Data is very well suited for when the data your app needs to work with is composed of multiple objects that all need to link together. For the app in this book, we just need to save chunks of raw text and attachments via file wrappers; however, if we were forced to not use file wrappers and had to store all of the components of the documents in a single file, Core Data might be a useful way of dealing with it.

If you want to learn more about Core Data, we highly recommend Marcus S. Zarra's *Core Data: Data Storage and Management for iOS, macOS, and iCloud* (Pragmatic Programmers); additionally, Apple's documentation (*http://apple.co/21UuYGV*) is extremely good.

There will now be an additional scheme in the scheme selector for Notes-iOS, at the top left of the window. Select it, and choose any simulator device you wish, so that pressing ⌘R will launch the app (Figure 7-8).

Figure 7-8. Selecting the scheme

Finally, we'll add the icon. All icons are available in the resources for this book; if you don't already have them, grab them by following the instructions in "Resources Used in This Book" on page ix.

iOS icons come in multiple sizes, and each one is designed for a different purpose. This is because of the diversity of devices that run iOS; in addition to iPhone and iPad, there's also the fact that different devices have different screen densities. Devices with a Retina display (that is, the devices with high-resolution screens, such as all iPhones after the iPhone 4 and all iPads after the iPad 3) need higher-resolution icons; in addition, larger models of iPhones, such as the iPhone 6 Plus and iPhone 6S Plus, have even higher resolutions.

To give your app an icon on iOS, you need multiple copies of the same image. Again, we've provided these in the downloadable resources.

To add the icon, follow these steps:

1. Open the iOS app's *Assets.xcassets* file, and select the AppIcon entry. You'll see a collection of slots—one for each of the different possible icon sizes.

2. Drag and drop the files from the downloadable resources into the slots. Use the names of each file to work out which slot they belong in; for example, *Icon-60@2x.png* belongs in the "60pt" category's "@2x" slot.

 If you accidentally add an image to the wrong icon category, you can remove it by selecting the errant image slot and pressing Delete.

When you're done, the asset catalog should look like Figure 7-9. If you need a reminder on asset catalogs, refer to "Adding the Icon" on page 110, when we added the icon to the macOS app.

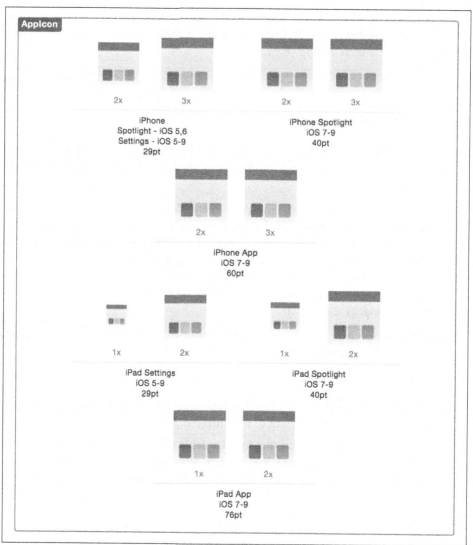

Figure 7-9. The asset catalog for the icons

Enabling the iOS App for iCloud

We'll now set up the project so that it has access to the same iCloud container as the macOS app. In particular, we need to enable the iCloud Documents feature, which will give the app access to the iCloud container.

You need to have a paid Apple developer account in order for your apps to access iCloud. If you don't have one, head to "The Apple Developer Program" on page 5 to learn how to set up your account.

1. Select the project at the top of the Project Navigator. The project properties will appear. Select the Notes-iOS target (Figure 7-10).

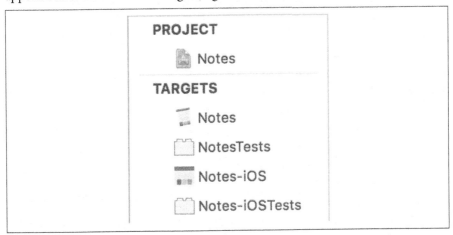

Figure 7-10. Selecting the target

2. Go to the Capabilities tab and find the iCloud section. Turn the switch on, and Xcode will add support for iCloud to the Notes-iOS target. It'll take a moment, so wait for the spinner to go away.

3. Once iCloud has been enabled, you need to enable access to iCloud Documents so that you can access the iCloud container folder that stores the files, and you need to configure the application to access the same container as the Mac app. We don't need the iOS application to have its own, separate container.

   Change the Services setting to only iCloud Documents, and change the Containers setting to "Specify custom containers." Next, select the iCloud container that you set up for the Mac app, and no others. See Figure 7-11.

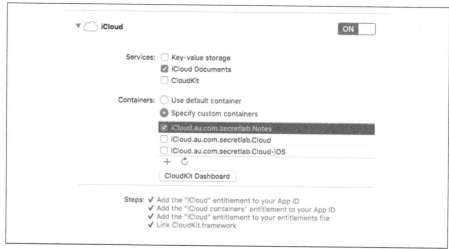

Figure 7-11. Enabling iCloud

Don't forget that iCloud can be used for more than just document storage. You can also store simple key/value data, as well as more complex database-oriented apps; for more info, see "iCloud" on page 177.

Next, we need to ensure that the app has access to iCloud. To do this, we'll ask the FileManager to tell us the location of the iCloud container on the disk; calling this will result in the creation of an iCloud container, if none previously existed.

Apple requires that you also have the ability to solely store files locally, if iCloud is not available or not turned on. We'll talk about this more in "iCloud Availability" on page 205.

1. Open *AppDelegate.swift*.

2. Add the following code to application(_,didFinishLaunchingWithOptions:):

```swift
// Ensure we've got access to iCloud
let backgroundQueue = OperationQueue()
backgroundQueue.addOperation() {
    // Pass 'nil' to this method to get the URL for the first
    // iCloud container listed in the app's entitlements
    let ubiquityContainerURL = FileManager.default
        .url(forUbiquityContainerIdentifier: nil)
```

```
    print("Ubiquity container URL: \(ubiquityContainerURL)")
}
```

Note that the call to url(forUbiquityContainerIdentifier:) is done in a background queue. This is because the first time you call this method, the system performs quite a bit of work to set up the container before the method returns. As a result, calling this on the main thread means that it will block anything else from happening, including responding to user input, so make sure to do it in the background.

 On iOS—indeed, on all modern operating systems—programs are divided into one or more *threads* of execution. Threads are executed simultaneously by the CPU, which means that running multiple threads means you can do multiple things at once. iOS and Mac apps always have at least one thread, called the *main* thread. All user interface work is done on the main thread, which means that if something takes a lot of time to finish—like preparing the iCloud container—then the app will appear to hang. We deal with this by creating a *background queue* and doing the work there.

Before you launch, you should sign in to iCloud on your iOS simulator.

 Testing iCloud in the Simulator

It's very strongly suggested that you create a new Apple ID and use that to do your testing; if you do, it's less of a problem if you accidentally erase all documents in the iCloud container. Apple's Documentation (*http://apple.co/21Uvdla*) provides guidance on this process.

3. To sign in to iCloud in the simulator, follow the same steps as you do on the device by using the Settings application, navigating to the iCloud section, and entering your username and password.

You can now test the application. To do this, you need to install it on a system that is signed in to iCloud. This can be either a simulator or a real device that's signed in to iCloud; it's up to you.

 Each device and simulator has its own settings, so to move between them you'll need to make sure they are signed in to iCloud with the account you are using.

4. Go back to Xcode and run the app; after a few seconds, it will log the location of the container!

 If you get a `nil` value instead of a URL, double-check the Settings app to make sure that you're signed in to iCloud. Additionally, check the project's Capabilities tab to make sure that the app is permitted to access iCloud.

Defining a Document Type

Now that the application has access to iCloud, we will set it up so it registers the Note document type with the system. Because iOS apps present their own methods for listing and opening documents, this isn't as critical to the whole document flow as it is in macOS, but it is necessary to support later features, such as Handoff. As a result, it's better to get it done sooner rather than later:

1. Go to the project properties, and select the Notes-iOS target.

2. Select the Info tab. Scroll down to the Document Type section, and click the triangle to open it.

3. Click the + button to create a new document type (Figure 7-12), and fill in the following fields:

    • Name: **Note**

    • Types: **au.com.secretlab.Note**

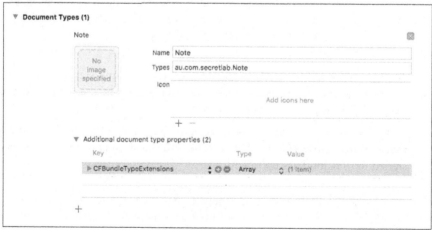

Figure 7-12. Adding a new document type

In place of `au.com.secretlab.Note` you will have to input your own identifier if you want it to work correctly with the macOS app you made earlier!

4. Add an entry to the "Additional document type properties" field by clicking the triangle inside the box, and then clicking in the field that's exposed. Name the entry `CFBundleTypeExtensions`, and set its type to `Array`.

5. Next, add an entry to this new array: a string, with the value `note`.

Now that the application has registered that it can open these documents, we need to expose a uniform type identifier (UTI) to the system that describes what the type actually is. Check back to "Defining a Document Type" on page 106, when we set up the document type for macOS, for more information on UTIs:

1. Open the Exported UTIs section, and click the + button to create a new type.

2. Fill in the fields as follows:

   - Description: **Note**
   - Identifier: **au.com.secretlab.Note**
   - Conforms to: **com.apple.package**

3. Add an entry to the "Additional exported UTI properties" field by clicking the triangle inside the box, and then clicking in the field that's exposed. Name it `UTType TagSpecification`, and set its type to `Dictionary`.

4. Add a single entry to this dictionary: **public.filename-extension**; set its type to **Array**.

5. Add a single element to this array: the string **note**.

Make sure that you type everything as written, with the same capitalization. If you used a different identifier back when you created the macOS application, use that here in place of `au.com.secret lab.Note`.

The app is now associated with this type (see Figure 7-13); when the app is installed, the iPhone will register the following things:

- A file format named Note exists.
- It has the file extension *.note*.

- It conforms to the `com.apple.package` format.

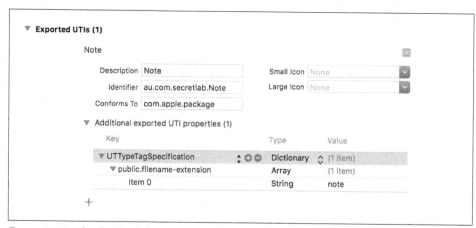

Figure 7-13. The finished document and exported UTI

Conclusion

In this chapter, we've laid the groundwork for our iOS counterpart to the macOS app. We've looked at the planned design of the app, consisting of wireframes and a planned feature set; created a new project for the iOS app to live in, adding it as a target alongside the macOS app; enabled iCloud document support; and set up the same document type we made for the macOS app in the iOS app.

In the next chapter, we'll build upon this foundation and start working on actually using the files in iCloud.

CHAPTER 8

Working with Files in iCloud

In this chapter, we'll discuss working with documents in iCloud on iOS. File management in iOS is handled by the apps themselves, rather than by a system-provided app like the Finder. As a result, we need to take care of tasks like providing a list of all available files to the user, opening the files, and saving changes.

This means that, when you work with documents in iOS, you need to do quite a bit more work. While you still have built-in automatic saving, you need to manually open and close documents; additionally, because bindings don't exist on iOS, you need to manually update the contents of the document object whenever the user provides input.

We'll start by listing whatever's already in iCloud, to demonstrate that we've got access to the same container as the Mac app and also to provide what will eventually become the user interface for opening these documents. Next, we'll implement the Document class, which is the iOS counterpart of the Mac app's Document class. Finally, we'll add support for creating new documents.

The App Sandbox

Apps on iOS are extremely limited in terms of the files that they're allowed to access. Any app that you install via the App Store—which means any third-party app—is *sandboxed*: the system will only permit it to read and write files in a single folder. This keeps any other app from reaching into the app's files and prevents your app from poking around the user's other files. The goal is to preserve user privacy: if apps can't get into files they shouldn't, it becomes a lot less likely for the user's data to be breached by a malicious app.

When installed, apps are placed inside a directory with a predefined structure that looks like Figure 8-1.

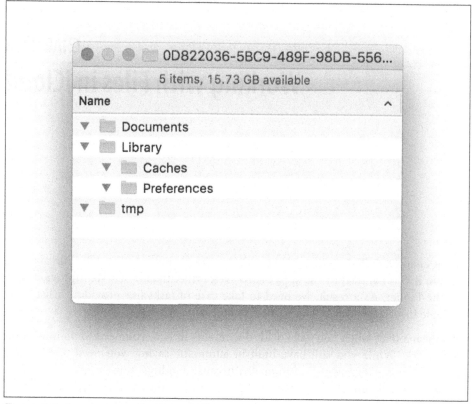

Figure 8-1. An empty application sandbox

The different folders that exist in the sandbox have special meaning to iOS:

- The *Documents* folder contains documents created by the user. Everything inside this folder is backed up to iCloud or to the user's computer if iCloud backups are disabled.

- The *Library* folder contains files that the app uses to operate. It has two subfolders:

  — The *Preferences* folder contains the user preferences, which are accessed via the UserDefaults class (more on this class later in this chapter!). These files are included in the backup.

  — The *Caches* folder stores data that the app stores locally to improve performance. This includes things like resources downloaded from the internet or files that can otherwise be regenerated if needed. These files are not included in the backup, and the system will delete the contents of the *Caches* folder when it begins to run low on storage space.

- The *tmp* folder is a temporary storage area that gives users a place to store files that they only need for a moment. This folder is not included in the backup; additionally, the system reserves the right to delete the contents of this folder at any time.

The sandbox also includes the iCloud container, which is a folder stored on disk. However, the specific location of the iCloud container is irrelevant to you as the developer, since you don't actually use the built-in filesystem management tools to work with it. Instead, as you'll see as we implement the application, you treat the whole thing as a separate layer of abstraction.

iCloud Availability

When you're writing an application, you can never assume that your app will always have access to iCloud. For example, consider the following scenarios:

- Your app is downloaded, but the user has no iCloud account.
- The user has an iCloud account, and is using your app to store documents in iCloud, but later signs out of the account.
- The user starts with no iCloud account, but later signs into iCloud.

Apps that use iCloud aren't allowed to *rely* on access to iCloud. If you're making an app, you're required to let users decline to store their files in iCloud; if they do, their files have to be stored locally.

This means that any code that works with files needs to work with both files saved locally and files saved inside iCloud. For this reason, we strongly recommend that you never store data *both* in iCloud and locally at the same time; for one reason, users should never care about the details of where the files they're looking at are stored (they should just be "on the phone"); and for another, you don't want to have to keep track of which file is local and which is remote.

There isn't a single solution to this problem, so we'll describe how the Notes application deals with it:

- When the application first launches (and *only* on the first launch), it asks if the user wants to use iCloud or use local files only. It saves the user's choice.
- Depending on whether the user chose to use iCloud or not, the app will store all documents in either iCloud or in local storage.
- The app will expose a setting to let users change their minds (which we'll cover in "Settings" on page 387).

- If the user previously chose to store files locally, and later opts to store them on iCloud instead, all files will be moved from local storage to iCloud.

With this in mind, let's get building!

Creating the Document List View Controller

The documents in the application's iCloud container need to be shown to the user so that they can be selected and opened. To do this, we'll need to create a user interface that can present this list.

There are three main options for presenting this sort of list in apps:

- A list, using `UITableView`, that looks similar to the list seen in the iOS Settings application (Figure 8-2)

Figure 8-2. The Settings list

- A grid, using `UICollectionView`, that looks similar to the iOS Photos application (Figure 8-3)
- Something entirely custom and handcoded

In this app, we'll use a `UICollectionView`. The main reason for this choice is that table views don't look good when they're very wide, which is what will happen on the iPad, whereas collection views can look good at any size.

Figure 8-3. The Photos grid

To get started, we'll first rename the view controller that the template starts with to something more descriptive. This is purely for our own convenience—the app will function the same way, but it's a lot clearer to refer to a "document list view controller" than to just a "view controller":

1. Find the *ViewController.swift* file in the Project navigator.

2. Rename *ViewController.swift* to *DocumentListViewController.swift* (Figure 8-4). Do this by clicking `ViewController.swift` and pressing Return.

3. Open this file, and rename the `ViewController` class to `DocumentListViewCon troller`. Make `DocumentListViewController` be a subclass of `UICollection ViewController`.

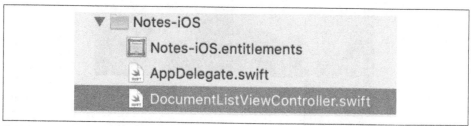

Figure 8-4. The newly renamed file

View Controllers and Storyboards

The code that runs the view controller is kept inside the *DocumentListViewController.swift* file. However, this is only half of the picture; in addition to the code, you also need to design the interface. To do this, you'll work with a storyboard.

A *storyboard* is a file that contains the interfaces for multiple view controllers, all linked together with *segues*. Storyboards allow you to work with your application's screens all in a single place, which gives you a much better idea of how the whole thing fits together. Storyboards are the preferred method of building apps for iOS, because the constraints placed upon the software by the device (such as the limited screen size) mean that what the user sees is limited to one screen at a time. Storyboards help you navigate the structure of your app.

When you created the project, a storyboard file was created for you. For most apps, you generally don't need to create a new storyboard beyond the first one.

The Navigation Controller

Now we'll start building the interface for the document list view controller:

1. Open *Main.storyboard*. You'll be looking at an empty view controller, which was created when the project was first created.

2. Select the existing view controller in the canvas and delete it. We'll replace it with our own in order to get a better picture of how these things come together.

3. Enter **navigation controller** in the Object library. The list will be reduced to just the navigation controller object, allowing you to quickly drag it out into the empty storyboard (see Figure 8-5).

Figure 8-5. Locating the navigation controller

4. Drag out a navigation controller into the storyboard. By default, it comes with a table view controller, which we don't need; we'll be using a collection view controller, so select the table view controller and delete it (Figure 8-6).

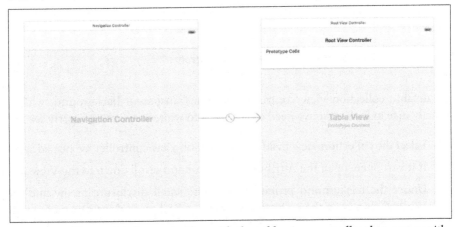

Figure 8-6. The navigation controller, with the table view controller that comes with it by default; you'll need to delete the table view controller

When the storyboard starts up, it needs to know what view controller to show first. This view controller, which Xcode calls the *initial view controller*, will be installed as the window's root view controller before the app is presented to the user.

Currently, there is no initial view controller, because we just deleted the earlier ones. This means that if you were to launch the app now, you'd simply get a black screen.

5. Select the navigation controller that you just added, and go to the Attributes Inspector. Select the Is Initial View Controller checkbox (Figure 8-7).

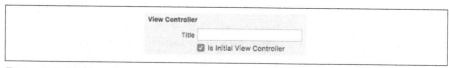

Figure 8-7. Making the navigation controller the initial view controller.

6. Go to the Object library, and search for a collection view controller. Drag it out into the storyboard (Figure 8-8).

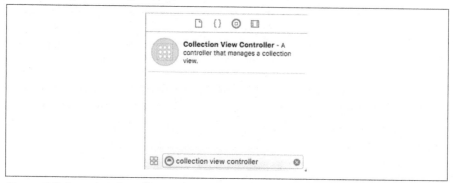

Figure 8-8. Locating the collection view controller

By default, collection view controllers have a transparent background, which isn't exactly nice to look at, so we need to change it to white so we can properly see it:

1. Select the collection view inside the collection view controller we just added.

2. If it isn't open, open the Attributes Inspector and scroll down to the View section.

3. Under the background property, press the small disclosure arrow and choose White Color. Now the collection view has a background we can more easily see (Figure 8-9).

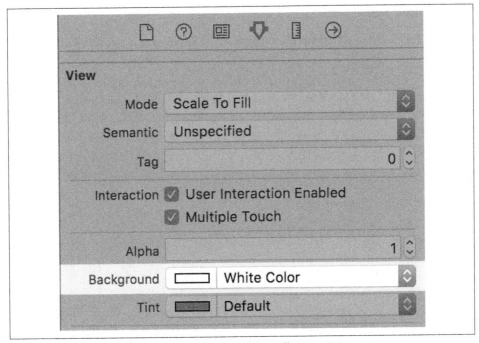

Figure 8-9. Changing the background color of the collection view

The entire purpose of a navigation controller is to present other view controllers. When it first appears, the navigation controller needs to have at least one view controller to present: the *root view controller*.

We'll now make the new collection view controller be the root view controller of the navigation controller:

1. Hold down the Control key, and drag from the navigation controller to the collection view controller. Select "root view controller" from the menu that appears.

Drag from the view controller, not the view. It's easiest to do this by zooming out first. You can also use the navigation controller and collection view controller representations in the outline if your prefer.

Now we need to link the new collection view controller up to our custom class we created.

2. Select the collection view controller and open the Identity Inspector.

3. Change the class to `DocumentListViewController`.

Collection Views

Collection views present a grid of *cells*; each cell contains views that present whatever information you want.

You don't create the individual cells in a collection view yourself; instead, you create a single *prototype* cell and prepare the views inside that. Typically, you also create a subclass of the base `UICollectionViewCell` class and set it as the custom class for the cell. Doing this allows you to create outlets in the custom class that link to the views you design in the interface builder.

To display its data, a collection view contacts an object, known as its *data source*, to ask questions about the information it should display. These questions include, "how many sections are there?", "how many items are there in each section?", and "what should I display for this specific item in this specific section?" This works exactly the same as the `NSCollectionView` we wrote in the macOS application, just with different method calls.

 When you use a collection view controller, the link between the collection view and the data source (which the view controller itself acts as) is automatically set up. If you're doing it yourself, you make your view controller—or any other object in the scene—conform to the `UICollectionViewDataSource` protocol (see "Protocols" on page 70).

Once you've designed the cell, you give it an *identifier*. This is used in the `collection View(_, cellForItemAt:)` method to prepare and return the correct type of cell for a given item in the collection view; we'll be creating this method later in the chapter.

Next, we'll set up the cell that will represent each note. To do that, we'll define the class that controls each cell, and then we'll set up the cell's interface:

1. Open *DocumentListViewController.swift*.

2. Add the `FileCollectionViewCell` class to the end of the file:

   ```swift
   class FileCollectionViewCell : UICollectionViewCell {
       @IBOutlet weak var fileNameLabel : UILabel?

       @IBOutlet weak var imageView : UIImageView?

       var renameHander : ((Void) -> Void)?

       @IBAction func renameTapped() {
           renameHander?()
       }
   ```

}

This code defines the class, a subclass of `UICollectionViewCell`, that specifies how each cell showing a note will behave. Right now it doesn't do much; it just has a `UIImageView` and some stubs to handle renaming in the future. But, now that the class exists, we can use it to set up the cell.

3. Open *Main.storyboard*, and select the collection view in the document list view controller (Figure 8-10).

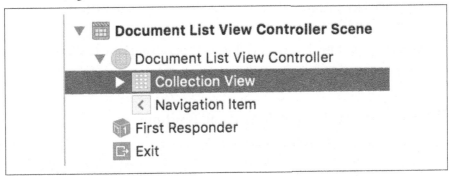

Figure 8-10. Locating the collection view in the outline

4. Open the Size Inspector, and set Cell Size to 180 × 180 (Figure 8-11). If you don't see any fields to change the cell size, change the cell size from Default to Custom in the drop-down box.

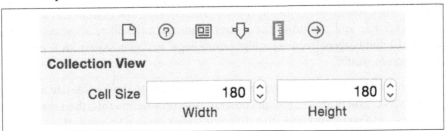

Figure 8-11. Setting the size of the cells

5. Select the cell. It looks like Figure 8-12.

Figure 8-12. The collection view cell

6. Open the Identity Inspector, and change its class from `UICollectionViewCell` to `FileCollectionViewCell`.

7. Open the Attributes Inspector and set the cell's Identifier to `FileCell`.

8. Drag in a `UILabel` and place it at the bottom of the view.

Using Constraints to Control Size and Position

When a view is added to the screen, it needs to know its size and position. Views on iOS are never shown in isolation—they're always displayed alongside other content, inside other views, and in cooperation with other stuff that the user cares about. This means that the position and size of any view depends upon where everything *else* on the screen is: content should never overlap other content, for example; and if you place a button in the bottom-right corner of a view, it should stay in that corner even when that view changes size.

This is where *constraints* come in. A constraint is a rule that defines some component of a view's size and position. These constraints are rules like, "view A's top edge is always 10 points away from view B's bottom edge" or, "view A's width is equal to half of the screen width."

The constraints of a view always need to be sufficient to define the size and position of that view. If there aren't enough constraints to fully define this, then the system will warn you, and you'll end up with a different layout to what you expect.

 If you add *no* constraints to a view, the system will automatically add the constraints that set its size and position, based upon where it was placed in the interface builder.

To add constraints, you select a view and click one of the buttons at the bottom right of the canvas (Figure 8-13).

Figure 8-13. The constraint buttons, at the bottom right of the canvas

The buttons in this collection are, from left to right:

Stack

This button allows you to quickly arrange a collection of views into a vertical or horizontal stack. We'll be working with stack views in Chapter 10.

Align

This button allows you to add constraints that align the selected view(s) to other views. For example, you can add constraints that say "the horizontal center of this view is the same as its containing view"; doing this will center the view along that line.

Pin

This button allows you to define the spacing between the selected view(s) to other views. For example, using this button, you can add constraints that say "the leading edge of this view is always 20 points away from the trailing edge of another view."

Resolve Auto Layout Issues

This button opens a menu that contains useful tools for resolving common problems with your constraints.

To place this label in the correct location, we need to add constraints to it that center it horizontally, keep it at the bottom of the container, and make it fill the width of the container while also ensuring that it has the correct height:

1. With the label selected, click the Align button, and turn on Horizontally in Center. Click Add Constraints.

2. Click the Pin button, and click the red bar icons at the left, right, and bottom. Additionally, set the Height to 20. Click Add Constraints.

By doing this, you've added the following constraints:

- Align center X to container
- Leading space to container margin = 0
- Trailing space to container margin = 0
- Bottom space to container margin = 0
- Height = 20

These constraints make the label take up the bottom section of the view.

3. Next, drag in a UIView. This will eventually be the preview image for the note documents.

4. Set its background color to something visible, like an orange color. (The precise color doesn't matter; this is just for your temporary use so that you can see the position and size of the view.)

5. Using the Align and Pin menus, add the following constraints:

- Leading space to container margin = 0
- Trailing space to container margin = 0
- Top space to container margin = 0
- Bottom space to the UILabel = 8

These constraints make the view take up the space above the label and ensure that there's a buffer between the view and the label.

6. Next, drag in a UIImageView, and place it inside the orange view.

7. Resize it to fill the entire view.

The cell should now look like Figure 8-14.

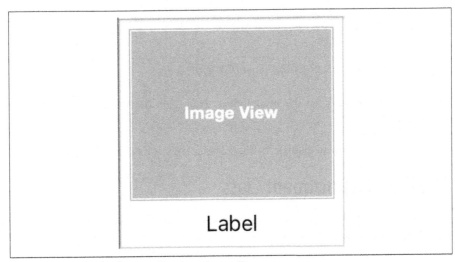

Figure 8-14. *The laid-out collection view cell*

8. Add the following constraints:

   - Leading space to superview = 0
   - Trailing space to superview = 0
   - Top space to superview = 0
   - Bottom space to superview = 0

 For this view, ensure that "Constrain to Margins" is off. This is because the view should be flush with the edges; we want the constraints to be relative to the edge, not to the margins. The view would be inset if the constraints were relative to the margins.

   These constraints make the image view fill its container.

   You can now connect the label and image view to the `FileCollectionView`
   `Cell`.

9. Open the Assistant, and ensure that it's got *DocumentListViewController.swift* open. If it doesn't, use the jump bar to navigate to Automatic→DocumentList-ViewController.swift.

10. Drag from the well—the small circle just to the left of the number 13 in Figure 8-15—at the left of the `fileNameLabel` property to the label in the cell. When you release the mouse button, the property will be connected to the label.

```
                                12 class FileCollectionViewCell : UICollectionViewCell {
  Label                         13      @IBOutlet weak var fileNameLabel : UILabel?
                    Label        14 }
```

Figure 8-15. Connecting from the outlet to the label

11. Repeat the process for the image view: drag from the `imageView` property to the image view.

Each document can now display its filename, as well as its preview image.

Creating the Document Class

We need a `Document` class for the iOS app. It's similar to the Mac app, but we subclass `UIDocument` instead of `NSDocument`, and implement different methods.

`NSDocument`, which we used earlier for the macOS app, behaves a bit differently than `UIDocument` on iOS. They provide the same fundamental features, but approach things a little differently.

One of the main differences is that `NSDocument` has some knowledge of the interface that the user will interact with, while `UIDocument` does not. The reason for this is that, on macOS, it's easy to take an interface and use bindings to connect it to the document's code, whereas we need to create a view controller on iOS to mediate the flow of information between the document and the interface.

There are a few minor API differences, as well. In `NSDocument`, you implement either `data(ofType:)` or `fileWrapper(ofType:)` to provide the ability to save the document; in `UIDocument`, you implement `contents(forType:)`, which can return either an `Data` object or an `FileWrapper` object.

1. Open the File menu and choose New→File.

2. Select "Cocoa Touch class" and click Next.

3. Set the name of the class to `Document` and set the "Subclass of" to `UIDocument` (see Figure 8-16). Click Next.

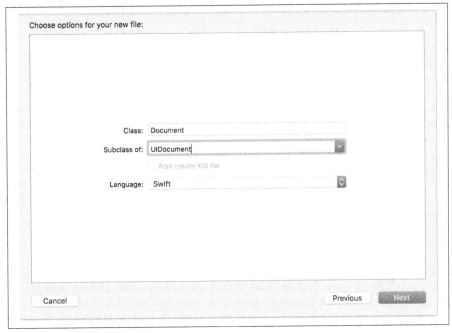

Figure 8-16. Adding the class

4. When saving the new class, make sure that it's added to the Notes-iOS target.

   Several important things need to be the same across the two different classes—for example, the names of the files in the file package. For this reason, we'll move the code that's common to both the Mac and iOS document classes into a separate file.

5. Right-click the project and select New Group. A new group will appear in the Project Navigator; name it **Common**.

6. Select this new group and go to the File Inspector.

7. Click the little folder icon to set its location (see Figure 8-17). An open dialog box will appear, showing the project.

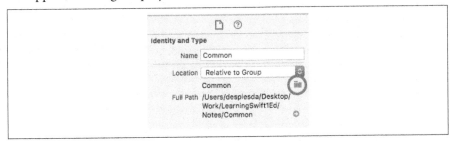

Figure 8-17. The location icon

8. In it, make a new folder called *Common* and then click Choose.

   You've just made a new folder in which to put files that are common to both projects.

A group in Xcode does not necessarily have to map to a folder on the filesystem. Here, we created a group and then assigned it to a folder location that happened to have the same name. Groups don't have to represent a real folder at all, and can simply exist within the project hierarchy. The metadata that says what files live in the group is maintained by Xcode when you drag a file into them.

9. Right-click the Common group and add a new Swift file.

Don't add a new Cocoa Touch class; you're adding a new, empty file. We're not using this file to make a Swift class; we're going to use it to store some variables that are common to both the iOS and macOS project, and we don't need a class to do that.

10. Name this new document *DocumentCommon.swift*.

11. With the *DocumentCommon.swift* file selected, open the File Inspector and add it to both the Notes and Notes-iOS targets by checking the boxes for each target in the Target Membership pane (see Figure 8-18).

A target in Xcode specifies a thing (called a *product*) to build and tells Xcode how to build it and what files to use. Because we want *DocumentCommon.swift* to be part of both the macOS and the iOS products, we add it to both targets.

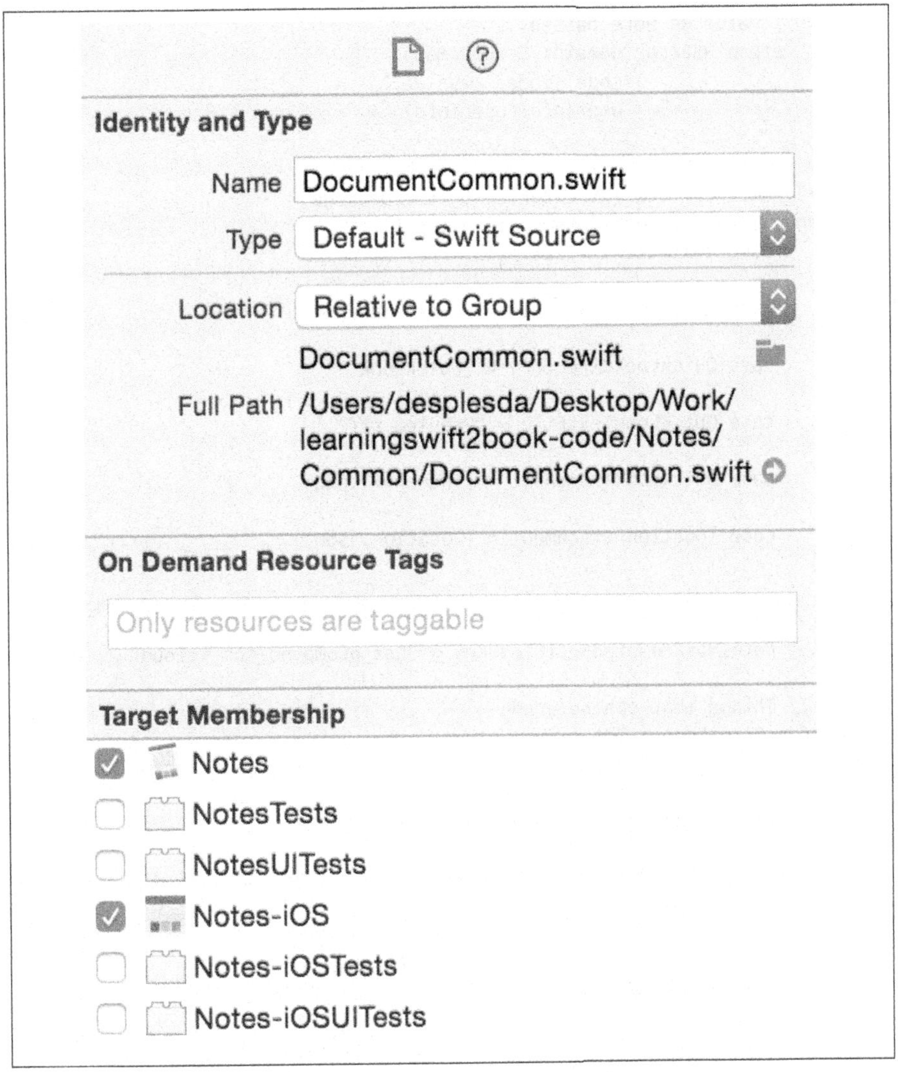

Identity and Type

Name: DocumentCommon.swift

Type: Default - Swift Source

Location: Relative to Group

DocumentCommon.swift

Full Path: /Users/desplesda/Desktop/Work/
learningswift2book-code/Notes/
Common/DocumentCommon.swift

On Demand Resource Tags

Only resources are taggable

Target Membership

☑ Notes
☐ NotesTests
☐ NotesUITests
☑ Notes-iOS
☐ Notes-iOSTests
☐ Notes-iOSUITests

Figure 8-18. Adding the file to the targets

12. Open the *DocumentCommon.swift* file, and add the following code to it:

```
// We can be throwing a lot of errors in this class, and they'll all
// be in the same error domain and using error codes from the same
// enum, so here's a little convenience func to save typing and space

let ErrorDomain = "NotesErrorDomain"

func err(_ code: ErrorCode,
        _ userInfo:[AnyHashable: Any]? = nil) -> NSError {
    // Generate an NSError object, using ErrorDomain, and using whatever
```

```
        // value we were passed.
        return NSError(domain: ErrorDomain,
                       code: code.rawValue,
                       userInfo: userInfo)
    }

    // Names of files/directories in the package
    enum NoteDocumentFileNames : String {
        case TextFile = "Text.rtf"

        case AttachmentsDirectory = "Attachments"

        case QuickLookDirectory = "QuickLook"

        case QuickLookTextFile = "Preview.rtf"

        case QuickLookThumbnail = "Thumbnail.png"

        case locationAttachment = "location.json"
    }

    let NotesUseiCloudKey = "use_icloud"
    let NotesHasPromptedForiCloudKey = "has_prompted_for_icloud"

    /// Things that can go wrong
    enum ErrorCode : Int {

        /// We couldn't find the document at all.
        case cannotAccessDocument

        /// We couldn't access any file wrappers inside this document.
        case cannotLoadFileWrappers

        /// We couldn't load the Text.rtf file.
        case cannotLoadText

        /// We couldn't access the Attachments folder.
        case cannotAccessAttachments

        /// We couldn't save the Text.rtf file.
        case cannotSaveText

        /// We couldn't save an attachment.
        case cannotSaveAttachment
    }
```

All this code contains is a convenience function for errors, an enumeration containing all the possible files inside the package of our Note document type, and the error codes we created earlier. Check back to "Package File Formats" on page 116, when we were setting up the macOS app, for a reminder.

Because we are building this application in stages, we have just rewritten a whole bunch of code that already existed inside *Document.swift*. We therefore need to delete the duplicated code. Open *Document.swift* and delete the ErrorDomain constant, err method, and NotesDocumentFileNames and ErrorCode enums.

 If you don't delete the duplicate code, you will get build errors.

If you've done everything correctly, the Mac app should still build with no errors. Double-check that now by changing the scheme to the Notes app and pressing ⌘-B. If it doesn't, double-check that the *DocumentCommon.swift* file's Target Membership settings include the Mac app.

You're now ready to set up the iOS document class:

1. Open the iOS app's *Document.swift* file.

2. Add the following code to the Document class:

```
var text = NSAttributedString(string: "") {
    didSet {
        self.updateChangeCount(UIDocumentChangeKind.done)
    }
}

var locationWrapper : FileWrapper?

var documentFileWrapper = FileWrapper(directoryWithFileWrappers: [:])

override func contents(forType typeName: String) throws -> Any {

    let textRTFData = try self.text.data(
        from: NSRange(0..<self.text.length),
        documentAttributes:
            [NSDocumentTypeDocumentAttribute: NSRTFTextDocumentType])

    if let oldTextFileWrapper = self.documentFileWrapper
        .fileWrappers?[NoteDocumentFileNames.TextFile.rawValue] {
        self.documentFileWrapper.removeFileWrapper(oldTextFileWrapper)
    }

    // checking if there is already a location saved
    let rawLocationVal = NoteDocumentFileNames.locationAttachment.rawValue
```

```
        if self.documentFileWrapper.fileWrappers?[rawLocationVal] == nil {
            // saving the location if there is one
            if let location = self.locationWrapper {
                self.documentFileWrapper.addFileWrapper(location)
            }
        }

        self.documentFileWrapper.addRegularFile(withContents: textRTFData,
            preferredFilename: NoteDocumentFileNames.TextFile.rawValue)

        return self.documentFileWrapper
    }

    override func load(fromContents contents: Any,
        ofType typeName: String?) throws {

        // Ensure that we've been given a file wrapper
        guard let fileWrapper = contents as? FileWrapper else {
            throw err(.cannotLoadFileWrappers)
        }

        // Ensure that this file wrapper contains the text file,
        // and that we can read it
        guard let textFileWrapper = fileWrapper
            .fileWrappers?[NoteDocumentFileNames.TextFile.rawValue],
            let textFileData = textFileWrapper.regularFileContents else {
            throw err(.cannotLoadText)
        }

        // Read in the RTF
        self.text = try NSAttributedString(data: textFileData,
            options: [NSDocumentTypeDocumentAttribute: NSRTFTextDocumentType],
            documentAttributes: nil)

        // Keep a reference to the file wrapper
        self.documentFileWrapper = fileWrapper

        // opening the location filewrapper
        let rawLocationVal = NoteDocumentFileNames.locationAttachment.rawValue
        self.locationWrapper = fileWrapper.fileWrappers?[rawLocationVal]

    }
```

This block of code:

- adds the NSAttributedString property text, which defaults to the empty attributed string.

- adds the FileWrapper property documentFileWrapper, which defaults to an empty directory file wrapper.

- implements `load(fromContents:)` to load the text.

- implements `contents(forType:)` to store the text. Importantly, in the `contents(forType:)` method, the app first checks to see if there's already an existing text file. If one exists, it's removed so that the new text file can replace it.

With this done, we've now implemented the text-related features of the Document system.

Listing Documents

We can now start listing documents in our `UICollectionView`. To show the user a list of available files, we need to have a way of finding out what files exist. As we discussed in "iCloud Availability" on page 205, there are two possible places where files can be found: in the iCloud container or locally on the device.

 Strictly speaking, files stored in iCloud are also stored locally on the device, but it's useful to think of them as existing outside the device. Doing this helps you to remember that the files may not yet have been downloaded and are therefore not ready to use.

To find files in iCloud, we use a class called `NSMetadataQuery` to compose a search query to return all files with a *.note* extension inside the iCloud container. Finding files stored locally simply involves asking the operating system to give us a list of files.

Regardless of how we find the list of files that are available, we need to keep track of this list so that it can be used to populate the list of documents that the user can see. To handle this, we'll create an array of `URL` objects:

1. Open *DocumentListViewController.swift*.

2. Add the `availableFiles` property:

    ```
    var availableFiles : [URL] = []
    ```

    This variable will store the `URL` for every file in the container that the app currently knows about. We'll now add code that will watch for changes to the list, so that if a new file is added—such as by another device—then the app will find out about it.

3. Add the `iCloudAvailable` property to the `DocumentListViewController` class:

    ```
    class var iCloudAvailable : Bool {

        if UserDefaults.standard
            .bool(forKey: NotesUseiCloudKey) == false {
    ```

```
        return false
    }

    return FileManager.default.ubiquityIdentityToken != nil
}
```

 This is a *class property*: one that's part of the class, and not attached to any specific instance of that class. You access this property by saying `DocumentListViewController.iCloudAvailable`; you don't need to have an instance of the class to access it.

This computed property returns `true` if the user is signed in to iCloud and has indicated that he or she wants to use iCloud; otherwise, it returns `false`. If you need a reminder on computed properties in Swift, flip back to "Properties" on page 66.

4. Add the `metadataQuery`, `queryDidFinishGatheringObserver`, and `queryDidUpdateObserver` properties:

```swift
var queryDidFinishGatheringObserver : AnyObject?
var queryDidUpdateObserver: AnyObject?

var metadataQuery : NSMetadataQuery = {
    let metadataQuery = NSMetadataQuery()

    metadataQuery.searchScopes =
            [NSMetadataQueryUbiquitousDocumentsScope]

    metadataQuery.predicate = NSPredicate(format: "%K LIKE '*.note'",
        NSMetadataItemFSNameKey)
    metadataQuery.sortDescriptors = [
        NSSortDescriptor(key: NSMetadataItemFSContentChangeDateKey,
            ascending: false)
    ]

    return metadataQuery
}()
```

This composes a `NSMetaDataQuery` query to look for files with our Notes file extension by making its `predicate` search for filenames ending in *.note*. You can customize and refine this search query by providing a different query; you can find more information on how to compose these queries in the Predicate Programming Guide (*http://apple.co/1q6hwUY*).

Note the parentheses at the end of the preceding code snippet and the equals sign before the opening brace near the top. This format means that, when the `DocumentListViewController` is created, the `metadataQuery` object will be created and prepared before any other code executes. This means that the rest of the code doesn't need to check to see if `metadataQuery` is ready to use or not—we're guaranteeing that it always will be ready.

5. Add the following code, which implements the `localDocumentsDirectoryURL` property. That property gives us the folder in which to store our local documents and implements the `ubiquitousDocumentsDirectoryURL` property, which in turn gives us the location of where to put documents in order for them to be stored in iCloud:

```
class var localDocumentsDirectoryURL : URL {
    return FileManager.default.urls(
        for: .documentDirectory,
        in: .userDomainMask).first!
}

class var ubiquitousDocumentsDirectoryURL : URL? {
    return FileManager.default
        .url(forUbiquityContainerIdentifier: nil)?
        .appendingPathComponent("Documents")
}
```

The `urls(for:in:)` method allows you to request a *type* of directory that you'd like—for example, `.documentDirectory` lets you request a place to store user documents. The method returns an array of URLs that you can use; on iOS, this will always point to the app sandbox's *Documents* folder. Because we specifically want the URL, and not an array of URLs, we return the `first` entry in the array; because this is optional, we must first unwrap it with `!`. It's worth pointing out that this will crash the program if, for some reason, `urls(for:in:)` returns an empty array; however, this won't happen, because all iOS apps are given a *Documents* directory when they're installed.

These two variables are `class` variables to ensure that they don't depend on the state of any specific instance of the `Docu mentListViewController` class. This isn't strictly necessary, but it helps to keep things tidier.

6. Make `viewDidLoad` set up the observers, which will be updated when the metadata query discovers new files:

```
override func viewDidLoad() {
    super.viewDidLoad()

    self.queryDidUpdateObserver = NotificationCenter.default
        .addObserver(forName: NSNotification.Name.NSMetadataQueryDidUpdate,
            object: metadataQuery,
            queue: OperationQueue.main) { (notification) in
                self.queryUpdated()
    }
    self.queryDidFinishGatheringObserver = NotificationCenter.default
    .addObserver(
        forName: NSNotification.Name.NSMetadataQueryDidFinishGathering,
        object: metadataQuery,
        queue: OperationQueue.main) { (notification) in
            self.queryUpdated()
}

}
```

When the document list controller's view loads, we need to register with the system the fact that if either NSMetadataQueryDidFinishGatheringNotification or NSMetadataQueryDidUpdateNotification is posted, we want to run some code in response. The NSMetadataQueryDidFinishGatheringNotification is sent when the metadata query finishes its initial search for content, and the NSMetadataQueryDidUpdateNotification is sent when any new files are discovered after this initial search. In both of these cases, we'll call a method called queryUpdated, which we'll add shortly.

7. Implement the refreshLocalFilesList method:

```
func refreshLocalFileList() {

    do {
        var localFiles = try FileManager.default
            .contentsOfDirectory(
                at: DocumentListViewController.localDocumentsDirectoryURL,
                includingPropertiesForKeys: [URLResourceKey.nameKey],
                options: [
                    .skipsPackageDescendants,
                    .skipsSubdirectoryDescendants
                ]
            )

        localFiles = localFiles.filter({ (url) in
            return url.pathExtension == "note"
        })

        if (DocumentListViewController.iCloudAvailable) {
            // Move these files into iCloud
```

```
                for file in localFiles {
                    if let ubiquitousDestinationURL =
                        DocumentListViewController
                            .ubiquitousDocumentsDirectoryURL?
                            .appendingPathComponent(file.lastPathComponent) {
                            do {
                                try FileManager.default
                                    .setUbiquitous(true,
                                                   itemAt: file,
                                                   destinationURL:
                                                   ubiquitousDestinationURL)
                            } catch let error as NSError {
                                NSLog("Failed to move file \(file) " +
                                    "to iCloud: \(error)")
                            }
                        }

                    }
                } else {
                    // Add these files to the list of files we know about
                    availableFiles.append(contentsOf: localFiles)
                }

            } catch let error as NSError {
                NSLog("Failed to list local documents: \(error)")
            }

        }
```

This looks for files stored locally. If it finds local files, and if iCloud is available, those files will be moved into iCloud for the NSMetadataQuery to find; if iCloud is not available, their URLs will be added to the availableFiles array so that the collection view displays them.

You'll notice that we use the FileManager class to access the list of files and also to move documents into iCloud. The FileManager class is your gateway to the filesystem. Just about anything you can do with files or folders can be done with FileManager, including creating, moving, copying, renaming, and deleting files.

Next, we need to make the viewDidLoad method ask users if they want to use iCloud; if they've been asked already, then it should either start searching iCloud or list the collection of local files.

8. Add the following code to the end of the viewDidLoad method:

```
override func viewDidLoad() {
    super.viewDidLoad()

    self.queryDidUpdateObserver = NotificationCenter.default
        .addObserver(forName: NSNotification.Name.NSMetadataQueryDidUpdate,
```

```
                    object: metadataQuery,
                    queue: OperationQueue.main) { (notification) in
                        self.queryUpdated()
        }
        self.queryDidFinishGatheringObserver = NotificationCenter.default
    .addObserver(
            forName: NSNotification.Name.NSMetadataQueryDidFinishGathering,
            object: metadataQuery,
            queue: OperationQueue.main) { (notification) in
                self.queryUpdated()
    }

>       let hasPromptedForiCloud = UserDefaults.standard
>           .bool(forKey: NotesHasPromptedForiCloudKey)
>
>       if hasPromptedForiCloud == false {
>           let alert = UIAlertController(title: "Use iCloud?",
>               message: "Do you want to store your documents in iCloud, " +
>               "or store them locally?",
>               preferredStyle: UIAlertControllerStyle.alert)
>
>           alert.addAction(UIAlertAction(title: "iCloud",
>               style: .default,
>               handler: { (action) in
>
>               UserDefaults.standard
>                   .set(true, forKey: NotesUseiCloudKey)
>
>               self.metadataQuery.start()
>           }))
>
>           alert.addAction(UIAlertAction(title: "Local Only", style: .default,
>               handler: { (action) in
>
>               UserDefaults.standard
>                   .set(false, forKey: NotesUseiCloudKey)
>
>               self.refreshLocalFileList()
>           }))
>
>           self.present(alert, animated: true, completion: nil)
>
>           UserDefaults.standard
>               .set(true, forKey: NotesHasPromptedForiCloudKey)
>
>       } else {
>           metadataQuery.start()
>           refreshLocalFileList()
>       }
```

}

This code displays an alert that, on the first launch of the application, asks users if they'd like to use iCloud. It first checks to see if the user has already seen the iCloud prompt. If not, then an alert is constructed from a `UIAlertController` object. There are two possible actions that the user can take: choose to use iCloud, or choose to save documents locally only. If the user chooses to save it in iCloud, then the iCloud-searching metadata query is started; if the user chooses to save locally, then the `refreshLocalFileList` method that you just wrote is called. In either case, the user's preference is recorded in the user preferences system. The alert is then presented, and the method records the fact that the user has seen this prompt.

If the user *has* previously seen the prompt, then the query is started *and* the file list is refreshed. This is done on purpose:

- If the user is not using iCloud, then the metadata query will find no files. This is fine, because checking for local files will happen immediately afterward.

- If the user *is* using iCloud, then the metadata query will begin searching for files; at the same time, by searching for local files, it will move any files that were stored locally into iCloud. This is useful for when the user previously elected to not use iCloud, but then changed his or her mind. We don't want any files to be stranded in local storage; we want to ensure that we sweep up any local files and store them in iCloud.

9. Implement the `queryUpdated` method, which is called if the `NSMetadataQuery` finds any files in iCloud. This method updates the list of known files in iCloud:

```
func queryUpdated() {
    self.collectionView?.reloadData()

    // Ensure that the metadata query's results can be accessed
    guard let items = self.metadataQuery.results as? [NSMetadataItem] else
{
    return
}

    // Ensure that iCloud is available—if it's unavailable,
    // we shouldn't bother looking for files.
    guard DocumentListViewController.iCloudAvailable else {
        return;
    }

    // Clear the list of files we know about.
    availableFiles = []
```

```
// Discover any local files, which don't need to be downloaded.
refreshLocalFileList()

for item in items {

    // Ensure that we can get the file URL for this item
    guard let url =
        item.value(forAttribute: NSMetadataItemURLKey) as? URL else {
        // We need to have the URL to access it, so move on
        // to the next file by breaking out of this loop
        continue
    }

    // Add it to the list of available files
    availableFiles.append(url)

}

}
```

We'll now add the two critical methods that provide data to the UICollection
View:

- collectionView(_, numberOfItemsInSection:), which is given a section
number (starting at zero) and returns the number of items in that section.

- collectionView(_, cellForItemAt: indexPath), which is given an Index
Path object, which contains a section number and an item number. It's
expected to return a UICollectionViewCell that's been prepared with the data
that should appear for this point in the grid.

There's also a third important method: numberOfSections(in:), which returns the
number of sections in the table view. However, if you don't implement it, the collection view assumes that there is one section. We only have one section in this collection view, so we'll save some typing and not include it:

1. Implement the numberOfItemsInSection and cellForItemAt:indexPath methods:

```
override func collectionView(_ collectionView: UICollectionView,
    numberOfItemsInSection section: Int) -> Int {

    // There are as many cells as there are items in iCloud
    return self.availableFiles.count
}

override func collectionView(_ collectionView: UICollectionView,
    cellForItemAt indexPath: IndexPath) -> UICollectionViewCell {
```

```
    // Get our cell
    let cell = collectionView
        .dequeueReusableCell(withReuseIdentifier: "FileCell",
            for: indexPath) as! FileCollectionViewCell

    // Get this object from the list of known files
    let url = availableFiles[indexPath.row]

    // Get the display name
    var fileName : AnyObject?
    do {
        try (url as NSURL).getResourceValue(&fileName,
                            forKey: URLResourceKey.nameKey)

        if let fileName = fileName as? String {
            cell.fileNameLabel!.text = fileName
        }
    } catch {
        cell.fileNameLabel!.text = "Loading..."
    }

    return cell


}
```

The `numberOfItemsInSections` is responsible for letting the collection view know how many items need to be displayed. There are always as many items in the collection view as there are URL objects in the list, so we just ask the `availa bleFiles` variable for its `count`.

The `cellForItemAt:indexPath` method is more complex. It's responsible for providing to the collection view each of its cells and making sure that each cell has the correct content.

You might notice that we don't actually create our own cells—that is, we never call the initializer for `FileCollectionViewCell`. Instead, we call the `dequeueReu sableCell(withReuseIdentifier: for:)` method on the collection view.

We do this for performance reasons. If you had a large number of items to display in the collection view, it's extremely inefficient to create all of the possible cells; and creating a cell on demand is bad as well, because memory allocation can be CPU-intensive.

Instead, the collection view system maintains a *reuse queue* system. When a cell is scrolled off-screen, it's not removed from memory; instead, it's simply taken off the screen and placed in the queue. When a new cell needs to appear, you call `dequeueReusableCell(withReuseIdentifier: for:)` to retrieve a cell from the queue. If the queue is empty, a new cell is allocated and created.

This approach to reusing a small number of UI elements is quite common in Cocoa and Cocoa Touch, where only a small number of elements ever exist and are simply reconfigured and reused as needed.

This, by the way, is why you gave the cell an identifier in the interface builder. The *reuse identifier* you pass in to the call to `dequeueReusableCell(withReuseI dentifier: for:)` is what the collection view uses to determine which queue of `UICollectionViewCells` to get a cell from.

2. Run the app! If there are documents in the container from before (when you were making the macOS app), they will appear—it might take a moment.

Creating Documents

Currently, the app can show documents that have been added to the iCloud container, but it can't create its own. Let's make that happen!

At this point, the icons shown in the document list will still be a flat color. Additionally, the code that actually makes the documents download from iCloud hasn't yet been added yet, so you'll just see the word "Loading..." under each of the icons. Don't panic—we'll be adding both of these in time.

In iOS, documents must be manually created by your code. You do this by creating a new instance of your `UIDocument` class, and then telling it to save; this will create the document on the disk.

This is the same method that is used to update an existing document on disk.

Now we can start creating new documents.

The way that saving works is this: we first create the document and save it to the local *Documents* directory. Once it's written, we can then move it into iCloud, where it will be synced to all devices.

Inside *DocumentListViewController.swift*, implement the `createDocument` function, which creates and saves the document:

```swift
func createDocument() {

    // Create a unique name for this new document by adding the date
    let formatter = DocumentListViewController.documentNameDateFormatter
    let documentDate = formatter.string(from: Date())
    let documentName = "Document \(documentDate).note"

    // Work out where we're going to store it, temporarily
    let documentDestinationURL = DocumentListViewController
        .localDocumentsDirectoryURL
        .appendingPathComponent(documentName)

    // Create the document and try to save it locally
    let newDocument = Document(fileURL:documentDestinationURL)
    newDocument.save(to: documentDestinationURL,
        for: .forCreating) { (success) -> Void in

        if (DocumentListViewController.iCloudAvailable) {

            // If we have the ability to use iCloud...
            // If we successfully created it, attempt to move it to iCloud
            if success == true, let ubiquitousDestinationURL =
                DocumentListViewController.ubiquitousDocumentsDirectoryURL?
                    .appendingPathComponent(documentName) {

                // Perform the move to iCloud in the background
                OperationQueue().addOperation { () -> Void in
                    do {
                        try FileManager.default
                            .setUbiquitous(true,
                                itemAt: documentDestinationURL,
                                destinationURL: ubiquitousDestinationURL)

                        OperationQueue.main
                            .addOperation { () -> Void in

                                self.availableFiles
                                    .append(ubiquitousDestinationURL)

                                self.collectionView?.reloadData()
                        }
                    } catch let error as NSError {
                        NSLog("Error storing document in iCloud! " +
                            "\(error.localizedDescription)")
                    }
                }
            }
        } else {
            // We can't save it to iCloud, so it stays in local storage.

            self.availableFiles.append(documentDestinationURL)
            self.collectionView?.reloadData()
```

```
            }
        }
    }
```

This code first creates the file locally, and then does different things depending on whether the user has access to iCloud or not:

- If the user has access to iCloud, it works out where it should exist in iCloud, and then moves it to that location. It does this in a background queue because it can take a moment to finish moving to the iCloud container.

- If the user has no access to iCloud, it manually adds the document to the list of files and reloads the list. It does this because, unlike when iCloud is available, there's no object watching the directory and keeping the file list up to date. Once that's done, the document is opened.

Now that we have the ability to create documents, we need a way to let the user initiate the process. We'll do this by adding a little button to the top of the screen, by adding a `UIBarButtonItem` to the view controller's `UINavigationItem`.

Every view controller that exists inside a `UINavigationController` has a `UINavigationItem`. This is an object that contains the content for the navigation bar for that view controller: its title and any buttons that should go in the bar. When the view controller is on screen, the navigation controller will use our `DocumentListView Controller`'s navigation item to populate the navigation bar (see Figure 8-19).

Figure 8-19. The Add button, which will be added to the top of the screen

 There's only ever one navigation bar in the entire navigation controller. When you switch from one view controller to another, the navigation controller notices this fact and updates the contents of the bar, animating it into place.

To create the button, we'll use a UIBarButtonItem. This is a button designed to go inside either a navigation bar or a toolbar. You can create one in the storyboard, but it's useful to know how to create one programmatically as well.

We'll use a UIBarButtonItem to show our Add button, which will look like a little + icon. When the button is tapped, the createDocument method that you just added will be run:

1. Add the following code to the viewDidLoad method:

```
let addButton = UIBarButtonItem(barButtonSystemItem: .add,
    target: self,
    action: #selector(DocumentListViewController.createDocument))
self.navigationItem.rightBarButtonItem = addButton
```

Notice the target and action parameters that are passed to the UIBarButton Item's initializer. When the user taps the button, iOS will call the action method on the target object. This means that tapping the Add button will call the crea teDocument method that you added earlier.

2. Run the app, click the + button, and add new files!

Downloading from iCloud

We've already got the app listing files, whether the user has chosen to get them locally or use iCloud. If the files are all stored locally, then we have no problem: the files are in place, and we can open them. However, if they're stored in iCloud, we hit a snag: the files that are in iCloud and are being reported by the NSMetadataQuery are not yet downloaded to the local device, which means we can't use them.

On macOS, this isn't a problem, because the system will automatically download every single file that's in the iCloud container. iOS doesn't do this, because there's significantly less storage space available on the smaller device, and the user may be on a cellular network.

If we want to be able to open the user's files, we need to download them. Additionally, we need to be able to tell whether a file is downloaded or not. Finally, we need to be able to convey to users that a file is not yet ready to be opened so that they don't get confused when they try to open a file that the system hasn't downloaded yet.

In this application, we're automatically downloading all files that we know about. This isn't the best approach for all apps, especially if the files can be quite large; in those situations, you should wait for the user to explicitly request for a file to be downloaded.

First, we need to show files that aren't yet downloaded:

1. Still inside *DocumentListViewController.swift*, implement `itemIsOpenable`, which tells us if we have downloaded the latest version of the file:

```
// Returns true if the document can be opened right now
func itemIsOpenable(_ url:URL?) -> Bool {

    // Return false if item is nil
    guard let itemURL = url else {
        return false
    }

    // Return true if we don't have access to iCloud (which means
    // that it's not possible for it to be in conflict - we'll always have
    // the latest copy)
    if DocumentListViewController.iCloudAvailable == false {
        return true
    }

    // Ask the system for the download status
    var resource : URLResourceValues
    do {
        resource = try itemURL.resourceValues(forKeys:
                                [.ubiquitousItemDownloadingStatusKey])
    } catch let error as NSError {
        NSLog("Failed to get downloading status for \(itemURL): \(error)")
        // If we can't get that, we can't open it
        return false
    }

    // Return true if this file is the most current version
    if resource.ubiquitousItemDownloadingStatus ==
                        URLUbiquitousItemDownloadingStatus.current {
        return true
    } else {
        return false
    }
}
```

The `itemIsOpenable` method returns `true` when the file is fit to be opened, and `false` otherwise. If the app doesn't have any access to iCloud, then the file must be openable; however, if the app *does* have access to iCloud, we have to do some additional checks.

First, we ask the URL to let us know what the *downloading status* is for the file. We do this by using the `resourceValues forKey:` method, which returns a collection of resources inside the URL determined by the keys parameter passed in, giving us control over what resources we want. In this case we only want a single value, .ubiquitousItemDownloadingStatusKey, which tells us the current download state of an iCloud resource, as the keys parameter is a set we can pass in more keys if we wanted more information; but in this case just the one is enough.

A file can be in one of several download states:

- URLUbiquitousItemDownloadingStatus.notDownloaded means we don't have it
- URLUbiquitousItemDownloadingStatus.downloaded means it's downloaded, but it's out of date
- URLUbiquitousItemDownloadingStatus.current means it's downloaded and up-to-date

We can only open files that are downloaded and up to date; otherwise, we have to tell the user that it's not openable.

2. Add checks in cellForItemAt indexPath to make unavailable documents transparent:

```
override func collectionView(_ collectionView: UICollectionView,
    cellForItemAt indexPath: IndexPath) -> UICollectionViewCell {

    // Get our cell
    let cell = collectionView
        .dequeueReusableCell(withReuseIdentifier: "FileCell",
            for: indexPath) as! FileCollectionViewCell

    // Get this object from the list of known files
    let url = availableFiles[indexPath.row]

    // Get the display name
    var fileName : AnyObject?
    do {
        try (url as NSURL).getResourceValue(&fileName,
                                forKey: URLResourceKey.nameKey)

        if let fileName = fileName as? String {
            cell.fileNameLabel!.text = fileName
        }
    } catch {
        cell.fileNameLabel!.text = "Loading..."
    }

    // If this cell is openable, make it fully visible, and
    // make the cell able to be touched
    if itemIsOpenable(url) {
        cell.alpha = 1.0
        cell.isUserInteractionEnabled = true
```

```
>      } else {
>          // But if it's not, make it semitransparent, and
>          // make the cell not respond to input
>          cell.alpha = 0.5
>          cell.isUserInteractionEnabled = false
>      }

       return cell

   }
```

To let the user know whether a document can be opened or not, we'll set the alpha property of the cell to 0.5 if the cell is not openable. The alpha property controls how transparent the view is: 1.0 means it's fully opaque, and 0.0 means it's entirely see-through.

3. Next, update queryUpdated to begin downloading any files that aren't already downloaded:

```
func queryUpdated() {
    self.collectionView?.reloadData()

    // Ensure that the metadata query's results can be accessed
    guard let items = self.metadataQuery.results as? [NSMetadataItem] else
{
    return
}

    // Ensure that iCloud is available - if it's unavailable,
    // we shouldn't bother looking for files.
    guard DocumentListViewController.iCloudAvailable else {
        return;
    }

    // Clear the list of files we know about.
    availableFiles = []

    // Discover any local files, which don't need to be downloaded.
    refreshLocalFileList()

    for item in items {

        // Ensure that we can get the file URL for this item
        guard let url =
            item.value(forAttribute: NSMetadataItemURLKey) as? URL else {
            // We need to have the URL to access it, so move on
            // to the next file by breaking out of this loop
            continue
        }
```

```
        // Add it to the list of available files
        availableFiles.append(url)

>       // Check to see if we already have the latest version downloaded
>       if itemIsOpenable(url) == true {
>           // We only need to download if it isn't already openable
>           continue
>       }
>
>       // Ask the system to try to download it
>       do {
>           try FileManager.default
>               .startDownloadingUbiquitousItem(at: url)
>
>       } catch let error as NSError {
>           // Problem! :(
>           print("Error downloading item! \(error)")
>
>       }

    }

}
```

When this code has been added, when you launch the iOS app, documents that have already been added to the iCloud container from other locations—such as from the macOS app—will start downloading. You'll see the "Loading…" text under the icons start gradually disappearing and being replaced with the actual filenames.

As you can see, there's not a huge amount of work that needs to be done for the app to ensure that files are available. All we have to do is first check to see if it's not already available; if it's not, then we ask the `FileManager` to start downloading the file. The `NSMetadataQuery` will update us later when the file finishes downloading.

4. Run the app. Any files that are not yet downloaded to the device will start downloading; until they're downloaded, they'll be semitransparent in the documents list.

Deleting Documents

Now we'll add some of the groundwork support for editing. We need to do two things to hook this up: first, we'll add an icon into the project that can be used for the Delete button, and then we'll add a button that will use that icon:

1. Open the *Assets.xcassets* asset catalog.

2. Drag the Delete icon, available in the *Design* folder in the downloaded resources (see "Resources Used in This Book" on page ix), into the list of assets. Unlike in the past where we've been dragging images into predetermined slots, we can just drag the image into anywhere in the asset pane.

3. Open *Main.storyboard* and select the `FileCollectionViewCell`.

4. Search for `UIButton` in the Object library and drag a new button into the cell.

5. Go to the Attributes Inspector, and change the button's Type from System to Custom.

6. Delete the button's title and set its image to Delete.

7. Position it at the top-right corner of the cell.

8. Open the Editor menu, and choose Resolve Auto Layout Issues→Reset to Suggested Constraints. The result is shown in Figure 8-20.

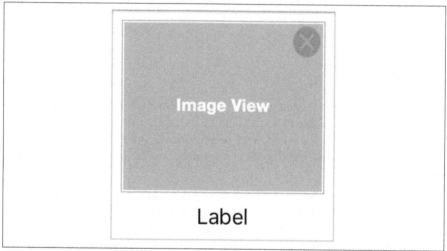

Figure 8-20. The delete button

9. Open *DocumentListViewController.swift* in the Assistant.

10. Hold down the Control key, and drag from the delete button into `FileCollectionViewCell`. Create a new outlet for the button called `deleteButton`.

11. Hold down the Control key again, and drag from the delete button into `FileCollectionViewCell`. Create a new action for the button called `deleteTapped`.

12. Add the following property to `FileCollectionViewCell`:

    ```
    var deletionHander : ((Void) -> Void)?
    ```

    This will be a closure that is run when the user taps the delete button.

13. Add the following code to the `deleteTapped` method:

```
@IBAction func deleteTapped() {
    deletionHander?()
}
```

This method calls the deletion closure; the actual content of the closure will be set up in collectionView(cellForItemAt:).

We want to draw the user's attention to the deletion buttons when they appear. To do this, we'll make the cells fade out, using iOS's animation system, when the deletion buttons are visible.

Animating a property of a UIView is as simple as telling the UIView class that you'd like to animate and indicating how long the animation should take. You also provide a closure, which the UIView class will run when it's ready to start animating content. Inside this closure, you make the changes you want: changing size, opacity, color, and mode.

Add the following method to FileCollectionViewCell:

```
func setEditing(_ editing: Bool, animated:Bool) {
    let alpha : CGFloat = editing ? 1.0 : 0.0
    if animated {
        UIView.animate(withDuration: 0.25, animations: { () -> Void in
            self.deleteButton?.alpha = alpha
        })
    } else {
        self.deleteButton?.alpha = alpha
    }
}
```

The setEditing method simply changes the opacity of the cell's deleteButton. When setEditing is called, it receives two parameters: first, whether the button should be visible or not, and second, whether the change in opacity should be animated.

The change in opacity should be animated if the cell is on screen. It doesn't look great for a view to suddenly *pop* from fully opaque to slightly transparent, so it should gradually fade, via an animation. However, if the view is off-screen, it *shouldn't* fade.

If the change in opacity needs to be animated, the second parameter of this method is set to true. This wraps the change to the deleteButton's alpha property inside a call to UIView's animate(withDuration: animations:); otherwise, it's simply assigned.

We'll now add a button that puts the collection of documents into Edit mode. There's actually an incredibly simple way to add an Edit button, and you can do it with a single line of code.

Add the following code to the bottom of the viewDidLoad method:

```
self.navigation.leftBarButtonItem = self.editButtonItem
```

The editButtonItem method returns a UIBarButtonItem that, when tapped, calls the setEditing method. We'll implement that now.

Inside *DocumentListViewController.swift*, implement the setEditing method to make all cells that are visible change their editing state:

```
override func setEditing(_ editing: Bool, animated: Bool) {

    super.setEditing(editing, animated: animated)

    for visibleCell in self.collectionView?.visibleCells
        as! [FileCollectionViewCell] {

        visibleCell.setEditing(editing, animated: animated)
    }
}
```

First, notice the call to super.setEditing. The superclass implementation of setEditing updates the class's editing property, which we'll make use of in a moment, and also updates the edit button that you added a moment ago to show either Edit or Done. Once it's done with that, it asks the collection view to provide an array of all visible FileCollectionViewCells. Each of these cells then has its setEditing method called.

Finally, we need to ensure that any cells that *aren't* visible also have their deletion button's opacity at the correct level. Remember, collection view cells that aren't visible don't actually exist; they're waiting in limbo to be added to the collection view on demand. This means that, in our cellForItemAtIndexPath method, we'll need to ensure that the deletion button's opacity is set correctly.

 This is why the FileCollectionViewCell's setEditing method allows you to control whether the change is animated or not. Cells that are being prepared in cellForItemAtIndexPath should not animate the change, because it would look a little odd for them to be fading in as you scroll. In addition, we'll give all cells a closure to call when the deletion button is tapped.

Add the following code to collectionView(_, cellForRowAt: indexPath) to add the deletion handler for cells. When the cell's delete button is tapped, we'll call the deleteDocumentAtURL method, which we'll add in a moment:

```
override func collectionView(_ collectionView: UICollectionView,
    cellForItemAt indexPath: IndexPath) -> UICollectionViewCell {

    // Get our cell
    let cell = collectionView
        .dequeueReusableCell(withReuseIdentifier: "FileCell",
            for: indexPath) as! FileCollectionViewCell
```

```
    // Get this object from the list of known files
    let url = availableFiles[indexPath.row]

    // Get the display name
    var fileName : AnyObject?
    do {
        try (url as NSURL).getResourceValue(&fileName,
                              forKey: URLResourceKey.nameKey)

        if let fileName = fileName as? String {
            cell.fileNameLabel!.text = fileName
        }
    } catch {
        cell.fileNameLabel!.text = "Loading..."
    }
>   cell.setEditing(self.isEditing, animated: false)
>   cell.deletionHander = {
>       self.deleteDocumentAtURL(url)
>   }

    // If this cell is openable, make it fully visible, and
    // make the cell able to be touched
    if itemIsOpenable(url) {
        cell.alpha = 1.0
        cell.isUserInteractionEnabled = true
    } else {
        // But if it's not, make it semitransparent, and
        // make the cell not respond to input
        cell.alpha = 0.5
        cell.isUserInteractionEnabled = false
    }

    return cell

}
```

Finally, add the `deleteDocumentAtURL` method, which actually deletes it:

```
func deleteDocumentAtURL(_ url: URL) {

    let fileCoordinator = NSFileCoordinator(filePresenter: nil)
    fileCoordinator.coordinate(writingItemAt: url,
        options: .forDeleting, error: nil) { (urlForModifying) -> Void in
        do {
            try FileManager.default
                .removeItem(at: urlForModifying)

            // Remove the URL from the list

            self.availableFiles = self.availableFiles.filter {
                $0 != url
```

```
            }

            // Update the collection
            self.collectionView?.reloadData()

    } catch let error as NSError {
        let alert = UIAlertController(title: "Error deleting",
            message: error.localizedDescription,
            preferredStyle: UIAlertControllerStyle.alert)

        alert.addAction(UIAlertAction(title: "Done",
            style: .default, handler: nil))

        self.present(alert,
                                        animated: true,
                                        completion: nil)
        }
    }
}
```

The deleteDocumentAtURL method, as its name suggests, removes a document from the system. However, you might notice that the line that actually does the deleting—that is, the call to FileManager's removeItem(at:url) method—is wrapped in a *lot* of other stuff. All of that is necessary, because the app is being extremely cautious about deleting the file at a safe time to do it. It does this through the use of an NSFileCoordinator.

The NSFileCoordinator class allows you to ensure that file-related tasks, such as opening, saving, deleting, and renaming files, are done in a way that won't interfere with any other task on the system trying to work with the same file. For example, if you happen to attempt to open a file at the same time it's deleted, you don't want both actions to happen at the same time.

The coordinate(writingItemAt:url) method lets you tell the system ahead of time what you intend to do with the file. In this case, we're passing the .ForDeleting flag, indicating that we'd like to remove the file entirely. We also pass in a closure, which is run after the system has ensured that it's safe to make changes. You'll notice that the closure itself receives a parameter, called urlForModifying. This is an URL that the file coordinator provides to you to make changes to. This may or may not be the same as the original URL that you passed in; it's possible that, in some cases, the file coordinator might provide you with a temporary URL for you to use instead.

Inside the closure, we remove the file by calling removeItem(at:url), passing in the URL that the file coordinator has given us. We also remove the original URL—*not* the one that the file coordinator has given us—from the list of available files. We do this by using the filter method on the array, which filters the array to only include items that are *not* url. We use the original URL because if `urlForModifying` is different from the original url variable, we may not actually remove the entry from the list.

Lastly, we update the list of files by calling the collection view's `reloadData` method.

Run the app, and tap the Edit button. The delete buttons will appear, and you can tap them to delete them.

Renaming Documents

Finally, we'll add the ability to rename documents when you tap their labels. The code for this will work in a similar way to deleting them: we'll give each cell a closure to run when the user taps the label; and in this closure, we'll present a box that lets the user enter a new name.

To detect taps on the label, we need to create a *gesture recognizer* and connect it. We'll be using a very simple "tap" gesture recognizer in this chapter, but we'll be using a more complex one later, in "Deleting Attachments" on page 310:

1. Open *Main.storyboard*, and locate the label in the collection view cell.

2. Select the label, and go to the Attributes Inspector. Scroll down to the View section in the inspector, and select the User Interaction Enabled checkbox. This will allow the label to respond to taps.

Let's now add the ability to detect when the user has tapped the label:

1. Add the following code to the `collectionView(_, cellForItemAt: indexPath)` method, after the deletion code:

```
override func collectionView(_ collectionView: UICollectionView,
    cellForItemAt indexPath: IndexPath) -> UICollectionViewCell {

    // Get our cell
    let cell = collectionView
        .dequeueReusableCell(withReuseIdentifier: "FileCell",
            for: indexPath) as! FileCollectionViewCell

    // Get this object from the list of known files
    let url = availableFiles[indexPath.row]

    // Get the display name
    var fileName : AnyObject?
    do {
        try (url as NSURL).getResourceValue(&fileName,
                                forKey: URLResourceKey.nameKey)

        if let fileName = fileName as? String {
            cell.fileNameLabel!.text = fileName
```

```
            }
        } catch {
            cell.fileNameLabel!.text = "Loading..."
        }

        cell.setEditing(self.isEditing, animated: false)
        cell.deletionHander = {
            self.deleteDocumentAtURL(url)
        }

>       let labelTapRecognizer = UITapGestureRecognizer(target:cell,
>               action: #selector(FileCollectionViewCell.renameTapped))))
>
>       cell.fileNameLabel?.gestureRecognizers = [labelTapRecognizer]
>
>       cell.renameHander = {
>           self.renameDocumentAtURL(url)
>       }

        // If this cell is openable, make it fully visible, and
        // make the cell able to be touched
        if itemIsOpenable(url) {
            cell.alpha = 1.0
            cell.isUserInteractionEnabled = true
        } else {
            // But if it's not, make it semitransparent, and
            // make the cell not respond to input
            cell.alpha = 0.5
            cell.isUserInteractionEnabled = false
        }

        return cell

    }
```

This code does several things:

- First, it removes any existing gesture recognizers from the label. This is necessary because cells get reused; if we don't remove existing recognizers, we'll end
up with labels that attempt to rename multiple files at once when they're
tapped.

- Next, it creates a new `UITapGestureRecognizer` and makes it call the cell's
`renameTapped` method. It then adds it to the label. Once this is done, tapping
the label will make the cell call the rename handler block, which is added next.
The rename block simply calls the `renameDocumentAtURL` method, which you'll
add in a second.

2. Add the following method to `DocumentListViewController`:

```swift
func renameDocumentAtURL(_ url: URL) {

    // Create an alert box
    let renameBox = UIAlertController(title: "Rename Document",
                                message: nil, preferredStyle: .alert)

    // Add a text field to it that contains its current name, sans ".note"
    renameBox.addTextField(configurationHandler: { (textField) -> Void in
        let filename = url.lastPathComponent
            .replacingOccurrences(of: ".note", with: "")
        textField.text = filename
    })

    // Add the cancel button, which does nothing
    renameBox.addAction(UIAlertAction(title: "Cancel",
        style: .cancel, handler: nil))

    // Add the rename button, which actually does the renaming
    renameBox.addAction(UIAlertAction(title: "Rename",
        style: .default) { (action) in

        // Attempt to construct a destination URL from
        // the name the user provided
        if let newName = renameBox.textFields?.first?.text
            {
                let destinationURL = url.deletingLastPathComponent()
                    .appendingPathComponent(newName + ".note")

                let fileCoordinator =
                    NSFileCoordinator(filePresenter: nil)

                // Indicate that we intend to do writing
                fileCoordinator.coordinate(writingItemAt: url,
                    options: [],
                    writingItemAt: destinationURL,
                    options: [],
                    error: nil,
                    byAccessor: { (origin, destination) -> Void in

                        do {
                            // Perform the actual move
                            try FileManager.default
                                .moveItem(at: origin,
                                    to: destination)

                            // Remove the original URL from the file
                            // list by filtering it out
                            self.availableFiles =
                                self.availableFiles.filter{$0 != url}
```

```
                            // Add the new URL to the file list
                            self.availableFiles.append(destination)

                            // Refresh our collection of files
                            self.collectionView?.reloadData()
                        } catch let error as NSError {
                            NSLog("Failed to move \(origin) to " +
                                "\(destination): \(error)")
                        }

                })

            }
        })

        // Finally, present the box.

        self.present(renameBox, animated: true, completion: nil)
    }
```

This method does several things:

- First, it creates a UIAlertController, which will be the interface through which the user actually renames the file.

- It adds a text field to it, using the addTextField method. This method takes a closure, which is called to fill the text field with content; in this case, it will contain the file's current name.

- It then adds two buttons: a cancel button, which does nothing except close the box, and a rename button.

The rename button, when tapped, gets the text that was entered and constructs a new URL for the document, representing where it will be moved to.

 In Unix-based operating systems, such as iOS, "renaming" a file really means moving it to a new location. If you move a file called *apples.txt* to a new location called *oranges.txt*, you've renamed that file.

Once it has the new URL, it creates an NSFileCoordinator and asks it to coordinate a writing operation that involves both the file's original location and the file's new location.

When the file coordinator is ready to perform the write, the FileManager is then used to move the file from its original location to the new location. The file's original URL is removed from the availableFiles list, and the new location is then added.

Finally, the collection view is asked to refresh its contents, and the user can view the result of the rename.

3. Now run the app and rename some files!

Conclusion

We have done a lot in this chapter, and we've added a whole lot of code! We've done the following:

- Implemented the iOS Document version of the document class, using UIDocument, as a counterpart to the macOS version of our document class, which uses NSDocu ment

- Added support for listing whatever note documents are stored in iCloud

- Added support for creating new documents and deleting or renaming existing documents

So we've covered lot of the ins and outs of working with iCloud on iOS for documents. In the next chapter, we'll add a new view to display the text content of notes and allow people to actually edit their notes, as well as save them.

CHAPTER 9

Working with Documents on iOS

In this chapter, we'll start making the iOS app feel more like an actual app: we'll add the ability to open notes and view their contents, as well as the ability to edit and save changes to notes.

Along the way, we'll create and connect up more new view controllers, create another new UI, and set up a segue to move between the list of notes and the note contents. We'll also use `UITextViewDelegate` to update the note document when the note text changes.

Adding a View to Display Notes

At the moment, the app has got the basics of note storage, but we don't have any ability to actually view or edit our notes on iOS. To add this, we'll create a view controller that lets you see and modify the content of note documents:

1. Open the File menu and choose New→File.

2. Ensure "Also create XIB file" is unchecked; we'll be using the storyboard we already have set up.

3. Select Cocoa Touch Class and click Next.

4. Name the new class `DocumentViewController`, and make it a subclass of `UIView Controller`. This will be responsible for the displaying the note, and eventually letting us edit the contents of notes.

5. Open *Main.storyboard*.

6. Go to the Object library and drag a new view controller into the canvas.

7. Select the new view controller, open the Identity Inspector, and set its class to DocumentViewController (see Figure 9-1). This connects the view controller in the storyboard to the view controller class that we just created.

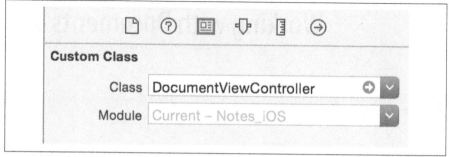

Figure 9-1. Setting the new view controller's class to DocumentViewController

8. Hold down the Control key and drag from the document list view controller to the new document view controller. A list of potential types of segues you can create will appear; click Show (see Figure 9-2).

 A segue is a transition between one view (and view controller) to another. Segues are used only with storyboards, not nibs. Segues are triggered, typically, by user interaction, and end when the new view controller is displayed. You construct the segue in the interface builder, and then it's either triggered automatically or manually through code using the performSe gue(withIdentifier:sender:) method. We'll be using this later in the chapter.

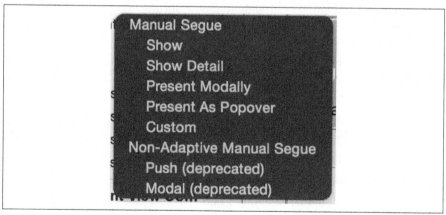

Figure 9-2. Creating the segue

9. Select the "Show segue to 'Document View Controller'" item in the outline, and go to the Attributes Inspector.

10. Set the Identifier of the segue to **ShowDocument** (Figure 9-3).

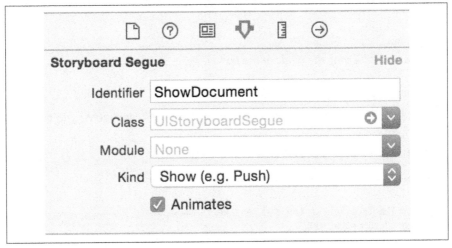

Figure 9-3. Configuring the segue

Next, we'll set up the user interface for the document view controller:

1. Add a UITextView to the document view controller. We'll use this to display the text contents of a note document.

2. Resize it to fill the entire screen, and add the following constraints to it:

   - Leading spacing to container's leading margin = 0
   - Trailing spacing to container's trailing margin = 0
   - Bottom spacing to bottom layout guide = 0
   - Top spacing to top layout guide = 0

   This will make the text view that we just added fill the majority of the screen.

3. Go to the Attributes Inspector, and change its mode from Plain to Attributed (Figure 9-4). We'll be displaying attributed text—text that has formatting attributes—so we need to make sure that the text view we're using knows how to display that.

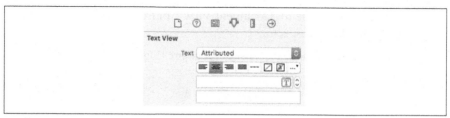

Figure 9-4. Setting the mode of the text view

4. Open *DocumentViewController.swift*.

5. Add the following code to implement the `textView`, document, and `documentURL` properties:

```
@IBOutlet weak var textView : UITextView!

fileprivate var document : Document?

// The location of the document we're showing
var documentURL:URL? {
    // When it's set, create a new document object for us to open
    didSet {
        if let url = documentURL {
            self.document = Document(fileURL:url)
        }
    }
}
```

The `textView` property will be used to connect this code to the text view that shows the document's text, while the `document` property holds the `Document` object that's currently open. The `documentURL` property stores the location of the document that the view controller is currently displaying; importantly, when it's set, it creates and prepares the `document` property with a `Document` object to use.

6. Open *Main.storyboard* and open *DocumentViewController.swift* in the Assistant. Connect the text view to the `textView` outlet.

For a quick reminder on how to connect views to outlets, see "Connecting the Code" on page 23.

7. Implement `viewWillAppear` to open the document and load information from it:

```
override func viewWillAppear(_ animated: Bool) {
    // Ensure that we actually have a document
    guard let document = self.document else {
        NSLog("No document to display!")
```

```
            _ = self.navigationController?.popViewController(animated: true)
        return
    }

    // If this document is not already open, open it
    if document.documentState.contains(UIDocumentState.closed) {
        document.open { (success) -> Void in
            if success == true {
                self.textView?.attributedText = document.text

            }
            else
            {
                // We can't open it! Show an alert!
                let alertTitle = "Error"
                let alertMessage = "Failed to open document"
                let alert = UIAlertController(title: alertTitle,
                    message: alertMessage,
                    preferredStyle: UIAlertControllerStyle.alert)

                // Add a button that returns to the previous screen
                alert.addAction(UIAlertAction(title: "Close",
                    style: .default, handler: { (action) -> Void in
                    _ = self.navigationController?
                        .popViewController(animated: true)
                }))

                // Show the alert
                self.present(alert,
                    animated: true,
                    completion: nil)
            }

            // checking if there isn't already a location file
            if self.document?.locationWrapper == nil {
                // determining our location permission status
                let status = CLLocationManager.authorizationStatus()

                if status != .denied && status != .restricted {
                    self.locationManager = CLLocationManager()
                    self.locationManager?.delegate = self

                    if status == .notDetermined {
                        self.locationManager?
.requestWhenInUseAuthorization()
                    else {
                        self.locationManager?.desiredAccuracy
                            = kCLLocationAccuracyBest
                        self.locationManager?.startUpdatingLocation()
                    }
```

```
                }
            }
            self.updateBarItems()
        }
    }

}
```

The code for opening documents is verbose but pretty straightforward. We first check to ensure that the view controller actually has a `Document` to open; if it doesn't, it tells the navigation controller to return to the document list.

Next, it asks if the document is currently closed. If it is, we can open it by calling `open(completionHandler:)`. This attempts to open the document and takes a closure that gets informed whether it was successfully opened or not. If opening succeeds, the `Document`'s properties now contain the data that we need, like its `text`; as a result, we can grab the note's text and display it in the `textView`.

If opening the document fails, we need to tell the user about it. To handle this, we create and display a `UIAlertController`.

Next, we'll make tapping a file in the document list view controller open that document:

1. Open *DocumentListViewController.swift*.

2. Implement the `didSelectItemAt:` to trigger the segue to the document:

```
override func collectionView(_ collectionView: UICollectionView,
    didSelectItemAt indexPath: IndexPath) {

    // Did we select a cell that has an item that is openable?
    let selectedItem = availableFiles[indexPath.row]

    if itemIsOpenable(selectedItem) {
        self.performSegue(withIdentifier: "ShowDocument",
                          sender: selectedItem)
    }

}
```

The `didSelectItemAt:` method is called when the user taps any item in the collection view, and receives as parameters the collection view that contained the item, plus an `IndexPath` that represents the position of the item in question. `IndexPath` objects are really just containers for two numbers: the *section* and the *row*. Collection views can be broken up into multiple sections, and each section can contain multiple rows.

To access the correct document, we need to figure out the URL representing the item the user just selected. Because we only have a single section in this collection view, we can just use the `row` property to get the URL from the `availableFiles` list. If that URL is openable (which we test by using the `itemIsOpenable` method), we ask the system to perform the `ShowDocument` segue, passing in the URL.

 We can also access the `row` property in `IndexPath` using the `item` property. They both represent the same value.

When we ask the system to perform a segue, the view controller at the other end of the segue will be created and displayed. Before it's shown, however, we're given a chance to prepare it with the right information that it will need. In this case, the `Docu mentViewController` at the other end of the segue will need to receive the correct URL so that it can open the document:

1. Open *DocumentListViewController.swift*.

2. Implement `prepare(for: sender:)` to prepare the next view controller:

```
override func prepare(for segue: UIStoryboardSegue, sender: Any?) {

    // If the segue is "ShowDocument" and the destination view controller
    // is a DocumentViewController...
    if segue.identifier == "ShowDocument",
        let documentVC = segue.destination
            as? DocumentViewController
    {

        // If it's a URL we can open...
        if let url = sender as? URL {
            // Provide the url to the view controller
            documentVC.documentURL = url
        } else {
            // it's something else, oh no!
            fatalError("ShowDocument segue was called with an " +
                "invalid sender of type \(type(of: sender))")
        }

    }
}
```

The `prepare(for:sender:)` method is called whenever the view controller is about to show another view controller, via a segue. It receives as its parameters the segue itself, represented by a `UIStoryboardSegue` object, as well as whatever object was responsible for triggering the segue. In the case of the `ShowDocument` segue, the sender is an URL, because we passed that in as the sender parameter to the performSegue(withIdentifier) method in didSelectItemAt.

To get the view controller that we're about to transition to, we ask the segue for its destinationViewController property and ask Swift to try to give it to us as a DocumentViewController. Next, we double-check the type of the sender and make sure that it's an URL. Finally, we give the view controller the URL.

Now's a great time to build and run the app. You should now be able to tap document thumbnails and segue to the editing screen, and get a "back" button to return to the document list, which is provided automatically by the navigation controller. Edits can be made, though they can't be saved yet. But, still! There's some good progress happening here.

Finally, we also want to open documents that we've just created. We'll do this by creating a method called openDocumentWithPath, which will receive a String that contains a path. It will prepare an NSURL, and then call performSegueWithIdentifier, passing the URL as the sender.

We'll be using this method from multiple different places later in this book, so we're putting it in a method.

1. Implement the openDocumentWithPath method, which takes a path and attempts to open it:

```
func openDocumentWithPath(_ path : String) {

    // Build a file URL from this path
    let url = URL(fileURLWithPath: path)

    // Open this document
    self.performSegue(withIdentifier: "ShowDocument", sender: url)

}
```

Next, when a document is created, we'll want the app to immediately open it for editing.

2. Add the calls to openDocumentWithPath to the createDocument method:

```
func createDocument() {

    // Create a unique name for this new document by adding the date
    let formatter = DocumentListViewController.documentNameDateFormatter
let documentDate = formatter.string(from: Date())
```

```
    let documentName = "Document \(documentDate).note"

    // Work out where we're going to store it, temporarily
    let documentDestinationURL = DocumentListViewController
        .localDocumentsDirectoryURL
        .appendingPathComponent(documentName)

    // Create the document and try to save it locally
    let newDocument = Document(fileURL:documentDestinationURL)
    newDocument.save(to: documentDestinationURL,
        for: .forCreating) { (success) -> Void in

        if (DocumentListViewController.iCloudAvailable) {

            // If we have the ability to use iCloud...
            // If we successfully created it, attempt to move it to iCloud
            if success == true, let ubiquitousDestinationURL =
                DocumentListViewController.ubiquitousDocumentsDirectoryURL?
                    .appendingPathComponent(documentName) {

                // Perform the move to iCloud in the background
                OperationQueue().addOperation { () -> Void in
                    do {
                        try FileManager.default
                            .setUbiquitous(true,
                                itemAt: documentDestinationURL,
                                destinationURL: ubiquitousDestinationURL)

                        OperationQueue.main
                            .addOperation { () -> Void in

                            self.availableFiles
                                .append(ubiquitousDestinationURL)

                            // Open the document
                            self.openDocumentWithPath(
> ubiquitousDestinationURL.path)

                            self.collectionView?.reloadData()
                        }
                    } catch let error as NSError {
                        NSLog("Error storing document in iCloud! " +
                            "\(error.localizedDescription)")
                    }
                }
            }
        } else {
            // We can't save it to iCloud, so it stays in local storage

            self.availableFiles.append(documentDestinationURL)
```

```
                    self.collectionView?.reloadData()

>                   // Just open it locally
>                   self.openDocumentWithPath(documentDestinationURL.path)
            }
        }
    }
```

We're now able to open documents, but not much else. Next, we'll add the ability to actually edit the document.

Editing and Saving Documents

The last critical feature of this app is to let the user make changes to the document. When you're using the UIDocument system, your documents are automatically saved when the user leaves your application or when you close the document. You don't need to manually save changes—the system will automatically take care of it for you. To signal to iOS that the user is done with the document, we'll close the document when the user leaves the DocumentViewController.

This means that, if the document was modified, the system will call contentsForType and ask the Document class to provide a FileWrapper containing the document's contents, which will be saved to disk.

However, the system has to know that changes were applied in the first place, so, in order to tell the document that changes were made, we need to use the updateChange Count method when the user makes a change to the text field. To find out *that* bit of information, we need to ask the text view to let the view controller know when a change is made:

1. Open *DocumentViewController.swift*.

2. Make DocumentViewController conform to UITextViewDelegate by adding UITextViewDelegate to the class's definition:

   ```
   class DocumentViewController: UIViewController, UITextViewDelegate {
   ```

   When an object conforms to the UITextViewDelegate protocol, it's able to act as the *delegate* for a text view. This means that it can be notified about events that happen to the text view, such as the user making changes to the content of the text view.

3. Implement the textViewDidChange method to store text in the document, and update the document's change count:

   ```
   func textViewDidChange(_ textView: UITextView) {

       document?.text = textView.attributedText
   ```

```
    document?.updateChangeCount(.done)
}
```

 Even though it's called the change "count," you don't really work with a number of changes. Rather, the change count is internal to the document system; your app doesn't need to know what the change count is; you just need to update it when the user modifies the content of the document.

With this method in place, the view controller is able to respond to a text view changing its content. We use this opportunity to update the Document's text property, and then call updateChangeCount to signal to the document that the user has made a change to its content. This indicates to the UIDocument system that the document has changes that need to be written to disk; when the system decides that it's a good time or when the document is closed, the changes will be saved.

Now that the document's contents are updated, we need to tell the document system to close the document when we leave the view controller:

1. Implement viewWillDisappear to close the document:

   ```
   override func viewWillDisappear(_ animated: Bool) {

       self.document?.close(completionHandler: nil)
   }
   ```

2. Open *Main.storyboard.*

3. Hold down the Control key, and drag from the text view to the document view controller (Figure 9-5). Select "delegate" from the menu that appears.

 Remember to drag to the view controller itself, not the view that the view controller is managing. If you drag to the little yellow circle icon above the view controller's interface, you'll always be connecting to the right thing.

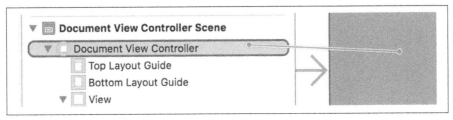

Figure 9-5. A drag in progress

4. Launch the app, open a document, make changes, close it, and reopen it—the changes are still there!

Conclusion

In this chapter, we've added the ability to open notes and view their contents, as well as the ability to actually edit and save the changes to notes. We did this by creating some new view controllers and their UI in storyboards and connecting them with segues.

In the next chapter, we'll add support for file attachments and update the interface to show a list of attachments.

CHAPTER 10

Working with Files and File Types

At the moment, the iOS app can work with the text content of note documents, but doesn't really know anything about attachments that might have been added through the macOS app.

In this chapter, we'll add support for working with attachments to the iOS app, as well as make its handling of note documents more robust. We'll do this by adding—you guessed it—more user interface to:

- Display any attachments
- Handle conflict resolution, for when a file is synced from multiple devices
- Add Quick Look support, to display a thumbnail preview of attachments

Setting Up the Interface for Attachments

First, we'll update the interface for the document view controller to support showing the list of attachments. This will involve reworking everything, as well as some reasonably complex constraints, so it's easier to start from scratch:

1. Open *Main.storyboard*.
2. Delete the text view from the document view controller's interface. We'll be reconstructing the interface, with room for the attachments to be displayed, so it's easier to remove everything than it is to rearrange.
3. It'll be easier to do this without the top bar in the way, so select the document view controller, and in the Simulated Metrics section of the Inspector, change Top Bar from Inferred to None (Figure 10-1).

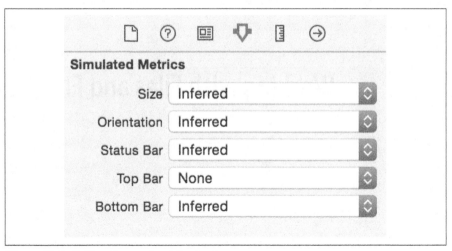

Figure 10-1. Setting the mode of the top bar

4. Drag a `UIScrollView` into the interface; this will enable us to display content larger than the view it's currently in (see Figure 10-2).

   We want the scroll view to fill the entire screen. By default, constraints are made relative to the margins, and to the layout guides at the top and the bottom. However, because the contents of the entire screen need to scroll, we want to take up *all* the space. This means that we need to add constraints differently.

5. Add constraints to the scroll view by selecting the scroll view and clicking the Pin button at the bottom right of the window. Turn off "Constrain to margins" and set all four of the numbers that appear to 0. Change Update Frames to Items of New Constraints, and click Add 4 Constraints. The scroll view will now fill the screen.

   We'll now add controls inside it. In particular, we'll be adding a stack view, which will contain the text editor and the collection view that will show the list of attachments. A stack view handles most of the work of laying out views in a horizontal or vertical *stack*. If all you care about is "these views should be next to each other," and you don't want to have to deal with more complex layouts, then stack views are exactly what you want.

> While `UIStackView` is a single class, it appears in the Object library twice: once for "vertical stack view," and once for "horizontal stack view."

Figure 10-2. The empty document view controller interface

6. Drag a vertical `UIStackView` into the scroll view.

7. With the stack view selected, click the Pin button, and set the top, leading, trailing, and bottom space to 0.

8. Next, resize the stack view so that it's the same width as the scroll view.

9. Hold down the Control key and drag from the stack view to the scroll view. A list of possible constraints will appear; choose Equal Widths.

It's important to make it the same width as the scroll view. This ensures that the scroll view doesn't collapse it to 0.

10. Inside the Attribute Inspector, ensure that the stack view's Alignment and Distribution are both set to Fill. This means that the stack view will make the size of its child views sufficient to fill up the stack view's boundaries.

11. Drag a UICollectionView into the stack view.

12. Hold down the Control key and drag from the collection view *to the collection view* itself. Choose Height from the menu that appears.

13. Select the collection view's cell and resize the cell size to 88 by 88.

14. Set the collection view's background color to 90% white (very slightly gray) in the Attributes Inspector.

    Next, we'll add (back) the text view, just like we did in the previous chapter.

15. Add a UITextView to the stack view.

    It needs no constraints, since the stack view will size and position it. Setting the height to 88 for the collection view, and adding no other constraints, will make the stack view do two things: position the collection view at the very top and make it fill the width of the screen, and make other views expand their height to fill the remaining space.

16. Connect the document view controller's textView outlet to this text view.

The textView property has the type UITextView, which means that the connection can only be made to a text view. The interface builder won't let you connect to any other type of view.

17. Make the text view use the document view controller as its delegate, by Control-dragging from the text view onto the document view controller in the outline.

18. Select the text view, and go to the Attributes Inspector. Set the text view to use attributed text and then turn Scrolling Enabled off—it's not necessary, because it's already contained inside a scroll view (see Figure 10-3).

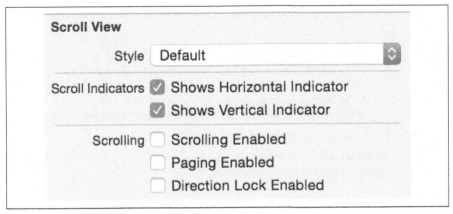

Figure 10-3. Disabling scrolling on the text view

19. Run the app; the text now appears underneath the collection view.

Listing Attachments

Now that the interface is set up, we'll add support for storing attachments in the iOS Document class:

1. Open *Document.swift*.

2. Add the following code to add the `attachmentsDirectoryWrapper` property, which returns the `FileWrapper` representing the folder where attachments are stored. If it doesn't exist, it creates it:

```
fileprivate var attachmentsDirectoryWrapper : FileWrapper? {

    // Ensure that we can actually work with this document
    guard let fileWrappers = self.documentFileWrapper.fileWrappers else {
        NSLog("Attempting to access document's contents, but none found!")
        return nil
    }

    // Try to get the attachments directory
    var attachmentsDirectoryWrapper =
        fileWrappers[NoteDocumentFileNames.AttachmentsDirectory.rawValue]

    // If it doesn't exist...
    if attachmentsDirectoryWrapper == nil {

        // Create it
        attachmentsDirectoryWrapper =
            FileWrapper(directoryWithFileWrappers: [:])
        attachmentsDirectoryWrapper?.preferredFilename =
```

```
NoteDocumentFileNames.AttachmentsDirectory.rawValue

    // And then add it
    self.documentFileWrapper
        .addFileWrapper(attachmentsDirectoryWrapper!)

    // We made a change to the file, so record that
    self.updateChangeCount(UIDocumentChangeKind.done)
}

    // Either way, return it
    return attachmentsDirectoryWrapper
}
```

The `attachmentsDirectoryWrapper` computed property first checks to make sure the `Document`'s file wrapper actually has a usable array of file wrappers to access. Generally, this is always true, but if it's not, we can't continue.

Next, we attempt to get the file wrapper for the *Attachments* directory. If that doesn't exist, then we first create it, and add it to the document's file wrapper. Either way, by the end of the method, we've got an *Attachments* directory to use, which we then return.

3. Add the `attachedFiles` property, which returns an array of `FileWrappers`, each of which represents an attached file:

```
dynamic var attachedFiles : [FileWrapper]? {

    // Get the contents of the attachments directory
    guard let attachmentsFileWrappers =
        attachmentsDirectoryWrapper?.fileWrappers else {
        NSLog("Can't access the attachments directory!")
        return nil
    }

    // attachmentsFileWrappers is a dictionary mapping filenames
    // to FileWrapper objects; we only care about the FileWrappers,
    // so return that as an array
    return Array(attachmentsFileWrappers.values)

}
```

To return the list of all attachments, we first ensure that we have an attachments directory to use. Next, we need to do a little bit of conversion. The `fileWrappers` property on `FileWrapper` objects returns a dictionary, in which strings are mapped to other `FileWrappers`. If we don't care about the filenames, and only care about the file wrappers, we need to ask the dictionary for its `values` value, and then ask Swift to convert it to an `Array`, which we then return.

4. Add the `addAttachmentAtURL` method, which adds an attachment to the document by copying it in:

```
@discardableResult func addAttachmentAtURL(_ url:URL) throws -> FileWrapper
{

    // Ensure that we have a place to put attachments
    guard attachmentsDirectoryWrapper != nil else {
        throw err(.cannotAccessAttachments)
    }

    // Create the new attachment with this file, or throw an error
    let newAttachment = try FileWrapper(url: url,
        options: FileWrapper.ReadingOptions.immediate)

    // Add it to the attachments directory
    attachmentsDirectoryWrapper?.addFileWrapper(newAttachment)

    // Mark ourselves as needing to save
    self.updateChangeCount(UIDocumentChangeKind.done)

    return newAttachment
}
```

Adding an attachment to the `Document` class works almost identically to the Mac version of the same method (seen in "Storing and Managing Attachments" on page 153). We first check to ensure that we have a file wrapper that we can place our attachments in, and then attempt to create a new file wrapper for the attachment. It's then added to the *Attachments* directory, and we record the fact that the document changed.

Determining Types of Attachments

To show attachments in the list, we need a way to visually represent them. This means that we need to show some kind of thumbnail image. We'll start by adding the default File image, which will be used as the fallback for when the app doesn't have special support for a type of file:

1. Open the *Assets.xcassets* file.
2. Drag the *File.pdf* image from the resources we provided on our website into the list of images to add it to the collection.

Next, we'll implement a way for the document to determine the type of the attachment, and a method to generate a thumbnail for the attachment. We'll do this by adding methods to the `FileWrapper` class that allow it to determine its file type and to return a `UIImage` that's appropriate for the type:

1. Open *Document.swift*.

2. Import the `MobileCoreServices` framework by adding this to the top of the file:

```
import MobileCoreServices
```

 MobileCoreServices framework gives us access to uniform type identifiers—unique identifiers for each type of data, such as PDF, text, or JPEG. By using UTIs we can determine what type of data is inside an attachment without having to guess based on the attachment's name.

3. Add a new extension to `FileWrapper` by adding the following code to *Document.swift*. We'll be putting our extra methods for `FileWrapper` into it:

```
extension FileWrapper {


}
```

4. Next, add the `fileExtension` property and the `conformsToType` method to this extension, which determines the file type:

```
var fileExtension : String? {
    return self.preferredFilename?
        .components(separatedBy: ".").last
}

func conformsToType(_ type: CFString) -> Bool {

    // Get the extension of this file
    guard let fileExtension = fileExtension else {
        // If we can't get a file extension, assume that it doesn't conform
        return false
    }

    // Get the file type of the attachment based on its extension
    guard let fileType = UTTypeCreatePreferredIdentifierForTag(
        kUTTagClassFilenameExtension, fileExtension as CFString, nil)?
        .takeRetainedValue() else {
        // If we can't figure out the file type from the extension,
        // it also doesn't conform
        return false
    }

    // Ask the system if this file type conforms to the provided type
    return UTTypeConformsTo(fileType, type)
}
```

The `fileExtension` property simply splits the file extension's `preferredFile` `name` wherever a `.` appears, and takes the last item from that array. This has the effect of getting the file extension.

The `conformsToType` method takes a UTI, stored in a `CFString`, and asks the type system to give us the UTI that applies to our file extension (using the `fileEx` `tension` property we just added). If that UTI conforms to the UTI that was passed in as a parameter, then we return `true`.

The `takeRetainedValue` method is necessary because the `UTType` collection of methods is written in C and isn't designed with Swift's memory management system. The `takeRetainedValue` method signals to Swift that it's responsible for disposing of the returned value from `UTTypeCreatePreferredIdentifierForTag` when it's all done.

Finally, we'll add the method `thumbnailImage` to the extension, which uses the information from `conformsToType` to figure out and return the image:

```
func thumbnailImage() -> UIImage? {

    if self.conformsToType(kUTTypeImage) {
        // If it's an image, return it as a UIImage

        // Ensure that we can get the contents of the file
        guard let attachmentContent = self.regularFileContents else {
            return nil
        }

        // Attempt to convert the file's contents to text
        return UIImage(data: attachmentContent)
    }

    // We don't know what type it is, so return nil
    return nil
}
```

The `thumbnailImage` property is one that we'll be adding to over time, as we continue to add support for additional types of attachments. At the moment, it simply checks to see if the file wrapper is an image file; if it is, it returns a `UIImage` based on the content of the file.

This is an early example of how UTIs can be powerful. To identify if the file wrapper is an image, we don't need to manually check to see if the file extension is *.png*, *.jpg*, *.jpeg*, and so on. We can simply ask the system. In addition, if iOS adds support for some additional image format, our code will automatically handle it.

Displaying Attachment Cells

Now that attachments are capable of providing an image, we'll make the attachments collection view show cells. We'll show one cell for each attachment, plus an additional "add new attachment" cell, which will add a new attachment when tapped.

First, we'll add the image for this "add attachment" cell, and then we'll connect up the collection view to the document view controller:

1. Open the *Assets.xcassets* file.

2. Add the *AddAttachment.pdf* image to the list of images. Next, we'll define the class that powers the collection view cells that represent each attachment.

3. In *DocumentViewController.swift*, add `AttachmentCell`. It's a subclass of `UICollectionViewCell` that has an outlet for an image view and for a label:

   ```
   class AttachmentCell : UICollectionViewCell {

       @IBOutlet weak var imageView : UIImageView?

       @IBOutlet weak var extensionLabel : UILabel?

   }
   ```

Manually Adding Attachments

Because the iOS app doesn't have a way to add attachments yet, if you're using the iOS simulator, the easiest way to test the feature we're about to build is to manually add some attachments yourself. This also gives you a peek into how your app is laid out in an iOS system. You can do this by opening the document package in the iCloud container and adding attachments:

1. Launch the app, and note the path that the app logs when it starts up. It should begin with something similar to *file:///Users/*.

2. Copy this URL excluding the *file://* at the start, and open the Terminal application. You'll find it in the *Applications→Utilities* folder on your Mac's hard drive.

3. Type **open**, type a **"** (double quotes), and then paste the URL. Type another **"** and press Enter. The container's folder will open in the Finder.

---

4. Open the *Documents* folder, and you'll find the list of documents that the iPhone simulator can access. Right-click one of them, and click Show Package Contents. (If you don't have any documents, create one in the iPhone app, and it will appear in the Finder window.)

5. Open the *Attachments* folder. If it doesn't exist, create it (taking care to spell it correctly and use the same capitalization).

6. Drag any file you like into this folder. For best results, use an image.

7. You're done! The document now has an attachment.

If you like, you can also add attachments using the macOS application we completed earlier in the book.

Next, let's make the view controller use this new class to show the list of all attachments:

1. Open *DocumentViewController.swift*.

2. Add an outlet for a `UICollectionView` called `attachmentsCollectionView`:

```
@IBOutlet weak var attachmentsCollectionView : UICollectionView!
```

3. Create an extension on `DocumentViewController` that conforms to `UICollectionViewDataSource` and `UICollectionViewDelegate`:

```
extension DocumentViewController : UICollectionViewDataSource,
    UICollectionViewDelegate {

}
```

 Putting the `UICollectionViewDelegate` and `UICollectionViewDataSource` methods in an extension allows us to keep these methods separate from the methods and properties that are specific to the `DocumentViewController` object. It's purely a stylistic choice.

4. Implement the `numberOfItemsInSection` method in this extension, which returns the number of attachments the document has, plus an additional cell (for the "add attachment" cell):

```
func collectionView(_ collectionView: UICollectionView,
    numberOfItemsInSection section: Int) -> Int {

    // No cells if the document is closed or if it doesn't exist
    if self.document!.documentState.contains(.closed) {
        return 0
    }
```

```
      guard let attachments = self.document?.attachedFiles else {
          // No cells if we can't access the attached files list
          return 0
      }

      // Return as many cells as we have, plus the add cell
      return attachments.count + 1
}
```

To figure out how many items need to exist in the attachments list, we need to
first check to see if the document is closed; if it is, then we can't display any
attachments, or the "add" cell. (This will be the case when the view controller has
appeared on screen, but the document hasn't finished opening yet.) We then ask
for the document's `attachedFiles` array and return its length, plus one. This
additional cell will be the "add attachment" cell.

5. Implement the `collectionView(cellForItemAt:)` method:

```
func collectionView(_ collectionView: UICollectionView,
    cellForItemAt indexPath: IndexPath) -> UICollectionViewCell {

    // Work out how many cells we need to display
    let totalNumberOfCells =
        collectionView.numberOfItems(inSection: indexPath.section)

    // Figure out if we're being asked to configure the Add cell,
    // or any other cell. If we're the last cell, it's the Add cell.
    let isAddCell = indexPath.row == (totalNumberOfCells - 1)

    // The place to store the cell. By making it 'let', we're ensuring
    // that we never accidentally fail to give it a value - the
    // compiler will call us out.
    let cell : UICollectionViewCell

    // Create and return the 'Add' cell if we need to
    if isAddCell {
        cell = collectionView.dequeueReusableCell(
            withReuseIdentifier: "AddAttachmentCell", for: indexPath)
    } else {

        // This is a regular attachment cell

        // Get the cell
        let attachmentCell = collectionView
            .dequeueReusableCell(withReuseIdentifier: "AttachmentCell",
                for: indexPath) as! AttachmentCell

        // Get a thumbnail image for the attachment
        let attachment = self.document?.attachedFiles?[indexPath.row]
```

```
    var image = attachment?.thumbnailImage()

    // Give it to the cell
    if image == nil {

        // We don't know what it is, so use a generic image
        image = UIImage(named: "File")

        // Also set the label
        attachmentCell.extensionLabel?.text =
            attachment?.fileExtension?.uppercased()

    } else {
        // We know what it is, so ensure that the label is empty
        attachmentCell.extensionLabel?.text = nil
    }
    attachmentCell.imageView?.image = image

    // Use this cell
    cell = attachmentCell
}

return cell

}
```

The collectionView(cellForItemAt:) method is very similar to its counterpart in the DocumentListViewController: the collection view will provide an index path, and we use it to grab a thumbnail image for the attachment, which is displayed in the cell. The only significant twist in this method is that if the index path refers to the last item in the collection view, we don't display an attachment but instead display the AddAttachmentCell.

We'll now create the interface for the attachment cells:

1. Open *Main.storyboard* and select the collection view.
2. Go to the Attributes Inspector, change the number of Items from 1 to 2, and set the Scroll Direction to Horizontal (Figure 10-4).

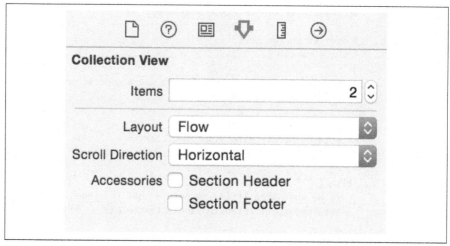

Figure 10-4. Updating the collection view's settings

3. Select the first cell and set its Identifier to `AttachmentCell`.

4. Go to the Identity Inspector, and set the class of this cell to `AttachmentCell`.

5. Select the second cell and set its Identifier to `AddAttachmentCell`.

6. Drag a `UIImageView` into both of these cells.

7. Make them both fill their cells—that is, resize them to fill the cell, and add constraints that pin the distances from all edges to 0.

8. Select the image view that you just added to the first cell—that is, `Attachment Cell`—and go to the Attributes Inspector. Set its Mode to Aspect Fill. This will make the image fill all of the image view.

9. Add a label to the first cell. Place it near the bottom of the cell, and resize it to fill the width:

   - Reduce the font size to 13.

   - Set its text alignment to Center.

   - Add constraints that pin the label to the bottom of the cell, and to the left and right edges.

10. Next, select the image view in the second cell (`AddAttachmentCell`). Set its Mode to Center. This will center the image in the middle of the view, without scaling.

11. Set the `AddAttachmentCell`'s image view's Image property to `AddAttachment`, as shown in Figure 10-5.

Figure 10-5. Setting the image view's image

The collection view's cells should now look like Figure 10-6.

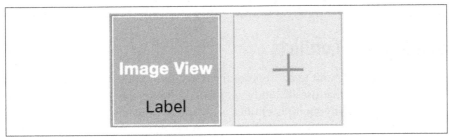

Figure 10-6. The configured collection view

12. Open *DocumentViewController.swift* in the Assistant.

13. Connect the empty image view in `AttachmentCell` to the `imageView` outlet of `AttachmentCell`.

14. Connect the label to the `extensionLabel` outlet.

15. Connect the `attachmentsCollectionView` outlet of the `DocumentViewControl ler` class to the collection view.

16. Hold down the Control key and drag from the collection view to the view controller, and then choose "data source" from the menu that appears.

17. Repeat the process, this time choosing "delegate" from the menu.

18. Open *DocumentViewController.swift*, and add the following code to the code in `viewWillAppear`:

```
// If this document is not already open, open it
if document.documentState.contains(UIDocumentState.closed) {
    document.open { (success) -> Void in
        if success == true {
            self.textView?.attributedText = document.text

>           self.attachmentsCollectionView?.reloadData()

        }
```

This code makes the view controller reload the contents of the collection view once the document is opened. This ensures that the list of attachments actually contains content.

19. Finally, add the following code to the end of `viewWillAppear` to make the attachments list refresh even if the document wasn't just freshly opened:

```
// And reload our list of attachments, in case it changed
// while we were away
self.attachmentsCollectionView?.reloadData()
```

20. Run the app. You'll see the list of attachments, plus an add cell!

Dealing with Conflicts

This is now a good point to address conflict resolution in the files. When you're making an application that uses iCloud—or, for that matter, *any* app that deals with files that can be opened by multiple entities at the same time—you need to handle situations in which a file is changed from two places at once.

Consider the following situation: you're about to board your flight, and you're editing a note. Your flight is called, so you hit Save and close your laptop. As a result, your file doesn't get saved to iCloud yet. On board the flight, you pull out your phone, and open your document. You make some changes and put your phone away. You later get off the plane, and your phone syncs its changes to iCloud. You then get home and open up your laptop, which finally has a chance to send your changes to iCloud. Suddenly, there's a problem: the file was changed from two places at once, which means that the file is in conflict. Which version of the file is *correct*? The file on your laptop, or the file on your phone? Or both?

It's up to your app to decide what to do. There are three main methods for resolving a conflict:

- Pick whichever file was most recently modified, and throw away all others. A variant of this technique is used by Dropbox.[1]

- Look at the contents of both files, and attempt to automatically merge them. This technique is used by source code management systems like Git.

- Present the user with the list of files that are in conflict, and ask them to choose the version to keep. This technique is used in Apple's productivity applications, like Pages and Keynote.

---

1 Dropbox doesn't throw away the other versions; instead, it sticks *Jon's conflicted copy* to the end of them so that you can later decide what you want to do.

Our app will pick the third option: if a document ends up in a conflicted state, then we'll simply show the list of possible options to users and let them decide. The advantage to doing this is that it's simple to think about and generally what the user wants; the downside is that it will always involve discarding data:

1. Add the following property to the `DocumentViewController` class:

```
var stateChangedObserver : AnyObject?
```

2. Add the following code to `viewWillAppear`:

```
// If this document is not already open, open it
if document.documentState.contains(UIDocumentState.closed) {
    document.open { (success) -> Void in
        if success == true {
            self.textView?.attributedText = document.text

            // Register for state change notifications
            self.stateChangedObserver = Notification.default
    .addObserver(
                forName: NSNotification.Name.UIDocumentStateChanged,
                object: document,
                queue: nil,
                using: { (notification) -> Void in
                    self.documentStateChanged()
                })

            self.documentStateChanged()

        }
```

This code registers a closure with the system, which will be run every time iOS receives a notification that the document's state has changed. In this case, all it will do is call the `documentStateChanged` method, which will handle conflicts for us.

Currently, the view controller will close the document when the view controller disappears. This can happen for a number of reasons, and we don't want the document to be closed except when the user taps the back button to go back to the document list. We therefore need to add some code to support this.

3. Add the following property to `DocumentViewController` to keep track of whether we should close the document when `viewWillDisappear` is called:

```
fileprivate var shouldCloseOnDisappear = true
```

We'll use a `UIAlertController` to present the list of possible actions the user can take. We've used `UIAlertControllers` before to present a message and possible actions for the user to take, but they've all been presented as *dialog boxes*—small windows that appear with buttons underneath. When you could have multiple options for the user to select from, or when the options might be quite wide, then an *action sheet* is better. Action sheets slide up from the bottom of the window and provide you room for multiple options. Functionally, there's no difference; the only way they differ is in their presentation.

4. Add the following method to `DocumentViewController`:

```
func documentStateChanged() {
    if let document = self.document
        , document.documentState.contains(UIDocumentState.inConflict) {

        // Gather all conflicted versions
        guard var conflictedVersions = NSFileVersion
            .unresolvedConflictVersionsOfItem(at: document.fileURL) else {
            fatalError("The document is in conflict, but no " +
                "conflicting versions were found. This should not happen.")
        }
        let currentVersion
            = NSFileVersion.currentVersionOfItem(at: document.fileURL)!

        // And include our own local version
        conflictedVersions += [currentVersion]

        // Prepare a chooser
        let title = "Resolve conflicts"
        let message = "Choose a version of this document to keep."

        let picker = UIAlertController(title: title, message: message,
            preferredStyle: UIAlertControllerStyle.actionSheet)

        let dateFormatter = DateFormatter()
        dateFormatter.dateStyle = .short
        dateFormatter.timeStyle = .short

        // We'll use this multiple times, so save it as a variable
        let cancelAndClose = { (action:UIAlertAction) -> Void in
            // Give up and return
            _ = self.navigationController?
.popViewController(animated: true)
        }

        // For each version, offer it as an option
        for version in conflictedVersions {
            let description = "Edited on " +
                "\(version.localizedNameOfSavingComputer!) at " +
                "\(dateFormatter.string(from: version.modificationDate!))"

            let action = UIAlertAction(title: description,
                                        style: UIAlertActionStyle.default,
                                        handler: { (action) -> Void in
```

```swift
                    // If it was selected, use this version
                    do {

                        if version != currentVersion {
        try version.replaceItem(at: document.fileURL,
            options: .byMoving)
        try NSFileVersion
            .removeOtherVersionOfItem(at: document.fileURL)
    }

                        document.revert(toContentsOf: document.fileURL,
                            completionHandler: { (success) -> Void in

                            self.textView.attributedText = document.text
                            self.attachmentsCollectionView?.reloadData()

                        })

                        for version in conflictedVersions{
                            version.isResolved = true
                        }

                    } catch let error as NSError {
                        // If there was a problem, let the user know and
                        // close the document
                        let errorView = UIAlertController(title: "Error",
                            message: error.localizedDescription,
                            preferredStyle: UIAlertControllerStyle.alert)

                        errorView.addAction(UIAlertAction(title: "Done",
                            style: UIAlertActionStyle.cancel,
                            handler: cancelAndClose))

                        self.shouldCloseOnDisappear = false
                        self.present(errorView,
                            animated: true,
                            completion: nil)
                    }

                })
                picker.addAction(action)
            }

            // Add a 'choose later' option
            picker.addAction(UIAlertAction(title: "Choose Later",
                style: UIAlertActionStyle.cancel, handler: cancelAndClose))

            self.shouldCloseOnDisappear = false
```

```
                // Finally, show the picker
                self.present(picker, animated: true, completion: nil)
        }
}
```

First, this method asks if the document is in a conflicted state. If it is, we've got some problems to solve! We ask the system to provide us with a list of all of the possible versions of this file. We then add the local device's current version of this file to the list.

We then create a closure, called `cancelAndClose`, which bails on the whole operation and returns to the document list view controller. This is kept in a variable, because it's used both for the Choose Later option (which we'll add in a moment), as well as for when there's a problem resolving the conflict.

Once this is done, we create a `UIAlertAction`, and, for each version of the file, we create a new action. This action displays the name of the computer that created the conflicting version, as well as the date and time that the version was created. When the action is selected, the app indicates to the system that we should use the action's associated version of the file and discard every other version.

If there's a problem, we present a separate alert controller, indicating to the user that something's gone wrong. This alert controller only has a single action, which, when tapped, runs the `cancelAndClose` code.

Finally, we add a final option, labeled Choose Later, which simply runs the `cancelAndClose` code (see Figure 10-7). The action sheet is then presented, letting the user choose what to do.

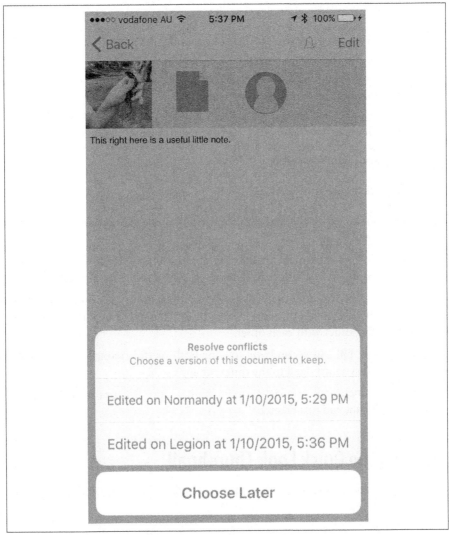

Figure 10-7. The interface that appears when resolving conflicts

5. Add the following code to viewWillDisappear to use the shouldCloseOnDisappear property to determine whether the document should be closed or not. Additionally, we'll clear the state changed observer:

```
override func viewWillDisappear(_ animated: Bool) {

>    if shouldCloseOnDisappear == false {
>        return
>    }
```

```
>       self.stateChangedObserver = nil

        self.document?.close(completionHandler: nil)
    }
```

6. Add the following code to the very end of `viewWillAppear` to reset the flag to true when the view controller reappears:

```
// We may be reappearing after having presented an attachment,
// which means that our 'don't close on disappear' flag has been set.
// Regardless, clear that flag.
self.shouldCloseOnDisappear = true
```

You can now test to see if it worked:

1. Open a document in the Mac application and make some changes. Don't save the changes yet.

2. Open the same document in the iOS application, ideally on a real device, and make some *different* changes to the ones you made on the Mac app.

3. Save and close the document in the Mac application, and then close the document in the iOS app. This will cause both of the apps to save their own versions, which will conflict with each other.

4. Wait a little bit—30 seconds or so—for both of the changes to be uploaded to iCloud and synchronized to the different apps.

5. Open the document one last time in the iOS app. Because it's in conflict, you'll see the UI that you just created!

Creating the Quick Look Thumbnail

Now that we can access the attachments, we'll add support for Quick Look in the iOS app.

We'll add a method to the `Document` class that generates a `Data` containing a PNG-encoded image that can be used for the app. This will generate the same kind of image as used in the Mac app (which we added in "Adding QuickLook" on page 166); the difference being that we need to use the iOS methods for drawing:

1. Add the following method to the `Document` class:

```
func iconImageDataWithSize(_ size: CGSize) -> Data? {
    UIGraphicsBeginImageContext(size)
    defer {
        UIGraphicsEndImageContext()
    }
```

```
    let entireImageRect = CGRect(origin: CGPoint.zero, size: size)

    // Fill the background with white
    let backgroundRect = UIBezierPath(rect: entireImageRect)
    UIColor.white.setFill()
    backgroundRect.fill()

    if (self.attachedFiles?.count)! >= 1 {
        // Render our text, and the first attachment
        let attachmentImage = self.attachedFiles?[0].thumbnailImage()

        let result = entireImageRect.divided(atDistance:
            entireImageRect.size.height / 2.0, from: CGRectEdge.minYEdge)

        self.text.draw(in: result.slice)
        attachmentImage?.draw(in: result.remainder)
    } else {
        // Just render our text
        self.text.draw(in: entireImageRect)
    }

    let image = UIGraphicsGetImageFromCurrentImageContext()
    return UIImagePNGRepresentation(image!)
}
```

To create the image in iOS, we first call `UIGraphicsBeginImageContext` to indicate that we'd like to start drawing in a canvas with the specified `size`. In addition, we need to be sure to tell iOS that we're done with this drawing once we are finished; to ensure that we don't forget, we'll use the `defer` keyword.

When you use `defer`, any code that you put in its associated block of code will be run when you exit the current scope. In this case, it means that just before we return from this method, we'll call `UIGraphicsEndImageContext`. `defer` is a great way to ensure that you clean up after yourself while keeping your cleanup code close to the code that actually creates the mess in the first place.

When we're drawing this icon, we use the `UIBezierPath` and `UIColor` classes to paint the entire canvas white. We then do the exact same thing as in the Mac version: if we have at least one attachment, we get its thumbnail image and draw it in the top half of the canvas while drawing the text in the lower half. If we don't have any attachments, we just draw the text.

Finally, we get the image from iOS by calling `UIGraphicsGetImageFromCurrentImageContext`, and convert it to a `Data` containing the PNG-encoded image by calling `UIImagePNGRepresentation`.

2. Add the following code to the `contentsForType` method to add the Quick Look files to the document package:

```
override func contents(forType typeName: String) throws -> Any {

    let textRTFData = try self.text.data(
        from: NSRange(0..<self.text.length),
        documentAttributes:
            [NSDocumentTypeDocumentAttribute: NSRTFTextDocumentType])

    if let oldTextFileWrapper = self.documentFileWrapper
        .fileWrappers?[NoteDocumentFileNames.TextFile.rawValue] {
        self.documentFileWrapper.removeFileWrapper(oldTextFileWrapper)
    }

>    // Create the QuickLook folder
>
>    let thumbnailImageData =
>        self.iconImageDataWithSize(CGSize(width: 512, height: 512))!
>
>    let thumbnailWrapper =
>        FileWrapper(regularFileWithContents: thumbnailImageData)
>
>    let quicklookPreview =
>        FileWrapper(regularFileWithContents: textRTFData)
>
>    let quickLookFolderFileWrapper =
>        FileWrapper(directoryWithFileWrappers: [
>        NoteDocumentFileNames.QuickLookTextFile.rawValue: quicklookPreview,
>        NoteDocumentFileNames.QuickLookThumbnail.rawValue: thumbnailWrapper
>        ])
>    quickLookFolderFileWrapper.preferredFilename =
>        NoteDocumentFileNames.QuickLookDirectory.rawValue
>
>    // Remove the old QuickLook folder if it existed
>    if let oldQuickLookFolder = self.documentFileWrapper
>        .fileWrappers?[NoteDocumentFileNames.QuickLookDirectory.rawValue] {
>            self.documentFileWrapper.removeFileWrapper(oldQuickLookFolder)
>    }
>
>    // Add the new QuickLook folder
>    self.documentFileWrapper.addFileWrapper(quickLookFolderFileWrapper)

    // checking if there is already a location saved
    let rawLocationVal = NoteDocumentFileNames.locationAttachment.rawValue
    if self.documentFileWrapper.fileWrappers?[rawLocationVal] == nil {
        // saving the location if there is one
        if let location = self.locationWrapper {
            self.documentFileWrapper.addFileWrapper(location)
        }
    }

    self.documentFileWrapper.addRegularFile(withContents: textRTFData,
```

```
    preferredFilename: NoteDocumentFileNames.TextFile.rawValue)

    return self.documentFileWrapper
}
```

Again, this is almost identical to the code seen in the Mac version: we create a file wrapper for the *QuickLook* folder, as well as file wrappers for both the thumbnail and preview file. We then remove the old *QuickLook* folder, if it exists, and add the new one to the document.

3. Run the app. When you close a document, it will update its Quick Look thumbnail.

Conclusion

We've now added a significant new feature to the iOS app. As a result, we're almost at feature parity with the Mac app; from now on, it's nothing but awesome new features. In the next chapter, we'll add the ability to create and add brand-new attachments, straight from the iOS app.

CHAPTER 11

Images and Deletion

In this chapter, we'll add the interface that allows the user to create new attachments in the iOS version. Once that's done, we'll create the first attachment viewing interface, for image attachments, and then add the ability to remove attachments from Notes documents.

Adding Attachments

First, we'll get started by letting users add new attachments to their documents.

To be able to create and add new attachments, we need to create an interface that lets the user choose which type of attachment to add. Initially, this will only present a single option. This will be a popover on iPad, and a modal display on iPhone; additionally, on the iPhone, we need to add the controls that will allow the user to cancel selecting it.

 A *popover* is a view that floats above the rest of your app. Popovers are great for presenting information about a specific item on the screen, or to provide access to tools, settings, or actions for a specific object. Popovers are most commonly used on the iPad, which is what we're doing here, where a modal view would really pull users out of what they're doing. We're using a modal view on non-iPad devices, where we have less available screen space.

1. Open *DocumentViewController.swift*.

2. Add a new method to the DocumentViewController class:

```swift
func addAttachment(_ sourceView : UIView) {

    let title = "Add attachment"
```

```
let actionSheet
    = UIAlertController(title: title,
                       message: nil,
                       preferredStyle: UIAlertControllerStyle
                           .actionSheet)

actionSheet.addAction(UIAlertAction(title: "Cancel",
    style: UIAlertActionStyle.cancel, handler: nil))

// If this is on an iPad, present it in a popover connected
// to the source view
if UI_USER_INTERFACE_IDIOM() == UIUserInterfaceIdiom.pad {

    actionSheet.modalPresentationStyle
        = .popover
    actionSheet.popoverPresentationController?.sourceView
        = sourceView
    actionSheet.popoverPresentationController?.sourceRect
        = sourceView.bounds
}

self.present(actionSheet, animated: true, completion: nil)

}
```

We'll be returning to this method several times, as we add support for other types of attachments. At the moment, all it does is present a UIAlertController that contains a single option, which closes it. However, note the sourceView parameter that gets passed to this method. This is used on the iPad, where the action sheet will be presented in a popover, which is visually attached to the source View's location on screen.

3. Add the collectionView(_, didSelectItemAt indexPath:) method to the extension that implements the UICollectionViewDelegate protocol. This method is run when the user taps a cell in the attachment view; to start, we'll detect if the user tapped the add cell and call the addAttachment method:

```
func collectionView(_ collectionView: UICollectionView,
    didSelectItemAt indexPath: IndexPath) {

    // Get the cell that the user interacted with; bail if we can't get it
    guard let selectedCell = collectionView
        .cellForItem(at: indexPath) else {
        return
    }

    // Work out how many cells we have
    let totalNumberOfCells = collectionView
```

```
        .numberOfItems(inSection: indexPath.section)

    // If we have selected the last cell, show the Add screen
    if indexPath.row == totalNumberOfCells - 1 {
        addAttachment(selectedCell)
    }
}
```

This method is run whenever the user taps a cell in the attachments list. Eventually, we'll extend this method to actually open attachments that the user taps; for now, we'll just detect whether the user has tapped the last cell in the list. We do this by asking the collection view to tell us how many cells exist in the collection, as well as asking for the actual `UICollectionViewCell` object that the user has tapped. If the index path of the selected cell represents the last item in the list, we call `addAttachment` method, passing in the cell.

 Remember, an `UICollectionViewCell` is a view, which means the `addAttachment` method is able to use it to present its popover relative to the cell's position. In other words, the popover can appear attached to the add button.

Run the app, and open a document. Tap the add button, and you'll get a modal screen on iPhone and a popover on iPad.

Adding Image Attachments

Currently, the list of possible attachments that users can add is empty; all they can do is dismiss the pop up. We'll add a method that shows the camera and lets the user take a photo, which is then added as an attachment.

To do this, we'll be using `UIImagePickerController`, which provides Apple-created interfaces for capturing images and movies, as well as the gallery of previously captured images and movies. All interaction in the `UIImagePickerController` is provided and handled for you, with the results passed to a delegate object.

UIImagePickerController can have different source types assigned to it: the camera, for taking new images or movies, or the photo library, for choosing from existing images and movies from which to choose. In this app, we only use the source type of UIImagePickerControllerSourceType.camera, but you could very easily extend it to support the photo gallery as well, by providing access to a UIImagePickerController with a source type of UIImagePickerControllerSourceType.photoLibrary. You can learn more in Apple's UIImagePickerController class reference (*http://apple.co/1PIdCG7*).

1. First, because captured images will arrive as raw chunks of data, we need a way to add them as attachments to the document. Open *Document.swift* and add the following method to the Document class:

```
func addAttachmentWithData(_ data: Data, name: String) throws {

    guard attachmentsDirectoryWrapper != nil else {
        throw err(.cannotAccessAttachments)
    }

    let newAttachment = FileWrapper(regularFileWithContents: data)

    newAttachment.preferredFilename = name

    attachmentsDirectoryWrapper?.addFileWrapper(newAttachment)

    self.updateChangeCount(.done)

}
```

This method takes a Data that should be added to the document, as well as its filename. Data objects on their own don't have any concept of a filename, so it needs to be a separate parameter.

To add the data, we construct a FileWrapper using the regularFileWithContents initializer, which takes the Data object. We then provide the new file wrapper with a name and add it to the *Attachments* folder, just like we do in addAttachmentAtURL. Finally, we update the change count, marking the document in need of saving.

2. Next, we'll add a method that presents a UIImagePickerController. Open *DocumentViewController.swift*, and add the following method to DocumentViewController:

```
func addPhoto() {
    let picker = UIImagePickerController()
```

```
picker.sourceType = .camera

picker.delegate = self

self.shouldCloseOnDisappear = false

self.present(picker, animated: true, completion: nil)
}
```

 You'll get a compiler error on the line that sets delegate to self, saying that the class doesn't conform to the protocol. Don't panic: we're about to tackle that next.

The addPhoto method creates a UIImagePickerController, which is a view controller that lets the user either take a photo using the built-in camera, or select a photo from the photo library. In this case, we're specifying that we want to use the camera. We then instruct it that we want it to contact this object when the user takes a photo, by setting its delegate to self; set the shouldCloseOnDisappear flag to false to prevent viewWillDisappear from closing the document when the image picker view controller appears; and then present the view controller.

3. Add the following extension to DocumentViewController, which adds support for dealing with the UIImagePickerController:

```
extension DocumentViewController : UIImagePickerControllerDelegate,
    UINavigationControllerDelegate {

    func imagePickerController(_ picker: UIImagePickerController,
        didFinishPickingMediaWithInfo info: [String : Any]) {
            do {

                let edited = UIImagePickerControllerEditedImage
                let original = UIImagePickerControllerOriginalImage
                if let image = (info[edited] as? UIImage
                    ?? info[original] as? UIImage) {

                    guard let imageData =
                        UIImageJPEGRepresentation(image, 0.8) else {
                        throw err(.cannotSaveAttachment)
                    }

                    try self.document?.addAttachmentWithData(imageData,
                        name: "Image \(arc4random()).jpg")

                    self.attachmentsCollectionView?.reloadData()
```

```
            } else {
                throw err(.cannotSaveAttachment)
            }
        } catch let error as NSError {
            NSLog("Error adding attachment: \(error)")
        }

        self.dismiss(animated: true, completion: nil)
    }

}
```

By extending the `DocumentViewController` to conform the `UIImagePicker ControllerDelegate` protocol, we're enabling the view controller to respond when the user takes a photo. When the user takes a photo, the `didFinishPicking MediaWithInfo` method is called, which receives a dictionary describing the media that the user selected. This dictionary can contain quite a lot of stuff, but we specifically want the photo that the user has taken.

The photo can be in one of two possible places in this dictionary. If the user took a photo and then edited it (such as by cropping it, which the `UIImagePicker Controller` supports), then the image will be in the dictionary under the `UIIma gePickerControllerEditedImage` key. Otherwise, if the user has not edited it, we can access the image through the `UIImagePickerControllerOriginalImage` key.

If the user edits the photo, *both* the edited and original images will be available. Absent a specific reason for doing otherwise, you should *always* use the edited version to avoid throwing away the user's editing efforts. However, unless the user actually *did* edit the image, `UIImagePickerControllerEdited Image` will be `nil`. For that reason, we try to access the edited image first and then fall back the original image if it's `nil`.

Once we have the image, we encode it to JPEG, using the `UIImageJPEGRepresen tation` function. This function takes a `UIImage`, as well as a compression factor, which is a float ranging from 0 (lowest size) to 1 (highest quality); a good compromise value is 0.8, which we're using here. This function returns a `Data` object, which means we can just call the `Document` object's `addAttachmentWithData` method.

Then we dismiss the entire image picker by calling `dismiss(animated:, comple tion:)`.

4. Lastly, we need to add the buttons that actually presents the camera. Go to the top of the file, and import the `AVFoundation` framework:

```
import AVFoundation
```

This isn't strictly necessary to access the camera, but it *is* required to determine whether you have permission to access the camera.

5. Add the following code to the `addAttachment` method to add the Camera entry to the attachment pop up. This button will either show the camera or ask the user for permission to go to the Settings app to enable access to the camera. In addition, we'll also add a cancel button that closes the pop up:

```
func addAttachment(_ sourceView : UIView) {

    let title = "Add attachment"

    let actionSheet
        = UIAlertController(title: title,
                            message: nil,
                            preferredStyle: UIAlertControllerStyle
                                .actionSheet)

>    // If a camera is available to use...
>    if UIImagePickerController
>        .isSourceTypeAvailable(UIImagePickerControllerSourceType.camera) {
>        // this variable contains a closure that shows the image picker,
>        // or asks the user to grant permission.
>        var handler : (_ action:UIAlertAction) -> Void
>
>        let authorizationStatus = AVCaptureDevice
>            .authorizationStatus(forMediaType: AVMediaTypeVideo)
>
>        switch authorizationStatus {
>        case .authorized:
>            fallthrough
>        case .notDetermined:
>            // If we have permission, or we don't know if it's been denied,
>            // then the closure shows the image picker.
>            handler = { (action) in
>                self.addPhoto()
>            }
>        default:
>
>            // Otherwise, when the button is tapped, ask for permission.
>            handler = { (action) in
>
>                let title = "Camera access required"
>                let message = "Go to Settings to grant permission to" +
```

```
>                       "access the camera."
>               let cancelButton = "Cancel"
>               let settingsButton = "Settings"
>
>               let alert = UIAlertController(title: title,
>                       message: message,
>                       preferredStyle: .alert)
>
>               // The Cancel button just closes the alert.
>               alert.addAction(UIAlertAction(title: cancelButton,
>                   style: .cancel, handler: nil))
>
>               // The Settings button opens this app's settings page,
>               // allowing the user to grant us permission.
>               alert.addAction(UIAlertAction(title: settingsButton,
>                   style: .default, handler: { (action) in
>
>                       if let settingsURL = URL(
>                           string: UIApplicationOpenSettingsURLString) {
>
>                           UIApplication.shared
>                               .openURL(settingsURL)
>                       }
>
>               }))
>
>               self.present(alert,
>                   animated: true,
>                   completion: nil)
>           }
>       }
>
>       // Either way, show the Camera item; when it's selected, the
>       // appropriate code will run.
>       actionSheet.addAction(UIAlertAction(title: "Camera",
>           style: UIAlertActionStyle.default, handler: handler))
>   }

    actionSheet.addAction(UIAlertAction(title: "Cancel",
        style: UIAlertActionStyle.cancel, handler: nil))

    // If this is on an iPad, present it in a popover connected
    // to the source view
    if UI_USER_INTERFACE_IDIOM() == UIUserInterfaceIdiom.pad {

        actionSheet.modalPresentationStyle
            = .popover
        actionSheet.popoverPresentationController?.sourceView
            = sourceView
        actionSheet.popoverPresentationController?.sourceRect
```

```
          = sourceView.bounds
  }

  self.present(actionSheet, animated: true, completion: nil)

}
```

This code does quite a bit. First, it asks the `UIImagePickerController` class to determine if a camera of any kind is available. If it's not—which is the case on the iOS simulator—then there's no point in offering the camera as an option.

Running Code on the Device

If you aren't already, now's a good time to run your app on the device. To do this, make sure that you're signed in to your iOS developer account by opening the Xcode menu, choosing Preferences, opening the Accounts tab, and adding your Apple ID. Once you've signed in, connect your device to your computer using the USB cable, and open the scheme selector at the top left of the Xcode window. Select your device and then click the Run button. Xcode will compile and install your app on your device.

We then create a variable that holds the action that will run when the user taps the Camera option in the list of possible attachments to add. The actual code that goes into this variable will depend on whether the user has granted permission to access the camera. If the app has explicit permission or the user hasn't yet decided, the closure will simply call the `addPhoto` method, which presents the `UIImagePickerController`. When it appears, the image picker will ask the user for permission to access the camera if it hasn't already been granted.

If the user has explicitly *denied* permission, then we can't present the image picker controller. If we did, the image picker won't ask for permission a second time, and as a result, the user would be looking at a useless, black screen. Instead, we prepare a dialog box that explains the situation and includes an action that, when tapped, takes the user to the Settings screen to enable the app to have access.

As we mentioned earlier, you could extend this to support using photos from the device photo gallery.

6. There is one final step before we can run the application: we need to set our project up to have permission to access the camera. As iOS is a privacy-conscious

platform, it is very important that everything we do as developers keeps user privacy in our minds. Sometimes this is enforced by the platform, and accessing the camera is one of those situations.

Open `info.plist`. In here we are going to add in a particular key-value pair that will do a few things. It will let our application access the camera (still with user permission) and will display a message explaining to the user why we need to access the camera. Without this key-value pair added to `info.plist`, the iOS ecosystem will simply refuse to allow our app access to the camera and won't even ask the user if he wants to give us permission.

Right-click in the editor below all the other key-value pairs and select Add Row.

Type **Privacy - Camera Usage Description**. As you are typing, Xcode should offer an autocompletion, and it is well worth using it to make sure you don't get the key wrong. Now the type of this value should be set to `String` automatically, but if it isn't, make sure to manually change it to `String`. Finally, in the Value column add a message you want to be shown to the user when he first tries to access the camera. For our application, we enter **We'll use the camera to take photos and videos, and add them as attachments.** but each app is different and will have different reasons, so choose your message wisely.

7. Run the app. You can now add images to documents, and they'll appear in the list of attachments.

Viewing Attachments

Because there are multiple different types of attachment, it doesn't make much sense to duplicate the "show a view controller" code for each one. We're going to create a new view controller for each type of attachment, but we don't want to have to write the same code over and over again for showing each different type of view controller. It doesn't make sense to repeat things like "if it's an image segue, then get the image view controller and give it the image."

Instead, we'll create a protocol for these view controllers, which means we can treat them all the same way: we'll just give them the `FileWrapper` that represents the attachment, and they can do whatever they need to it. This way we only need to write the code to show an attachment once:

1. Open *DocumentViewController.swift*.

2. Add the `AttachmentViewer` protocol:

```
protocol AttachmentViewer : NSObjectProtocol {

    // The attachment to view. If this is nil,
    // the viewer should instead attempt to create a new
```

```
    // attachment, if applicable.
    var attachmentFile : FileWrapper? { get set }

    // The document attached to this file
    var document : Document? { get set }
}
```

Classes that conform to the `AttachmentViewer` protocol need to have two properties: the `attachmentFile` property, which is an optional `FileWrapper`, and the
`document` property, which is an optional `Document`. Each of the view controllers
that we'll be making will conform to this protocol, meaning that they can all be
treated in the same way, and the `DocumentViewController` won't have to care
about the specific type of each attachment view controller it presents.

Next, we'll implement the view controller that displays the image:

1. Open the File menu and choose New→File.

2. Select Cocoa Touch Class and click Next.

3. Name the new class **ImageAttachmentViewController** and make it a subclass of
   `UIViewController`.

4. Open *ImageAttachmentViewController.swift*, and make the class conform to the
   `AttachmentViewer` protocol:

   ```
   class ImageAttachmentViewController: UIViewController, AttachmentViewer {
   ```

 Doing this will simplify how `DocumentViewController` works
with the view controller, when we get to it later in this chapter.

5. Add an `imageView` outlet:

   ```
   @IBOutlet weak var imageView : UIImageView?
   ```

6. Add an `attachmentFile` and `document` property to conform to the `Attachment
   Viewer` protocol:

   ```
   var attachmentFile : FileWrapper?

   var document : Document?
   ```

7. Implement `viewDidLoad` to load the image from the data:

   ```
   override func viewDidLoad() {
       super.viewDidLoad()

       // If we have data, and can make an image out of it...
       if let data = attachmentFile?.regularFileContents,
   ```

```
        let image = UIImage(data: data) {
        // Set the image
        self.imageView?.image = image

    }
}
```

When the view loads, we need to present whatever image is represented by the attachment given to this view controller by the DocumentViewController. We'll be making DocumentViewController actually give the view controller its attachment shortly.

To display it, we grab whatever Data is inside the file wrapper and attempt to make a UIImage out of it. If this succeeds, we pass this image to the UIImageView for it to display.

Next, we'll set up the interface for this new view controller:

1. Open *Main.storyboard* and add a new UIViewController.

2. Select the new view controller and go to the Identity Inspector.

3. Change its class to **ImageAttachmentViewController**.

4. Select the view and go to the Attributes Inspector.

5. Change the background color to black (Figure 11-1).

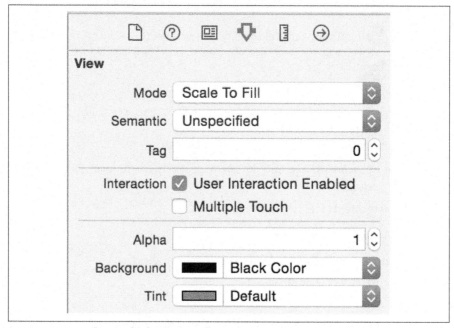

Figure 11-1. Updating the background color

6. Drag in a UIImageView and add constraints to make it fill the screen.

7. Go to the Attributes Inspector and set its Content Mode to Aspect Fit.

8. Hold down the Control key and drag from the image attachment view controller in the outline to the image view. Select the imageView outlet from the list that appears.

The interface should now look like Figure 11-2.

Figure 11-2. The laid-out image view

We'll now create a segue that connects this image attachment view controller to the document view controller:

1. In the outline, hold down the Control key and drag from the document view controller to the image attachment view controller. When prompted, choose to make a "present as popover" segue.

2. Select the new segue and go to the Attributes Inspector.

3. Set the identifier of the new segue to ShowImageAttachment.

4. Drag from the well in the Anchor slot in the Attributes Inspector to the document view controller's view. The Anchor is the view that the popover will be attached to.

Next, we'll add support for triggering a segue when an attachment is tapped. Importantly, we need to detect the type of the attachment and use that to determine which segue to use:

1. Open *DocumentViewController.swift* and add the following line of code to the top of the file, next to the other import statements:

```
import MobileCoreServices
```

2. Next, add code in didSelectItemAt indexPath to detect the type of the attachment and trigger a segue:

```
func collectionView(_ collectionView: UICollectionView,
    didSelectItemAt indexPath: IndexPath) {

>       // Do nothing if we are editing
>       if self.isEditingAttachments {
>           return
>       }

        // Get the cell that the user interacted with; bail if we can't get it
        guard let selectedCell = collectionView
            .cellForItem(at: indexPath) else {
            return
        }

        // Work out how many cells we have
        let totalNumberOfCells = collectionView
            .numberOfItems(inSection: indexPath.section)

        // If we have selected the last cell, show the Add screen
        if indexPath.row == totalNumberOfCells - 1 {
            addAttachment(selectedCell)
        }
>       else {
>           // Otherwise, show a different view controller based on the type
>           // of the attachment
>           guard let attachment = self.document?
```

```
>                .attachedFiles?[(indexPath as IndexPath).row] else {
>
>                NSLog("No attachment for this cell!")
>                return
>            }
>
>        let segueName : String?
>
>        if attachment.conformsToType(kUTTypeImage) {
>            segueName = "ShowImageAttachment"
>
>        }
>
>        } else {
>
>            segueName = nil
>        }
>
>        // If we have a segue, run it now
>        if let theSegue = segueName {
>            self.performSegue(withIdentifier: theSegue,
>                sender: selectedCell)
>        }
>
>    }
 }
```

Our earlier implementation of didSelectItemAt indexPath simply detected if the user was tapping the last cell, which resulted in the *new attachment* list appearing. However, we now need to handle what to do when the user taps any of the actual attachment cells.

First, we attempt to get whatever attachment the selected cell represents by asking the document's attachedFiles array to give us the appropriate FileWrapper. Next, we need to decide what segue to run, based on the type of the attachment. Different types of attachments will require different view controllers, and each view controller will need a different segue to reach it.

At the moment, the only type of attachment that we have is images, so we simply ask the attachment if it conforms to the "image" type. If it does, then the name of the segue we need to run is ShowImageAttachment.

 We'll be adding more to this part of the method as we add more attachment types.

Finally, if we have a segue to run, we perform it:

1. Add the `prepare(for segue:, sender:)` method to the `DocumentViewControl ler` class, which gives the attachment to the view controller:

```swift
override func prepare(for segue: UIStoryboardSegue, sender: Any?) {

    // If we're going to an AttachmentViewer...
    if let attachmentViewer
        = segue.destination as? AttachmentViewer {

        // Give the attachment viewer our document
        attachmentViewer.document = self.document!

        // If we were coming from a cell, get the attachment
        // that this cell represents so that we can view it
        if let cell = sender as? UICollectionViewCell,
            let indexPath =
                self.attachmentsCollectionView?.indexPath(for: cell),
            let attachment = self.document?.attachedFiles?[indexPath.row] {

            attachmentViewer.attachmentFile = attachment
        } else {
            // we don't have an attachment
        }

        // Don't close the document when showing the view controller
        self.shouldCloseOnDisappear = false

        // If this has a popover, present it from the the attachments list
        if let popover =
            segue.destination.popoverPresentationController {

            popover.sourceView = self.attachmentsCollectionView
            popover.sourceRect = self.attachmentsCollectionView.bounds

        }
    }
    else if segue.identifier == "ShowLocationSegue" {
        if let destination =
    segue.destination as? LocationAttachmentViewController {
            destination.locationAttachment = self.document?.locationWrapper
        }
    }
}
```

It's in this method that we can take advantage of the `AttachmentViewer` protocol. Remember, `ImageAttachmentViewController` is an `AttachmentViewer`, and so will be every other view controller that can display an attachment. As a result, the prepare(for segue:, sender:) method doesn't have to be able to tell the difference between the different view controllers that will be presenting the attachment; all it needs to do is give the attachment viewer its attachment.

To do this, it first checks to see if the sender of this segue—that is, the object that was passed in as the sender parameter to performSegue—is a UICollectionViewCell. If it is, we can figure out the attachment by asking the collection view for its index path and use that to get the attachment filewrapper.

 If there's no attachment available, then that's not a problem—instead, the attachment view controller will be presented with no attachment and will let the user create a new one. This doesn't apply to the image view controller, because images get created by one type of view controller and viewed by another, but it will apply to other types of attachments.

2. Run the app. You can now tap image attachments and view them!

However, there's a problem on the iPhone: it lacks any way to close the view controller. The view will appear, but there won't be a close button. Let's add that.

3. In the prepare(for segue:, sender:) method, set up the view controller to make the popover controller its delegate. You'll get a compiler error, saying that DocumentViewController doesn't conform to the necessary protocol. Don't worry—we'll fix that in a moment:

```
override func prepare(for segue: UIStoryboardSegue, sender: Any?) {

    // If we're going to an AttachmentViewer...
    if let attachmentViewer
        = segue.destination as? AttachmentViewer {

        // Give the attachment viewer our document
        attachmentViewer.document = self.document!

        // If we were coming from a cell, get the attachment
        // that this cell represents so that we can view it
        if let cell = sender as? UICollectionViewCell,
            let indexPath =
                self.attachmentsCollectionView?.indexPath(for: cell),
            let attachment = self.document?.attachedFiles?[indexPath.row] {

            attachmentViewer.attachmentFile = attachment
        } else {
            // we don't have an attachment
        }

        // If this has a popover, present it from the the attachments list
```

```
            if let popover =
                segue.destination.popoverPresentationController {

>               // Ensure that we add a close button to the popover on iPhone
>               popover.delegate = self

                popover.sourceView = self.attachmentsCollectionView
                popover.sourceRect = self.attachmentsCollectionView.bounds

            }
        }
>       else if segue.identifier == "ShowLocationSegue" {
>           if let destination =
>   segue.destination as? LocationAttachmentViewController {
>               destination.locationAttachment = self.document?.locationWrapper
>           }
>       }
    }
```

4. Next, add the extension to DocumentViewController that makes it conform to UIPopoverPresentationControllerDelegate:

```
extension DocumentViewController : UIPopoverPresentationControllerDelegate
{
    // called by the system to determine which view controller
    // should be the content of the popover
    func presentationController(_ controller: UIPresentationController,
        viewControllerForAdaptivePresentationStyle
        style: UIModalPresentationStyle) -> UIViewController? {

        // Get the view controller that we want to present
        let presentedViewController = controller.presentedViewController

        // If we're showing a popover, and that popover is being shown
        // as a full-screen modal (which happens on iPhone)...
        if style == UIModalPresentationStyle.fullScreen && controller
            is UIPopoverPresentationController {

            // Create a navigation controller that contains the content
            let navigationController = UINavigationController(
    rootViewController: controller.presentedViewController)

            // Create and set up a "Done" button, and add it to the
            // navigation controller.
            // It will call the 'dismissModalView' button, below
            let closeButton = UIBarButtonItem(title: "Done",
                style: UIBarButtonItemStyle.done, target: self,
                action: #selector(DocumentViewController.dismissModalView))

            presentedViewController.navigationItem
```

```
            .rightBarButtonItem = closeButton

        // Tell the system that the content should be this new
        // navigation controller.
        return navigationController
    } else {

        // Just return the content
        return presentedViewController
    }
}

func dismissModalView() {
    self.dismiss(animated: true, completion: nil)
}
}
```

When a view controller is shown in a popover, the popover is managed by a `UIPo` `poverPresentationController`. This object manages the contents of the popover and gives us an opportunity to make changes to how the view controller is presented.

Specifically, if the view controller is being presented on an iPhone, we want to wrap the view controller in a navigation controller. Doing this means that the view controller will have a navigation bar at the top, in which we can place a Done button. When this button is tapped, we want the current view controller—that is, the `DocumentViewController`—to dismiss the attachment view controller.

However, on the iPad, we don't need to do this, because when you tap outside the view controller, the popover is closed. We therefore *shouldn't* do this extra work of adding and configuring a Done button if we're not running on the iPad.

There's one last consideration we need to take. So far in this chunk of code, we've been mostly talking about how we need to perform differently when we're on the iPad, but that's not precisely correct. The reason this needs to behave differently is because, on the iPhone, when you request a popover, it will slide up from the bottom of the screen, covering everything else. This is due to the extremely limited screen space available on the phone: there's no point in wasting the space around the edges of the screen.

This is usually not a concern on the iPad, but things can change when the iPad is displayed in a split-screen view. If you're in another app, and you swipe from the righthand side of the screen, you can summon the Notes application and place it in a little bar, roughly one-third the width of the screen. When this happens, the app is practically just a tall iPhone.

Because applications can change their presentation styles, it's almost always better to ask yourself what is the specific behavior you're trying to deal with. Don't simply assume that the iPad behaves one way, and the iPhone behaves another.

So, rather than simply ask, "Are we on the iPad?" we'll instead check to see what style of presentation the popover is using. If it's .fullScreen, then we need to add the Done button.

The most straightforward way to add a navigation bar to the top of the content view controller is to put that view controller in a navigation controller. While it's *possible* to reach into the content view controller and insert a UINavigationBar into the top of the screen, you would then have to ensure that the navigation bar you've just added doesn't cover anything else up. It's easier to simply get a navigation controller, which takes care of resizing the content view controller's view to make room for the navigation bar.

So, we do this and embed the content view controller in the new navigation controller. We then create a new UIBarButtonItem and add it to the content view controller's UINavigationItem, which causes the button to appear at the top right. When the button is being created, we set its target to self (that is, the DocumentViewController) and the action to dismissModalView. This is a new method that simply calls dimiss(animated:, completion:); when this happens, the popover is dismissed.

Lastly, the navigation controller that now contains the content view controller is returned.

5. Run the application. You'll now have a close button when on the iPhone.

Deleting Attachments

We'll use the standard deleting gesture: when you tap and hold an attachment, we'll display a delete button. To detect when the user touches and holds on a cell, we'll use a gesture recognizer. Just as with the tap gesture recognizer that we added to the labels in the DocumentListViewController in "Renaming Documents" on page 247, we'll add a long-press gesture recognizer to detect when the user holds a finger down on the attachment. When the user does this, deletion buttons will appear, allowing the user to remove attachments. When these delete buttons appear, we also need a way to cancel deletion.

So far in this book, we've seen tap gesture recognizers, and we're about to start looking at long-press recognizers. There are several other types of recognizers available:

- Pan recognizers detect when a finger drags over the screen.
- Pinch recognizers detect when two fingers are placed on the screen and are moved together or away from each other.
- Rotation recognizers detect when two fingers are placed on the screen and then rotated around a central point.
- Swipe recognizers detect when a finger makes a swiping motion.
- Screen-edge swipe recognizers detect when a finger makes a swiping motion that begins off-screen.

We'll add a delegate protocol that lets cells notify their delegate that they've been deleted:

1. Add the `AttachmentCellDelegate` protocol to *DocumentViewController.swift*:

   ```
   protocol AttachmentCellDelegate {
       func attachmentCellWasDeleted(_ cell: AttachmentCell)
   }
   ```

2. Go to the `AttachmentCell` class, also in *DocumentViewController.swift*.

3. Add the following code to the class:

   ```
   class AttachmentCell : UICollectionViewCell {

       @IBOutlet weak var imageView : UIImageView?

       @IBOutlet weak var extensionLabel : UILabel?

   >   @IBOutlet weak var deleteButton : UIButton?
   >
   >   var editMode = false {
   >       didSet {
   >           // Full alpha if we're editing, zero if we're not
   >           deleteButton?.alpha = editMode ? 1 : 0
   >       }
   >   }
   >
   >   var delegate : AttachmentCellDelegate?
   >
   >   @IBAction func delete() {
   >       self.delegate?.attachmentCellWasDeleted(self)
   >   }
   ```

```
>
}
```

4. Add the `isEditingAttachments` property to `DocumentViewController`, which keeps track of whether the delete button attached to each cell should appear or not:

```
fileprivate var isEditingAttachments = false
```

5. In `cellForItemAt`, set the `editMode` property of `AttachmentCell` to `true` if the view controller is in Edit mode:

```swift
func collectionView(_ collectionView: UICollectionView,
    cellForItemAt indexPath: IndexPath) -> UICollectionViewCell {

    // Work out how many cells we need to display
    let totalNumberOfCells =
        collectionView.numberOfItems(inSection: indexPath.section)

    // Figure out if we're being asked to configure the Add cell,
    // or any other cell. If we're the last cell, it's the Add cell.
    let isAddCell = indexPath.row == (totalNumberOfCells - 1)

    // The place to store the cell. By making it 'let', we're ensuring
    // that we never accidentally fail to give it a value - the
    // compiler will call us out.
    let cell : UICollectionViewCell

    // Create and return the 'Add' cell if we need to
    if isAddCell {
        cell = collectionView.dequeueReusableCell(
            withReuseIdentifier: "AddAttachmentCell", for: indexPath)
    } else {

        // This is a regular attachment cell

        // Get the cell
        let attachmentCell = collectionView
            .dequeueReusableCell(withReuseIdentifier: "AttachmentCell",
                for: indexPath) as! AttachmentCell

        // Get a thumbnail image for the attachment
        let attachment = self.document?.attachedFiles?[indexPath.row]
        var image = attachment?.thumbnailImage()

        // Give it to the cell
        if image == nil {

            // We don't know what it is, so use a generic image
            image = UIImage(named: "File")
```

```
                    // Also set the label
                    attachmentCell.extensionLabel?.text =
                        attachment?.fileExtension?.uppercased()

                } else {
                    // We know what it is, so ensure that the label is empty
                    attachmentCell.extensionLabel?.text = nil
                }
                attachmentCell.imageView?.image = image

>               // The cell should be in edit mode if the view controller is
>               attachmentCell.editMode = isEditingAttachments
>
                // Use this cell
                cell = attachmentCell
            }

        return cell

    }
```

This ensures that all newly created attachment cells have their deletion button's
visibility correctly set.

6. Add the beginEditMode action method; this makes all visible cells enter their
   Edit mode and adds a Done button to the navigation bar:

```
func beginEditMode() {

    self.isEditingAttachments = true

    UIView.animate(withDuration: 0.1, animations: { () -> Void in
        for cell in self.attachmentsCollectionView!.visibleCells {

            if let attachmentCell = cell as? AttachmentCell {
                attachmentCell.editMode = true
            } else {
                cell.alpha = 0
            }
        }
    })

    let doneButton = UIBarButtonItem(barButtonSystemItem:
        UIBarButtonSystemItem.done, target: self,
                action: #selector(DocumentViewController.endEditMode))
    self.navigationItem.rightBarButtonItem = doneButton

}
```

This does three things. First, it causes every attachment cell to change its Edit mode, causing its delete button to appear. At the same time, it causes every *non*-attachment cell (that is, the *add* cell) to fade out to nothing.

Finally, it creates and adds a new bar button item, labeled Done, which calls the endEditMode method that we're about to add. It places it at the righthand side of the navigation bar.

7. Add the endEditMode method:

```
func endEditMode() {

    self.isEditingAttachments = false

    UIView.animate(withDuration: 0.1, animations: { () -> Void in
        for cell in self.attachmentsCollectionView!.visibleCells {

            if let attachmentCell = cell as? AttachmentCell {
                attachmentCell.editMode = false
            } else {
                cell.alpha = 1
            }
        }
    })

    self.navigationItem.rightBarButtonItem = nil
}
```

This method does the reverse of the beginEditMode method by making all visible AttachmentCells leave Edit mode, ensuring the add cell is visible, and removing the Done button.

8. Add code at the start of didSelectItemAt to ensure that we don't try to view an attachment if we're in Edit mode:

```
// Do nothing if we are editing
if self.isEditingAttachments {
    return
}
```

Next, we'll add the button to the AttachmentCell, which will appear when the cell enters Edit mode (that is, when the user long-presses it):

1. Open *Main.storyboard*, and locate the AttachmentCell in the document view controller.

2. Drag a UIButton into the AttachmentCell.

3. Go to the Attributes Inspector and change its type to Custom.

4. Remove the button's label and set the image to Delete (Figure 11-3).

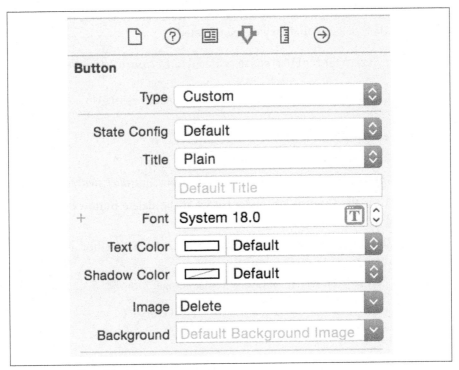

Figure 11-3. The delete button

5. Position the button at the top right of the cell, and add constraints that pin the top and right edges to the container.

6. Open *DocumentViewController.swift*, and locate the `AttachmentCell` class. Drag from the well next to the `deleteButton` outlet to the button you just added.

7. Hold down the Control key and drag from the `deleteButton` outlet to this button.

8. Add code in the `DocumentViewController`'s `collectionView(_, cellForItemAt indexPath:)` method to add a long-press gesture recognizer that enters Delete mode:

```
// The cell should be in edit mode if the view controller is
attachmentCell.editMode = isEditingAttachments

> // Add a long-press gesture to it, if it doesn't
> // already have it
> let longPressGesture = UILongPressGestureRecognizer(target: self,
>     action: #selector(DocumentViewController.beginEditMode))
> attachmentCell.gestureRecognizers = [longPressGesture]
```

Now we make the buttons actually delete stuff. We'll add a delegate protocol that lets cells notify their delegate that they've been deleted:

1. Add the `AttachmentCellDelegate` protocol to *DocumentViewController.swift*:

```
protocol AttachmentCellDelegate {
    func attachmentCellWasDeleted(_ cell: AttachmentCell)
}
```

2. Add the `delegate` property on `AttachmentCell`:

```
var delegate : AttachmentCellDelegate?
```

3. Open *Main.storyboard*, and open *DocumentViewController.swift* in the Assistant.

4. Hold down the Control key and drag from the delete button onto the `delete` method in the `AttachmentCell` class.

5. Open *Document.swift* and add the `deleteAttachment` method to the `Document` class, which removes an attachment:

```
func deleteAttachment(_ attachment:FileWrapper) throws {

    guard attachmentsDirectoryWrapper != nil else {
        throw err(.cannotAccessAttachments)
    }

    attachmentsDirectoryWrapper?.removeFileWrapper(attachment)

    self.updateChangeCount(.done)

}
```

6. Go back to *DocumentViewController.swift*, and add an extension to `Document` `ViewController` that conforms to `AttachmentCellDelegate`. We're adding this in an extension mostly to keep these methods visually separated in the code; it's purely a stylistic choice:

```
extension DocumentViewController : AttachmentCellDelegate {

    func attachmentCellWasDeleted(_ cell: AttachmentCell) {
        guard let indexPath = self.attachmentsCollectionView?
            .indexPath(for: cell) else {
            return
        }

        guard let attachment = self.document?
            .attachedFiles?[indexPath.row] else {
            return
        }
        do {
            try self.document?.deleteAttachment(attachment)
```

```
                  self.attachmentsCollectionView?
                      .deleteItems(at: [indexPath])

                  self.endEditMode()
              } catch let error as NSError {
                  NSLog("Failed to delete attachment: \(error)")
              }

          }
      }
```

7. Add code to collectionView(_, cellForItemAt indexPath:) that sets the cell's delegate to self:

```
// Add a long-press gesture to it, if it doesn't
// already have it
let longPressGesture = UILongPressGestureRecognizer(target: self,
    action: #selector(DocumentViewController.beginEditMode))
attachmentCell.gestureRecognizers = [longPressGesture]

> // Contact us when the user taps the delete button
> attachmentCell.delegate = self
```

8. Run the app—you can now delete attachments!

Conclusion

In this chapter, we created the interface that allows the user to create new attachments in the iOS version. We also added support for viewing images attached to note documents and the ability to remove attachments from Notes documents.

CHAPTER 12

Supporting the iOS Ecosystem

In this chapter, we'll add support for sharing, handoffs (so users can resume what they're doing on other iOS devices or in the macOS app), and search (so the iOS search system can be used to find text within note documents). All three of these features help to integrate your app into the wider context of the user's phone, which means that your app is no longer an island.

Sharing with UIActivityController

We'll start by adding sharing support to the image attachment view controller, as shown in Figure 12-1.

Figure 12-1. The standard iOS share sheet

Sharing on iOS is handled by `UIActivityViewController`, which provides a standard view controller offering system services, such as copy and paste, as well as sharing to social media, email, or text messaging. Other apps can also provide share destinations.

1. Open *Main.storyboard* and go to the image attachment view controller.

2. Add a `UIToolBar` from the Object library to the view and place it at the bottom of the screen. This will also include a `UIBarButtonItem`, which works pretty much exactly like our old friend `UIButton`, but is customized to work in toolbars.

3. Resize the toolbar to make it fit the width of the screen. Next, click the Pin menu, and pin the left, right, and bottom edges of the view. This will keep it at the bottom of the screen and make it always fill the width of the screen.

4. Select the button and set its System Item property to Action, as shown in Figure 12-2. This will change its icon to the standard iOS share icon.

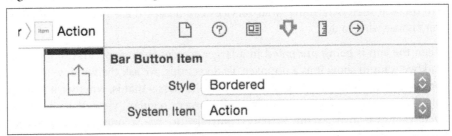

Figure 12-2. Setting the button to the Action mode

5. Open *ImageAttachmentViewController.swift* in the Assistant editor.

6. Hold down the Control key and drag from the toolbar button you just added into `ImageAttachmentViewController`. Create a new action called `shareImage`.

7. Add the following code to the `shareImage` method. Note that the type for the `sender` parameter is `UIBarButtonItem`—you'll need to change it when you start writing the code:

```
@IBAction func shareImage(_ sender: UIBarButtonItem) {

    // Ensure that we're actually showing an image
    guard let image = self.imageView?.image else {
        return
    }

    let activityController = UIActivityViewController(
        activityItems: [image], applicationActivities: nil)

    // If we are being presented in a window that's a Regular width,
    // show it in a popover (rather than the default modal)
    if UIApplication.shared.keyWindow?.traitCollection
        .horizontalSizeClass == UIUserInterfaceSizeClass.regular {
        activityController.modalPresentationStyle = .popover

        activityController.popoverPresentationController?
            .barButtonItem = sender
    }
```

```
        self.present(activityController, animated: true,
            completion: nil)
```

```
    }
```

When the share button is tapped, we want to prepare and present a `UIActivityCon` `troller`, which will allow the user to do something with the image. What that *something* actually is depends upon the capabilities of the system and the apps that the user has installed. To create it, you pass in an array of `activityItems`, which can be a wide variety of things: URLs, images, text, chunks of data, and so on. The `UIActivityCon` `troller` will then determine what services can accept these items, and then let the user choose what to do.

When the app is being presented in a larger screen, such as on an iPhone 6 Plus or iPad, we want to show it as a popover. To detect this, we ask the window in which the app is running to tell us about its horizontal *size class*—that is, whether it is in a horizontally "compact" view, or a horizontally larger "regular" view. If it's in a regular-sized view, we instruct the activity controller to use a popover, and we set the `barButtonItem` property on the `popoverPresentationController` to the `sender`, which will visually connect the popover to the share button in the toolbar.

Handoffs

Let's imagine that your user's on a bus, tapping out a note. She arrives at her stop, gets off the bus, and walks into the office, still writing the note. Eventually, she reaches her desk, and she wants to finish up the note. She *could* finish it up on the phone, but she's right in front of a dedicated workstation. Rather than deal with a tiny touchscreen, she instead uses *Handoff* to move her work from her phone to the desktop.

Handoff is a technology on the Mac, iOS, and watchOS that allows the user to start an activity on one device and seamlessly move to another device (see Figure 12-3). The way it works is this: applications register *activity types* with the system, which are simple text strings that are the same across all of the different apps that can receive the handoff. When the user opens a document, she marks it as the current *activity*; this makes the operating system broadcast this fact to all nearby devices. When the user decides to activate Handoff on another device, the originating device and the receiving device quickly swap information about what he wants to do, and the receiving device's app delegate is then given the opportunity to continue the activity.

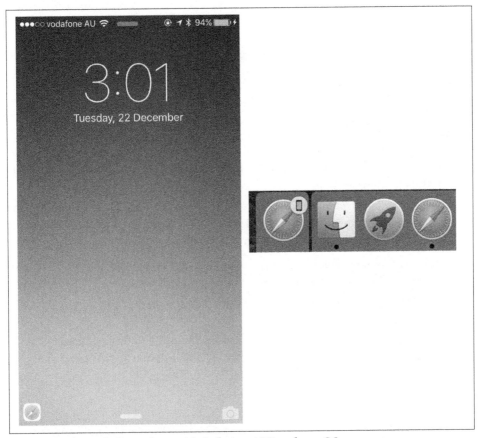

Figure 12-3. Handoffs working with Safari on iOS and macOS

Because we're using NSDocument and UIDocument, lots of the details of this get taken care of for you. If you weren't using the document system, you'd need to manually create your own NSUserActivity objects before calling becomeCurrent. For more information, see the Handoff Programming Guide (*http://bit.ly/handoff_program ming_guide*) in the Xcode documentation.

To get started using Handoff, we need to describe to the system the type of "activity" that is associated with editing this document. When we do this, the device will inform all other devices that belong to the same person that this specific document is being edited:

1. Select the project at the top of the Project Navigator (Figure 12-4).

Figure 12-4. Selecting the project in the Project Navigator

2. Go to the Notes target settings (that is, the macOS app) and scroll down to the Document Types section.

3. Add a new entry in "Additional document type properties" by expanding the "Additional document type properties" triangle, selecting the `CFBundleTypOS Types` entry, and clicking the + button that appears.

4. Call the new entry **NSUbiquitousDocumentUserActivityType** and set its type to `String`. Set its value to **au.com.secretlab.Notes.editing**.

5. Now go to the same place in Notes-iOS, and add the same entry.

 If you have been using a custom bundleID throughout, make sure you use that here with `.editing` appended at the end. If you don't do this, handoffs will not work.

Once you've done this, the two applications will associate a Handoff-able activity with their document types. When the document is open, the app will be able to simply say to the system, "Begin broadcasting the fact that this document is open."

6. Open the *AppDelegate.swift* file that belongs to the Notes-iOS target (not the macOS one!).

7. Implement the following method, which returns to the list of documents and then signals that that view controller should resume an activity:

```swift
func application(_ application: UIApplication,
    continue userActivity: NSUserActivity,
    restorationHandler: @escaping ([Any]?) -> Void) -> Bool {

    // Return to the list of documents
    if let navigationController =
        self.window?.rootViewController as? UINavigationController {

        navigationController.popToRootViewController(animated: false)
```

```
        // We're now at the list of documents; tell the restoration
        // system that this view controller needs to be informed
        // that we're continuing the activity
        if let topViewController = navigationController.topViewController {
            restorationHandler([topViewController])
        }

        return true
    }
    return false
}
```

The `continueUserActivity` method is called when the user has decided to hand off the activity from one device to the next. The `userActivity` object contains the information describing what the user wants to do, and this method is responsible for telling the app what needs to happen to let the user pick up from where the last device left off.

It does this through the `restorationHandler` closure that it receives as a parameter. This closure takes an array of objects that the app should call the `restoreU serActivityState` method on; this method receives the `NSUserActivity` as a parameter, which can be used to continue the state.

The reason for doing this is to move as much of the logic that drives the continuation of the activity to the view controllers, instead of making the app delegate have to know about the details of how documents get opened.

The way that we'll handle this in this app is to return to the `DocumentListView Controller`, and then indicate that the view controller should be told about the handoff by passing it to the `restorationHandler`.

8. Open *DocumentListViewController.swift*.

9. Add the following method to the `DocumentListViewController` class:

```
override func restoreUserActivityState(_ activity: NSUserActivity) {
    // We're being told to open a document

    if let url = activity.userInfo?[NSUserActivityDocumentURLKey] as? URL {

        // Open the document
        self.performSegue(withIdentifier: "ShowDocument", sender: url)
    }

}
```

This method is called as a result of passing the `DocumentListViewController` to the `restorationHandler` in `continueUserActivity`. Here, we extract the URL for the document that the user wants to open by getting it from the `NSUserActiv ity`'s `userInfo` dictionary, and then performing the `ShowDocument` segue, passing in the URL to open. This means that when the application is launched through the Handoff system, the document list will immediately open the document that the user wants.

10. Finally, add the following code to the `viewWillAppear` method of `DocumentView Controller` to make the activity current:

```
// If this document is not already open, open it
if document.documentState.contains(UIDocumentState.closed) {
    document.open { (success) -> Void in
        if success == true {
            self.textView?.attributedText = document.text

            self.attachmentsCollectionView?.reloadData()

>           // We are now engaged in this activity
>           document.userActivity?.becomeCurrent()

            // Register for state change notifications
            self.stateChangedObserver = Notification.default
    .addObserver(
                forName: NSNotification.Name.UIDocumentStateChanged,
                object: document,
                queue: nil,
                using: { (notification) -> Void in
                self.documentStateChanged()
            })

            self.documentStateChanged()

    }
```

Every `UIDocument` has an `NSUserActivity`. To indicate to the system, and to every other device that the user owns, that the user's current task is editing this document, we call `becomeCurrent` on the document's `userActivity`. This causes the current device to broadcast to all other devices in range, letting them know that we're offering to hand off this activity.

You can now test handoffs. Launch the iOS app on your phone, and then launch the macOS app. Open a document on your phone, and a Handoff icon will appear at the left of the dock on your Mac, as shown in Figure 12-5.

Figure 12-5. Handoff on macOS

The reverse will also work on iOS: open a document on your Mac, and the iOS app's icon will appear on the lock screen (Figure 12-6).

Figure 12-6. Handoff on iOS—the handoff icon is shown in the bottom-left corner

Searchability

Spotlight, shown in Figure 12-7, is iOS's built-in searching system. When you pull down on the icons on the home screen, you enter Spotlight, where you can type and search for content inside your device and on the web.

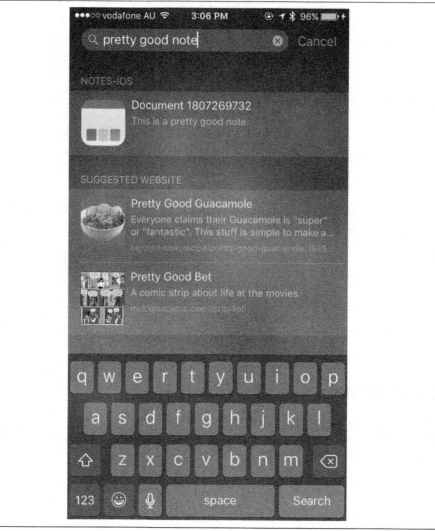

Figure 12-7. Searching with Spotlight on iOS

The next feature we'll add is the ability for users to search the phone to find documents that they've written. There are three different searching technologies that we can use to support this: NSUserActivity objects, Core Spotlight, and web indexing:

- NSUserActivity allows you to index parts of your app—for example, if you have an app that downloads and shows recipes, every time the user views a recipe, you record that as an activity and describe how to get back to this screen; Spotlight indexes this activity and displays it if the user searches for things that match the activity's description.

- Core Spotlight gives you control over the search index: you manually submit metadata items into the index. We'll be covering using Core Spotlight in "Indexing Activities" on page 329.
- Web indexing allows you to mark up websites for Apple's search crawler to view.

 Because we're not building web apps in this book, we won't be covering web archiving. If you're interested in it, you can read more about it in the App Search Programming Guide (*http://apple.co/ 22UCur2*), in the Xcode documentation.

We'll be covering marking `NSUserActivity` objects as searchable in this chapter. We'll also talk about creating a Spotlight indexing extension, which provides additional search functionality by registering the contents of *all* documents in the app with Core Spotlight.

Indexing Activities

We'll start by adding support for indexing the app through `NSUserActivity`:

1. Open *DocumentViewController.swift*.

2. Import the Core Spotlight framework at the top of the file:

   ```
   import CoreSpotlight
   ```

3. Update the `viewWillAppear` method to add searchable metadata to the document's user activity when the document is opened:

   ```
   // If this document is not already open, open it
   if document.documentState.contains(UIDocumentState.closed) {
       document.open { (success) -> Void in
           if success == true {
               self.textView?.attributedText = document.text

               self.attachmentsCollectionView?.reloadData()

               // Add support for searching for this document
               document.userActivity?.title = document.localizedName

               let contentAttributeSet
                   = CSSearchableItemAttributeSet(
                       itemContentType: document.fileType!)

               contentAttributeSet.title = document.localizedName
               contentAttributeSet.contentDescription = document.text.string

               document.userActivity?.contentAttributeSet
   ```

```
>                    = contentAttributeSet
>
>              document.userActivity?.isEligibleForSearch = true

              // We are now engaged in this activity
              document.userActivity?.becomeCurrent()

              // Register for state change notifications
              self.stateChangedObserver = Notification.default
    .addObserver(
                  forName: NSNotification.Name.UIDocumentStateChanged,
                  object: document,
                  queue: nil,
                  using: { (notification) -> Void in
                  self.documentStateChanged()
              })

              self.documentStateChanged()

          }
```

This code adds further metadata to the document's userActivity. First, it provides a name for the document, which will appear in the Spotlight search results. In addition, we create a CSSearchableItemAttributeSet, which is the (overcomplicated) term for "stuff the search system uses to decide if it's what the user's looking for." In this case, we provide two pieces of information: the name again and the text of the document.

We then provide this to the userActivity and mark it as available for searching.

You can now test searching. Run the app and open a document. Type some words into the document, close the app, and go to the Search field (swipe down while on the home screen). Type in some of the words that you added to the document, and your document will appear! When you tap the search result, the app will launch, and you'll be taken to the document.

Spotlight Extensions

If you want your app's contents to appear in Spotlight, you need to add information about that content to the *searchable index*. The searchable index is the search database used to locate everything on the device; if it's not in the index, it won't appear when you search for it.

In "Searchability" on page 327, we added some initial support for searchability by marking the NSUserActivities that represent the documents as searchable. However, the limitation of this is that documents only become searchable when they're

---

opened, and if users change their content on another device, the search index won't get updated to reflect their new contents until they're opened.

To address this, we'll add a Spotlight indexing app extension. This is periodically awakened by the system and asked to update the searchable index. The specifics of what this involves are entirely up to your app; in our case, we'll scan the entire collection of documents.

App Extensions

An app extension is a program that's embedded in an app and used by the system for some auxiliary role. There are many different app extension types available, in addition to the Spotlight extension that we're adding in this chapter:

Action extension
> Appear as entries in a `UIActivityController`, allowing your app to receive and process content. Dropbox's "Save to Dropbox" feature is an action extension.

Audio unit extensions
> Allow an app to provide an *audio unit*, which is a plug-in that audio-processing apps can use to generate, modify, or receive audio.

Content blocker extensions
> Allow an app to provide a list of URLs and URL patterns from which Safari will refuse to load resources. Content blockers are primarily designed to let apps provide ad-blocking functionality to Safari by filtering out content from specific sites, such as ads hosted on ad-providing servers.

Custom keyboard extensions
> Allow your app to provide an entirely customized keyboard for the user to use. A famous example is the gesture-driven keyboard Swype.

Document providers
> Allow other applications to access files stored in your app's sandbox. For example, the Git version control app Working Copy allows other applications to access files under its control and make changes.

Photo editing extensions
> Loaded by the Photos application and can be used to create a processed version of a photo in the user's photo library. The app Waterlogue is an excellent example of this: users can create a watercolor version of any photo without having to leave the Photos app.

Share extensions
> Closely related to action extensions and allow your app to receive content for sharing. The Twitter, Facebook, and Pinterest apps all provide share extensions.

Shared Links extensions

Allow apps to place links in the Safari "Shared Links" section. For example, the Twitter app provides one of these extensions, which makes any links from people you follow appear in Safari.

Let's get started by adding the extension to the project:

1. Open the File menu, and choose New→Target.

2. Choose iOS→Application Extension→Spotlight Index Extension (see Figure 12-8).

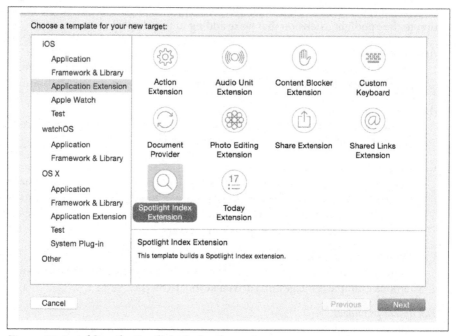

Figure 12-8. Adding the Spotlight Index Extension target

The reason we're adding a new target is because extensions are technically entirely separate programs, which means they're compiled and linked separately from their container application.

3. Name the new target **Notes-SpotlightIndexer**.

Once you click Finish, Xcode will pop up a little window asking if you want to activate the new scheme created. When you created the Spotlight extension, Xcode also made a new scheme for us to use to build the extension.

4. Click Activate to move to the new scheme.

We now need to give the extension access to the iCloud container, because to access the user's documents, we need access to the container in which they're located:

1. Go to the target's properties and then the Capabilities tab.

2. Turn on iCloud and wait for it to finish spinning.

3. Turn on iCloud Documents.

4. Select the iCloud container used by the Mac and iOS apps, and ensure that no other container is selected. To do this, change "Use default container" to "Specify custom container."

The extension now has permission to access the container.

Next, we need to ensure that the Notes-SpotlightIndexer target is able to use the enumeration that defines the names of important files:

1. Open the *DocumentCommon.swift* file, and open the File Inspector by choosing View→Utilities→Show File Inspector.

2. Ensure that the checkbox next to "Notes-SpotlightIndexer" is selected (Figure 12-9).

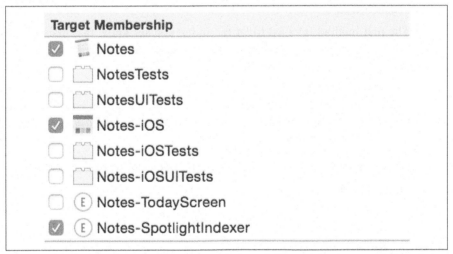

Figure 12-9. Adding the DocumentCommon.swift file to the Notes-SpotlightIndexer target

The order of the list of targets in your project might look slightly different. This is OK, as long as the file is added to the right targets.

Next, we'll implement the Spotlight indexer itself:

1. Open *IndexRequestHandler.swift*, which was created when you added the target —it's provided as part of the template code that Xcode generates. This file implements the core functionality of the indexer by implementing the `IndexReques tHandler` class.

2. Add the following line of code to the top of the file:

```
import UIKit
```

There are two main methods in the index request handler:

- `searchableIndex(_,reindexAllSearchableItemsWithAcknowledgementHandler:)`

- `searchableIndex(_,reindexSearchableItemsWithIdentifiers:, acknowledgementHandler:)`

The first method is called to let the index updater know that it should rescan the entire collection of data and add it to Spotlight. The second is called to let the updater know that it should rescan certain specific files.

To allow the extension to function, we first need to be able to get the collection of all documents known to the app. To do this, we'll implement a computed property that looks for all documents, in both the local *Documents* folder and in the iCloud container.

3. Add the following computed property to the `IndexRequestHandler` class:

```
var availableFiles : [URL] {

    let fileManager = FileManager.default

    var allFiles : [URL] = []

    // Get the list of all local files
    if let localDocumentsFolder
        = fileManager.urls(for: .documentDirectory,
            in: .userDomainMask).first {
        do {

            let localFiles = try fileManager
                .contentsOfDirectory(atPath: localDocumentsFolder.path)
                .map({
```

```
                localDocumentsFolder.appendingPathComponent($0,
                    isDirectory: false)
            })

        allFiles.append(contentsOf: localFiles)
    } catch {
        NSLog("Failed to get list of local files!")
    }
}

// Get the list of documents in iCloud
if let documentsFolder = fileManager
    .url(forUbiquityContainerIdentifier: nil)?
    .appendingPathComponent("Documents", isDirectory: true) {
    do {

        // Get the list of files
        let iCloudFiles = try fileManager
            .contentsOfDirectory(atPath: documentsFolder.path)
            .map({
                documentsFolder.appendingPathComponent($0,
                    isDirectory: false)
            })

        allFiles.append(contentsOf: iCloudFiles)

    } catch  {
        // Log an error and return the empty array
        NSLog("Failed to get contents of iCloud container")
        return []
    }

}

// Filter these to only those that end in ".note",
// and return NSURLs of these

return allFiles
    .filter({ $0.lastPathComponent.hasSuffix(".note") })


}
```

This method builds an array of URL objects, first by looking in the local *Documents* folder, and second by accessing the iCloud folder if it's able to. It then filters this array to include only files ending in *.note*.

Each document that we want to add to the index needs to be represented by a CSSearchableItem object. This object contains the actual information that will be added to the Spotlight index and contains three critical pieces of information: the title of the document, its contents, and its URL.

4. Add the following method to `IndexRequestHandler`:

```swift
func itemForURL(_ url: URL) -> CSSearchableItem? {

    // If this URL doesn't exist, return nil
    if (url as NSURL).checkResourceIsReachableAndReturnError(nil) == false
{
        return nil
    }

    // Replace this with your own type identifier
    let attributeSet = CSSearchableItemAttributeSet(
        itemContentType: "au.com.secretlab.Note")

    attributeSet.title = url.lastPathComponent

    // Get the text in this file
    let textFileURL = url.appendingPathComponent(
        NoteDocumentFileNames.TextFile.rawValue)

    if let textData = try? Data(contentsOf: textFileURL),
        let text = try? NSAttributedString(data: textData,
            options:
    [NSDocumentTypeDocumentAttribute: NSRTFTextDocumentType],
            documentAttributes: nil) {

            attributeSet.contentDescription = text.string

    } else {
        attributeSet.contentDescription = ""
    }

    let item =
        CSSearchableItem(uniqueIdentifier: url.absoluteString,
        domainIdentifier: "au.com.secretlab.Notes",
        attributeSet: attributeSet)

    return item
}
```

You'll need to change the `domainIdentifier` from `au.com.secretlab.Notes` to your own app's bundle identifier.

This method generates a `CSSearchableItem` for a given URL. It does this by attempting to reach into the document and extract the text content from the *Text.rtf* file it contains. It then combines this with the document's name and its

URL, which it uses as the searchable item's unique identifier, and returns the item. If the file that the URL points to doesn't exist, it returns nil.

Next, we need to implement the method that updates the entire index. This method is passed an acknowledgementHandler parameter, which is a closure that the method needs to call when the work of updating the index is complete.

 This method, and the reindexSearchableItemsWithIdentifiers method, *must* call the acknowledgementHandler. If it doesn't, then iOS will assume that the attempt to update the index has failed.

1. Delete the searchableIndex(_, reindexAllSearchableItemsWithAcknowledge mentHandler:) method, and replace it with the following code:

```
override func searchableIndex(_ searchableIndex: CSSearchableIndex,
    reindexAllSearchableItemsWithAcknowledgementHandler
        acknowledgementHandler: @escaping () -> Void) {

    // Reindex all data with the provided index

    let files = availableFiles

    var allItems : [CSSearchableItem] = []

    for file in files {
        if let item = itemForURL(file) {
            allItems.append(item)
        }
    }

    searchableIndex.indexSearchableItems(allItems) { (error) -> Void in
        acknowledgementHandler()
    }

}
```

This method simply gets the list of all available files and creates a CSSearchableI tem for them. It then provides this list of searchable items to the index; when this is complete, a closure is run that calls the acknowledgementHandler.

Finally, we need to implement the method that takes a specific set of CSSearcha bleItems and refreshes the index with their contents.

2. Delete the searchableIndex(_, reindexSearchableItemsWithIdentifiers:, acknowledgementHandler:) method, and replace it with the following code:

```
override func searchableIndex(_ searchableIndex: CSSearchableIndex,
            reindexSearchableItemsWithIdentifiers identifiers: [String],
                    acknowledgementHandler: @escaping () -> Void) {

    // Reindex any items with the given identifiers and the provided index

    var itemsToIndex : [CSSearchableItem] = []
    var itemsToRemove : [String] = []

    for identifier in identifiers {

        if let url = URL(string: identifier), let item = itemForURL(url) {
            itemsToIndex.append(item)
        } else {
            itemsToRemove.append(identifier)
        }
    }

    searchableIndex.indexSearchableItems(itemsToIndex) { (error) -> Void in
        searchableIndex
            .deleteSearchableItems(withIdentifiers: itemsToRemove) {
                (error) -> Void in
                acknowledgementHandler()
            }
    }

}
```

When this method is called, it receives a list of identifiers for CSSearchableI
tems. Because the identifiers are URLs, we can use them to access the specific
documents that need reindexing. To reindex a document, we just generate a new
CSSearchableItem with the same identifier; when it's submitted to the indexer, it
will replace the older one.

We also need to use this opportunity to remove items from the index. If the user has
deleted a document, we need to remove its corresponding entry from the index. We
do this by detecting when we fail to create a CSSearchableItem; if we do, then the
document is missing, and we add the document's identifier to a list of items to
remove.

Finally, we'll make the app capable of opening documents after the user has selected
them:

1. Open *DocumentListViewController.swift*.

2. Import the Core Spotlight framework at the top of the file:

   ```
   import CoreSpotlight
   ```

3. Add the following code to the restoreUserActivityState method:

```
override func restoreUserActivityState(_ activity: NSUserActivity) {
    // We're being told to open a document

    if let url = activity.userInfo?[NSUserActivityDocumentURLKey] as? URL {

        // Open the document
        self.performSegue(withIdentifier: "ShowDocument", sender: url)
    }
    // We're coming from a search result
    if let searchableItemIdentifier = activity
            .userInfo?[CSSearchableItemActivityIdentifier] as? String,
        let url = URL(string: searchableItemIdentifier) {
        // Open the document
        self.performSegue(withIdentifier: "ShowDocument", sender: url)
    }

}
```

When the user taps a search result in Spotlight, the app is launched just as if the user used Handoff (see Figure 12-10): an NSUserActivity is given to the app delegate's continueUserActivity method, which summons the document list. The document list, in its restoreUserActivityState method, can then check to see if the activity is actually a search result. If it is, we get the result's identifier, using the CSSearchableItemActivityIdentifier key. Remember that this is a URL, so we can immediately load it.

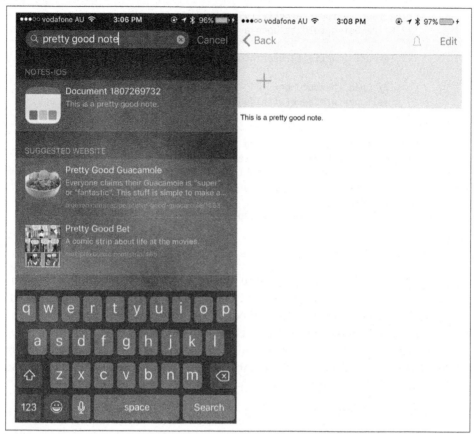

Figure 12-10. Search results and a corresponding note open in the app

You're done! The app will now periodically index all of its documents, making them appear in the search results.

Low Power Mode

The indexing extension will run in the background, even when the phone is locked. This means that the app is consuming power, which can be a problem when the battery is low.

Low power mode is a feature of iOS, introduced in iOS 9, that helps to extend the available battery power of the device by disabling as many features as it can, while still preserving basic device operation. When enabled, low power mode disables:

- Background apps
- Background mail fetch
- Certain animated UI elements and visual effects

iOS devices will automatically offer to enter low power mode when they hit 20% battery, but users can choose to activate it at any time in Settings.

Your application should respect a user's low power mode settings and postpone any CPU- or network-intensive operations until low power mode is turned off. To do this, listen for `NSProcessInfoPowerStateDidChangeNotification` notifications, in this case by adding a new observer to our app's `NSNotificationCenter`.

When our selector method is called, we can then check if `NSProcessInfo.processInfo().lowPowerModeEnabled` is `true`, and take steps to reduce our power consumption if it is.

In the case of background-running extensions like the Spotlight indexing extension, you don't generally need to respond to low power mode, because iOS will simply not run the background extension while low power mode is active. However, it's useful to know about low power mode when your app is in the foreground.

Conclusion

When an application participates in the wider iOS ecosystem, it feels like it "belongs" on the user's device. When you take advantage of as many system features as possible, rather than reinventing new systems from whole cloth, it's more likely that users will consider your apps an indispensable part of their device use.

CHAPTER 13

Multimedia and Location Attachments

In this chapter, we'll improve the iOS app by adding more capabilities to the attachment system. We'll add support for audio and video attachments as well as an attachment to store where the note was created.

In Notes, each attachment is represented by a file that's added to the document's *Attachments* directory and is managed by a view controller. Because of the architecture of the application, all we need to do to add support for different attachment types is to create a new view controller for it and add code to a couple of existing methods in `DocumentListViewController` to make them open the necessary view controller for each attachment type.

Let's get started by building support for adding audio attachments.

Audio Attachments

This attachment we'll add gives us the ability to record audio and play it back. We'll do this by using the AVFoundation framework, which includes two classes: `AVAudio Recorder` will be used to record the audio, and `AVAudioPlayer` will be used to play it back.

 We're just scratching the surface of the iOS audio capabilities. You can learn more about the audio frameworks on iOS in Apple's documentation (*http://apple.co/22UK1pM*).

First, we'll add some icons that will be needed for this additional screen:

1. Open *Assets.xcassets*.

2. Add the Audio, Record, Play, and Stop icons to the asset catalog.

Next, we'll add an entry to the list of attachment types for audio:

1. Add the following code to the `addAttachment` method:

```
func addAttachment(_ sourceView : UIView) {

    let title = "Add attachment"

    let actionSheet
        = UIAlertController(title: title,
                            message: nil,
                            preferredStyle: UIAlertControllerStyle
                                .actionSheet)

    // If a camera is available to use...
    if UIImagePickerController
        .isSourceTypeAvailable(UIImagePickerControllerSourceType.camera) {
        // This variable contains a closure that shows the image picker,
        // or asks the user to grant permission.
        var handler : (_ action:UIAlertAction) -> Void

        let authorizationStatus = AVCaptureDevice
            .authorizationStatus(forMediaType: AVMediaTypeVideo)

        switch authorizationStatus {
        case .authorized:
            fallthrough
        case .notDetermined:
            // If we have permission, or we don't know if it's been denied,
            // then the closure shows the image picker.
            handler = { (action) in
                self.addPhoto()
            }
        default:

            // Otherwise, when the button is tapped, ask for permission.
            handler = { (action) in

                let title = "Camera access required"
                let message = "Go to Settings to grant permission to" +
                    "access the camera."
                let cancelButton = "Cancel"
                let settingsButton = "Settings"

                let alert = UIAlertController(title: title,
                    message: message,
                    preferredStyle: .alert)
```

```
                // The Cancel button just closes the alert.
                alert.addAction(UIAlertAction(title: cancelButton,
                    style: .cancel, handler: nil))

                // The Settings button opens this app's settings page,
                // allowing the user to grant us permission.
                alert.addAction(UIAlertAction(title: settingsButton,
                    style: .default, handler: { (action) in

                        if let settingsURL = URL(
                            string: UIApplicationOpenSettingsURLString) {

                            UIApplication.shared
                                .openURL(settingsURL)
                        }

                }))

                self.present(alert,
                        animated: true,
                        completion: nil)
            }
        }

        // Either way, show the Camera item; when it's selected, the
        // appropriate code will run.
        actionSheet.addAction(UIAlertAction(title: "Camera",
            style: UIAlertActionStyle.default, handler: handler))
    }

>   actionSheet.addAction(UIAlertAction(title: "Audio",
>       style: UIAlertActionStyle.default, handler: { (action) -> Void in
>       self.addAudio()
>   }))

    actionSheet.addAction(UIAlertAction(title: "Cancel",
        style: UIAlertActionStyle.cancel, handler: nil))

    // If this is on an iPad, present it in a popover connected
    // to the source view
    if UI_USER_INTERFACE_IDIOM() == UIUserInterfaceIdiom.pad {

        actionSheet.modalPresentationStyle
            = .popover
        actionSheet.popoverPresentationController?.sourceView
            = sourceView
        actionSheet.popoverPresentationController?.sourceRect
            = sourceView.bounds
    }
```

```
        self.present(actionSheet, animated: true, completion: nil)
    }
```

Just like when we added support for photo attachments, we also need to add a new entry for audio attachments.

2. Add the `addAudio` method to `DocumentViewController`:

```
func addAudio() {
    self.performSegue(withIdentifier: "ShowAudioAttachment", sender: nil)
}
```

Additionally, we need to trigger the right segue when the user decides to add an audio attachment.

3. Open the File menu and choose New→File.

4. Create a new `UIViewController` subclass named `AudioAttachmentViewController`.

5. Open *AudioAttachmentViewController.swift*.

6. Import the `AVFoundation` framework into view controller; this framework includes everything we could possibly need for loading, playing, and pausing audio and video content.

7. Make `AudioAttachmentViewController` conform to the `AttachmentViewer` and `AVAudioPlayerDelegate` protocols:

```
class AudioAttachmentViewController: UIViewController, AttachmentViewer,
        AVAudioPlayerDelegate
```

8. Add the `attachmentFile` and `document` properties, which are required by the `AttachmentViewer` protocol:

```
var attachmentFile : FileWrapper?
var document : Document?
```

9. Add outlet properties for the record, play, and stop buttons that we're about to add:

```
@IBOutlet weak var stopButton: UIButton!
@IBOutlet weak var playButton: UIButton!
@IBOutlet weak var recordButton: UIButton!
```

10. Finally, add an audio player and audio recorder:

```
var audioPlayer : AVAudioPlayer?
var audioRecorder : AVAudioRecorder?
```

Time to create the user interface!

11. Open *Main.storyboard*.

12. Drag in a new view controller, and set its class to `AudioAttachmentViewControl`ler in the Identity Inspector.

13. Hold down the Control key and drag from the document view controller to this new view controller. Choose "popover" from the list of segue types:

    - Set the newly created segue's Anchor View to the document view controller's view.

    - Set the identifier for this segue to `ShowAudioAttachment`.

      We'll use a stack view to manage the three different buttons. Only one of them will appear at a time, and we want the currently visible button to appear in the center of the screen. Rather than overlay the buttons, we'll put them all in a centered stack view.

14. Search for `UIStackView` in the Object library and drag a vertical stack view into the audio attachment view controller's interface (Figure 13-1).

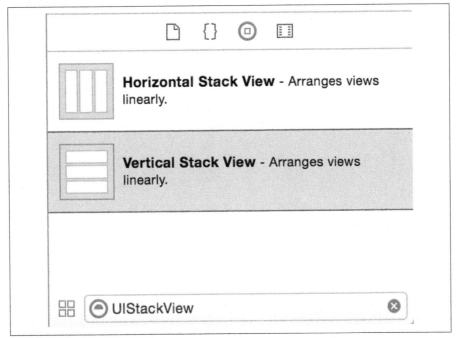

Figure 13-1. A vertical stack view

15. Center the stack view in the screen. Next, click the Align button at the lower-right corner, and turn on both "Horizontally in container" and "Vertically in container." Click Add 2 Constraints; this will add centering constraints to the stack view.

16. Drag a new `UIButton` into the stack view. In the Attributes Inspector, set type to Custom, delete the label text, and set image to Record.

 The stack view will resize to match the size of the button when you add the button. This is expected!

17. Repeat this process, adding two more buttons, with Play and Stop icons.

When you're done, the stack view should look like Figure 13-2.

Figure 13-2. The view controller's interface

The order of the buttons doesn't matter, so if you added the buttons in different positions and you like that, stick with it.

18. Next, connect each button to its corresponding outlet; the record button should be connected to `recordButton`, and so on for the rest.

19. Connect each button to new actions in `AudioAttachmentViewController`, called `recordTapped`, `playTapped`, and `stopTapped`:

```
@IBAction func recordTapped(_ sender: AnyObject) {
    beginRecording()
}
@IBAction func playTapped(_ sender: AnyObject) {
    beginPlaying()
}
@IBAction func stopTapped(_ sender: AnyObject) {
    stopRecording()
    stopPlaying()
}
```

These methods simply respond to the buttons being tapped. The stop button serves a dual purpose—when tapped, it stops both the recorder and the player.

20. Implement the `updateButtonState` method:

```
func updateButtonState() {
    if self.audioRecorder?.isRecording == true ||
        self.audioPlayer?.isPlaying == true {

        // We are either recording or playing, so
        // show the stop button
        self.recordButton.isHidden = true
        self.playButton.isHidden = true

        self.stopButton.isHidden = false
    } else if self.audioPlayer != nil {

        // We have a recording ready to go
        self.recordButton.isHidden = true
        self.stopButton.isHidden = true

        self.playButton.isHidden = false
    } else {

        // We have no recording.

        self.playButton.isHidden = true
        self.stopButton.isHidden = true
```

```
            self.recordButton.isHidden = false
        }

    }
```

The `updateButtonState` method is called from multiple places in this class. All it does is ensure that the right button is visible, based on whether the audio player is playing, or whether the audio recorder is recording.

21. Implement the `beginRecording` and `stopRecording` methods:

```
func beginRecording () {

    // Ensure that we have permission. If we don't,
    // we can't record, but should display a dialog that prompts
    // the user to change the settings.

    AVAudioSession.sharedInstance().requestRecordPermission {
        (hasPermission) -> Void in

        guard hasPermission else {

            // We don't have permission. Let the user know.
            let title = "Microphone access required"
            let message = "We need access to the microphone" +
                    "to record audio."
            let cancelButton = "Cancel"
            let settingsButton = "Settings"

            let alert = UIAlertController(title: title, message: message,
                preferredStyle: .alert)

            // The Cancel button just closes the alert.
            alert.addAction(UIAlertAction(title: cancelButton,
                style: .cancel, handler: nil))

            // The Settings button opens this app's settings page,
            // allowing the user to grant us permission.
            alert.addAction(UIAlertAction(title: settingsButton,
                style: .default, handler: { (action) in

                    if let settingsURL
                        = URL(string: UIApplicationOpenSettingsURLString) {
                        UIApplication.shared
                            .openURL(settingsURL)
                    }

            }))

            self.present(alert,
```

```
            animated: true,
            completion: nil)
        return
    }

    // We have permission!

    // Try to use the same filename as before, if possible

    let fileName = self.attachmentFile?.preferredFilename ??
    "Recording \(Int(arc4random())).wav"

    let temporaryURL = URL(fileURLWithPath: NSTemporaryDirectory())
        .appendingPathComponent(fileName)

    do {
        self.audioRecorder = try AVAudioRecorder(url: temporaryURL,
            settings: [:])

        self.audioRecorder?.record()
    } catch let error as NSError {
        NSLog("Failed to start recording: \(error)")
    }

    self.updateButtonState()
}

}
func stopRecording () {
    guard let recorder = self.audioRecorder else {
        return
    }
    recorder.stop()

    self.audioPlayer = try? AVAudioPlayer(contentsOf: recorder.url)

    updateButtonState()
}
```

The beginRecording method first determines if the user has granted permission
to access the microphone. If permission is *not* granted, we create and display an
alert box letting the user know that it's not possible to record. If it is, we create a
URL that points to a temporary location, and ask the audio recorder to begin
recording.

Much like what we had to do with the camera permissions, we need to set a specific key inside the applications info.plist—without this key-value pair, iOS
will refuse to let our app use the microphone. Inside info.plist add a new row
into the dictionary. Type **Privacy - Microphone Usage Description** for the

key and type a message you want to be displayed when the app first tries to use the microphone. We used **We'll use the microphone to record audio attachments**, but you should go with whatever works best for you.

You can't assume that the user has given permission to access the microphone. As a result, if you want to record audio, you need to first check if the app has permission by calling the AVSession method requestRecordPermission. This method takes a closure as a parameter, which receives as *its* parameter a bool value indicating whether the app has permission to record.

This closure may not be called immediately. If it's the first time the app has ever asked for permission, then iOS will ask if the user wants to grant your app permission. After the user answers, the closure will be called.

If you *really* need the user to grant permission, and it's been previously withheld, you can send the user to the app's Settings page, which contains the controls for granting permission. Be careful about annoying the user about this, though!

1. Implement the beginPlaying and stopPlaying methods:

```
func beginPlaying() {
    self.audioPlayer?.delegate = self
    self.audioPlayer?.play()

    updateButtonState()
}

func stopPlaying() {
    audioPlayer?.stop()

    updateButtonState()
}
```

The beginPlaying and stopPlaying methods are quite straightforward: they start and stop the audio player, and then call updateButtonState to ensure that the correct button is appearing. Importantly, beginPlaying also sets the delegate of the audio player so that the AudioAttachmentViewController receives a method call when the audio finishes playing.

2. Implement the prepareAudioPlayer method, which works out the location of the file to play from and prepares the audio player:

```
func prepareAudioPlayer() {

    guard let data = self.attachmentFile?.regularFileContents else {
```

```
        return
    }

    do {
        self.audioPlayer = try AVAudioPlayer(data: data)
    } catch let error as NSError {
        NSLog("Failed to prepare audio player: \(error)")
    }

    self.updateButtonState()

}
```

The prepareAudioPlayer method checks to see if the AudioAttachmentViewCon
troller has an attachment to work with; if it does, it attempts to create the audio
player, using the data stored inside the attachment.

3. Implement the audioPlayerDidFinishPlaying method, which is part of the
AVAudioPlayerDelegate protocol:

```
func audioPlayerDidFinishPlaying(_ player: AVAudioPlayer,
    successfully flag: Bool) {
    updateButtonState()
}
```

When the audio finishes playing, we have a very simple task to complete: we
update the state of the button. Because the audio player is no longer playing, it
will change from the "stop" symbol to the "play" symbol.

4. Finally, implement the viewDidLoad and viewWillDisappear methods:

```
override func viewDidLoad() {

    if attachmentFile != nil {
        prepareAudioPlayer()
    }

    // Indicate to the system that we will be both recording audio,
    // and also playing back audio
    do {
        try AVAudioSession.sharedInstance()
            .setCategory(AVAudioSessionCategoryPlayAndRecord)
    } catch let error as NSError {
        print("Error preparing for recording! \(error)")
    }

    updateButtonState()
}
override func viewWillDisappear(_ animated: Bool) {
    if let recorder = self.audioRecorder {
```

```
    // We have a recorder, which means we have a recording to attach
    do {
        attachmentFile =
            try self.document?.addAttachmentAtURL(recorder.url)

        prepareAudioPlayer()

    } catch let error as NSError {
        NSLog("Failed to attach recording: \(error)")
    }
}
```

The `viewDidLoad` method first gets the audio player prepared, if an audio attachment is present. It then signals to the system that the application will be both playing back and recording audio; this enables the microphone, and permits simultaneous use of the microphone and the speaker. Finally, it updates the button to whatever state is appropriate, depending on whether we have audio to play.

The `viewWillDisappear` method is responsible for saving any recorded audio. Because the `AVAudioRecorder` saves directly to a temporary URL, we simply need to copy it into the `Document` by calling `addAttachmentAtURL`.

Now we'll add support for working with audio attachments in the document view controller. First, we'll make the `Document` class return a suitable image for audio attachments, and then we'll make the `DocumentViewController` present the `AudioAttachmentViewController` when an audio attachment is tapped:

1. Open *Document.swift*, and add the following code to FileWrapper's thumbnail Image method:

```
func thumbnailImage() -> UIImage? {

    if self.conformsToType(kUTTypeImage) {
        // If it's an image, return it as a UIImage

        // Ensure that we can get the contents of the file
        guard let attachmentContent = self.regularFileContents else {
            return nil
        }

        // Attempt to convert the file's contents to text
        return UIImage(data: attachmentContent)
    }
>    if (self.conformsToType(kUTTypeAudio)) {
>        return UIImage(named: "Audio")
>    }
```

```
    // We don't know what type it is, so return nil
    return nil
}
```

All we're doing here is making the `FileWrapper` return the *Audio.pdf* image if it represents an audio file of any kind.

2. Open *DocumentViewController.swift*, and add the following code to `Document ViewController`'s `collectionView(_, didSelectItemAt indexPath:)` method:

```
func collectionView(_ collectionView: UICollectionView,
    didSelectItemAt indexPath: IndexPath) {

    // Do nothing if we are editing
    if self.isEditingAttachments {
        return
    }

    // Get the cell that the user interacted with; bail if we can't get it
    guard let selectedCell = collectionView
        .cellForItem(at: indexPath) else {
        return
    }

    // Work out how many cells we have
    let totalNumberOfCells = collectionView
        .numberOfItems(inSection: indexPath.section)

    // If we have selected the last cell, show the Add screen
    if indexPath.row == totalNumberOfCells - 1 {
        addAttachment(selectedCell)
    }
    else {
        // Otherwise, show a different view controller based on the type
        // of the attachment
        guard let attachment = self.document?
            .attachedFiles?[(indexPath as IndexPath).row] else {

            NSLog("No attachment for this cell!")
            return
        }

        let segueName : String?

        if attachment.conformsToType(kUTTypeImage) {
            segueName = "ShowImageAttachment"

        }
>       else if attachment.conformsToType(kUTTypeAudio) {
>           segueName = "ShowAudioAttachment"
>       }
```

```
        } else {

            // We have no view controller for this.
            // Instead, show a UIDocumentInteractionController

            self.document?.URLForAttachment(attachment,
                completion: { (url) -> Void in

                if let attachmentURL = url {
                    let documentInteraction
                      = UIDocumentInteractionController(url: attachmentURL)

                    documentInteraction
                      .presentOptionsMenu(from: selectedCell.bounds,
                          in: selectedCell, animated: true)
                }

            })

            segueName = nil
        }

        // If we have a segue, run it now
        if let theSegue = segueName {
            self.performSegue(withIdentifier: theSegue,
                sender: selectedCell)
        }

    }
}
```

Again, there's not a huge amount of stuff we need to add here; we simply need to run the ShowAudioAttachment segue when the user selects an audio attachment.

 Unfortunately, the simulator doesn't allow you to record audio, as it doesn't have any actual recording hardware. It will, however, allow you to play back any audio you recorded on other devices.

You can now add and play back audio attachments!

Video Attachments

iOS has extensive video capture abilities, so we're now going to add support for recording video to our app. Unlike with the first two types of attachments that we've implemented, we don't need to implement our own view controller; instead, we'll make use of iOS-provided view controllers. We'll make the UIImagePicker Controller—which we first mentioned back in "Adding Image Attachments" on page 293—record video, and we'll make use of a new view controller, AVPlayerViewCon troller, to actually play the video back:

1. First, we'll add an icon to represent this type of attachment. Open *Assets.xcassets* and add the Video icon to it.

2. Next, we'll add support to the Document class to make it return an image for videos. Open *Document.swift,* and add the following code to FileWrapper's thumb nailImage method:

```swift
func thumbnailImage() -> UIImage? {

    if self.conformsToType(kUTTypeImage) {
        // If it's an image, return it as a UIImage

        // Ensure that we can get the contents of the file
        guard let attachmentContent = self.regularFileContents else {
            return nil
        }

        // Attempt to convert the file's contents to text
        return UIImage(data: attachmentContent)
    }

    if (self.conformsToType(kUTTypeAudio)) {
        return UIImage(named: "Audio")
    }

>   if (self.conformsToType(kUTTypeMovie)) {
>       return UIImage(named: "Video")
>   }

    // We don't know what type it is, so return nil
    return nil
}
```

As you might have guessed, this detects whether the file wrapper is any type of movie, and returns the *Video.pdf* image you just added.

3. We'll now make changes to the addPhoto method that allows the user to record video in addition to taking photos. Open *DocumentViewController.swift* and add the following code to the addPhoto method:

```swift
func addPhoto() {
    let picker = UIImagePickerController()

    picker.sourceType = .camera
```

```
>     picker.mediaTypes = UIImagePickerController
>         .availableMediaTypes(
>             for: UIImagePickerControllerSourceType.camera)!

    picker.delegate = self

    self.shouldCloseOnDisappear = false

    self.present(picker, animated: true, completion: nil)
}
```

By default, a `UIImagePickerController` will only support taking photos—in the overwhelming majority of all use cases, that's all you need. However, you can control what types of media the image picker will accept by modifying the `medi aTypes` property. In this case, we're asking the image picker class for *all* types of media that the camera can produce, and then telling the image picker that we'll take them all.

4. Next, we'll make the document picker capable of detecting when the user recorded a video. If the user did, we get a URL that points at the recorded video, which means that we can add it as an attachment. Update the `imagePickerControl ler(_, didFinishPickingMediaWithInfo:)` method with the following code:

```
func imagePickerController(_ picker: UIImagePickerController,
    didFinishPickingMediaWithInfo info: [String : Any]) {
        do {

            let edited = UIImagePickerControllerEditedImage
            let original = UIImagePickerControllerOriginalImage
            if let image = (info[edited] as? UIImage
                ?? info[original] as? UIImage) {

                guard let imageData =
                    UIImageJPEGRepresentation(image, 0.8) else {
                    throw err(.cannotSaveAttachment)
                }

                try self.document?.addAttachmentWithData(imageData,
                    name: "Image \(arc4random()).jpg")

                self.attachmentsCollectionView?.reloadData()

>           } else if let mediaURL
>               = (info[UIImagePickerControllerMediaURL]) as? URL {
>
>               try self.document?.addAttachmentAtURL(mediaURL)
            } else {
                throw err(.cannotSaveAttachment)
            }
```

```
    } catch let error as NSError {
        NSLog("Error adding attachment: \(error)")
    }

    self.dismiss(animated: true, completion: nil)
}
```

When we first implemented the ability to take photos, we used the UIImagePick erControllerOriginalImage and UIImagePickerControllerEditedImage to retrieve the photo from the info dictionary. However, we now need to be able to get videos as well. We can detect if the user took a video by checking to see if there's any value in the info dictionary for the UIImagePickerControllerMe diaURL key. This URL points to the location on disk of the video the user took; this makes it extremely convenient, since we can then use it with the addAttach mentAtURL method to add the attachment.

5. Run the app—you can now capture video!

Next, we'll make it possible to view the recorded video. We'll do this by preparing a built-in view controller type, called AVPlayerViewController, and using that to show the video. This will also enable us to show the video in Picture in Picture mode, which lets users opt to view a video playing in their apps in a movable and resizeable window that sits on top of other content, allowing them to use other apps while they watch videos.

The AVPlayerViewController is the view controller used in the built-in Videos appli-cation. It's capable of playing any video format that iOS can natively play.

To work, AVPlayerViewController requires a URL that points to the video file the user wants to play. Up until now, we've been able to work directly with the data inside the attachment FileWrappers, but that won't work for video. Part of the reason for this is that video files can be *huge*—we don't want to have to load them into memory in the form of a Data in order to work with them.

We therefore need to be able to ask the Document class to provide us with a URL for a given attachment. This has a complication, however: if we ask for the URL for an attachment that has just been added, *before* the document is saved, then the attach-ment may not yet have been written to disk, which means it has no URL.

To solve this, we'll force the Document to save itself to disk before we attempt to get the URL. However, this has its *own* complication: saving the document is an asyn-chronous task, meaning that it might take some time to complete. Therefore, any method that asks for the URL of an attachment must *itself* be asynchronous: it needs to take a closure as a parameter that, after the document finishes saving, is called. This closure will receive as *its* parameter the URL for the attachment.

1. Open *Document.swift* and add the following method to the `Document` class:

```swift
// Given an attachment, eventually returns its URL, if possible.
// It might be nil if 1. this isn't one of our attachments or
// 2. we failed to save, in which case the attachment may not exist
// on disk.
func URLForAttachment(_ attachment: FileWrapper,
    completion: @escaping (URL?) -> Void) {

    // Ensure that this is an attachment we have
    guard let attachments = self.attachedFiles
            , attachments.contains(attachment) else {
        completion(nil)
        return
    }

    // Ensure that this attachment has a filename
    guard let fileName = attachment.preferredFilename else {
        completion(nil)
        return
    }

    self.autosave { (success) -> Void in
        if success {

            // We're now certain that attachments actually
            // exist on disk, so we can get their URL
            let attachmentURL = self.fileURL
                .appendingPathComponent(
                    NoteDocumentFileNames.AttachmentsDirectory.rawValue,
                    isDirectory: true).appendingPathComponent(fileName)

            completion(attachmentURL)

        } else {
            NSLog("Failed to autosave!")
            completion(nil)
        }
    }

}
```

Now that we can get the URL for an attachment, we can work with the `AVPlayer` `ViewController`.

2. Import the AVKit framework at the top of *DocumentViewController.swift*:

```swift
import AVKit
```

3. Update DocumentViewController's collectionView(_, didSelectItemAt indexPath:) method to show an AVPlayerViewController when a video attachment is tapped:

```swift
func collectionView(_ collectionView: UICollectionView,
    didSelectItemAt indexPath: IndexPath) {

    // Do nothing if we are editing
    if self.isEditingAttachments {
        return
    }

    // Get the cell that the user interacted with; bail if we can't get it
    guard let selectedCell = collectionView
        .cellForItem(at: indexPath) else {
        return
    }

    // Work out how many cells we have
    let totalNumberOfCells = collectionView
        .numberOfItems(inSection: indexPath.section)

    // If we have selected the last cell, show the Add screen
    if indexPath.row == totalNumberOfCells - 1 {
        addAttachment(selectedCell)
    }
    else {
        // Otherwise, show a different view controller based on the type
        // of the attachment
        guard let attachment = self.document?
            .attachedFiles?[(indexPath as IndexPath).row] else {

            NSLog("No attachment for this cell!")
            return
        }

        let segueName : String?

        if attachment.conformsToType(kUTTypeImage) {
            segueName = "ShowImageAttachment"

        }
        else if attachment.conformsToType(kUTTypeAudio) {
            segueName = "ShowAudioAttachment"
        }
>       else if attachment.conformsToType(kUTTypeMovie) {
>
>           self.document?.URLForAttachment(attachment,
>               completion: { (url) -> Void in
```

```
>
>                   if let attachmentURL = url {
>                       let media = AVPlayerViewController()
>                       media.player = AVPlayer(url: attachmentURL)
>
>                       self.present(media, animated: true,
>                           completion: nil)
>                   }
>           })
>
>           segueName = nil
        } else {

            // We have no view controller for this.
            // Instead, show a UIDocumentInteractionController

            self.document?.URLForAttachment(attachment,
                completion: { (url) -> Void in

                if let attachmentURL = url {
                    let documentInteraction
                        = UIDocumentInteractionController(url: attachmentURL)

                    documentInteraction
                        .presentOptionsMenu(from: selectedCell.bounds,
                            in: selectedCell, animated: true)
                }

            })

            segueName = nil
        }

        // If we have a segue, run it now
        if let theSegue = segueName {
            self.performSegue(withIdentifier: theSegue,
                sender: selectedCell)
        }

    }
  }
```

When the user selects a video, we don't actually want to use a segue to move to a view controller that we've made. Instead, we create a new `AVPlayerViewControl ler` and give it the URL of the attachment. We then manually present it, using `present(viewController:, animated:)`, and set `segueName` to `nil`, indicating that we don't want to actually run a segue. You can now tap videos and play them back.

Finally, we'll now enable support for Picture in Picture mode:

1. Go to the Notes-iOS target's Capabilities, and scroll down to the Background Modes section.

2. Turn on "Audio, AirPlay and Picture in Picture" (see Figure 13-3).

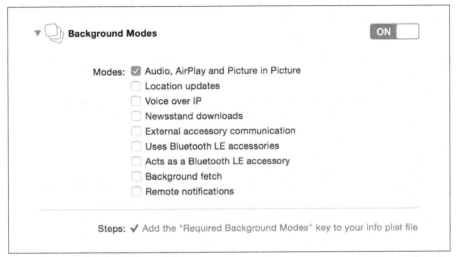

Figure 13-3. Enabling the "Audio, AirPlay and Picture in Picture" background mode

3. Finally, add the following line of code to the code you just added in didSelectItemAt indexPath:

```
else if attachment.conformsToType(kUTTypeMovie) {

    self.document?.URLForAttachment(attachment,
        completion: { (url) -> Void in

            if let attachmentURL = url {
                let media = AVPlayerViewController()
                media.player = AVPlayer(url: attachmentURL)

>               let _ = try? AVAudioSession.sharedInstance()
>                   .setCategory(AVAudioSessionCategoryPlayback)

                self.present(media, animated: true,
                    completion: nil)
            }
    })

    segueName = nil
```

By setting the application's audio session category to AVAudioSessionCategory Playback, you're indicating to the system that the application is simply playing back content. This will enable Picture in Picture mode for the player.

Users can now tap the Picture in Picture button while watching a video, and it will scale down into the corner. This view will stick around, even if they leave the app.

Location Attachment

iOS devices have a whole slew of clever sensors on them, and the one we care the most about now is the GPS. When it comes time to determine the location of the device, however, iOS doesn't rely solely on the GPS! It has a whole bag of tricks that allow it to more accurately and rapidly pinpoint a location.

The Core Location framework provides a whole suite of location-based features for you to use—everything from a quick and efficient way to get the current location, to monitoring entry and exit from specific regions, looking for Bluetooth beacons, to significant change location alerts.

We're only going to be using a tiny portion of the features of Core Location here. If you'd like to know more, check out Apple's Location and Maps Programming Guide (*http://apple.co/22UHNXD*).

There are three ways that iOS can figure out its location on the planet:

- Using the positioning radios, by receiving a GPS or GLONASS signal from orbiting satellites
- Using WiFi location, in which the iOS device uses a crowd-sourced database of hotspot physical locations; depending on the hotspots the device can see, the device can estimate where it is in the world
- Using cell towers, which work in essentially the same way as WiFi locations, but with towers that provide cellular phone and data coverage

The Core Location system is designed so you don't need to know the details of *how* the device is figuring out its location. Instead you simply ask the iOS device to start tracking the user's location, and it will provide it to you. It will use whatever hardware it thinks necessary, based on how precise a measurement you've asked for.

The user's location is private. Your app won't have access to it without user permission, and the user isn't required to give it to you. This means that any app that works with user location has to be prepared for the user saying no.

We'll now add the ability to attach locations to documents. The way location attachments work will be a little bit different from other attachments, as it doesn't really make a lot of sense to *add* a location to a note. Instead, much like what we did in the macOS application, we will set it up so that when creating a new note we will store the location it was created. This won't be an attachment like the images or audio attachments; rather, it will be its own special file inside the document. This means this attachment, unlike the others, will be read only, and we will view it as a pin on a map using MapKit.

 There are few standard file formats for storing location information, such as KML or GeoJSON, but they are both designed for features much larger than what we need, so we'll make our own. Our location attachments will just be a little JSON file that stores a latitude and longitude coordinate pair, following the same lines as the macOS app.

We'll be using MapKit to handle viewing the attachment and showing the map. MapKit provides fully featured maps, created by Apple, for you to use in your apps. Maps can include pretty much everything the Maps app that ships with iOS and macOS can do, from street-level map information to satellite view to 3D buildings. MapKit also supports custom annotations, as well as automatic support to easily zoom and pan the map.

Custom annotations can be defined by a single point (a lat/long pair) or as an overlay that is defined by a number of points that form a shape. Annotations and overlays behave as you'd expect, and are not just unintelligent subviews; they move and resize appropriately when the user pans, zooms, or otherwise manipulates the map.

First, we'll set up the application to use location services:

1. Open the application's *Info.plist* file.

2. Add a new string value to the dictionary: `NSLocationWhenInUseUsageDescription`. Set its value to the string `We'll use your position to show where you were when you created your notes.`. This string will be shown to the user in a pop up when the app first tries to determine location.

 Much like with the camera and microphone, don't ever ask to access a user's location when you don't really need it. Apple frowns upon this, and users will come to distrust you. Treat access to a user's location with care.

3. Open the *Assets.xcassets* file.

4. Drag the *Current Location.pdf* image into the list of images.

5. Rename it to be *Position*.

We now have an image ready to display for when we hook up the location attachment code, and we are correctly configured to ask the user's permission to use location.

Next we will need to add the code to handle looking after the location JSON file to our document model:

1. Open *Document.swift*.

2. Add a new `FileWrapper` property into the `Document` class:

```
var locationWrapper : FileWrapper?
```

This will be used to store our location JSON file when we get around to creating it.

3. Add the following to the `contents forType` method:

```
override func contents(forType typeName: String) throws -> Any {

    let textRTFData = try self.text.data(
        from: NSRange(0..<self.text.length),
        documentAttributes:
            [NSDocumentTypeDocumentAttribute: NSRTFTextDocumentType])

    if let oldTextFileWrapper = self.documentFileWrapper
        .fileWrappers?[NoteDocumentFileNames.TextFile.rawValue] {
        self.documentFileWrapper.removeFileWrapper(oldTextFileWrapper)
    }

    // Create the QuickLook folder

    let thumbnailImageData =
        self.iconImageDataWithSize(CGSize(width: 512, height: 512))!

    let thumbnailWrapper =
        FileWrapper(regularFileWithContents: thumbnailImageData)

    let quicklookPreview =
        FileWrapper(regularFileWithContents: textRTFData)

    let quickLookFolderFileWrapper =
        FileWrapper(directoryWithFileWrappers: [
        NoteDocumentFileNames.QuickLookTextFile.rawValue: quicklookPreview,
        NoteDocumentFileNames.QuickLookThumbnail.rawValue: thumbnailWrapper
        ])
    quickLookFolderFileWrapper.preferredFilename =
        NoteDocumentFileNames.QuickLookDirectory.rawValue
```

```
// Remove the old QuickLook folder if it existed
if let oldQuickLookFolder = self.documentFileWrapper
    .fileWrappers?[NoteDocumentFileNames.QuickLookDirectory.rawValue] {
        self.documentFileWrapper.removeFileWrapper(oldQuickLookFolder)
}

// Add the new QuickLook folder
self.documentFileWrapper.addFileWrapper(quickLookFolderFileWrapper)

> // checking if there is already a location saved
> let rawLocationVal = NoteDocumentFileNames.locationAttachment.rawValue
> if self.documentFileWrapper.fileWrappers?[rawLocationVal] == nil {
>     // saving the location if there is one
>     if let location = self.locationWrapper {
>         self.documentFileWrapper.addFileWrapper(location)
>     }
> }

self.documentFileWrapper.addRegularFile(withContents: textRTFData,
    preferredFilename: NoteDocumentFileNames.TextFile.rawValue)

return self.documentFileWrapper
}
```

This will check if we need to save a location and store it; otherwise, do nothing.

4. Add the following to load fromContents:

```
override func load(fromContents contents: Any,
    ofType typeName: String?) throws {

    // Ensure that we've been given a file wrapper
    guard let fileWrapper = contents as? FileWrapper else {
        throw err(.cannotLoadFileWrappers)
    }

    // Ensure that this file wrapper contains the text file,
    // and that we can read it
    guard let textFileWrapper = fileWrapper
        .fileWrappers?[NoteDocumentFileNames.TextFile.rawValue],
        let textFileData = textFileWrapper.regularFileContents else {
        throw err(.cannotLoadText)
    }

    // Read in the RTF
    self.text = try NSAttributedString(data: textFileData,
        options: [NSDocumentTypeDocumentAttribute: NSRTFTextDocumentType],
        documentAttributes: nil)

    // Keep a reference to the file wrapper
    self.documentFileWrapper = fileWrapper
```

```
>    // opening the location filewrapper
>    let rawLocationVal = NoteDocumentFileNames.locationAttachment.rawValue
>    self.locationWrapper = fileWrapper.fileWrappers?[rawLocationVal]

    }
```

This will load our location; now all we need to do is write some code to let us save a location once we determine it.

5. Add the following new method to Document:

```
func addLocation(withData data: Data) {
    // making sure we don't already have a location
    guard self.locationWrapper == nil else {
        return
    }

    let newLocation = FileWrapper(regularFileWithContents: data)
    newLocation.preferredFilename
  = NoteDocumentFileNames.locationAttachment.rawValue

    self.locationWrapper = newLocation

    self.updateChangeCount(.done)
}
```

Next, we'll create the view controller that we will use to show our attachment. First we'll set up the code, and then we'll build the interface:

1. Create a new file by going to to the File menu and choosing File→New.

2. Select Cocoa Touch Class and click Next.

3. Name the new class **LocationAttachmentViewController** and make it a subclass of UIViewController.

4. Open the *LocationAttachmentViewController.swift* file that was added to your project.

5. Import the MapKit frameworks:

```
import MapKit
```

6. Create an outlet for our location attachment property. This will be passed in when the view controller is called to appear:

```
var locationAttachment: FileWrapper?
```

7. Then create an outlet for our map view:

```
@IBOutlet weak var mapview: MKMapView?
```

8. Open *Main.storyboard* and drag in a new UIViewController.

9. Go to the Identity Inspector, and change the class of the view controller to `Loca tionAttachmentViewController`.

10. Drag an `MKMapView` into the view controller's interface.

11. Add constraints that make it fill the entire interface.

12. Go to the Attributes Inspector and select the Shows User Location checkbox. This will make the small blue user location appear on the map should the user be near the note's annotation. While this isn't necessary, it is a nice touch.

13. Hold down the Control key and drag from the view controller to the map view. Choose "mapView" from the menu that appears.

Now it is time to implement the code to draw an annotation on the map based on the JSON file passed into the `attachmentFile` property. Open *LocationAttachmentView-Controller.swift* and implement the `viewWillAppear` method:

```
override func viewWillAppear(_ animated: Bool) {
    if let data = locationAttachment?.regularFileContents {
        do {
            guard let loadedData =
                try JSONSerialization.jsonObject(with: data,
                        options: JSONSerialization.ReadingOptions())
                    as? [String:CLLocationDegrees] else {
                return
            }

            if let latitude = loadedData["lat"],
                let longitude = loadedData["long"] {
                let coordinate = CLLocationCoordinate2D(latitude: latitude,
                                        longitude: longitude)

                // create a new annotation to show on the map
                let annotation = MKPointAnnotation()
                annotation.coordinate = coordinate
                annotation.title = "Note created here"

                self.mapview?.addAnnotation(annotation)

                // moving the map to focus on the annotation
                self.mapview?.setCenter(coordinate, animated: true)
            }
        }
        catch let error as NSError {
            print("failed to load location: \(error)")
        }
    }
}
```

This will create a new `MKPointAnnotation`, which is the default pin style annotation on maps. Now we could create a custom annotation and draw our own picture, but for our app the built-in point annotation will do nicely. We set a title that appears when the user taps the pin. This code finishes up by moving the center of the map to be the same position as where the annotation is.

 In our code, we don't zoom the map at all; we just pan it to the pin. Zooming a map is a bit stranger than it might seem, as the map is being displayed as a rectangle on our device but the Earth is a sphere (mostly). iOS uses what is called the Mercator projection to map the surface of the Earth onto a rectangular display. This has some interesting side effects such as how far zoomed-in the map appears, changing depending on how far north or south you go. Keep this in mind if you expect your app users to be moving around the world a great deal.

Now it is time to hook up the code to actually determine the user's location, and save that as a JSON attachment in the document. Core Location works by creating a manager, configuring it, and then waiting for it to tell its delegate about what is happening. We don't directly talk to the location services; we only talk to the manager as its delegate.

1. Open *DocumentViewController.swift*. We will need the Core Location framework to determine the location, so let's do that first:

   ```
   import CoreLocation
   ```

2. Next we need to conform to the `CLLocationManagerDelegate` protocol; this will give us all the methods and callbacks we will need to determine users location:

   ```
   extension DocumentViewController: CLLocationManagerDelegate {
   ```

   We are doing this in an extension just to keep our code neat and tidy. This is where we will put all our `CLLocationManagerDelegate` methods.

3. Now we will need a new property that will hold our location manager:

   ```
   var locationManager : CLLocationManager?
   ```

4. It's time to set up our location manager. Add the following to the bottom of the `viewWillAppear` method, inside the `document.open` closure:

   ```
   // checking if there isn't already a location file
   if self.document?.locationWrapper == nil {
       // determining our location permission status
       let status = CLLocationManager.authorizationStatus()

       if status != .denied && status != .restricted {
           self.locationManager = CLLocationManager()
           self.locationManager?.delegate = self

           if status == .notDetermined {
   ```

```
            self.locationManager?.requestWhenInUseAuthorization()
        }
        else {
            self.locationManager?.desiredAccuracy
                = kCLLocationAccuracyBest
            self.locationManager?.startUpdatingLocation()
        }
    }
}
self.updateBarItems()
```

In this code, we first we check if there is already a location set for this note; if there is then we do nothing. If there isn't, then we need to see if we have permission to access the location services. If we don't, we ask permission; if permission has previously been given, we tell the location manager to start checking our location. We also have a call to update the navigation bar items, which we'll handle in a moment. As far as the location is concerned, however, from this point onward it is up to the location manager and its delegate methods.

Now we want to update the updateBarItems method to show either a spinning activity indicator, using the UIActivityIndicatorView class, while we are working out location, or a button to segue to the attachment view controller we made earlier:

```
// the button to segue to the attachment view controller
let image = UIImage(named: "Position")
let showButton = UIBarButtonItem(image: image, style: .plain,
                        target: self, action: #selector(showLocation))

// if there is already a location
if self.document?.locationWrapper != nil {
    // we show the segue button
    rightButtonItems.append(showButton)
} else {
    // if we don't have permission or permission is denied
    let status = CLLocationManager.authorizationStatus()

    if status == .denied || status == .restricted {
        // we don't have permission
        rightButtonItems.append(showButton)
    } else {
        // the activity indicator to show when determining location
        let spinner = UIActivityIndicatorView(activityIndicatorStyle: .gray)
        spinner.startAnimating()
        let spinItem = UIBarButtonItem(customView: spinner)
        rightButtonItems.append(spinItem)
    }
}
```

If you are wondering what the showLocationAttachment selector is, don't worry—we will implement that shortly.

You might have noticed how we have wrapped our UIActivity IndicatorView inside a UIBarButtonItem. That's because the navigation bar can only show UI elements that are UiBarButtonItems and our spinner is not, so we have to wrap it inside one before we can show it.

Now it is time to implement all the location manager delegate methods we need:

1. The first location manager delegate we need to handle is when the authorization changes. This will get called after the user first chooses whether or not to allow location services. Implement the locationManager didChangeAuthorization status: method:

```
func locationManager(_ manager: CLLocationManager,
                     didChangeAuthorization status: CLAuthorizationStatus) {
    if status == .authorizedWhenInUse {
        self.locationManager?.desiredAccuracy = kCLLocationAccuracyBest
        self.locationManager?.startUpdatingLocation()
    }
    self.updateBarItems()
}
```

All we are doing in here is looking to see if we have permission to start tracking location; if we do, we ask the location manager to start; otherwise, we do nothing. In some apps you may really need location more than a note app does, so in here you may want to let the user know if permission is declined. For us, not worrying about it is fine.

2. Now that we are set up and have asked the location manager to determine our location, we need to handle when a location is determined. Implement the loca tionManager didUpdateLocations method:

```
func locationManager(_ manager: CLLocationManager,
                     didUpdateLocations locations: [CLLocation]) {
    self.locationManager?.stopUpdatingLocation()
    guard let location = locations.last else {
        return
    }

    // creating a json representation of our location
    let latitude = location.coordinate.latitude
    let longitude = location.coordinate.longitude

    let locationData = ["lat":latitude, "long":longitude]

    do {
        let json = try JSONSerialization.data(withJSONObject: locationData,
                        options: JSONSerialization.WritingOptions())
```

```
        // saving our location to the document
        self.document?.addLocation(withData: json)
    }
    catch let error as NSError
    {
        print("unable to save location: \(error)")
        self.locationManager?.startUpdatingLocation()
    }
    self.updateBarItems()
}
```

This method gets called whenever the location manager has determined a location from the location hardware. Because of how the hardware works, it is possible that we have determined multiple locations within a few moments, so the results are passed in as an array called locations. From this array we grab the latest location determined and use this to build up our JSON, which we then store. Finally, because the location hardware can be quite battery intensive, we make sure to turn it off when we are no longer using it.

This will be ready to go, with just one more feature: we need to be able to trigger an appropriate segue when the user chooses to view the location:

1. Implement the showLocation method we said we'd make earlier:

   ```
   func showLocation() {
       self.performSegue(withIdentifier: "ShowLocationSegue", sender: self)
   }
   ```

   This will trigger the location segue ShowLocationSegue, which we will now set up.

2. Open *main.storyboard*.

3. Hold down the Control key and drag from the document view controller to the location attachment view controller. Choose "show" from the list that appears. Normal attachments are presented as popovers, but because the location attachment is a bit different, we will signal this by using a different segue style.

4. Give the segue the identifier ShowLocationSegue.

5. Add the following to the prepare(for segue: sender:) method after where we check if the segue is for an attachment:

   ```
   else if segue.identifier == "ShowLocationSegue" {
       if let destination = segue.destination as?
           LocationAttachmentViewController {
           destination.locationAttachment = self.document?.locationWrapper
       }
   }
   ```

Now that we have the segue hooked up, we can run our app and add a location attachment to our notes!

Conclusion

In this chapter, we've improved the iOS app by adding support for richer attachments, audio, video, and locations. To do this we've added new view controllers for the different attachment types and connected our new views and controllers to our existing views.

CHAPTER 14

Polishing the iOS App

Our iOS notes application is now largely feature-complete. It's fully operational, but could do with a few more finishing touches to add some polish. In this chapter, we'll add support for opening links in the provided web browser view controller, overall app settings, undo, and image filters.

Opening Links in SFSafariViewController

Links in the text are currently tappable, but this functionality is not ideal, for two reasons:

- It's available only when the text view is not editable.
- Tapping links launches Safari, taking users out of the app. This is probably something they don't want.

To fix the first problem, we'll add support for moving between an "editing" mode and a "viewing" mode for the `DocumentViewController`. To fix the second, we'll override the existing behavior for opening links, and instead open them in the `SFSafariViewController`.

There are three ways in which an app can display web content: creating a custom mini-browser by using `WKWebView` or `UIWebView`, pushing the user out of the app by opening Safari using `openURL`, or using `SFSafariViewController` to display a compact version of Safari within the app.

`WKWebView` or `UIWebView` are outside the scope of this book, as these days they're only necessary if you're doing something complex with web views, or you're making your own web browser for iOS (like Chrome, Firefox, Mercury Browser, or similar). In the past, most apps implemented their own custom mini-browser using either `UIWebView` or the newer `WKWebView` to display web content. This wasn't ideal for a number of reasons, chief among them the fact that each in-app mini-browser ended up with its own unique UI and didn't have access to iCloud Keychain, among other Safari features.

We cover `SFSafariViewController` here because it's the best way for apps to allow users to open web content: it behaves like Safari, it looks like Safari, it's easy to use, and it has access to all of Safari's features, such as content blockers and iCloud Keychain. It also easily allows users to open the web page you send them to in full Safari if they wish (see Figure 14-1).

Figure 14-1. SFSafariViewController showing the authors' website

This ensures that the contents of the navigation bar are appropriately set up, both when the document is opened and when the view controller reappears after returning from another view controller.

When the document opens, we want to begin in the "viewing" state:

1. Add the following code to `viewDidLoad`:

```
override func viewDidLoad() {

    super.viewDidLoad()

>   self.editing = false

}
```

2. Next, override the `setEditing` method to make the text view editable or not:

```
override func setEditing(_ editing: Bool, animated: Bool) {
    super.setEditing(editing, animated: animated)

    self.textView.isEditable = editing

    if editing {
        // If we are now editing, make the text view take
        // focus and display the keyboard
        self.textView.becomeFirstResponder()
    }

    updateBarItems()
}
```

When you run the app, you can now tap the Edit button, which will change to Done. At that point, you can make changes to the document.

We'll now make the text view detect links:

1. Open *Main.storyboard*, and go to the document view controller.
2. Select the text view and go to the Attributes Inspector.
3. Turn on Links in the Detection section (see Figure 14-2).

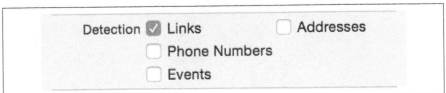

Figure 14-2. Turning on link detection for the text field

Now, any links in the text view will become tappable when you leave Edit mode.

Finally, we'll intercept the link taps and open them in an `SFSafariViewController`:

1. Open *DocumentViewController.swift*.

2. Import the SafariServices framework at the top of the file:

   ```
   import SafariServices
   ```

3. Implement `textView(_, shouldInteractWith URL:, inRange:)` to present an `SFSafariViewController` (see Figure 14-3):

   ```
   func textView(_ textView: UITextView, shouldInteractWith URL: URL,
       in characterRange: NSRange) -> Bool {

       let safari = SFSafariViewController(url: URL)
       self.present(safari, animated: true, completion: nil)

       // return false to not launch in Safari
       return false
   }
   ```

 This method is called because we've already set the text view's delegate—we set that up earlier in "Editing and Saving Documents" on page 262.

Figure 14-3. SFSafariViewController showing the O'Reilly website

3D Touch

If you're using an iPhone 6S, 6S Plus, or any iPhone 7 model, you can use 3D Touch to get a quick preview of any link inside the SFSafariViewController by pressing firmly on a link.

Certain iOS devices are able to detect and make use of the pressure applied to the screen when a user touches it, in order to provide quick access to application functionality. There are a couple of ways you can use this: home screen quick actions and Peek and Pop.

Home Screen Quick Actions

A home screen quick action is a menu item that appears when the user presses firmly on your app's icon. Quick actions make your app quickly perform an action in the background, or jump straight to a common target in the app.

There are two kinds of home screen quick actions: *static* and *dynamic*. Static actions never change, while dynamic actions can be added at runtime.

To add a static action, you add an array to your app's *Info.plist* called UIApplication ShortcutItems; this is an array of dictionaries, which each contain the following items:

UIApplicationShortcutItemType: *Required*
 The app will receive this string.

UIApplicationShortcutItemTitle: *Required*
 The user will see this label.

UIApplicationShortcutItemSubtitle: *Optional*
 The user will see this label under the title.

UIApplicationShortcutItemIconFile: *Optional*
 Provide your own file.

UIApplicationShortcutIconType: *Optional*
 Use a system-provided icon.

UIApplicationShortcutItemUserInfo: *Optional*
 Dictionary that will be passed to the app.

A dynamic action is an instance of the UIApplicationShortcutItem object; the app's shared UIApplication object has an array called shortcutItems, which you can control. When you add a shortcut action object to this array, a new menu item will appear when the app's icon is firmly pressed. For our app let's make a static action that will allow you to create a new note from the home menu:

1. The first thing we need to do is modify our *info.plist* to support our create note action. Open *info.plist* and insert a new key-value pair into the plist; the key should be UIApplicationShortcutItems and the type should be Array.

2. Modify the first and only item in the array to be a Dictionary; this is where we will add the information iOS will use to build up the Quick Action.

3. Add a new key-value pair to the Dictionary, set the key to be `UIApplication ShortcutItemTitle`, and the value to be a `String` saying `New Note`.

4. Now we need to add in the type of action for the shortcut. Add in another key-value pair with the key `UIApplicationShortcutItemType` and make the value a string saying `au.com.secretlab.Notes.new-note`. Make sure to replace `au.com.secretlab.Notes` with the bundle identifier for your app. The app will use this type later so we can determine when the app was launched by the Quick Action or not.

5. Finally, add one more key-value pair to the dictionary, set the key to `UIApplicationShortcutItemIconType` and the value to the `String` `UIApplicationShortcutIconTypeCompose`. This will show the default creation icon used throughout iOS next to the text `New Note` when your user performs the quick action.

With that done, we can start writing the code to handle when the user performs a quick action:

1. Inside *AppDelegate.swift* we will add a new property to handle the action type:

   ```
   let createNoteActionType = "au.com.secretlab.Notes.new-note"
   ```

2. This will just give us a reference so we don't misspell it later on, as this string is the identifier we get told about when the quick action occurs. Now we need to add a small check to the bottom of `application didFinishLaunchingWithOptions` method to check if we were launched by the quick action:

   ```
   // Did we launch as a result of using a shortcut option?
   if let shortcutItem =
     launchOptions?[.shortcutItem] as? UIApplicationShortcutItem
   {

           // We did! Was it the 'create note' shortcut?
           if shortcutItem.type == createNoteActionType {
               // Create a new document.
               createNewDocument()
           }

           // Return false to indicate that 'performActionForShortcutItem'
           // doesn't need to be called
           return false
   }
   ```

3. This code checks if the app was launched by a quick action; if it was we then check if it was the quick action we defined earlier. If all that is the case, we run a method called `createNewDocument`, which we are about to write, to handle the actual creation of a new note.

4. The last thing we have to do is write the `createNewDocument` function. Add a new function to `AppDelegate.swift`:

```swift
func createNewDocument() {

    // Ensure that the root view controller is a navigation controller
    guard let navigationController =
        self.window?.rootViewController as? UINavigationController else {
        fatalError("The root view controller is not a navigationcontroller")
    }

    // Ensure that the navigation controller's root view controller is the
    // Document List
    guard let documentList = navigationController.viewControllers.first
                             as? DocumentListViewController else {
        fatalError("first view controller isn't DocumentListViewController")
    }

    // Move back to the root view controller
    navigationController.popToRootViewController(animated: false)

    // Ask the document list to create a new document
    documentList.createDocument()
}
```

This method is pretty straightforward: it grabs the app's navigation controller, then grabs the document list view controller from the navigation controller, and then finally tells the document list view controller to create a new note. With that done we can run the app on your 3D Touch–enabled phone and you can create a new note straight from the home screen! You can see what this looks like in Figure 14-4.

Figure 14-4. The home screen quick action

 While we always recommend you use the actual device for testing your apps, 3D Touch is still a new feature that most iPhones don't have. Much like with the camera or other hardware features, the simulator can't emulate it, with one exception. If your Macbook is equipped with a Force Trackpad you can use its pressure detection to simulate 3D Touch. Open the iOS Simulator, go to Hardware→Touch Pressure→Use Trackpad Force, and this will enable 3D Touch simulation via your trackpad. However, this is still not as good as testing on the real hardware!

Peek and Pop

Peek and Pop is a feature that allows the user to get a quick preview of content by pressing firmly on an element on the screen; if the user pushes harder, the content opens. For example, in the Mail app, if you press firmly on an email, you get a quick preview; if you press harder, the preview "pops" up and fills the screen, as though you'd tapped the email in the list. For our application we will make it so that when you peek on a note inside the document list view controller, it shows a small preview, and when you fully commit and push a little harder it will pop open the full note:

1. To add support for Peek and Pop, the first thing we need to do is add an identifier to the *DocumentViewContoller* inside the Storyboard. We will use the identifier later on to summon a preview of the note.

2. Open up *main.storyboard* and select the *DocumentViewController* inside the storyboard. Open up the Inspectors and go to the Identity Inspector tab, then under the Identity section add `DocumentViewController` to the Storyboard ID.

 In addition to the higher-level interactions the system provides, you can also directly access force information from `UITouch` objects as the system receives them. To access this, use the `force` property on the `UITouch` object.

Now with that done, the next step is to register the document list view controller as supporting Peek and Pop:

1. Open *DocumentListViewController.swift* and add the following to the bottom of `viewDidLoad`:

```
// Mark the collection view as preview-able, if our current device supports
// 3D Touch.
if self.traitCollection.forceTouchCapability == .available {
    self.registerForPreviewing(with: self,
                             sourceView: self.collectionView!)
}
```

This method does a check to see if the device the app is running on is capable of using 3D Touch; if so, it registers the collection view showing all the notes as ready to support Peek and Pop. They aren't yet but we will add that functionality in next.

2. To participate in Peek and Pop, you provide an object that conforms to `UIView ControllerPreviewingDelegate`. This delegate receives calls to the methods `previewingContext viewControllerForLocation` and `previewingContext viewControllerToCommit`. The first method is called when the user starts pressing firmly on the view, and returns a view controller to display; the second is called when the user presses even harder, preparing for a transition to the preview view controller. We will implement these as an extension on the `Documen tListViewController` to keep it all tidy:

```
extension DocumentListViewController : UIViewControllerPreviewingDelegate {
    func previewingContext(
```

```swift
        _ previewingContext: UIViewControllerPreviewing,
        viewControllerForLocation location: CGPoint) -> UIViewController? {

        // Determine which cell was tapped; if we can't
        // return nil to indicate that we can't offer a preview
        guard let indexPath =
                self.collectionView?.indexPathForItem(at: location) else {
            return nil
        }

        // Get the cell object for this location
        guard let cell =
                self.collectionView?.cellForItem(at: indexPath) else {
            fatalError("We have an index path, but not a cell")
        }

        // Determine the document URL that this cell represents
        let selectedItem = availableFiles[indexPath.item]

        // Tell the previewing context about
        // the shape that should remain unblurred
        previewingContext.sourceRect = cell.frame

        // Create a DocumentViewController for showing this file
        guard let documentVC = self.storyboard?.instantiateViewController(
                            withIdentifier: "DocumentViewController")
                                    as? DocumentViewController else
        {
            fatalError("Expected to get a DocumentViewController here " +
                "- make sure that the Document View Controller's" +
                "storyboard identifier is set up correctly")
        }

        // Give the document URL to the document view controller
        documentVC.documentURL = selectedItem

        // Create a navigation controller to embed this in
        let navigationVC =
            UINavigationController(rootViewController: documentVC)

        // Return this navigation controller
        return navigationVC
    }

    func previewingContext(_ previewingContext: UIViewControllerPreviewing,
            commit viewControllerToCommit: UIViewController)
    {
        // The viewControllerToCommit is a navigation controller
        // that contains a document view controller.
        // Ensure that this is the case.
```

```
    guard let navigationVC = viewControllerToCommit as?
                                    UINavigationController else {
        fatalError("Expected the preview view controller" +
            "to be a navigation controller")
    }

    guard let documentVC = navigationVC.viewControllers.first
                            as? DocumentViewController else {
        fatalError("View controller is not a document view controller")
    }

    // Get the document view controller's URL
    guard let url = documentVC.documentURL else {
        fatalError("Expected the document view controller" +
            "to have a document set")
    }

    // Present the segue, just as if we'd tapped the cell
    self.performSegue(withIdentifier: "ShowDocument", sender: url)
    }
}
```

There is a fair bit of code here, but it is all pretty simple. First we add an extension to the DocumentListViewController class to say we support Peek and Pop. Then we implement the two required methods.

previewingContext viewControllerForLocation: first gets the cell and note inside the collection view that the user wants to preview. We use the cell frame to tell the previewing system not to blur the cell itself; this will also have the effect of blurring everything that isn't the cell. Then we use the Storyboard identifier set up earlier to create a new document view controller, and we pass it the selected note. Finally we create a new navigation controller to wrap around the Document View Controller as the Document View Controller requires it, and this all gets returned. The previewing system will then show a preview of this note through the returned view controller.

previewingContext commit viewControllerToCommit: is the second method and is called when the user commits to the note after seeing the preview popping it into existence and working otherwise exactly the same as if the user had tapped the note cell. An important parameter of this method is the viewControllerToCommit; this is the same view controller the user started to preview earlier. This method does some checks to make sure that the viewControllerToCommit is a valid DocumentViewCon troller with a surrounding navigation controller. If it is, we can then grab the note out of the view controller and use it as part of the normal segue to view a note.

With all this done, we can now run the app and peek and pop on our notes!

For more information on how to use 3D Touch in your apps, check out the Adopting 3D Touch on iPhone (*http://apple.co/22UQbX4*) guide.

Settings

We'll now add a setting to our app, one that controls whether documents are in the Edit state that we just set up when they're opened.

Settings are stored in the UserDefaults class, which works like a giant dictionary that sticks around, even when the application quits. This is one of myriad ways that an app can store data—it's probably the simplest, least powerful, least flexible way, but it gets the job done when it comes to storing very small pieces of information, such as settings.

UserDefaults can only store certain kinds of objects, which happen to be the same kinds that a property list can store. These objects are called *property list values*, and consist of the types String, Number, Date, Array, Data, and Dictionary. UserDe faults should only be used for storing very small pieces of information:

1. Open the File menu and choose New→File.

2. Add a new iOS→Resource→Settings Bundle. Name it **Settings** and add it to the Notes-iOS target.

3. Open the *Settings.bundle* that was just added, and open the *Root.plist* file inside it.

4. Remove all items from the Preference Items list.

5. Select the Preferences Items and press Enter to create a new one.

6. Set the Type of the new item to Toggle Switch.

7. Set the Title to "Documents are editable when opened."

8. Set the Identifier to "document_edit_on_open."

We'll now make the app actually use the preference:

1. Open *DocumentViewController.swift*.

2. Remove this line of code from viewDidLoad:

    ```
    self.editing = false
    ```

3. Replace it with this:

    ```
    self.isEditing = UserDefaults.standard.bool(forKey:"document_edit_on_open")
    ```

Install the app on your device (or in the simulator) and then go to the Settings app. Change the settings and then go back into the app. Note the difference in behavior! (See Figure 14-5.)

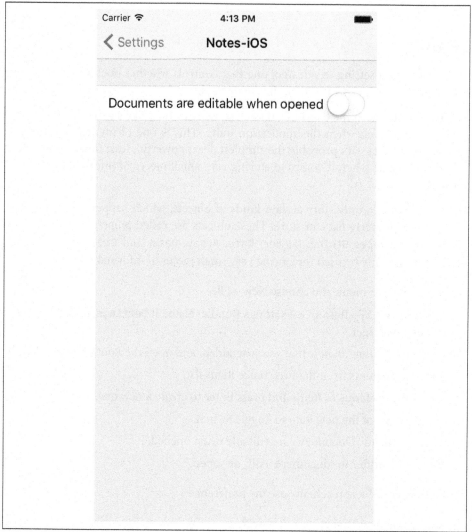

Figure 14-5. The app settings

Undo Support

Next we'll add support for undoing changes to the text view via the built-in undo manager. This means that we'll ask the undo system to notify us about changes in the ability to undo; we'll also add a button that can trigger undo actions. Undo on iOS is provided by UndoManager, which allows you to register things that the user might want to undo, and how to undo them. It also takes care of redoing anything that is undone, if needed.

UITextView provides its own UndoManager, so we'll make use of that:

1. Add the following properties to DocumentViewController:

```
var undoButton : UIBarButtonItem?
var didUndoObserver : AnyObject?
var didRedoObserver : AnyObject?
```

2. Add the following code to viewDidLoad to register changes to the ability to undo or redo a change:

```
let respondToUndoOrRedo = { (notification:Notification) -> Void in
    self.undoButton?.isEnabled = self.textView.undoManager?.canUndo == true
}

didUndoObserver = NotificationCenter.default
    .addObserver(forName: NSNotification.Name.NSUndoManagerDidUndoChange,
                 object: nil,
                 queue: nil,
                 using: respondToUndoOrRedo)

didRedoObserver = NotificationCenter.default
    .addObserver(forName: NSNotification.Name.NSUndoManagerDidRedoChange,
                 object: nil,
                 queue: nil,
                 using: respondToUndoOrRedo)
```

We want to run the same code when the user performs either an undo or a redo. Because the addObserver forName: method takes a closure as its parameter, we can just write the code once, and use it twice.

3. Add the following code to updateBarItems to change the Undo button's enabled state:

```
  func updateBarItems() {
      var rightButtonItems : [UIBarButtonItem] = []
      rightButtonItems.append(self.editButtonItem)

>     if isEditing {
>         undoButton = UIBarButtonItem(barButtonSystemItem: .undo,
>                                       target: self.textView?.undoManager,
>                                       action: #selector(UndoManager.undo))
>
>         undoButton?.isEnabled = self.textView?.undoManager?.canUndo == true
>         rightButtonItems.append(undoButton!)
>     }
```

```
        // the button to segue to the attachment view controller
        let image = UIImage(named: "Position")
        let showButton = UIBarButtonItem(
    image: image,
    style: .plain,
    target: self,
    action: #selector(showLocation))

        // if there is already a location
        if self.document?.locationWrapper != nil {
            // we show the segue button
            rightButtonItems.append(showButton)
        } else {
            // if we don't have permission or permission is denied
            let status = CLLocationManager.authorizationStatus()

            if status == .denied || status == .restricted {
                // we don't have permission
                rightButtonItems.append(showButton)
            } else {
                // the activity indicator to show when determining location
                let spinner
    = UIActivityIndicatorView(activityIndicatorStyle: .gray)
                spinner.startAnimating()
                let spinItem = UIBarButtonItem(customView: spinner)
                rightButtonItems.append(spinItem)
            }
        }

        self.navigationItem.rightBarButtonItems = rightButtonItems

    }
```

When the bar items are updated, we need to add an Undo button to the right-hand side of the navigation bar if the document is in editing mode. In addition, we need to ensure that the Undo button is disabled if it's not possible to perform an undo. We check this by asking the text view's undo manager if it's currently possible.

4. Add the following code to `textViewDidChange`:

```
    func textViewDidChange(_ textView: UITextView) {

>       self.undoButton?.isEnabled = self.textView.undoManager?.canUndo == true

        document?.text = textView.attributedText
        document?.updateChangeCount(.done)
    }
```

Every time the text view changes, we need to check to see if it's possible for the text view to undo a change. We can then use this to update whether or not the Undo button should be available.

5. Update the code in the `documentStateChanged` method with the following code to update the Undo button:

```
document.revert(toContentsOf: document.fileURL,
    completionHandler: { (success) -> Void in

        self.textView.attributedText = document.text
        self.attachmentsCollectionView?.reloadData()

>       self.updateBarItems()
})

for version in conflictedVersions{
    version.isResolved = true
}
```

This gets called when a conflict is detected between the local copy and the iCloud copy. All this code is doing is ensuring that, when the text view has changed due to the document's contents being updated, the Undo button is or is not available.

6. Run the app. When you enter Edit mode, an Undo button will appear; it will be disabled if you can't undo, and if you make changes, you can tap it to undo those changes.

Images with Filters

Everyone loves filters! We're going to add the ability for users to apply filters to their images. When the user is viewing an image, we'll also show three different, filtered versions of the image as buttons along the bottom of the screen. When the user taps these buttons, the main image view will change to show the filtered version of the image.

The filters available to you are very similar to the filters available in Instagram: they make the photo look like it was shot on film or through cheaper lenses.

We're going to use Core Image to apply the filters. Core Image is a framework provided by Apple that provides image filtering, enhancement, editing, and other useful nondestructive or pipeline-based image editing capabilities. Core Image underpins the photo editing provided by Apple's Photos app on both iOS and macOS. You can learn more about Core Image in Apple's Core Image Programing Guide (*http://apple.co/1RR35x3*).

1. Open *Main.storyboard*, and go to the image attachment view controller.

2. Add a `UIView` to the interface.

3. Make it fill the width of the screen and 80 points tall.

4. Pin it to the bottom and sides.

5. Set its background color to black, with 0.5 alpha.

6. Add three buttons to it and place them at the left, center, and right. Make them all the same height as the view they're contained in, and make them square.

7. Set their content mode to "aspect fit."

 If you are having trouble seeing the buttons on the black background, feel free to use a different background color. We chose black because we think it looks the best for this, but it's your app, so go wild!

8. Open *ImageAttachmentViewController.swift* in the Assistant.

   Because there are multiple buttons, it doesn't make much sense to create separate outlets for each of them. Instead, we'll use an *outlet collection*.

 An outlet collection is an outlet that lets you point to a bunch of different things, rather than just a single thing. This is useful here because all the buttons that change the filter are essentially doing the same thing, but each applies a different filter. Instead of creating a single outlet for each button, it's easier to deal with them as an array rather than as separate properties.

9. Add the following `filterButtons` property to `ImageAttachmentViewController`:

   ```
   @IBOutlet var filterButtons: [UIButton]!
   ```

 Note the square brackets for the creation of the array of `UIButton` objects! This is an array of buttons, not a single button.

10. Drag from the well at the left of the `filterButtons` property to each of the three buttons. This will add them to the array.

11. Connect them all to a new action called showFilteredImage. (Only create a single action—after creating the method, Control-drag from the second and third buttons onto the method.)

12. Add the following code to the showFilteredImage method:

```swift
@IBAction func showFilteredImage(_ sender: UIButton) {

    self.imageView?.image = sender.image(for: UIControlState())
    self.imageView?.contentMode = .scaleAspectFit

}
```

13. Add the prepareFilterPreviews method to ImageAttachmentViewController:

```swift
func prepareFilterPreviews() {

    let filters : [CIFilter?] = [
        CIFilter(name: "CIPhotoEffectChrome"),
        CIFilter(name: "CIPhotoEffectNoir"),
        CIFilter(name: "CIPhotoEffectInstant"),
    ]

    guard let image = self.imageView?.image else {
        return
    }

    let context = CIContext(options: nil)

    for (number, filter) in filters.enumerated() {

        let button = filterButtons[number]

        let unprocessedImage = CIImage(image: image)

        filter?.setValue(unprocessedImage, forKey: kCIInputImageKey)

        if let processedCIImage =
            filter?.value(forKey: kCIOutputImageKey) as? CIImage{

                // Render the result into a CGImage
            let image = context.createCGImage(processedCIImage,
                from: CGRect(origin: CGPoint.zero, size: image.size))

            button.setImage(UIImage(cgImage: image!),
                        for: UIControlState())
        }
    }
}
```

In this method, we're updating the images in the three `filterButtons` by running the source image through three filters. These filters are `CIFilter` objects, which we create by naming them.

You can find the full list of available filters in the Core Image Filter Reference (*http://apple.co/1RR3MpY*), available in the Xcode documentation.

To generate them, we create a Core Image context and then iterate through the three filters. We do this using the `enumerate` function, which, for each item in the list, returns a tuple (see "Tuples" on page 47) containing the index number of the item, and the item itself. For example, the first time the loop runs, you'll get the number 0 and the `CIPhotoEffectChrome` filter. We'll be using this to work with the `filterButtons` array.

For each filter, we grab the corresponding button. We then create a new `CIImage` using the original image and pass it into the filter. Once it's in the filter, we can extract the processed image; once we have that, we need to convert it first into a `CGImage`, and then convert *that* into a `UIImage` for the button to use.

It's possible to go straight from a `CIImage` to a `UIImage`, bypassing the `CGImage` step. However, if you do this, you'll end up with an image that just behaves oddly—for example, the image will *always* be stretched to fill the contents of whatever image view you place it in.

14. Add the following code to the `viewDidLoad` method:

```
override func viewDidLoad() {
    super.viewDidLoad()

    // If we have data, and can make an image out of it...
    if let data = attachmentFile?.regularFileContents,
        let image = UIImage(data: data) {
        // Set the image
        self.imageView?.image = image

>       prepareFilterPreviews()
    }
}
```

All we're adding here is the call to `prepareFilterPreviews`, which updates the filter buttons.

15. Run the application. When you view an Image attachment, you'll see three different versions underneath it (see Figure 14-6). Tap them to view a larger version of that filtered image.

Figure 14-6. The image filters

Worldwide Apps

Not all of your users are going to speak your language. There's an unfortunate tendency among software developers in the English-speaking world to assume that all users speak their language. This significantly reduces the number of people who can use their software.

However, making an app support multiple languages is easier than you think. There are two parts to making an app multilingual: internationalization and localization.

Internationalization

Internationalization is the process of preparing an app for localization. You do this by separating the text used in your app from the app itself, making it load any user-facing language resources at runtime based on the user's language preferences, and adjusting your user interface to support different lengths of text. In addition, your app should take into account whether the user's language displays text in a left-to-right direction (such as English and French), or in a right-to-left direction (such as Hebrew and Arabic).

> The possibility of your app running in a different language direction than your own is the reason the horizontal constraints applied to views refer to "leading" and "trailing" space rather than "left" or "right" space. In a left-to-right language, leading space is on the left and trailing on the right, while in a right-to-left language, leading space is on the right and trailing on the left. Both iOS and macOS will automatically use the appropriate direction for the user's language.

There are two major tasks involved in internationalizing your app: replacing all text in your code with calls to methods that load localized text at runtime, and testing and adjusting your interface to support the text in your app being a different width than your development language.

To make your app load the text that the user will read at runtime, use the `NSLocali zedString` function. This function allows you to leave the text in the code for you to read (and therefore understand what the text is *for*), while also ensuring that the app isn't actually hardcoding a specific language.

Let's take a look at how to do this by internationalizing a string in the Notes app. Open *DocumentViewController.swift* and replace the line of code where we set a title with the following line of code at the top of the `addAttachment` method:

```
let title = NSLocalizedString("Add attachment", comment:"Add attachment title")
```

The `NSLocalizedString` function takes two parameters. The first is the key, which indicates to the system which string you want; the second is the `comment`, a piece of text that explains what the string is for to people who do the translating.

NSLocalizedString works by searching the application for any *strings tables* that are targeted at the user's current language. If it finds an entry for key in the strings tables, the function returns the string it found. If it can't find any strings tables for the user's current language, or if it can't find the key in the strings tables it did find, then the function returns the key string.

If you run the app and access the string (by selecting some text and looking at the menu that appears), you won't see any difference. However, in the next section, we'll begin localizing the app into French, and this call to NSLocalizedString will change its behavior.

Until you receive translated text from whomever's doing your translating, it's usually not possible to accurately determine how your application's interface will need to change to suit the new language. For example, German text tends to be significantly longer than Chinese.

However, there's a useful rule of thumb: generally, text in different languages will never be more than twice as long as your native development language. Xcode is aware of this and lets you test your application in a fake "language" that simply repeats every piece of text twice. For example, the string "New Document" would appear as "New Document New Document". If every piece of text in your app is doubled, you can see how your interface might need to adjust to account for wider-than-expected text.

To use this double-length localization, you'll need to ask Xcode to launch your app using a new language as follows:

1. Open the Product menu and choose Scheme→Edit Scheme.
2. Go to the Run section and choose the Options tab.
3. Open the Application Language menu, shown in Figure 14-7.

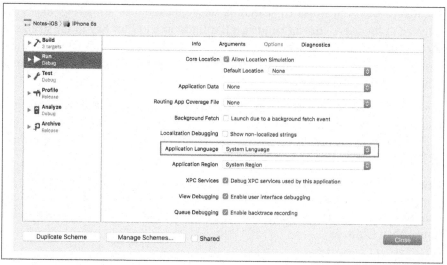

Figure 14-7. Changing the scheme language

4. Choose Double Length Pseudolanguage (Figure 14-8).

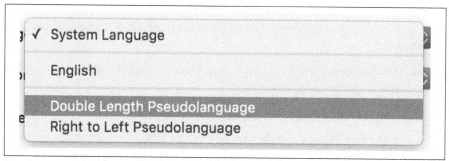

Figure 14-8. Using the double length localization

5. Click Close and then run your app. All text will be double-length (Figure 14-9).

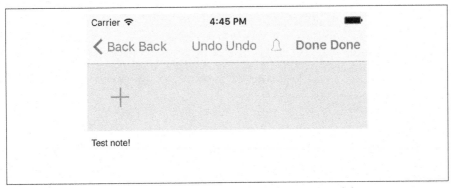

Figure 14-9. The application running in the double-length pseudolanguage

You can also use the Right to Left Pseudolanguage option, which reverses the writing order of your text, allowing you to test the layout and behavior of your app in right-to-left languages.

Localization

Once you've internationalized your application, you can *localize* it into a specific language. The majority of this work involves providing new text for your internationalized strings. In the previous section, we internationalized the add attachment title; next, we'll localize this into French:

1. Add a new Strings file to the app by opening the New File window and choosing iOS→Resources→Strings File (Figure 14-10).

Figure 14-10. Adding a Strings file

2. Name the new file *Localizable.strings*.

Xcode allows you to localize resource files, which means instructing Xcode to create a new copy of the file; the new copy is used only when the app is being run in a specific language. Resource files can have as many localizations as you like.

First, we'll localize the *Localizable.strings* file for your current development language; next, we'll add a new localization to this file for French:

1. Select the *Localizable.strings* file in the Project Navigator, and then go to the File Inspector.

2. Click the Localize button (Figure 14-11).

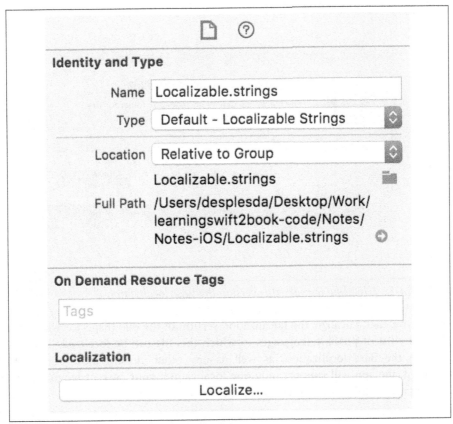

Figure 14-11. Localizing the Localizable.strings file

Xcode will ask you what you want to do with this file. You can either make the current version of the file the "Base" version, or you can make this file the localized version for your current language. Choose Base, and click Localize (Figure 14-12).

The Base localization is the version of the file that the app will fall back to if it can't find a string in the user's current language. If it can't find a string in the Base localization either, then the call to NSLocalizedString will return the key that was passed to it.

Figure 14-12. Choosing to make this version the Base localization

When you click Localize, the Localization section of the File Inspector will change to show the list of possible languages to which this file can be localized. This list will include the Base localization, as well as any other current localizations. At the moment, the app will support only one localization: your current language. (In our case, that's English, which is why it appears in Figure 14-13.)

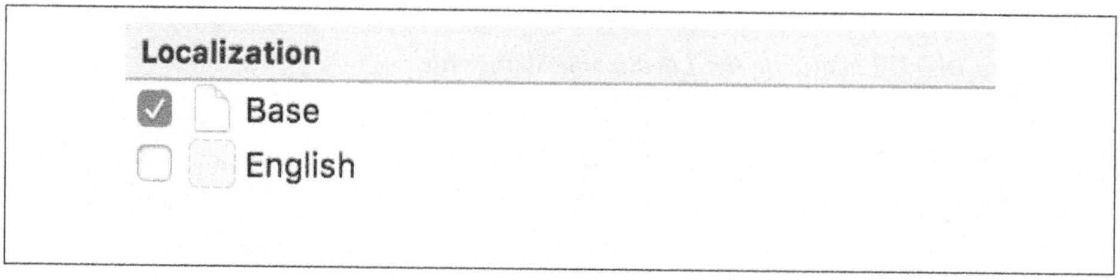

Localization
- ☑ 📄 Base
- ☐ 📄 English

Figure 14-13. The Localization list, showing the Base localization and the available localizations

To add support for another language, you must first mark the project as capable of using it:

1. Go to the Project info page. Scroll down to the Localizations list. You'll find one entry in there: the Development language. Click the + button at the bottom of the list, and choose "French (fr)" from the menu that appears (Figure 14-14).

Figure 14-14. Adding the French language

A window will appear, asking you which files should be localized (Figure 14-15). The files available will include all storyboards and *.xib* files, as well as any files that you've manually localized (which includes the *Localizable.strings* file).

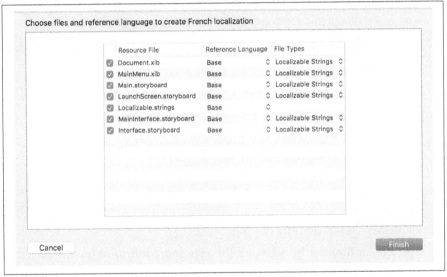

Figure 14-15. Selecting file to localize

2. Click Finish.

This registers French as a language into which the app can be localized.

If you look at the Project Navigator, you'll notice that these files have a disclosure indicator next to them. If you click this, you'll see that they now exist as multiple files; the original Base language version, and a French *.strings* file (Figure 14-16).

Localization

☑ Base

☐ English

Figure 14-16. The list of different localizations for the file

3. Open the *Localizable.strings (Base)* file. It's inside the *Localizable.strings* file. Add the following text to it:

```
"Add attachment" = "Add attachment";
```

4. Next, open the *Localizable.strings (French)* file. Add the following text to it:

```
"Add attachment" = "Ajouter une pièce jointe";
```

The Add attachment view controller title is now localized! We can test this by asking Xcode to launch the app in the French language.

5. Return to the Edit Scheme window by opening the Product menu and choosing Scheme→Edit Scheme.

6. Go to the Run section and go to the Options tab.

7. Change the Application Language to French.

"French" now appears in this menu because you've added it as a language that your app supports.

8. Close the window, and run the app.

9. Test the localization by selecting the text and confirming that French appears when adding an attachment (Figure 14-17).

Figure 14-17. The app, localized into French

You've now localized one piece of the app! The next step is to localize *all* strings into French. This is left, as they say, as an exercise for the reader.

 Luckily for us, a lot of the work of localizing an app is handled for us by the system. Because the app uses standard controls provided by the system, such as the Edit and Back buttons, they'll be displayed in French as well.

Accessibility

Not everyone is able to see your app. The ability to read the contents of the screen varies from person to person; some users may have no trouble at all, while some are totally blind, and some are partially sighted. On top of this, there are users who have good vision but have trouble reading text, such as people with dyslexia.

Both iOS and macOS have support for *VoiceOver*, a built-in screen reader. VoiceOver is able to read text that appears on the screen, as well as describe nontextual elements, like the layout of a screen.

The good news is that your app doesn't need to do much to support VoiceOver. The components from which your app is made—buttons, labels, text fields, and so on— are already set up to work with VoiceOver. However, it's very important to test how your app would be used by a person who can't see your app.

To start testing an application with VoiceOver, you'll first need to set up your phone to make it easy to turn VoiceOver on or off. VoiceOver changes the way that iOS responds to touches; for example, when using VoiceOver, tapping a button *selects* that button rather than triggering the action.

1. Launch the Settings app on your iOS device.

2. Go to General→Accessibility→Accessibility Shortcut.

   The Accessibility Shortcut is triggered when you triple-click the home button.

    There are several accessibility features that can be triggered by the home button, including inverting all colors on the screen and turning on a screen zoom feature. While these are useful, they're not something that you as a developer have much control over, so we'll focus on VoiceOver.

3. Turn on VoiceOver and turn everything else off.

4. Launch the app on your iPhone and triple-click the home button. VoiceOver will turn on (Figure 14-18).

   When you tap the screen, iOS selects whatever's under your finger and describes it to you. You can swipe left and right to select the previous or next item, and double-tap to "open" the currently selected item.

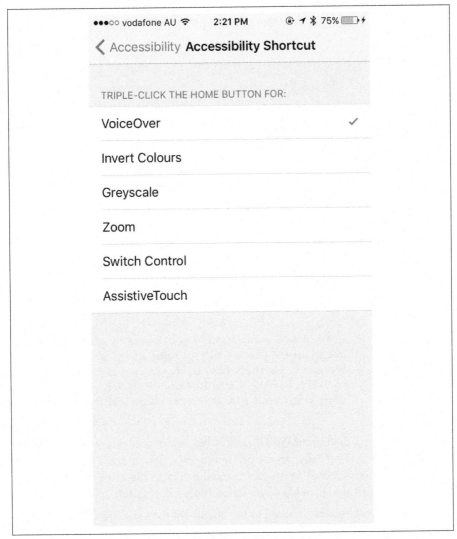

Figure 14-18. Configuring the Accessibility shortcut

5. Tap the + button once. iOS will select the button.

6. Double-tap anywhere on the screen. A new document will be created (Figure 14-19).

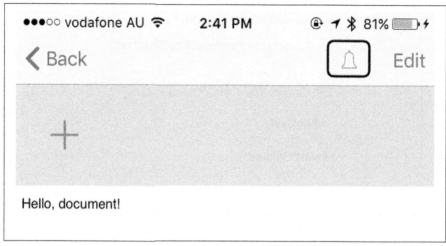

Figure 14-19. VoiceOver in the Notes app

7. Exit the new document by tapping the Back button once, and then double-tapping the screen to exit the document.

 If your vision is fine, it's difficult to accurately gauge what it's like to use the phone while not being able to see the screen, because it's extremely hard to keep your eyes closed or not sneak a peek at the screen. To disable the screen entirely while using VoiceOver, tap the screen three times with three fingers.

8. Try to open a document. You'll notice that, while you can select the document's name, you can't actually tap the cell to open the document. The reason for this is that VoiceOver doesn't know that the cell works in the same way as a button. To fix this, we need to provide some accessibility information.

9. Open *Main.storyboard*, and go to the document list view controller.

10. Find the `FileCell` in the document collection view.

11. Select the view that contains the image view. When users tap the cell, they'll generally be tapping this view. We need to tell VoiceOver that this view is interactive.

12. Go to the Identity Inspector and scroll down to the Accessibility section.

13. Select the Accessibility Enabled checkbox, as well as the User Interaction Enabled and Button checkboxes (Figure 14-20).

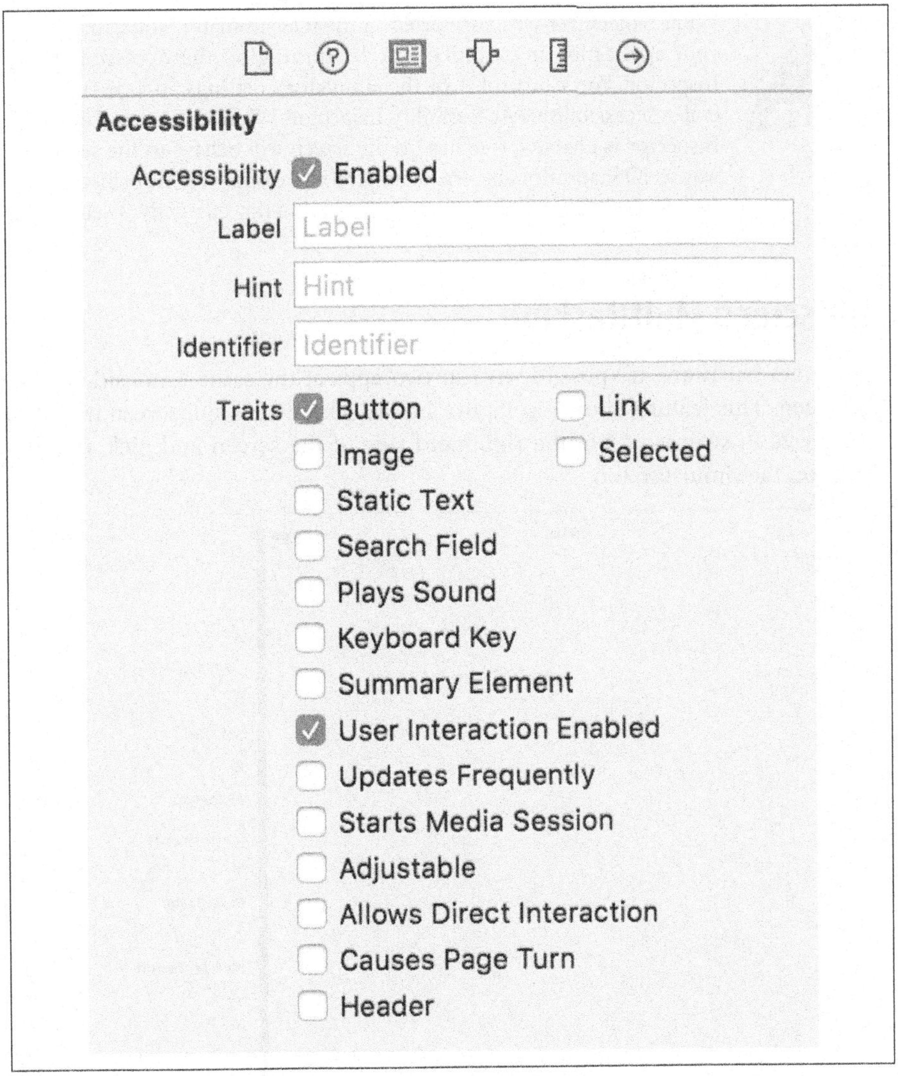

Figure 14-20. Enabling accessibility for the document cell

14. Rerun the application on your phone. You can now select and open documents.

While VoiceOver isn't supported in the iOS simulator, you can test your application in a similar way by turning on the Accessibility Inspector. You can find it in the simulator's Settings app, in General→Accessibility→Accessibility Inspector. While the Accessibility Inspector is enabled, touches on the *screen* will behave in the same way as iOS; additionally, the simulator will display the information that would be provided to the user about the currently selected item.

Splitscreen Multitasking

On certain hardware, it's possible to run two apps at the same time, side by side on the screen. This feature, shown in Figure 14-21, is known as splitscreen multitasking. To activate it, swipe in from the righthand side of the screen and pick an app. This works on the simulator, too.

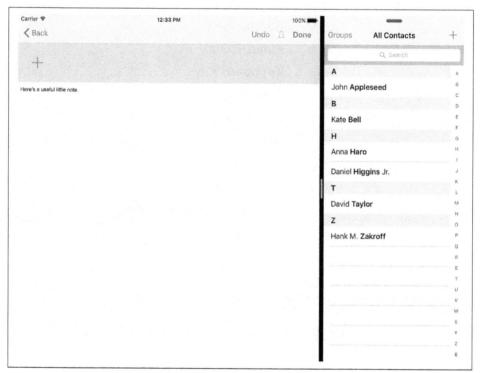

Figure 14-21. Splitscreen multitasking

Splitscreen multitasking is fully available only on iPad Air 2, iPad Mini 4, and the iPad Pro; it's available in a limited mode on earlier devices.

You don't actually need to do anything to support it; because this app is using constraints, the interface will lay itself out appropriately.

This view can be resized, so your constraints will handle it (and also change size classes when needed).

Conclusion

In this chapter, we added the following collection of finishing touches to our iOS app:

- We added text-to-speech support, and along the way learned how to add things to the menu that appears when text is selected.
- We detected links inside the text content of notes, and added the ability for users to tap links and open them in the provided web browser view controller, `SFSafar iViewController`.
- We added app settings, available via the iOS Settings application.
- We added undo support, using `NSUndoManager`.
- We added image filters, using Core Image.
- Finally, we looked at how you can add localization and accessibility support into your apps.

In Part IV, we'll add Apple Watch support to the iOS app, explore a selection of more advanced iOS features, and touch on debugging and problem tracing with your Swift code.

Extending Your Apps

CHAPTER 15

Building a watchOS App

In Part I of this book we explored the Apple developer ecosystem and the developer tools, as well as the basics of programming with Swift and how to structure apps for Apple's platforms. In Parts II and III, we learned the fundamentals of Swift by creating an app for both macOS and iOS, respectively; our app shares data through iCloud, lets us makes notes with a variety of attachment types, and generally behaves as a good, modern application for Mac, iPhone, or iPad. But Apple's platforms don't just stop at conventional computers and handheld computers—they also extend to wearable computers: Apple Watch.

It's important to remember that you can't build a watchOS app without also building and distributing an iOS app. watchOS apps are supplied to a tethered Apple Watch via an application users install on their iPhone.

Apple Watch runs watchOS. watchOS is quite similar to iOS in many ways, and has many of the same frameworks and basic building blocks that you've come to expect. In this chapter, we'll extend our Notes app to also support the Apple Watch.

Of course, Apple also ships the Apple TV, which runs another variant of iOS called tvOS. tvOS is beyond the scope of this book, since it's mostly targeted at entertainment apps and games, and we're here to learn Swift through app development. Everything you've learned in this book about Swift, and much of the Cocoa and Cocoa Touch frameworks, applies to tvOS, too; it just has its own set of frameworks, as well as variants on the ones we've used here. The best place for learning more about tvOS is Apple's documentation (*https://developer.apple.com/tvos/documentation/*).

We'll begin working with watchOS by first discussing how to design for it—from both a visual and a software standpoint. We'll then build out a very simple app, making use of the various features of watchOS, including glances and communicating with iOS.

 If you want to learn more about building apps for the Apple Watch, we recommend the book *Swift Development for the Apple Watch* (O'Reilly), by some of the same authors who wrote this book (hello!). Apple's documentation (*https://developer.apple.com/watchos/*) is also a good reference.

Designing for the Watch

Before we start looking at building the Notes application for the Apple Watch, let's take a closer look at the Apple Watch itself (see Figure 15-1).

Just by looking at the device, we can immediately see a number of constraints that are placed upon all software:

- The screen is extremely small. This limits both the amount of content that can be displayed at once, and also the area in which the user can interact with that content.

- Because the screen is small, touching the screen means covering up a large percentage of the visible content. The Digital Crown, on the side of the device, is therefore used to scroll the screen up and down while still keeping everything visible.

- The device is strapped to the wrist. Because we can't move our lower arms with the same precision as our fingers, the device will be moving around underneath the user's fingers. At the same time, the user might be doing some other activity, or holding something, further complicating how the device is moving. Compare this to the phone or tablet, in which users have a *lot* of control in the off-hand that holds the device.

Figure 15-1. The Apple Watch

In addition to these physical constraints, there are a number of technical constraints imposed on your apps. The watch is a very low-powered device and relies on communication with an iPhone to access a number of resources. This means that the archi-tecture of the watchOS app is distinct to the Apple Watch.

There are three components at play when working with a watchOS app: the container iOS app, the WatchKit app, and the WatchKit extension:

- The *WatchKit app* contains the resources (interface, UI, etc.) used by the watchOS application.

- The *WatchKit extension* contains the code; both are installed on the watch.

- Both the WatchKit app and the WatchKit extension are embedded in an iOS application, which is distributed through the App Store. When the user down-loads the app from the App Store, the app and extension are transferred to the user's Apple Watch.

Designing Our watchOS App

The watchOS app for Notes needs to be very careful in terms of how it's designed. We can't replicate the entire feature set of the iOS app, nor should we: users are not going to want to access every single thing that they can do on their phone. Instead, we need to focus on the *most important* and *most frequently accessed* features.

In our opinion, there are precisely two things that the user will want to do:

- Look at a note
- Make a new note

We'll therefore gear the entire design around these two features. Just as with the Mac and iOS apps, we created wireframes as part of our thinking about how the watchOS app should work.

To access notes, the user needs a way to see the list of available notes. To enable this, we need a screen that presents a list of buttons that, when tapped, displays the note (see Figure 15-2).

Figure 15-2. The note list on the watch

Displaying the note itself is easy; we just need to display a bunch of text (see Figure 15-3). We're specifically excluding attachments from the Apple Watch application, because it's our opinion that the user will care more about the note's text rather than the things attached to it.

Figure 15-3. The note content on the watch

Creating the watchOS Extension

The first thing we need to do to create an app for the watch is add a WatchKit app extension to our project. We do this by adding yet another new target. Let's get started:

1. Open the File menu and choose New→Target.
2. In the watchOS section, choose WatchKit App and click Next (Figure 15-4).

You'll notice that there's also a template called "WatchKit App for watchOS 1"; watchOS 1 did not allow apps to actually run on the watch, and instead everything was done via network to the phone, with the watch handling display only. watchOS 2 and beyond, which is what we're using here, actually allows apps to run on the watch. You shouldn't ever use the watchOS 1 template at this point.

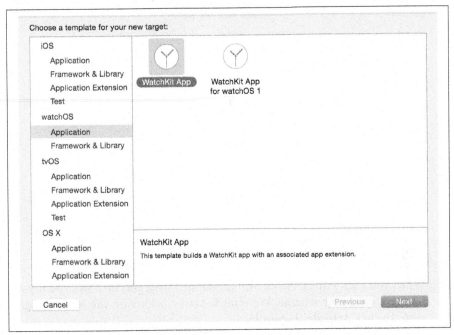

Figure 15-4. Creating the watchOS app

3. Name the application **Watch1**.

The name "Watch" is only for our internal use. On the Apple Watch, it will take the name of the container iOS app. Xcode will make the bundle identifier the same as iOS app's, with .Watch appended. This is because Watch apps are embedded inside iOS app.

4. Ensure that Include Glance Scene is turned on (Figure 15-5). We'll be adding a *glance*, which is a single-screen view of your app that users can access from their watch face, in "Glances" on page 455.

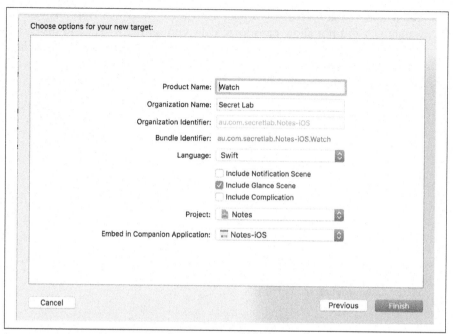

Figure 15-5. Configuring the watchOS app target

5. When you click Finish, Xcode will create the target and then ask you if you want to activate the new scheme. We want to start working on the watchOS app right away, so click Activate (Figure 15-6).

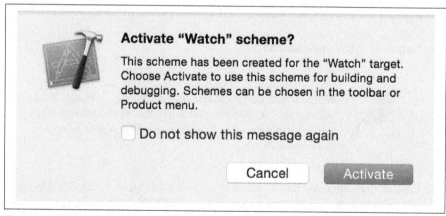

Figure 15-6. Activating the scheme

Now that the application has been set up, we'll add the watchOS app's icons to its asset catalog. Adding icons to an asset catalog should be very familiar at this point!

1. Open the *Assets.xcassets* file inside the Watch group (not the one in the Watch Extension group).

The images to use for the icons are provided in the resources that accompany this book. If you don't have them already, follow the instructions in "Resources Used in This Book" on page ix to get them.

2. Select the AppIcon image set, and drag and drop the images into the slots, as shown in Figure 15-7. Remember to use the filenames to determine the correct slot for each image—for example, the slot "Apple Watch Companion Settings 29pt 2x" should use the image *Icon-AppleWatch-Companion-Settings@2x.png*.

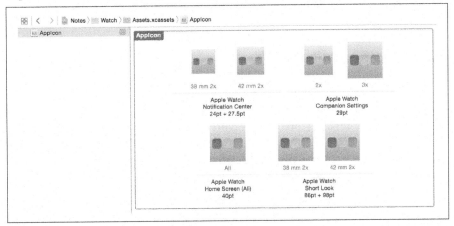

Figure 15-7. Adding the icons for the project

When you're building a watchOS application, you need to use the same developer identity for both the iOS app and the watchOS app. If you only have a single developer account, you're fine. If you use more than one, then double-check the Team setting in the General tab of the Watch and Notes-iOS project info.

3. In the Scheme Selector at the top left of the Xcode window, set the active scheme to a simulator plus a watch. Any combination of iPhone and Watch will do.

If you have an iPhone and an Apple Watch (that is, the real devices, not just the simulator), you can build and run straight onto your watch; watches don't have to leave your wrist for you to install stuff. Note that testing on the simulator is a *lot* easier. If you're testing on an Apple Watch, you may have to go to the home screen and tap the icon to launch it.

4. Press ⌘-R to build and run the app.

Because you're about to install the app onto a new simulator, the simulated iPhone on which you're going to install won't be signed in to iCloud. To fix this, once the iPhone appears, sign it into iCloud by opening the Settings application, selecting iCloud, and tapping Sign In.

Communicating with the iPhone

By default, the app is blank. Let's fix that and let the app retrieve the notes from the phone.

To get access to any data stored on its paired iPhone, you use the WatchConnectivity framework, which allows you to communicate with the phone by sending messages. These messages are simply dictionaries containing very small chunks of information, like strings and numbers.

First, we'll define the different messages that can be sent back and forth between the Apple Watch and the iPhone. There are three different types of messages that will be sent:

List all notes
> The watch wants to receive the list of notes. The iPhone should send back an array of dictionaries; each dictionary will contain the name of the note and its URL.

Open note
> The watch wants to display the content of a note. It will pass the URL of a note; the iPhone should open it, retrieve its text, and send it back.

Create note
> The watch wants to create a note. It will pass the text that the note should contain; the iPhone will create the note and return the updated list of all notes (that is, it will have the same reply as "list all notes").

The actual data that's transferred between the watch and the phone is simply a dictionary; the contents of this dictionary will depend on what type of message it is, which is indicated by the value of the "name" entry in the dictionary.

We now need to define the actual messages that will be sent back and forth. Because a message is just a dictionary, to distinguish between the three different types of messages, the dictionary will need to contain an entry that describes the "name" of the message. Additionally, each value that can be sent in either direction needs a name as well so that it can be retrieved from the dictionaries that are sent back and forth.

The best place to define these is in *DocumentCommon.swift*, which is the Swift file that's currently shared among all of the different targets. We'll add it to the Watch extension target, too:

1. Select *DocumentCommon.swift* and open the File Inspector. Set its Target Membership to include the Watch Extension.

   Doing this includes the *DocumentCommon.swift* file in the watchOS application.

2. Next, add the following code to the end of *DocumentCommon.swift*:

   ```
   let WatchMessageTypeKey = "msg"
   let WatchMessageTypeListAllNotesKey = "list"
   let WatchMessageTypeLoadNoteKey = "load"
   let WatchMessageTypeCreateNoteKey = "create"

   let WatchMessageContentNameKey = "name"
   let WatchMessageContentURLKey = "url"
   let WatchMessageContentTextKey = "text"
   let WatchMessageContentListKey = "list"
   ```

   These strings will be used in the messages that are sent back and forth between the iPhone and the watch.

In this application, multiple different screens will need to access the iPhone via WatchConnectivity. Rather than spreading this work over all of the app, it's better to centralize it into a single object. To that end, we'll create a class that handles all iPhone/watch communication:

1. Open *ExtensionDelegate.swift*.

2. Import the WatchConnectivity framework by adding it to the list of imports:

   ```
   import WatchConnectivity
   ```

This framework enables the Apple Watch and the iPhone to which it's tethered to talk to each other over the network. The practicalities of how this happens are handled for you: sometimes it might be over Bluetooth, sometimes it might be over WiFi, and sometimes it'll be a combination of both. The iPhone to which the watch is tethered doesn't even need to be on the same network for this to work.

3. Add the following class to the end of the file. Note that it conforms to WCSession Delegate:

```
class SessionManager : NSObject, WCSessionDelegate {

}
```

The WCSessionDelegate protocol defines methods that are called when the device receives a message. Both the watchOS app and the iOS app will have a class that implements WCSessionDelegate, since they'll both need to respond to messages.

We want this class to be a *singleton*—that is, a class of which there's only ever one instance, and everyone accesses the same instance. We've seen this pattern before —for example, the NSFileManager class's defaultManager property provides access to a single, shared instance of the class.

To make a shared instance of this class available, we'll define a *static* constant property that, when then application loads, is initialized to an instance of the class.

4. Add the following property to SessionManager:

```
static let sharedSession = SessionManager()
```

Additionally, when the instance is created, we'll get in touch with the shared WCSession and tell it to use this instance as its delegate. Doing this means that we'll receive messages from the session.

This won't happen on the watch, but it will happen on the iPhone, so now's a good time to introduce it.

5. Add the following code to SessionManager:

```
var session : WCSession { return WCSession.default() }

override init() {
    super.init()
    session.delegate = self
    session.activate()
}
```

When the SessionManager class is created—which happens when the sharedSes sion variable is created—then the shared WCSession class is told to use the Ses sionManager as its delegate. This means that the SessionManager will be notified when a message arrives. We then activate the session, enabling communication between the watch and the iPhone.

However, the session won't activate immediately. Instead, the session will take a moment before it's ready; when it is, or if it encounters a problem, it will call a method on its delegate, called session(_, activationDidCompleteWith: error:). This method indicates that activation either completed successfully, or failed.

This poses a minor problem for our design. Other objects in the Watch Extension shouldn't have to know or care about whether the session is active or not; they should simply try to send messages, and get back a reply (or an error).

To deal with this, we'll set up a simple message queue in the SessionManager class. When the SessionManager is asked to send a message, and the session is not yet active, it will instead store the message call in a closure, which it keeps in an array. When the session becomes active, all closures in this array are called. This has the effect of delaying any attempt to deliver a message until the session becomes active.

We'll begin by adding the array that stores these deferred tasks. Add the following type alias and property to the SessionManager class:

```
// To save us some typing, we'll define a type called
// 'DeferredSessionTask', which is a closure that accepts an
// optional error and returns nothing
typealias DeferredSessionTask = (Error?) -> Void

// The 'deferredTasks' array is a list of all tasks that are
// waiting for the session to activate
var deferredTasks : [DeferredSessionTask] = []
```

Next, we'll add the method that queues up a task. If the session is already active, then the task will be run right away; otherwise, it will be added to the array. Add the following method to the SessionManager class:

```
// Runs a closure when the session becomes active. If the session is
// already active, the closure is run immediately.
func runTaskWhenSessionActive(completionBlock: @escaping DeferredSessionTask) {

    // If the session is already active, run the block immediately
    // with no error
    if session.activationState == .activated {
        completionBlock(nil)
    } else {
        // Otherwise, add this task to the list,
        // and request that the session activate
        deferredTasks.append(completionBlock)
        session.activate()
    }
}
```

Finally, we'll implement the session(_, activationDidCompleteWith: error:) method. In this method, the queued up tasks are all run. If there was a problem, the error that this method receives as a parameter is passed to the tasks. Add the following method to the SessionManager class:

```
func session(_ session: WCSession,
  activationDidCompleteWith activationState: WCSessionActivationState,
  error: Error?) {

    // Either the session was activated, or error != nil.
    // Call each task, passing the current value of error.
    for task in deferredTasks {
        task(error)
    }

    // Clear the list.
    deferredTasks = []

}
```

We now need to have some way for the watch to keep track of the notes that it knows about. We don't need to have a complete representation of the entire note—we just need to know about the names and URLs of notes that exist on the phone.

To that end, we'll create a struct that just stores the name as a String, and the URL as a NSURL. Because the iPhone will be passing information about the notes as dictionaries, we'll also add an initializer to this struct that allows it to use a dictionary to set itself up.

Finally, it's worth pointing out that this struct will be *inside* the SessionManager class. This decision is entirely a stylistic one; it's slightly nicer to keep related stuff together:

1. Add the following code to SessionManager:

```
struct NoteInfo : Equatable {
    var name : String
    var URL : Foundation.URL?

    init(dictionary:[String:AnyObject]) {

        let name
            = dictionary[WatchMessageContentNameKey] as? String
                ?? "(no name)"

        self.name = name

        if let URLString = dictionary[WatchMessageContentURLKey] as? String
        {
            self.URL = Foundation.URL(string: URLString)
        }

    }
```

```
        static func == (lhs: NoteInfo, rhs: NoteInfo) -> Bool {
            return lhs.name == rhs.name && lhs.URL == rhs.URL
        }
    }
```

The NoteInfo struct is used on the watch to represent a single note. It's a very simple, pared-back version of the Document class, which stores two critical things: the name of the document, which is shown to the user, and the URL of the document as it exists on the iPhone. We also provide an initializer that lets it use a dictionary to get its initial values.

2. Next, we'll add an array to store this collection of notes. Add the following property to SessionManager:

```
    var notes : [NoteInfo] = []
```

Then, because there are two different messages that can result in us receiving a list of notes, we'll break out the code that updates the notes array into its own method. This will help to keep the code tidy, since we can then just call this method and pass in the information we got from the phone to it as a parameter, rather than having to write the same code twice.

3. Add the following method to SessionManager:

```
    func updateLocalNoteListWithReply(_ reply:[String:Any]) {

        // Did we receive a dictionary in the reply?
        if let noteList = reply[WatchMessageContentListKey]
            as? [[String:AnyObject]] {

            // Convert all dictionaries to notes
            self.notes = noteList.map({ (dict) -> NoteInfo in
                return NoteInfo(dictionary: dict)
            })

        }
    }
```

This method simply takes the dictionary that we've received and turns it into an array of notes, which is stored in the notes property.

We can now add the methods that send messages to the iPhone and receive the results. The users of these methods will need to provide a closure, which will be called when the information has been loaded, and serves as the means for the information to be passed back.

We'll start with the method that asks for the list of notes.

4. Add the following method to SessionManager:

```
    func updateList(_ completionHandler: @escaping ([NoteInfo], NSError?)->Void)
    {
```

```
let message = [
    WatchMessageTypeKey : WatchMessageTypeListAllNotesKey
]

self.runTaskWhenSessionActive { (error) in

    if error != nil {
        completionHandler([], error as NSError?)
        return
    }

    self.session.sendMessage(message, replyHandler: {
        reply in

        self.updateLocalNoteListWithReply(reply as [String:AnyObject])

        completionHandler(self.notes, nil)

    }, errorHandler: { error in
        print("Error! \(error)")
        completionHandler([], error as NSError?)

    })
}

}
```

When the `updateList` method is called, we prepare a message by creating a dictionary. We then ask the `WCSession` to send the message to the iPhone and provide a closure that's called when the iPhone's reply arrives. When it does, we simply call `updateLocalNoteListWithReply`. Additionally, this method has its *own* completion handler, allowing our UI to be notified about when it's time to update what the user can see.

5. Next, we'll implement the method that asks for a specific note by its URL and receives its text:

```
func loadNote(_ noteURL: URL,
    completionHandler: @escaping (String?, Error?) -> Void) {

    let message = [
        WatchMessageTypeKey: WatchMessageTypeLoadNoteKey,
        WatchMessageContentURLKey: noteURL.absoluteString
    ]

    self.runTaskWhenSessionActive { (error) in
        if error != nil {
            completionHandler(nil, error)
            return
```

```
        }

        self.session.sendMessage(message, replyHandler: {
            reply in

            let text = reply[WatchMessageContentTextKey] as? String

            completionHandler(text, nil)
        },
                            errorHandler: { error in
                                completionHandler(nil, error)

        })
    }

}
```

This method is extremely similar to the `updateList` method, except that it requests a specific note from the iPhone. The iPhone will return the text of the note, which is then given to `updateList`'s completion handler.

6. Finally, we'll implement the method that asks the iPhone to create a new note with provided text (which will eventually come from the Apple Watch's built-in dictation system) and that receives an updated list of notes:

```
func createNote(_ text:String,
    completionHandler: @escaping ([NoteInfo], Error?)->Void) {

    let message = [
        WatchMessageTypeKey : WatchMessageTypeCreateNoteKey,
        WatchMessageContentTextKey : text
    ]

    self.runTaskWhenSessionActive { (error) in

        if error != nil {
            completionHandler([], error)
            return
        }

        self.session.sendMessage(message, replyHandler: {
            reply in

            self.updateLocalNoteListWithReply(reply)

            completionHandler(self.notes, nil)

        }, errorHandler: {
            error in

            completionHandler([], error)
```

```
          })
        }

    }
```

The createNote method simply takes the text to be used in a new note and fires it off to the iPhone. The iPhone will create the document and then return the updated list of documents available, allowing us to refresh the list immediately after creating a new note.

We're done with the watch side of things. The messages are sent, and the reply is interpreted and used. Next, we need to add support for these messages to the iPhone. We'll do this by extending the AppDelegate class to act as the delegate for the WCSession, which will allow it to receive messages from the watch. We'll then implement code, in the iOS app, that allows it to reply to the messages that it's received:

1. Open the iOS app's *AppDelegate.swift* file.

2. Add the WatchConnectivity framework to the list of imports:

   ```
   import WatchConnectivity
   ```

3. Next, add the extension that makes AppDelegate conform to WCSessionDelegate. We're doing this to keep the WCSessionDelegate methods separate from the rest of the methods, for ease of reading. First, we'll include some methods that are called when the state of the WCSession changes:

   ```
   extension AppDelegate : WCSessionDelegate {

       public func session(_ session: WCSession,
                           activationDidCompleteWith
                               activationState: WCSessionActivationState,
                           error: Error?) {
           NSLog("Watch session is now in activation state \(activationState)")
       }

       public func sessionDidDeactivate(_ session: WCSession) {
           NSLog("Watch session deactivated")
       }

       public func sessionDidBecomeInactive(_ session: WCSession) {
           NSLog("Watch session is now inactive")
       }

   }
   ```

Next, we need to receive messages from the Apple Watch and determine what to do with them. To do this, we need to implement the method session(_, didReceive

---

Message:, replyHandler:) in the extension. This method will receive the message that was sent from the watch and determine what to do about it.

To keep things tidy, we'll implement a handler method for each of the three different types of messages that can be received.

One of the parameters that the didReceiveMessage method receives is a closure, which must be called in order to reply to the message; therefore, this closure will be passed to the handler methods.

Let's get started by implementing didReceiveMessage:

1. Add the following method to the AppDelegate's WCSessionDelegate extension:

```
func session(_ session: WCSession,
    didReceiveMessage message: [String : Any],
    replyHandler: @escaping ([String : Any]) -> Void) {

    if let messageName = message[WatchMessageTypeKey] as? String {

        switch messageName {
        case WatchMessageTypeListAllNotesKey:
            handleListAllNotes(replyHandler)
        case WatchMessageTypeLoadNoteKey:
            if let uString = message[WatchMessageContentURLKey] as? String,
        let url = URL(string: uString) {
        handleLoadNote(url, replyHandler: replyHandler)
            } else {
                // If there's no URL, then fall through to the
                // default case fallthrough
            }
        case WatchMessageTypeCreateNoteKey:
            if let textForNote = message[WatchMessageContentTextKey]
                as? String {

                handleCreateNote(textForNote, replyHandler: replyHandler)
            } else {
                // No text provided? Fall through to the default case
                fallthrough
            }

        default:
            // Don't know what this is, so reply with the empty dictionary
            replyHandler([:])
        }
    }
}
```

When we receive a message from the watch, we check the value of the message's WatchMessageTypeKey. Based on the value, we call either the handleListAll

Notes, handleLoadNote, or handleCreateNote method. In each case, we pass the replyHandler closure to these methods, allowing the method to send a reply.

2. Next, implement the handleListAllNotes method, which uses an NSFile Manager to list the current contents of the iCloud container, builds an array of dictionaries that represents the contents, and passes this dictionary as a reply to the message:

```
func handleListAllNotes(_ replyHandler: ([String:Any]) -> Void) {

    let fileManager = FileManager.default

    var allFiles : [URL] = []

    do {

        // Add the list of cloud documents
        if let documentsFolder = fileManager
            .url(forUbiquityContainerIdentifier: nil)?
            .appendingPathComponent("Documents", isDirectory: true)  {
            let cloudFiles = try fileManager
                .contentsOfDirectory(atPath: documentsFolder.path)
                .map({
                    documentsFolder.appendingPathComponent($0,
                        isDirectory: false)
                })
            allFiles.append(contentsOf: cloudFiles)
        }

        // Add the list of all local documents

        if let localDocumentsFolder
            = fileManager.urls(for: .documentDirectory,
                in: .userDomainMask).first {

            let localFiles =
                try fileManager
                .contentsOfDirectory(atPath: localDocumentsFolder.path)
                .map({
                    localDocumentsFolder.appendingPathComponent($0,
                        isDirectory: false)
                })
            allFiles.append(contentsOf: localFiles)
        }

        // Filter these to only those that end in ".note",

        let noteFiles = allFiles
            .filter({
                $0.lastPathComponent.hasSuffix(".note")
```

```
    })

    // Convert this list into an array of dictionaries, each
    // containing the note's name and URL
    let results = noteFiles.map({ url in

        [
            WatchMessageContentNameKey: url.lastPathComponent,
            WatchMessageContentURLKey: url.absoluteString
        ]

    })

    // Bundle up this into our reply dictionary
    let reply = [
        WatchMessageContentListKey: results
    ]

    replyHandler(reply as [String : AnyObject])

} catch let error as NSError {
    // Log an error and return the empty array
    NSLog("Failed to get contents of Documents folder: \(error)")
    replyHandler([:])
}

}
```

In this method, we're querying for the list of all documents and filtering that list down to only those whose filenames end in *.note*. We then use this list to create a reply dictionary, which we pass to the `replyHandler`. As a result, the watch will receive the list of available notes.

3. Next, implement the `handleLoadNote` method, which receives the URL of a note to load, opens that document, and retrieves its text, which it passes back as the reply:

```
func handleLoadNote(_ url: URL,
    replyHandler: @escaping ([String:Any]) -> Void) {
    let document = Document(fileURL:url)
    document.open { success in

        // Ensure that we successfully opened the document
        guard success == true else {
            // If we didn't, reply with an empty dictionary and bail out
            replyHandler([:])
            return
        }

        // Extract the plain, nonattributed text from the document
```

```
        let text = document.text.string

        // Build the reply with this response
        let reply = [
            WatchMessageContentTextKey: text
        ]

        // Close the document; don't provide a completion handler,
        // because we're not making changes and therefore don't care
        // if a save succeeds or not
        document.close(completionHandler: nil)

        replyHandler(reply as [String : AnyObject])
    }

}
```

To return the text of a note, we first need to open the Document and ask it for its
text. Before we return it, we close the document; note that we don't provide a closure to closeWithCompletionHandler, since we're not making any changes to the
document, and therefore don't need to worry about whether saving the document
when it was closed succeeded.

4. Finally, implement the handleCreateNote method, which receives some text to
   save in a new note; it creates the new document, gives it the text, and saves it; it
   then calls handleListAllNotes, passing the reply handler, so that the watch
   receives the updated list of documents:

```
func handleCreateNote(_ text: String,
    replyHandler: @escaping ([String:Any]) -> Void) {

    let formatter = DocumentListViewController.documentNameDateFormatter
    let documentDate = formatter.string(from: Date())
    let documentName = "Document \(documentDate) from Watch.note"

    // Determine where the file should be saved locally
    // (before moving to iCloud)
    guard let documentsFolder = FileManager.default
        .urls(for: .documentDirectory,
        in: .userDomainMask).first else {
            self.handleListAllNotes(replyHandler)
            return
    }

    let documentDestinationURL = documentsFolder
        .appendingPathComponent(documentName)

    guard let ubiquitousDocumentsDirectoryURL =
        FileManager.default.url(forUbiquityContainerIdentifier: nil)?
        .appendingPathComponent("Documents") else {
```

```
            self.handleListAllNotes(replyHandler)
            return
    }

    // Prepare the document and try to save it locally
    let newDocument = Document(fileURL:documentDestinationURL)
    newDocument.text = NSAttributedString(string: text)

    // Try to save it locally
    newDocument.save(to: documentDestinationURL,
        for: .forCreating) { (success) -> Void in

            // Did the save succeed? If not, just reply with the
            // list of notes.
            guard success == true else {
                self.handleListAllNotes(replyHandler)
                return
            }

            // OK, it succeeded!

            // Move it to iCloud
            let ubiquitousDestinationURL = ubiquitousDocumentsDirectoryURL
                .appendingPathComponent(documentName)

            // Perform the move to iCloud in the background
            OperationQueue().addOperation { () -> Void in
                do {
                    try FileManager.default
                        .setUbiquitous(true,
                            itemAt: documentDestinationURL,
                            destinationURL: ubiquitousDestinationURL)

                } catch let error as NSError {
                    NSLog("Error storing document in iCloud! " +
                        "\(error.localizedDescription)")
                }

                OperationQueue.main
                    .addOperation { () -> Void in
                    // Pass back the list of everything currently
                    // in iCloud
                    self.handleListAllNotes(replyHandler)
                }
            }

    }
}
```

The last method to implement involves creating a new note. This is very similar to the `createDocument` method we implemented back in "Creating Documents" on page 234, but with one change: when we successfully finish creating the document, we call `handleListAllNotes`, which results in the Apple Watch receiving the updated list of documents.

Finally, we need to make the `WCSession` use the app delegate, which is now capable of receiving and replying to messages from the watch, as its delegate.

5. Add the following code to `AppDelegate`'s `didFinishLaunchingWithOptions` method to set up and activate the session:

```
WCSession.default().delegate = self
WCSession.default().activate()
```

Just as on the Apple Watch, we need to configure the `WCSession` to let us know when we receive a message. We also call `activateSession` to turn on the two-way communication between the two devices.

Congratulations! The iPhone and Apple Watch are now able to talk to each other. We don't have a user interface on the watch yet, so it's not very useful!

Let's put this new functionality to use by building the Watch app's interface.

User Interfaces for the Apple Watch

We'll now start making the interface that the user works with on the watch. The watch app will be composed of two `WKInterfaceController` subclasses: one that displays the list of notes, and one that displays the content of a single note.

By default, the Xcode template contains a single `WKInterfaceController`, called `InterfaceController`. This name isn't the greatest, since it doesn't describe what the interface controller is *for*, so we'll start by renaming it:

1. Rename the file *InterfaceController.swift* to *NoteListInterfaceController.swift*.

2. Open this file and rename the `InterfaceController` class to `NoteListInterface Controller`.

Because the Apple Watch app is configured to look for an interface controller class called `InterfaceController` at startup, we need to change this setting:

1. Open the Watch extension's *Info.plist* file and find the `RemoteInterfacePrinci palClass` entry.

2. Change this entry from `$(PRODUCT_MODULE_NAME).InterfaceController` to `$(PRODUCT_MODULE_NAME).NoteListInterfaceController`.

Next, we'll create the class that controls the second screen (the one that shows the contents of a note). Each separate interface controller should be a separate class so that each screen can operate independently.

1. Open the File menu and choose New→File.

2. Choose the Source category in the watchOS section, and select "WatchKit class." Click Next.

Remember, creating a new class really means creating a Swift file; the advantage of using this method is that some of the setup will be taken care of for you.

3. Name the new class **NoteInterfaceController**, and make it a subclass of WKIn terfaceController (see Figure 15-8).

Figure 15-8. Configuring the new class

We'll now set up the storyboard that the watchOS application uses. We used story-boards for the iOS app, back in Part III, and we'll be using them again here for the watchOS app:

1. Open the *Interface.storyboard* file and find the interface controller. Select it.

2. Open the Identity Inspector and change its class from `InterfaceController` to `NoteListInterfaceController`.

This will make the new interface controller use the `NoteListInterfaceControl ler` class that we just created.

3. Open the Attributes Inspector and change its title to **Notes**.

This updates the label at the top of the screen to Notes.

We're finally ready to build the interface. The note list will show, as its name suggests, a list of notes. In watchOS, you use a *table* to show lists of content; each row in the table can have its interface customized to your requirements.

The contents of each row are controlled by a *row controller*, which is a custom object that you create. Each type of row requires a new row controller class.

Unlike `UICollectionViews` and `UITableViews`, there's no special class for the row controllers that you should subclass. You just subclass the generic `NSObject` class:

1. Go to the Object library, and search for a `table` (Figure 15-9).

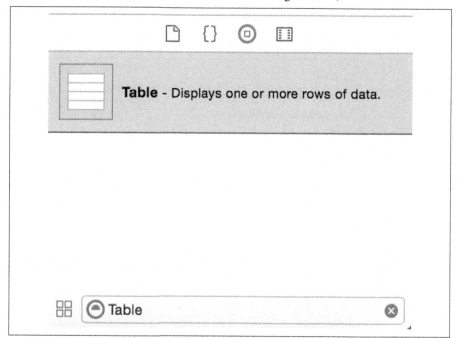

Figure 15-9. A Table in the Object library

2. Drag a table into the interface controller. It will fill the width of the screen (Figure 15-10).

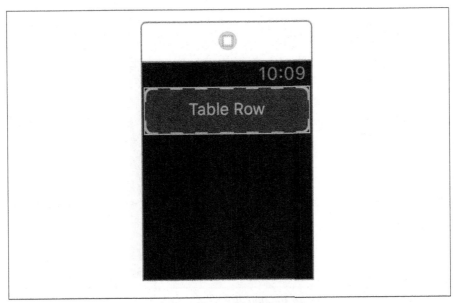

Figure 15-10. A Table object, filling the width of the screen

Next, we'll create the row controller class for the rows. Remember, each row will represent a note that the watch knows about:

1. Open *NoteListInterfaceController.swift* in the Assistant Editor.

2. Add the following NoteRow class to the bottom of the file:

   ```
   class NoteRow : NSObject {

   }
   ```

3. Select the row controller in the outline and go to the Identity Inspector. Set its class to NoteRow.

4. Go to the Attributes Inspector and set its identifier to NoteRow as well. We'll use this to populate the table's contents.

5. Search for Label in the Object library and drag it into the table's row.

6. Select the new label and set its text to Note Name.

The interface for the note list is now fully designed and should look like Figure 15-11.

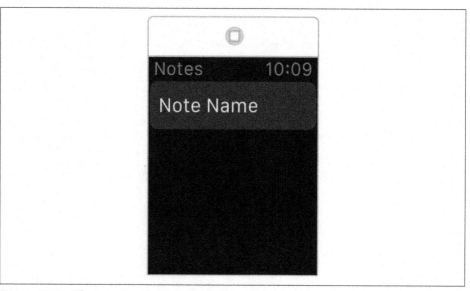

Figure 15-11. The interface for the note list

We'll now connect the interface to the code. First, we need to connect the label in the table's row to an outlet in the `NoteRow` class; next, we need to connect the table itself to the interface controller:

1. Hold down the Control key and drag from the label into the `NoteRow` class. Create a new outlet called `nameLabel`.

2. Hold down the Control key a second time and drag from the table into the `Note ListInterfaceController` class. Create a new outlet, `noteListTable`, by dragging from the table entry in the outline.

 Drag from the outline, not from the table in the canvas. If the drag starts from the canvas, you'll end up creating an outlet for the wrong type of object.

We can now set up the `NoteInterfaceController` to request a list of notes from the watch, via the `SessionManager`, and populate the table.

Because there will eventually be *two* reasons for updating the table (both when the app starts up, and when the user has added a new note), we'll break out the code that updates the table into its own function, `updateListWithNotes`:

1. Add the following method to `NoteListInterfaceController`:

```
func updateListWithNotes(_ notes: [SessionManager.NoteInfo]) {

    // Have the notes changed? Don't do anything if not.
    if notes == self.displayedNotes {
        return
    }

    self.noteListTable.setNumberOfRows(notes.count, withRowType: "NoteRow")

    for (i, note) in notes.enumerated() {
        if let row = self.noteListTable.rowController(at: i) as? NoteRow {
            row.nameLabel.setText(note.name)
        }
    }

    self.displayedNotes = notes
}
```

This method will be called by the willActivate method, which we'll add to shortly. It receives a list of NoteInfo objects, which it uses to populate the contents of the table view.

When the interface controller first appears, we need to query the iPhone for the list of notes and then call updateListWithNotes.

2. Add the following method to NoteListViewController:

```
override func willActivate() {
    SessionManager.sharedSession.updateList() { notes, error in
        self.updateListWithNotes(notes)
    }
}
```

When the interface controller appears on screen, it needs to get the list of notes to display. To get this, we ask the SessionManager to request the list of notes from the iPhone; when we receive the reply, we call updateListWithNotes to make it appear.

We can now test the app.

3. Run the application. The list of notes will appear (see Figure 15-12).

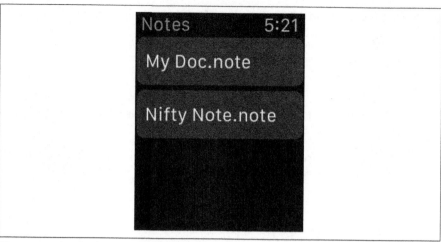

Figure 15-12. The list of notes

Showing Note Contents

Next, we'll create a new interface controller that shows the contents of a single note. When the user taps a note in the NoteListInterfaceController, we'll use a segue to transition to this new interface controller, which will then request the text of a note from the iPhone. Once it receives the text, it will display it in a label.

Let's start by creating the interface for the new interface controller:

1. Go to the Object library, and search for Interface Controller. A few different options will appear; the one you want is the base Interface Controller, which should appear at the top of the list (see Figure 15-13).

   The other options are the Glance Interface Controller, which allows you to create a custom UI for glances (screens that appear when the user swipes up from the bottom of the watch screen), and the Notification Interface Controller, which allows you to create a custom UI for notifications that your app receives. We want a generic, simple interface controller to add to the app.

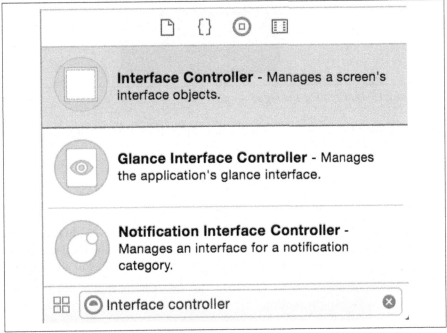

Figure 15-13. Searching for Interface Controller in the Object library—the base Interface Controller, which is the one we want, is selected

2. Drag in a new interface controller.

3. Select it and go to the Identity Inspector. Change its class from `WKInterfaceCon troller` to `NoteInterfaceController` to make it use that class's code.

4. Go to the Attributes Inspector and change its title to **Note**.

Next, we'll create the segue that connects the note list interface controller to the note interface controller:

1. Hold down the Control key and drag from the Note Row—that is, the single row in the table view—to the note interface controller. When you release the mouse button, a menu will appear with the available types of segue (Figure 15-14). Choose Push.

   The alternative is to create a modal segue, which slides an interface controller up from the bottom of the screen. It's designed for alerts and other modal content.

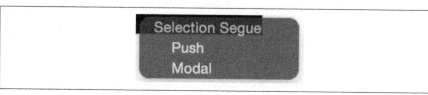

Figure 15-14. Creating the segue

2. Select this new segue and go to the Attributes Inspector. Change its identifier to ShowNote.

We can now create the interface for the interface controller:

1. Drag a label into the interface controller.

2. Go to the Attributes Inspector and set the Lines value to 0. This will make the label resize to fit all of the text; if the lines value is 0, then the label resizes itself to fit *all* lines of text, rather than truncating after a fixed number of allowed lines.

3. Set the Text value to **Note Content**. This text will be replaced with the actual content of the note at runtime.

The entire interface, for both interface controllers, should now look like Figure 15-15.

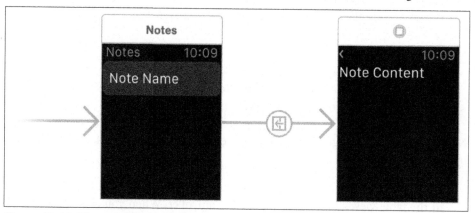

Figure 15-15. The completed interface

Finally, we can connect the label in the note interface controller to the code:

1. Open NoteInterfaceController in the Assistant. Hold down the Control key and drag from the Note Content label into the NoteInterfaceController class. Create a new outlet called noteContentLabel.

2. Run the application, and tap one of the notes. You'll be taken to the new interface controller!

Next, we'll make the `NoteListInterfaceController` respond to the user tapping the cell and make it pass along the selected note's URL to the `NoteInterfaceController`. This will allow the `NoteInterfaceController` to request the contents of the document.

To do this, we'll implement the `contextForSegueWithIdentifier` method, which watchOS calls when a table row is tapped. This method is expected to return a *context object*, which can be of any type; this object is passed to the next interface controller's `awakeWithContext` method as a parameter.

1. Open *NoteListInterfaceController.swift* and add the following method to it:

```
override func contextForSegue(withIdentifier segueIdentifier: String,
    in table: WKInterfaceTable, rowIndex: Int) -> Any? {

    // Was this the ShowNote segue?
    if segueIdentifier == "ShowNote" {
        // Pass the URL for the selected note to the interface controller
        return SessionManager.sharedSession.notes[rowIndex].URL
    }

    return nil
}
```

This code works in the same way as the `prepareForSegue` method that `UIView` `Controllers` implement. It checks to make sure that we're running the `ShowNote` segue, and if we are, we pass the URL of the note that the user has selected.

2. Next, we'll implement `awakeWithContext` in the `NoteInterfaceController` to make it use this `NSURL` to request the note text. The `NoteInterfaceController` will give this `NSURL` to the `SessionManager`, which will give it to the iPhone to retrieve the content of the document.

3. Open *NoteInterfaceController.swift* and update `awakeWithContext` to look like the following code:

```
override func awake(withContext context: Any?) {

    // We've hopefully received an NSURL that points at a
    // note on the iPhone we want to display!

    if let url = context as? URL {

        // First, clear the label - it might take a moment for
        // the text to appear.
        self.noteContentLabel.setText(nil)
```

```
SessionManager.sharedSession.loadNote(url,
    completionHandler: { text, error -> Void in

    if let theText = text {
        // We have the text! Display it.
        self.noteContentLabel.setText(theText)
    }
})
}

}
```

In the `NoteInterfaceController`'s `awakeWithContext` method, the context is whatever object was returned by the `contextForSegueWithIdentifier` method. If this is an `NSURL`, then we use it to request the text of the note. If we receive the text, we display it in the `noteContentLabel`.

4. Run the app. When you tap a note, its contents will now appear! (See Figure 15-16.)

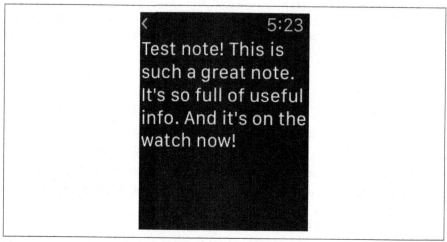

Figure 15-16. A note being tapped in the list, and then displayed

There's one last thing to do. It's possible that the transfer of the text might fail; if this happens, we should show an alert to the user to indicate that something's gone wrong. Add the following code to `awakeWithContext`:

```
override func awake(withContext context: Any?) {

    // We've hopefully received an NSURL that points at a
    // note on the iPhone we want to display!

    if let url = context as? URL {
```

```
            // First, clear the label - it might take a moment for
            // the text to appear.
            self.noteContentLabel.setText(nil)

            SessionManager.sharedSession.loadNote(url,
                completionHandler: { text, error -> Void in

>               if let theError = error {
>                   // We have an error! Present it, and add a button
>                   // that closes this screen when tapped.
>
>                   let closeAction = WKAlertAction(title: "Close",
>                       style: WKAlertActionStyle.default,
>                       handler: { () -> Void in
>                           self.pop()
>                       })
>
>                   self.presentAlert(withTitle: "Error loading note",
>                       message: theError.localizedDescription,
>                       preferredStyle: WKAlertControllerStyle.alert,
>                       actions: [closeAction])
>
>                   return
>               }

                if let theText = text {
                    // We have the text! Display it.
                    self.noteContentLabel.setText(theText)
                }
            })
        }

    }
```

The completion handler passed to loadNote receives either the text content or an NSError object. If we have an error, then we show an alert interface controller by calling presentAlertControllerWithTitle.

 We aren't using do-catch here because the error comes from outside this method, rather than being created by calling a method that throws.

When you run the application again, if there's ever an error in displaying the contents of the note, an alert will appear (see Figure 15-17).

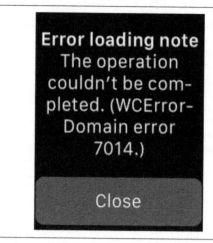

Figure 15-17. The alert that appears when there's an error displaying the contents of the note

Creating New Notes

Next, we'll add the ability to create new notes on the Apple Watch. We'll do this through a *menu item*: when the user force-touches the note list screen (that is, presses hard on the watch's surface), a button will appear that allows him or her to write a new note. If this button is tapped, the watch will allow the user to dictate some text; once this is done, the NoteListInterfaceController will send this text to the iPhone to create the note.

The only meaningful way to do text input on the Apple Watch is with voice recognition.

First, we'll create the menu item:

1. Go to the *Interface.storyboard* file.

2. Search for Menu in the Object library and drag it onto the NoteListInterfaceCon troller.

3. Select the menu item that comes by default, and go to the Attributes Inspector.

4. Set its image to **Add**, and its title to **Create Note**.

5. Hold down the Control key and drag from the Menu item into NoteListInterfa ceController. Create a new action called createNote.

6. Add the following code to the `createNote` method:

```
@IBAction func createNote() {

    let suggestions = [
        "Awesome note!",
        "What a great test note!",
        "I love purchasing and reading books from O'Reilly Media!"
    ]

    self.presentTextInputController(withSuggestions: suggestions,
        allowedInputMode: WKTextInputMode.plain) {
        (results) -> Void in

            if let text = results?.first as? String {
                SessionManager
                    .sharedSession
                    .createNote(text, completionHandler: { notes, error in
                    self.updateListWithNotes(notes)
                })
            }
        }
    }
}
```

This method displays a text input view controller, which permits the user to either select from an array of options that you provide or dictate a response.

 If you pass in `nil` for the list of suggestions, the text input controller will go straight to dictation, instead of letting the user pick from a list of options. Dictation doesn't work on the simulator, so if you want to test it without a device, always pass in some suggestions.

7. Run the application and force-touch the note list to start dictating. When you're done, new notes will be created (see Figure 15-18).

Figure 15-18. The force-touch menu

Adding Handoff Between the Watch and the iPhone

We'll now add the ability to hand off from the Apple Watch to the iPhone. If a user is viewing a note on the watch and then turns on the iPhone, a Handoff icon will appear in the bottom left of the screen; if the user swipes up from this icon, the document will open in the iOS app.

This functionality is provided through the same system that makes Handoff work between the iPhone and the Mac: a *user activity* is broadcast by the watch, and when the user decides to continue the activity on the phone, they exchange information.

There's only one snag when it comes to the Apple Watch/iPhone handoff: unlike the Mac/iPhone handoff, we aren't able to take advantage of the fact that NSDocument/ UIDocument deal with passing the URL for the document for us. We'll need to pass it along ourselves. This means adding a little bit of extra information into the user activity on the watch, and looking for that information on the iPhone.

Handoff works only on a physical device. You'll need to build and run the app on your actual Apple Watch and iPhone to test this:

1. Open *DocumentCommon.swift*.

2. Add the following line of code to the file:

   ```
   let WatchHandoffDocumentURL = "watch_document_url_key"
   ```

   We'll use this key to find the URL of the document when handing off from the watch to another device.

3. Next, open *DocumentListViewController.swift* and add the following code to the `restoreUserActivityState` method:

```
override func restoreUserActivityState(_ activity: NSUserActivity) {
    // We're being told to open a document

    if let url = activity.userInfo?[NSUserActivityDocumentURLKey] as? URL {

        // Open the document
        self.performSegue(withIdentifier: "ShowDocument", sender: url)
    }

>   // This is coming from the watch
>   if let urlString = activity
>           .userInfo?[WatchHandoffDocumentURL] as? String,
>       let url = URL(string: urlString) {
>           // Open the document
>           self.performSegue(withIdentifier: "ShowDocument", sender: url)
>   }

    // We're coming from a search result
    if let searchableItemIdentifier = activity
            .userInfo?[CSSearchableItemActivityIdentifier] as? String,
        let url = URL(string: searchableItemIdentifier) {
        // Open the document
        self.performSegue(withIdentifier: "ShowDocument", sender: url)
    }

}
```

If the handoff dictionary contains a value for the key `WatchHandoffDocumentURL`, we extract the URL from it and use it to open the document.

Finally, we'll make the `NoteInterfaceController` let other devices know that the user is looking at a document. This will cause the user's other devices to show the app's icon either on the lock screen (for iOS devices) or in the Dock (on Macs):

1. Open *NoteInterfaceController.swift* and add the following code to the `awakeWith Context` method:

```
override func awake(withContext context: Any?) {

    // We've hopefully received an NSURL that points at a
    // note on the iPhone we want to display!

    if let url = context as? URL {

        // First, clear the label - it might take a moment for
        // the text to appear.
        self.noteContentLabel.setText(nil)
```

```
>      let activityInfo = [WatchHandoffDocumentURL: url.absoluteString]
>
>      // Note that this string needs to be the same as
>      // the activity type you defined in the Info.plist for the iOS
>      // and Mac apps
>      updateUserActivity("au.com.secretlab.Notes.editing",
>          userInfo: activityInfo, webpageURL: nil)

    SessionManager.sharedSession.loadNote(url,
        completionHandler: { text, error -> Void in

        if let theError = error {
            // We have an error! Present it, and add a button
            // that closes this screen when tapped.

            let closeAction = WKAlertAction(title: "Close",
                style: WKAlertActionStyle.default,
                handler: { () -> Void in
                    self.pop()
            })

            self.presentAlert(withTitle: "Error loading note",
                message: theError.localizedDescription,
                preferredStyle: WKAlertControllerStyle.alert,
                actions: [closeAction])

            return
        }

        if let theText = text {
            // We have the text! Display it.
            self.noteContentLabel.setText(theText)
        }
    })
  }

}
```

First, we create a dictionary that contains the note's URL. We then call updateU
serActivity, which broadcasts the fact that the user is looking at this particular
document to the user's other devices.

2. Run the app on your Apple Watch and open a Note. Turn your iPhone on, and
   see the iOS app's icon in the lower-left corner. Swipe up, and the document you're
   viewing on your watch will be opened in the iOS app! (See Figure 15-19.)

You'll also see the Mac app's icon appear in the Dock, with an Apple Watch icon. This means that you can hand off from your watch to your Mac as well as to your iPhone.

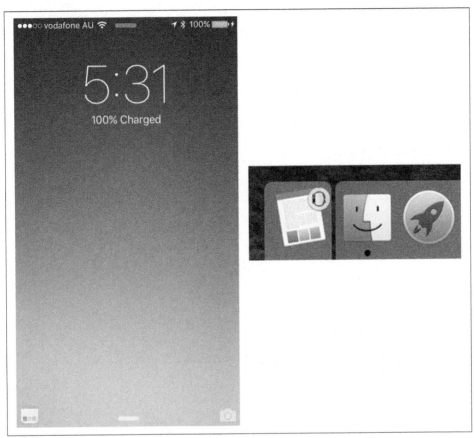

Figure 15-19. The Handoff icon on an iPhone's home screen, and in the Mac's Dock

Glances

Glances allow users to quickly view information while they're using their watch, without having to launch the watchOS app. Glances can display custom content, but cannot be interactive and are limited to one screen. Tapping a glance can launch the watchOS app, though.

Glances are simple but powerful. Learn more about them in Apple's WatchKit documentation (*https://developer.apple.com/watchos/resources/*).

We're going to add a glance to our watchOS app that allows users to very quickly jump into the watchOS app and begin dictating a new note.

When you tap a glance, its corresponding app is launched on the watch. There's no direct way to communicate between a glance and its app; instead, your glance's interface controller creates a user activity—in exactly the same way as you do for Handoff —when it appears. If the user taps the glance, the app is opened; it should then check to see what the current user activity is, and respond accordingly.

The design of the glance is a single, large Add image, to make it unambiguous that tapping the glance will make a new note (Figure 15-20). The image is available in the book's resources (see "Resources Used in This Book" on page ix).

Figure 15-20. The image we'll be using for the watchOS glance

First, we'll add this image:

1. Open the *Assets.xcasset* file in the Watch group (not the one in the Watch extension group).
2. Drag the Watch Glance Add image from the resources that accompany this book into the list of image sets.

We'll now add the code to the GlanceController class to make it set the current user activity to one that will make the NoteListInterfaceController start creating a new note when it appears:

1. Open *GlanceController.swift*, which is a file that Xcode created for you when you created the app.

2. Update the willActivate method to look like the following code:

```swift
override func willActivate() {
    // This method is called when watch view controller is
    // about to be visible to user
    updateUserActivity("au.com.secretlab.Notes.creating",
                       userInfo: ["editing":true], webpageURL: nil)
    super.willActivate()
}
```

By calling updateUserActivity, we're indicating to the larger watchOS system that the user is about to create a document if the glance is tapped.

Next, we'll make the NoteListInterfaceController detect this user activity and begin creating a note. If the glance is tapped, the watchOS app is launched, and the first interface controller that appears will have the handleUserActivity method called on it. At this point, we can grab information from that activity and figure out if the user wants to begin creating a note:

1. Open NoteListInterfaceController.swift.

2. Add the following method to the *NoteListInterfaceController* class:

```swift
override func handleUserActivity(_ userInfo: [AnyHashable: Any]?) {
    if userInfo?["editing"] as? Bool == true {
        // Start creating a note
        createNote()

        // Clear the user activity
        invalidateUserActivity()
    }
}
```

If the user activity contains the editing flag, which we set in the GlanceControl ler's willActivate method, then we call createNote to begin creating a new note. We then call invalidateUserActivity to clear the user's current activity, tidying up after ourselves.

Finally, we'll implement the user interface for the glance.

Glances have a very specific layout pattern. There's a smaller top section and a larger lower section. You don't have a huge amount of flexibility in this, primarily for efficiency reasons: by constraining what your layout looks like, the watch is able to save quite a bit of power.

1. Open *Interface.storyboard* and go to the glance interface controller.

2. Select the interface controller. Set the Upper section's interface to the option that contains a single small label. Set the Lower section's interface to the option that contains a single image.

3. Select the label in the upper section. In the Attributes Inspector, set its text to **Notes**.

4. Select the image object that now appears in the lower section of the glance's interface. In the Attributes Inspector, set its image to Watch Glance Add, and set its mode to Center.

The interface is now ready; see Figure 15-21.

Figure 15-21. The glance interface

You can now test the glance by running it on your Apple Watch; when you tap the glance, the app will launch, and immediately enter dictation mode to let you create the note.

 You may need to manually add the glance to your watch through the Watch app on your iPhone.

To test the glance in the simulator, use the scheme selector to select the "Glance - Watch" scheme. If the target is a simulator, the simulated watch will show the glance.

Conclusion

In this chapter, we extended the iOS app to add support for the Apple Watch. We built a simple watchOS app that allows users to look at their notes and create new notes on the Apple Watch. To do this, we worked with the WatchKit, the framework for building watchOS apps, and the communication system between the watch and the phone. We also added support for handoffs to the watchOS app, so users can work with the same information when moving between the devices.

CHAPTER 16

Code Quality and Distribution

In this chapter, we'll talk about some tools and techniques you can use to ensure that your code is as good as it can be. Specifically, we'll be talking about how to monitor your app and find ways to improve its performance, how to track down and fix bugs, and how to set up your application to run automatic tests on itself, which will help you make changes to the code without accidentally breaking its features.

After that, we'll talk about how to use automated tools to ensure that every piece of the app works every step of the way as you continue to build your project. Finally, we'll talk about how to deal with the App Store, including code signing requirements and delivering your product to Apple for distribution, as well as how to ensure that only the assets that the user's device actually needs are downloaded.

Debugging

Sometimes, your code just doesn't work the way you want it to: either you have a crash, or a more subtle behavioral difference. To track down these problems, you can use Xcode's built-in *debugger*. A debugger is a program that can interrupt the execution of an app, gather data from its variables, and help you figure out what the app's doing.

To use the debugger, you add *breakpoints*. A breakpoint is a point in the program at which the debugger should stop, allowing the developer (that's you!) to inspect the program's current state.

When a program is stopped at a breakpoint, you can step through its execution, line by line, observing the data stored in both the local variables and in the properties of the classes change. By carefully observing the behavior of your app, you can track down the causes of problems and fix them.

In addition, you can make the debugger automatically jump in the moment the application crashes, allowing you to figure out the cause of the crash.

To add a breakpoint to your application, simply click inside the gray area at the left of the code. When you do, a small blue arrow will appear, representing the point at which the program will stop (Figure 16-1).

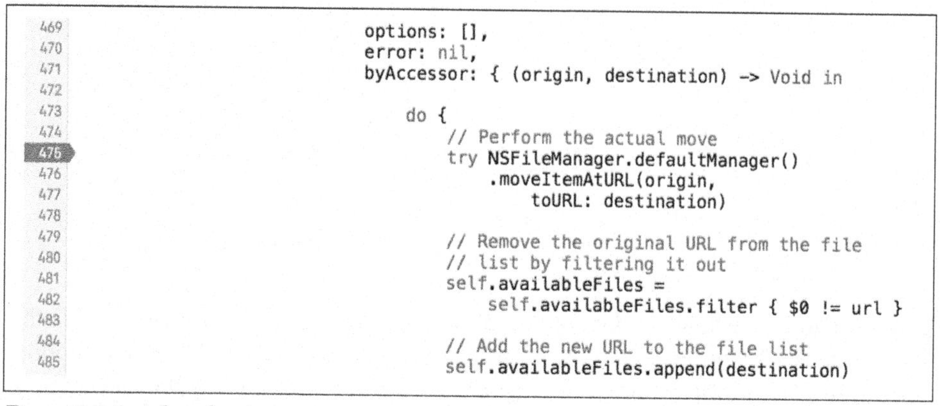

```
469         options: [],
470         error: nil,
471         byAccessor: { (origin, destination) -> Void in
472
473             do {
474                 // Perform the actual move
475                 try NSFileManager.defaultManager()
476                     .moveItemAtURL(origin,
477                         toURL: destination)
478
479                 // Remove the original URL from the file
480                 // list by filtering it out
481                 self.availableFiles =
482                     self.availableFiles.filter { $0 != url }
483
484                 // Add the new URL to the file list
485                 self.availableFiles.append(destination)
```

Figure 16-1. A breakpoint

If you run the application and trigger the code that has the breakpoint, your program will pause and Xcode will appear, showing the debug view (Figure 16-2).

When the debugger is active, a number of things appear:

- The Debug Inspector, at the left of the Xcode window, shows a *stack trace*, indicating where in the program the execution has stopped, and which methods were called to reach this point.

- The debug view appears and is split into two sections:

  — On the left, the list of all local variables is displayed. From here, you can see the current value of all local variables, as well as access the current object's properties in the self variable.

  — On the right, the LLDB console appears. From here, you can type commands for the debugger to interpret. The most useful command is po, which causes the debugger to print the value of the specified expression.

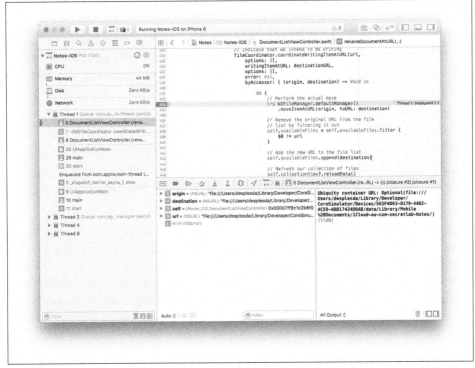

Figure 16-2. *The program, stopped in the debugger*

At the top of the debug view, you can find buttons that control the execution of the debugger (see Figure 16-3). The most important are the first six:

- The first button closes the debug view.
- The second button enables or disables breakpoints.
- The third button resumes execution of the program.
- The fourth button moves to the next line of code.
- The fifth button steps into the next method call.
- The sixth button continues until the current method returns, and then stops.

Figure 16-3. *The debug view's controls*

The debugger is an essential tool for diagnosing problems in your app. Don't hesitate to stick a breakpoint in to figure out what your code is actually doing!

Instruments

The *Instruments* tool tracks the activity of an application. You can monitor just about every single aspect of an application, from high-level metrics like how much data it's transferring over the network, down to low-level information about the OpenGL commands that the app executed in a single frame.

If your app is running slowly, Instruments lets you figure out which part of your application is responsible for taking up the majority of the time; if your app is consuming too much memory, you can work out what's responsible for allocating it.

There are two ways to use Instruments. First, you can get a high-level summary of the behavior of your app in Xcode (see Figure 16-4); if you need more information, you can launch the separate Instruments app.

To access the high-level summary of how your app is performing, simply run it and go to the debug navigator. Underneath the app's name, you'll find four entries—CPU, Memory, Disk, and Network—showing the current performance status of the app: how much of the system's CPU capacity it's using, how much total memory, how much data is being read and written to disk, how much network traffic the app is getting. When you select these, you'll be shown a more detailed picture of the selected aspect.

 If you're testing on a Mac, or on an iOS device—that is, not the simulator—then you'll also see energy consumption data. If you're on a Mac, you'll also see iCloud usage data.

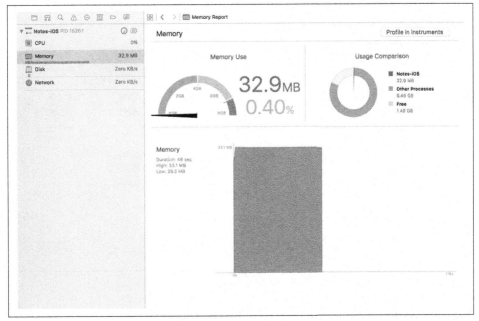

Figure 16-4. Performance data in Xcode

You'll notice a button labeled "Profile in Instruments" at the top-right corner of the view. If you click this, Xcode will offer to transfer control of the application to Instruments, allowing you to gather a more detailed view of the application.

You can use Instruments to profile both the simulator and a real device. However, the simulator has different performance characteristics than real devices, and real users don't use the simulator. Always test the performance of your app on an actual device before shipping to the App Store.

You can also launch your app directly into Instruments, allowing you to gather data through the entire run of your app from start to finish. To do this, open the Product menu and choose Profile.

To demonstrate, let's profile the Notes application to identify performance hotspots when viewing image attachments:

1. Choose Product → Profile, or press ⌘-I.

2. If Instruments is not already open, it will ask you which tools in Instruments you want to use to gather data about your app (Figure 16-5). Select the Time Profiler, and click Choose. (If Instruments is already profiling your app, it will start a new run using the existing tools, and you should close it and try again.)

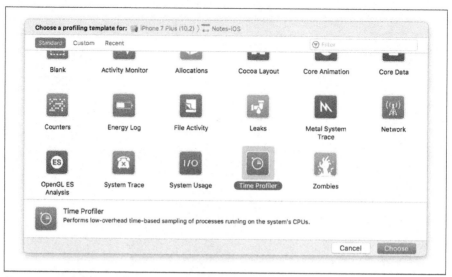

Figure 16-5. Selecting the Time Profiler tool

3. Click the Record button at the top left of the window.

4. Instruments will launch, showing the CPU Usage tool (Figure 16-6).

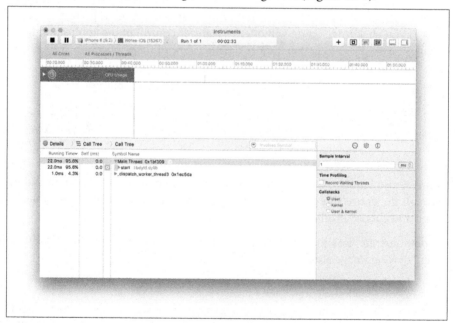

Figure 16-6. Instruments, using the CPU Usage tool

As you use the application, the CPU usage will be logged. We'll now perform some tests to determine which methods are taking up most of the time:

1. Open a document. Once the document is open, go to Instruments and press the Pause button.

2. Look at the Call Tree pane, which takes up the majority of the bottom section of the window. This window shows the amount of CPU time taken up by each thread; additionally, you can dive into each thread to find out which *methods* took up the most CPU time.

The less time spent on the CPU, the better your performance.

When you're tuning the performance of your application, there's not much sense in wading through the huge collection of methods that you didn't write. To that end, we can filter this view to show only the code that you have control over:

1. Find the Display Settings button, at the top of the panel in the bottom right of the screen. Click it, and you'll see a collection of options to control how the data is displayed.

2. Turn off everything except Hide System Libraries. When you do this, the Call List will be reduced to just your methods. Additionally, they'll be ordered based on how much each time each method took (see Figure 16-7).

Figure 16-7. Instruments, after the display has been filtered

The content of the detail area, which is the lower half of the screen, depends on which instrument you're working with. For the CPU Usage instrument, the columns in the Detail Area's Call Tree view are:

Running Time
> The total amount of time taken by the current row, including any of the methods that it calls.

Self (ms)
> The total amount of time taken by the current row, *not* including any of the methods it calls.

Symbol Name
> The name of the method in question.

> You'll notice that main is taking up the majority of the time. This makes sense, because main is the function that kicks off the entirety of the application. If you open the list of methods, you'll see the methods that main calls; each one can in turn be opened.

 You can double-click a line in this table to be taken to a view of the source code, which shows the most CPU-heavy lines of code.

This process of measuring the work done by the app, determining the point that needs changing, and optimizing it can be applied many times, and in different ways. In this section, we've only looked at reducing the time spent on the CPU; however, you can use the same principles to reduce the amount of memory consumed, data written to and read from disk, and data transferred over the network.

Testing

While simple apps are easy to test, complex apps get very difficult to properly test. It's simple enough to add some code and then check that it works; but the more code you add, the more you increase the chance that a change in one part of the code will break something elsewhere. To make sure that all of the app works, you need to test all of the app. However, this has many problems:

- It's tedious and boring, which means you'll be less likely to do it thoroughly.
- Because it's repetitious, you'll end up testing a feature in the same way every time, and you may not be paying close attention.
- Some problems appear only if you use the app in a certain way. The more specific the use case, the less you'll test it.

To address these problems, modern software development heavily relies on automated testing. Automated testing solves these problems immediately, by running the same tests in the same way every time, and by checking every step of the way; additionally, automated testing frees up your mental workload a lot.

There are two types of automated tests in Xcode: *unit tests* and *user interface tests*.

Unit Testing

Unit tests are small, isolated, independent tests that run to verify the behavior of a specific part of your code. Unit tests are perfect for ensuring that the output of a method you've written is what you expect. For example, the code that we wrote all the way back in "Location" on page 171 to load a location from JSON is very straightforward to test: given some valid JSON containing values for lat and lon, we expect to be able to create a CLLocationCoordinates; additionally, and just as importantly, if we give it invalid JSON *or* JSON that *doesn't* contain those values, we should expect to *fail* to get a coordinate.

Unit tests are placed inside a unit test *bundle*. You can choose to either include unit tests when you create the project, or you can add one to an existing project by opening the File menu and choosing New→Target, then opening the Tests section and choosing Unit Tests (see Figure 16-8).

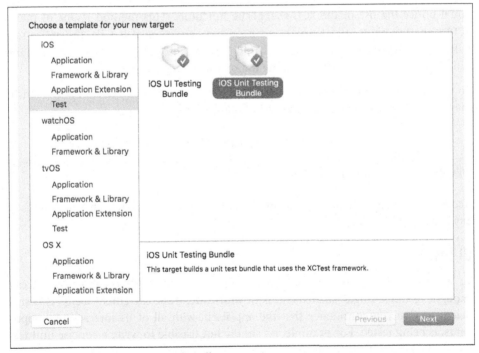

Figure 16-8. Adding a Unit Test bundle to a project

Test bundles contain one or more *test cases*; each test case is actually a subclass of XCTestCase, which itself contains the individual unit tests. A test case looks like this:

```
func testDocumentTypeDetection() {

    // Create an NSFileWrapper using some empty data
    let data = NSData()
    let document = NSFileWrapper(regularFileWithContents: data)

    // Give it a name
    document.preferredFilename = "Hello.jpg"

    // It should now think that it's an image
    XCTAssertTrue(document.conformsToType(kUTTypeImage))

}
```

The tests inside XCTestCase class are its methods. When Xcode runs the tests, which we'll show in a moment, it first locates all subclasses of XCTestCase, and then finds all methods of each subclass that begin with the word test. Each test is then run: first, the test case's setUp method is run, then the test itself, followed by the test case's tear Down method.

You'll notice the use of the XCTAssertTrue functions. This method is one of many XCTAssert functions, all of which test a certain condition; if it fails, the entire test fails, and Xcode moves on to the next test. You can find the entire list of XCTAssert functions in the Xcode testing documentation (*http://apple.co/22VaRyg*).

To run the unit test for your current target, press ⌘-U, or click the icon at the left of the top line of a specific test, as shown in Figure 16-9.

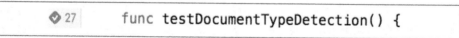

Figure 16-9. Running a specific test

Xcode will launch your app, perform the test(s), and report back on which tests, if any, failed.

UI Testing

To get a complete picture of how your app works, unit tests on their own aren't enough. Testing a single isolated chunk of your code, while extremely useful, isn't sufficient to give you confidence that the app itself, with all of its interacting components, is being tested. For example, it's simply not feasible to write a concise unit test for "create a document, edit it, and save it."

Instead, you can use UI tests to verify that the app is behaving the way you want it to as it's used. A UI test is a recording of how the user interacts with the user interface; however, these recordings are done in a very clever way. While a UI test is being recorded, Xcode notes every interaction that you perform, and adds a line of code that reproduces that step.

The result is code that looks like this (we've added comments to describe what's going on):

```
func testCreatingSavingAndClosingDocument() {

    // Get the app
    let app = XCUIApplication()

    // Choose File->New
    let menuBarsQuery = XCUIApplication().menuBars
    menuBarsQuery.menuBarItems["File"].click()
    menuBarsQuery.menuItems["New"].click()

    // Get the new 'Untitled' window
    let untitledWindow = app.windows["Untitled"]

    // Get the main text view
    let textView = untitledWindow.childrenMatchingType(.ScrollView)
        .elementBoundByIndex(0).childrenMatchingType(.TextView).element

    // Type some text
    textView.typeText("This is a useful document that I'm testing.")

    // Save it by pressing Command-S
    textView.typeKey("s", modifierFlags:.Command)

    // The save sheet has appeared; type "Test" in it and press return
    untitledWindow.sheets["save"].childrenMatchingType(.TextField)
        .elementBoundByIndex(0).typeText("Test\r")

    // Close the document
    app.windows["Test"].typeKey("w", modifierFlags:.Command)
}
```

UI tests are run the same way as your unit tests. When they're run, the system will take control over your computer and perform the exact steps as laid down in the test. This ensures that your app is tested in the exact same way, every time.

You can also record your interactions with an app directly into a UI test. This is extremely useful, since it means that you don't have to learn the API involved—you can just use the app as you would normally, and Xcode will note what you did. For more information, see Writing Tests (*http://apple.co/22VbeJ1*) in the Xcode documentation.

Build Bots

A build bot is a program running on a server that watches for changes in your source code, and automatically builds, tests, and packages your software. Build bots are great for reducing the load on your main development computer, and for ensuring that your tests are always run.

To create a build bot, you'll first need to have a Mac running the Apple-provided macOS Server application, which you can purchase from the App Store. You can find more information on how to set up build bots in the Xcode Server and Continuous Integration Guide (*http://apple.co/22VblV3*).

Using Objective-C and Swift in the Same Project

If you're making a new project from scratch, you'll likely have the opportunity to write all of your code in Swift. However, if you have an existing project written in Objective-C, and want to write code in Swift, you need a way to bridge the two. The same thing applies in reverse, for when you have a project written in Swift and need to add some Objective-C code.

Using Swift Objects in Objective-C

To make objects written in Swift available in Objective-C, you need to add the @objc tag in front of them. For example, if you have a class written in Swift called Cat, you write the class as normal and prepend @objc to its name:

```
@objc class Cat : NSObject {
    var name : String = ""

    func speak() -> String {
        return "Meow"
    }
}
```

Classes that are defined in Swift are available to Objective-C only if they're a subclass of NSObject (or any of NSObject's subclasses).

In your Objective-C code, you import an Xcode-generated header file that makes all of your @objc-tagged Swift code available to Objective-C:

```
#import "MyAppName-Swift.h"
```

Once it's imported, you can use the class as if it had originally been written in Objective-C:

```
Cat* myCat = [[Cat alloc] init];
myCat.name = @"Fluffy";
[myCat speak];
```

Using Objective-C Objects in Swift

To use classes and other code written in Objective-C in your Swift code, you fill out a *bridging header*. When you add an Objective-C file to a project containing Swift files, or vice versa, Xcode will offer to create and add a bridging header to your project.

Inside this header, you add #import statements for all of the Objective-C files you want to export to Swift. Then, inside your Swift code, you can use the Objective-C classes as if they had been originally written in Swift.

This method is actually how your code accesses the majority of the Cocoa and Cocoa Touch APIs, which are mostly written in Objective-C.

For example, consider a class written in Objective-C, like so:

```
@interface Elevator

- (void) moveUp;
- (void) moveDown;

@property NSString* modelName;

@end
```

All you need to do is import the class's header file into the bridging header that Xcode generates for you:

```
#import "Elevator.h"
```

Once that's done, you can use the class in Swift as if it were originally written in Swift:

```
let theElevator = Elevator()

theElevator.moveUp()
theElevator.moveDown()

theElevator.modelName = "The Great Glass Elevator"
```

Interoperation between Swift and Objective-C is a large and complex topic, and there's much more that you should know if you plan on making the two work together. Apple has written an entire book on the topic, *Using Swift with Cocoa and Objective-C* (*http://apple.co/22Vea8G*), which is available for free both online and on the iBooks Store.

The App Store

Once you've written your app, it's time to get it out to the world. To do this, you need to submit it to the App Store.

The App Store is the only way that Apple permits third-party iOS apps to be distributed to the public. To submit to the App Store, you need the following things:

- An app, ready to go out to the public
- A distribution certificate, signed by Apple
- The text and images for the app's page on the App Store

iOS devices run only signed code. This means that, in order to run your app on an actual device, and to submit to the App Store, you need to get a certificate from Apple. Getting a certificate is free if you just want to make apps that run on your own devices; if you want to submit to the App Store, you need to join the Apple Developer Program (*https://developer.apple.com/programs/*), which is $99 USD per year.

Because the App Store submission process mostly takes place on websites, it's difficult to write a book that stays up to date with it. We therefore strongly encourage you to read Apple's App Distribution Guide (*http://apple.co/22VepR3*), which discusses both the technical requirements as well as the information you need to provide for the App Store.

When you submit an application to the App Store, it is first checked by automated systems and then by a human. The automated systems perform checks that are easily computer-run, such as making sure that the app has all of the necessary icons for the platform that it runs on. Once the automated checks have passed, the app goes into a queue while it waits for a human being to look at it. This is what Apple refers to as *app review.* App review isn't a scary process, and the review team is not there to judge you on the quality of your app; instead, the review checks to see if your app violates any of the App Store Review Guidelines (*http://apple.co/2nwiR6R*). These reviews are generally common sense and exist to help Apple maintain the overall quality of the App Store.

After Apple has approved your application, you'll receive an automated email indicating whether the app has passed review or has been rejected. If your app is rejected, don't worry! Almost all app rejections are due to a simple thing that's easily changed; the most common one that we've heard has been forgetting to test an app with flight mode turned on, which cuts off access to all internet services, including iCloud. Simply fix the issue and resubmit your app.

If your app has been approved, you just need to press the button in iTunes Connect to release it. A few hours later, your app will be in the App Store!

App Thinning

While it's important to design your app to work on as many devices as possible, the fact remains that when an app is downloaded onto a specific type of device, it will never make use of the resources that are necessary for it to work on *other* devices. For example, an app that runs on both the iPad and the iPhone needs an icon for both, and you need to include it in your app when you deliver it to the App Store. However, when you download it onto your iPhone, there's no point in downloading the iPad version of the icon.

To deal with this issue, Xcode has support for *app thinning*. App thinning involves marking certain files with information about what kinds of devices will use the different resources included in the app. For example, if you select an image set in an asset catalog, you can specify which types of devices the image will appear in (such as iPhone only, iPad only, and so on); however, you can also be extremely specific with the conditions in which the asset will be included (see Figure 16-10). These include specifying the minimum amount of memory that must be available for the image to be downloaded, or the minimum graphics hardware capability.

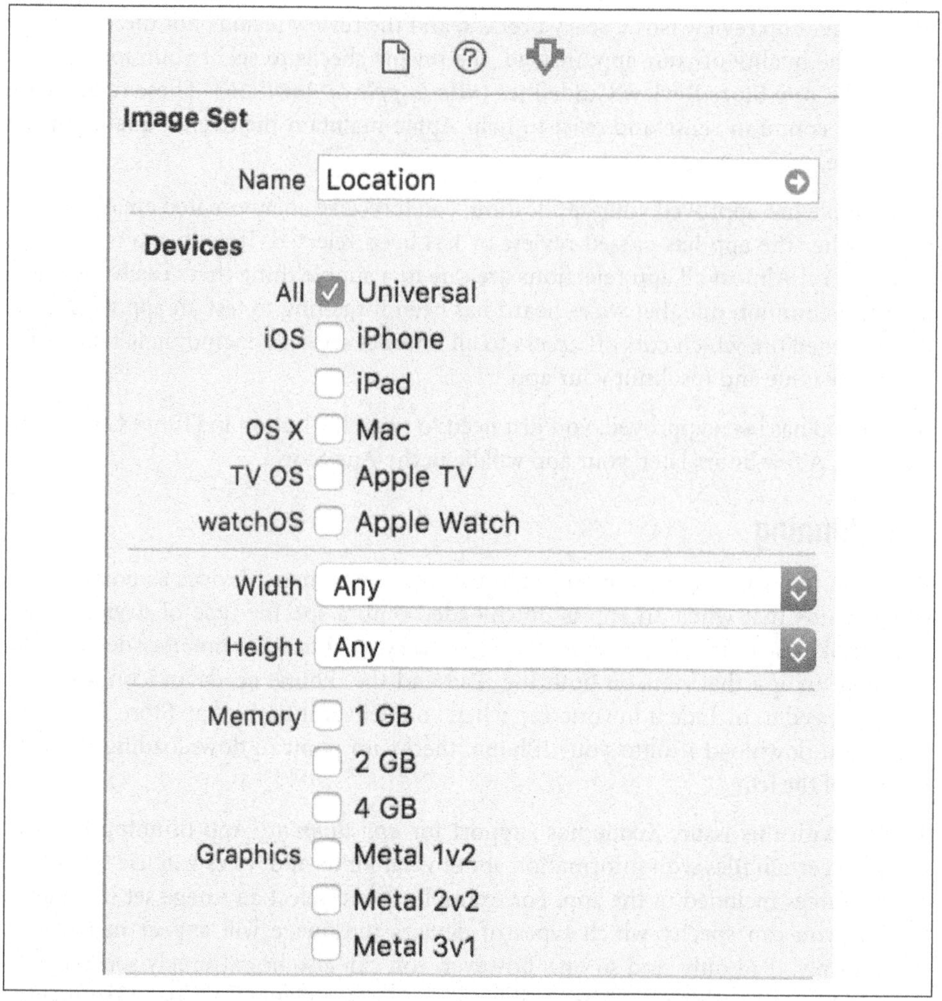

Figure 16-10. App thinning options for an image set in an asset catalog

Testing iOS Apps with TestFlight

TestFlight is a service operated by Apple that allows you to send copies of your app to people for testing. TestFlight allows you to submit testing builds to up to 25 people who are members of your Developer Program account. You can also send the app to up to 1,000 additional people for testing, once the app is given a preliminary review by Apple.

To use TestFlight, you configure the application in iTunes Connect by providing information like the app's name, icon, and description. You also create a list of users who should receive the application. You then upload a build of the app through Xcode, and Apple emails them a link to download and test it.

We're not covering TestFlight in detail in this book, as the user interface and steps for distributing via TestFlight change frequently.

For more information on how to use TestFlight, see the iTunes Connect documentation (*http://bit.ly/testing_w_testflight*).

Conclusion

If you've read this far, congratulations. You've built three complete, complex apps from start to finish for a variety of platforms, and you're ready to build even bigger.

We hope that you've enjoyed your journey through this book. If you've made something, we'd love to hear about it! Send us an email at *learningswift@secretlab.com.au*.

Index

About the Authors

Paris Buttfield-Addison is an author and a designer of games at Secret Lab, which he co-founded with Jon. Paris has a PhD in computing and a degree in medieval history. Paris can be found online at *www.paris.id.au* (*https://blog.paris.id.au*) and on Twitter as @parisba.

Jon Manning is an iOS software engineer, independent game developer, and author. In addition to writing books like these, he designs and builds games at Secret Lab, which he cofounded with Paris. Jon has a PhD in computing, in which he studied the manipulation of ranking systems in social media sites. Jon can be found on Twitter as @desplesda.

Tim Nugent pretends to be a mobile app developer, game designer, PhD student, and now he even pretends to be an author. When he isn't busy avoiding being found out as a fraud, he spends most of his time designing and creating little apps and games he won't let anyone see. Tim spent a disproportionately long time writing this tiny little bio, most of which was spent trying to stick a witty sci-fi reference in, before he simply gave up. Tim can be found as @The_McJones on Twitter.

Colophon

The animal on the cover of *Learning Swift* is a fairy martin (*Petrochelidon ariel*), a member of the swallow family that breeds in Australia. This migratory bird winters through most of Australia, though some instead reach New Guinea and Indonesia.

The fairy martin averages 12 centimeters in length and weighs up to 11 grams. It is dumpy with a square tail; adults are iridescent blue on their backs with brown wings and tail, and a whitish behind. Its pale rump distinguishes this species from other Australian swallows. Males and females have similar coloring, but younger birds have duller coloring and paler foreheads and fringes. The fairy martin has a high-pitched twitter and a *chrrrr* call.

During breeding season—from August to January—fairy martins gather in tens of nests; the largest known colony contained 700 nests. They traditionally nest near cliff faces, natural holes in dead trees, riverbanks, or rock crevices, but are increasingly found in manmade sites such as culverts, pipes, bridges, or buildings. Both sexes help build the nests, which consist of up to 1,000 mud pellets and are lined with dried grass and feathers. Fairy martins breed in clutches, which usually consist of up to four or five eggs.

Fairy martins feed in large flocks, catching flying insects in the air or in swarms over water. This is a highly gregarious species that often gathers in large groups that include tree martins.

Learn from experts.
Find the answers you need.

Sign up for a **10-day free trial** to get **unlimited access** to all of the content on Safari, including Learning Paths, interactive tutorials, and curated playlists that draw from thousands of ebooks and training videos on a wide range of topics, including data, design, DevOps, management, business—and much more.

Start your free trial at:
oreilly.com/safari

(No credit card required.)

CPSIA information can be obtained
at www.ICGtesting.com
Printed in the USA
BVOW09s2221020417

480001BV00001B/1/P

9 781491 967065